A NEW HYMNAL FOR COLLEGES AND SCHOOLS

YALE UNIVERSITY PRESS

New Haven and London

in association with the

YALE INSTITUTE OF SACRED MUSIC

A NEW HYMNAL FOR COLLEGES AND SCHOOLS

Edited by

JEFFERY ROWTHORN

and

RUSSELL SCHULZ-WIDMAR

WITHDRAWN
Fresno Pacific College - M.B. Seminary
Fresno, CA 93702

The members of the Editorial Board and Yale University Press acknowledge with great appreciation the financial support and generous encouragement given by Mrs. Robert S. (Clementine) Tangeman during the preparation of this hymnal.

Music and hymn texts set by David Budmen at Abraham Botvinick Publishing.
Text set in Times Roman type by The Composing Room of Michigan, Inc.
Printed in the United States of America by Vail-Ballou Press, Binghamton, New York.

Library of Congress Cataloging-in-Publication Data

A New hymnal for colleges and schools / edited by Jeffery Rowthorn and Russell Schulz-Widmar.
1 close score.
Rev. ed. of: Hymnal for colleges and schools, 1956.
Includes index.
ISBN 0-300-05113-1
1. Hymns, English—United States. I. Rowthorn, Jeffery W. II. Schulz-Widmar, Russell. III. Hymnal for colleges and schools.
M2117.N522 1992 91-5026 CIP M

A catalogue record for this book is available from the British Library.

The paper in this book meets the guidelines for permanence and durability of the Committee on Production Guidelines for Book Longevity of the Council on Library Resources.

10 9 8 7 6 5 4 3 2 1

EDITORIAL BOARD

CONTENTS

HOPE FOR THE WORLD

PREFACE

Within the covers of this book is a rich selection of congregational psalms, hymns, and spiritual songs for use at occasions of worship in academic communities. Many college and school chaplains and musicians have expressed their desire for a new hymnal which would be both scholarly in its standards and useful in its range of contents. With this collection we hope to answer that need.

This book is indebted to its much appreciated predecessor, the *Hymnal for Colleges and Schools,* which Yale University Press published in 1956. For many years it provided a rich resource for worshiping communities in academic settings across the country. Yet every hymnal, however imaginatively edited and sensitively employed, must eventually show its age. Each passing decade will diminish its capacity to address the needs, express the aspirations, and deepen the faith experience of those who use it. Hymnal revision is thus a necessary and desirable dimension of our worship of God, and the preparation of this book is a recognition of that.

In the past generation the landscape of daily life has altered dramatically within and beyond the walls of every school and college in North America. The world at large, communities of faith, our understanding of the life of witness and service, and our self-perception as individuals have all been subject to far-reaching changes. This new hymnal is responsive to the shaking of the foundations of campus life primarily in three ways:

We have provided a broad repertoire of material to take into account the greater religious and ethnic diversity in academic settings. For that reason we have drawn on Roman Catholic, evangelical, African American, and Hispanic sources. The international character of this collection is further evidenced by the inclusion of hymns from Africa and Asia in addition to Protestant and Anglican hymnody from both sides of the Atlantic. In this ecumenical age we hope that songs beloved by one part of the Christian family will come to be appreciated and treasured by other parts as well. We have also included a number of Jewish hymns and religious songs, and provided hymns suitable for use in interfaith settings at which faculty members and students representing a range of religious traditions from around the world come together in prayer.

We have sought to be particularly sensitive to the need for a more inclusive language of praise. In this regard we have been greatly helped by the work of editors of other recent hymnals, and we have made our own contribution to this process. The Psalter in this book depends heavily on inclusive-language versions prepared by the United Methodist Church and the National Council of Churches. In the hymns, taken as a whole, masculine references have been significantly reduced, and some hymns which use feminine imagery in speaking to or about God have been included. However, we have declined to be rigorously consistent in this matter of inclusive language. Thus, while changing the familiar opening line of some hymns in order to help assure the continued use of those texts, we have on other occasions consciously retained the biblical titles of "Father," "Lord," and "King." To be consistent—either by making no changes at all or by making every conceivable change—was not, we felt, either an attainable or a desirable goal.

We have drawn widely on the extraordinary flowering of new hymn texts and tunes in the past quarter-century. This new repertoire is, we believe, one of the most promising signs of religious vitality in our times. In these hymns the pressing issues of today and tomorrow and the experiences which shape and challenge the faith of each successive student generation can be more adequately and directly addressed. Because of that we believe this to be a hymnal which will help those who use it to live the life of faith in our day and at the same time to have their faith strengthened by the experience of their forebears who also journeyed in uncertain times.

This hymnal, therefore, includes among its contents:

- Hymns for many kinds of worship services and occasions in the academic calendar.
- The great bulk of the psalms as appointed for use on Sundays in the Common (Ecumenical) Lectionary, together with optional tones and newly composed seasonal antiphons which will help in recovering the ancient tradition of chanting psalmody. These antiphons may be reprinted without cost in the worship bulletins of congregations or institutions purchasing multiple copies of this book. The psalms are, however, set out in such a manner that they can also be read aloud in a variety of ways, including but not limited to responsive reading by leader and congregation.
- A selection of service music which will enable congregations to participate more fully in the principal act of worship on the Lord's Day, by whatever name that service may be known (Lord's Supper, Holy Communion, Mass, Eucharist, or Divine Liturgy).
- A generous selection of music from the many rich traditions of hymnody, freshly edited in the light of recent scholarship. Chants, chorales, psalter tunes, eighteenth-century tunes, nineteenth-century choral hymnody, and folkloric hymnody are some of the primary fields represented. Though the tone of the book is catholic and international, we believe a special richness is the music it includes by American composers.
- Poetry of distinction not before set as hymns as well as new texts and tunes specially commissioned for this book.

The broadened scope of the present hymnal makes it impossible to include detailed notes on each selection. However, we have provided as much basic information as is practicable. The table of contents and the running head at the top of each page will help in the choice of hymns appropriate to particular occasions. Each seasonal section of the hymnal is amplified with a list of additional hymns suitable for use at that time in the Church Year. The psalms, together with some metrical psalm paraphrases, can be found in the main body of hymns because we wish to emphasize their primary identity as songs of Israel.

The evolution of many hymns is surprisingly complicated. Because the folkloric impulse is so central to the nature of hymnody, and because hymns are integrally related to the living enterprise of corporate worship, most do not and cannot remain indefinitely the same. The majority of texts and tunes—certainly far more than most of us realize—have been altered in some way over the course of decades or centuries. For example, John Wesley altered the words of Isaac Watts, and J. S. Bach harmonized changed versions of historic chorales and changed some himself. Sometimes the changes in hymns have been minor (a single word or note); in other instances the words or music have been essentially rewritten. In this book we have accepted many revised versions as worthy improvements on the originals. However, we have also restored many original or older versions. This restoration will reveal itself in language and thought patterns and in melodic forms and harmonizations that are richer and more characteristic and captivating than the commonly known versions. Our intent has always been to be respectful of the original work, and to make decisions informed by current scholarship and perceived needs.

We believe the practice of signaling changes by printing *alt.* (altered) after the name of the writer or source has become unhelpful and sometimes misleading, and therefore we have abandoned it. Today, with the exception of some copyrighted hymns, it must be assumed that most hymns are not printed exactly in the way that their original authors or composers first made them available.

We are grateful to many publishers and individuals for their consent to reproduce copyrighted material. In many instances, living authors have revised their own words at our request, and copyright holders have allowed us to incorporate such changes as commended themselves to us. Every effort has been made to identify and contact the owners of copyrighted material, and acknowledgment notices are printed elsewhere in the book. We ask to be excused if any rights have inadvertently been overlooked. The publishers have gladly undertaken to make any necessary corrections in future editions of the hymnal.

This enterprise was first broached as a possibility in the late summer of 1984. Now that it has been completed, it is appropriate to express our gratitude to those who have contributed to the funding, preparation, and publication of *A New Hymnal for Colleges and Schools*:

- the chaplains of Brown, Cornell, and Princeton universities, who responded enthusiastically to the initiative taken by Rev. John Vannorsdall while serving as chaplain of Yale University;
- the members of the Editorial Board, who volunteered their musical, theological, and literary gifts and for several years gladly contributed time, energy, pastoral experience, humor, faith, and hope to the shaping of this hymnal;
- John Ryden, director of Yale University Press, who from the first has shown a commitment to and enthusiasm for the book which has greatly encouraged all who have worked on its preparation;
- John Cook, director of the Yale Institute of Sacred Music, who has been associated with the hymnal since its inception, together with the faculty and staff of the institute, and in particular Constance Wentzel, who has given generously of her time and expertise in administering the prepublication budget of the hymnal;
- Harry Haskell, music editor of Yale University Press, who has expended much time and skill in preparing the manuscript to be printed;
- those who have given invaluable help in matters large and small over many months of detailed, exhilarating, and exhausting work: Nancy Mourette Bose, Ellen Little, and Susan Ransom, along with Charlene Alling, Kate Harrigan, Sarah Hinman, James E. Mooney, Sam Smith, and Hans Venable;
- Mrs. Robert S. (Clementine) Tangeman, who, as a generous benefactress and valued contributor at Editorial Board meetings, has been unwaveringly supportive throughout the preparation of the book; apart from her gracious support and active encouragement, there would not now be a *New Hymnal for Colleges and Schools*.

Our hope is that this book, made possible by the willing collaboration and support of so many gifted and generous people, will provide many diverse communities of faith with a worthy vehicle of praise. For praise is the intent of this collection, and from start to finish it echoes the call contained in the final stanza of one of the most widely sung new hymns of our day:

Let every instrument be tuned for praise!
Let all rejoice who have a voice to raise!
And may God give us faith to sing always
  Alleluia!
—F. Pratt Green, "When in our music God is glorified"

Jeffery Rowthorn
Russell Schulz-Widmar
Coeditors

1 All people that on earth do dwell

Psalm 100

William Kethe, 1561; translations: French, Roger Chapal, 1970; German, after Cornelius Becker (1561–1604) and David Denicke (1603–1680); Indonesian, Yayasan Musik Gerejani, 1973; Italian, E. Costa, 1973; Japanese, *Sanbika*, 1955; Spanish, Federico J. Pagura, 1960; Swahili, *Nyimbo* (Standart)

Music: *Old Hundredth*, 8888; melody composed or adapted by Louis Bourgeois for Psalm 134 in *Genevan Psalter*, 1551

1 All peo - ple that on earth do dwell, sing to the
2 The Lord, ye know, is God in - deed; with - out our
3 O en - ter then his gates with praise; ap - proach with
4 For why? the Lord our God is good; his mer - cy
Lord with cheer - ful voice; him serve with mirth, his
aid he did us make; we are his folk, he
joy his courts un - to; praise, laud, and bless his
is for ev - er sure; his truth at all times
praise forth tell, come ye be - fore him and re - joice.
doth us feed, and for his sheep he doth us take.
name al - ways, for it is seem - ly so to do.
firm - ly stood, and shall from age to age en - dure.

French

1 Vous qui sur la terre habitez,
chantez à pleine voix, chantez.
Réjouissez-vous au Seigneur,
égayez-vous à son honneur.

2 Lui seul est notre souverain,
c'est lui qui nous fit de sa main:
nous le peuple qu'il mènera,
le troupeau qu'il rassemblera.

3 Dans sa maison dès aujourd'hui,
tous présentez-vous devant lui;
célébrez son nom glorieux,
exaltez-le jusques aux cieux.

4 Pour toi, Seigneur, que notre amour
se renouvelle chaque jour:
ta bonté, ta fidélité,
demeurent pour l'éternité.

German

1 Nun jauchzt dem Herren alle Welt,
kommt her, zu seinem Dienst euch stellt,
kommt mit Frohlocken, säumet nicht,
kommt vor sein heilig Angesicht.

2 Erkennt, daß Gott ist unser Herr,
der uns erschaffen ihm zur Ehr,
und nicht wir selbst; durch Gottes Gnad
ein jeder Mensch sein Leben hat.

3 Die ihr nun wollet bei ihm sein,
kommt, geht zu seinen Toren ein
mit Loben durch der Psalmen Klang,
zu seinem Vorhof mit Gesang.

4 Er ist voll Güt und Freundlichkeit,
voll Lieb und Treu zu jeder Zeit;
sein Gnade währet dort und hier
und seine Wahrheit für und für.

Italian

1 Tutta la terra cantia te,
Dio dell' universo;
tutto il creato viene a te
annuncia la tua gloria.

2 Unico Dio sei per noi,
fatti dalla tua mano;
Padre, noi siamo figli tuoi,
popolo che tu guidi.

3 Nella tua casa accoglierai
l'inno delle nazioni;
a chi ti cerca tu darai
di lodarti per sempre.

4 Si, ogni uomo lo dirà:
Buono è il Signore Dio;
l'amore suo è verità,
nei secoli fedele.

Spanish

1 Oh pueblos todos alabad,
en alta voz a Dios cantad,
regocijáos en su honor,
servid alegres al Señor.

2 El soberano Creador
de nuestra vida es el autor;
el pueblo suyo somos ya,
rebaño que El pastoreará.

3 A su santuario pues entrad,
y vuestras vidas ofrendad;
al nombre augusto dad loor,
que al mundo llena de esplendor.

4 Incomparable es su bondad,
y para siempre su verdad;
de bienes colma nuestro ser
su gracia no ha de fenecer.

Swahili

1 Enyi mkaao nchi,
mwimbieni Mungu sana,
msifuni kwa sauti kuu,
mbele zake mwakutana.

2 Mungu mwamjua, kwani
aliyetuumba ndiye,
atuchunga malishani,
na tu kundi lake Yeye.

3 Haya! malangoni mwake,
hata nyuani, imbeni;
mulikuze Jina lake,
Jina la Bwana si duni.

4 Kwani, Jehova ni mwema
ana rehema milele;
kweli yake yasimama
leo na kesho vivile.

Indonesian

1 Hai bumi Tuhan, soraklah!
Baktikan diri padaNya:
datang menghadap Yang Kudus,
nyanyi bersukaria t'rus!

2 Akuilah dengan teguh:
Tuhanmu ini Allahmu!
OlehNya kita adalah
dan jadi kawan dombaNya.

3 Masukilah gapuraNya,
puji-syukurma naik serta:
halaman Tuhan b'ri penuh
alunan haleluyamu!

4 Kar'na Tuhanmu mahabaik;
kasihNya pun kekal ajaib
dan setiaNya 'kan teguh
turun-temurun bagimu!

Japanese

1 よろずのくにびと、
わが主にむかいて、
こころのかぎりに、
よろこびたたえよ。

2 主こそはかみなれ、
われらはその民、
主はわがかいぬし、
みまきのひつじぞ。

3 もろごえあわせて、
みかどに入りゆき、
大御名ほめつつ、
みまえに近づかん。

4 めぐみはゆたかに、
こよなきまことは、
あわれみつきせず、
ときわにかわらじ。

2 **Another harmonization (adapted from Claude Goudimel, 1565):**

3 I'll praise my Maker while I've breath

Isaac Watts, 1719, based on Psalm 146

Music: *Old 113th*, 888888; melody in *Strasburger Kirchenamt*, 1525, probably by Matthäus Greiter; abridged during the 18th century; harmony by V. Earle Copes, 1966

1 I'll praise my Ma - ker while I've breath, and when my voice
2 Hap - py are they whose hopes re - ly on Is - rael's God,
3 The Lord pours eye - sight on the blind; the Lord sup - ports
4 I'll praise my God who lends me breath; and when my voice
is lost in death, praise shall em - ploy my no - bler powers.
who made the sky and earth and seas, with all their train;
the faint - ing mind and sends the la - boring con-science peace.
is lost in death, praise shall em - ploy my no - bler powers.
My days of praise shall ne'er be past, while life and thought
whose truth for - ev - er stands se - cure, who saves the op - pressed,
God helps the strang - er in dis - tress, the wid - ow and
My days of praise shall ne'er be past while life and thought
and be - ing last, or im - mor - tal - i - ty en - dures.
and feeds the poor, and none shall find God's prom - ise vain.
the fa - ther - less, and grants the pris - oner sweet re - lease.
and be - ing last, or im - mor - tal - i - ty en - dures.

4 Come, O come, our voices raise

George Wither, *The Hallelujah*, 1641

Music: *Sonne der Gerechtigkeit*, 77774; melody in *Kirchengeseng*, Berlin, 1566; harmony by Jan O. Bender, 1969

1 Come, O come, our voic - es raise, sound - ing God Al -
2 Sound the trum - pet, touch the lute, let no tongue nor
3 Come ye all be - fore God's face, in this cho - rus
4 Let, in praise of God, the sound run a nev - er -
might - y's praise; hith - er bring in one con - sent
string be mute, nor a voice - less crea - ture found,
take your place; and, a - mid the mor - tal throng,
end - ing round, that our songs of praise may be
heart, and voice, and in - stru - ment. Al - le - lu - ia!
that hath nei - ther note nor sound. Al - le - lu - ia!
be ye mas - ters of the song. Al - le - lu - ia!
ech - o - ing e - ter - nal - ly. Al - le - lu - ia!

5 So this huge wide orb we see
shall one choir, one temple be;
where in such a praiseful tone
we will sing what God hath done.
Alleluia!

6 Thus our song shall overclimb
all the bounds of space and time;
come, then, come, our voices raise,
sounding God Almighty's praise.
Alleluia!

5 Maoz tsur y'shuati

Rock of ages

Jewish traditional; translation by Marcus Jastrow and Gustave Gottheil, 20th century

Music: *Maoz tsur*, 767666336; Jewish traditional melody; harmony by Erik Werner (1901–1988)

1 *Ma - oz tsur y' - shu - a - ti l'-cha na - eh l'-sha - bei - ach,*
1 Rock of a - ges, let our song praise your sav - ing pow - er;
2 Chil-dren of the Ho - ly God, wheth - er free or fet - tered,
ti - kon beit t' - fi - la - ti v'-sham to - dah n'-za - bei - ach.
you, a - mid our rag - ing foes, were our shel - tering tow - er.
wake the ech - oes of that song where you may be scat - tered.
L'-eit ta - chin mat - bei - ach mi - tzar ham'-na - bei - ach,
Fur - ious they as - sailed us, but your arm a - vailed us,
Yours the mes - sage cheer - ing that the time is near - ing
az eg - mor b'-shir miz - mor cha - nu - kat ha-miz - bei - ach.
and your word broke their sword when our own strength failed us.
which will see all set free, ty - rants no more fear - ing.
(♭)

6 O worship the King

Robert Grant, 1833, based on Psalm 104

Music: *Hanover*, 10.10.11.11; melody in *A Supplement to the New Version*, London, 1708; probably by William Croft

1 O wor - ship the King, all glo - rious a - bove,
2 O tell of God's might, O sing of God's grace,
3 The earth, with its store of won - ders un - told,
4 Thy boun - ti - ful care, what tongue can re - cite?
O grate - ful - ly sing God's pow - er and love;
whose robe is the light, whose can - o - py space;
Al - might - y, thy power hath found - ed of old,
It breathes in the air, it shines in the light;
our Shield and De - fend - er, the An - cient of Days,
whose char - iots of wrath the deep thun - der - clouds form,
hath stab - lished it fast by a change - less de - cree,
it streams from the hills, it de - scends to the plain,
pa - vil - ioned in splen - dor, and gird - ed with praise.
for dark is God's path on the wings of the storm.
and round it hath cast, like a man - tle, the sea.
and sweet - ly dis - tills in the dew and the rain.

5 Frail children of dust, and feeble as frail,
in thee do we trust, nor find thee to fail;
thy mercies, how tender, how firm to the end,
our Maker, Defender, Redeemer, and Friend.

7 We sing to you, O God

Gracia Grindal, 1985, 1989

Music: *Camano*, 66664444; Richard Proulx, 1979

1 We sing to you, O God, the Rock who gave us birth, let our re-joic-ing
2 We wan-dered far from home out in a des-ert land, you shield-ed with your
3 You bear us through the world, an ea-gle to her young, who ris-es on her
4 O God, e-ter-nal God, we hide with-in your wings, the ev-er-last-ing
sing your name in all the earth. To you, O God, let
love our fear-ful pil-grim band. You kept us safe with-
wings and bears us toward the sun. We ride the vaults of
arms to whom our prais-es ring. Your word is true, your
songs be raised, in joy-ful hymns, our feast of praise.
in your arms and shel-tered us a-gainst the storm.
light and air and trust in your un-fail-ing care.
way is just, you are the God in whom we trust.

8 We sing of God, the mighty source

Christopher Smart; adapted from "A Song to David," 1763

Music: *Glorious*, 886886; William Albright, 1983

These words can also be sung to *Cornwall*, no. 490.

1 We sing of God, the might - y source, glo - rious in
2 Glo - rious the sun in mid ca - reer; glo - rious the as -
3 Glo - rious, more glo - rious is the crown of Christ who
power, stu - pen - dous force on which all strength de - pends;
sem - bled fires ap - pear; glo - rious the com - et's train:
brought sal - va - tion down by meek - ness, Da - vid's son;
from whose right arm, be - neath whose eyes, all per - iod,
glo - rious the trum - pet and a - larm; glo - rious the al -
seers that stu - pen - dous truth be - lieved, and now the
all per - iod,
glo - rious the al -
and now the
power, and en - ter - prise com - men - ces, reigns, and ends.
might - y stretched - out arm; glo - rious the en - rap - tured main:
match - less deed's a - chieved, de - ter - mined, dared, and done.

9 Thy strong word did cleave the darkness

Martin H. Franzmann, 1954

Music: *Ebenezer*, 8787D; Thomas J. Williams, 1890

These words can also be sung to *Blaenwern*, no. 522.

1 Thy strong word did cleave the dark-ness; at thy speak-ing it was done;
2 Lo, on those who dwelt in dark-ness, dark as night and deep as death,
3 Thy strong word be-speaks us right-eous; bright with thine own ho - li - ness,
4 From the cross thy wis-dom shin-ing break-eth forth in con-quering might;
for cre - a - ted light we thank thee, while thine or-dered sea-sons run:
broke the light of thy sal - va-tion, breathed thine own life - giv - ing breath:
glo-rious now, we press toward glo - ry, and our lives our hopes con-fess:
from the cross for - ev - er beam-eth all thy bright re - deem-ing light.
Al - le - lu - ia, al - le - lu - ia! Praise to thee who light dost send!
Al - le - lu - ia, al - le - lu - ia! Praise to thee who light dost send!
Al - le - lu - ia, al - le - lu - ia! Praise to thee who light dost send!
Al - le - lu - ia, al - le - lu - ia! Praise to thee who light dost send!
Al - le - lu - ia, al - le - lu - ia! Al - le - lu - ia with - out end!
Al - le - lu - ia, al - le - lu - ia! Al - le - lu - ia with - out end!
Al - le - lu - ia, al - le - lu - ia! Al - le - lu - ia with - out end!
Al - le - lu - ia, al - le - lu - ia! Al - le - lu - ia with - out end!

5 God Almighty, Light-Creator,
to thee laud and honor be;
to thee, Light of Light begotten,
praise be sung eternally;

Holy Spirit, Light-Revealer,
glory, glory be to thee;
mortals, angels, now and ever
praise the Holy Trinity.

10 O for a thousand tongues

"For the Anniversary Day of One's Conversion," Charles Wesley, 1739

Music: *Northfield*, 8686 extended; Jeremiah Ingalls (1764–1828);
in *Hymn and Tune Book of the Methodist Episcopal Church, South*, Nashville, 1889

1 O for a thou-sand tongues to sing my dear Re-deem-er's praise,
2 My gra-cious Mas-ter, and my God, as - sist me to pro- claim,
the glo - ries of my God and King, the
to spread through all the earth a - broad the
the glo - ries of my
to spread through all the
the
to
the glo - ries of my God and King, the glo - ries of my
to spread through all the earth a - broad, to spread through all the
tri - umphs of his grace,
hon - ors of your name,
God and King,
earth a - broad
the tri - umphs of his grace!
the hon - ors of your name.
glo - ries of my God and King,
spread through all the earth a - broad
God and King,
earth a - broad

11 O for a thousand tongues

"For the Anniversary Day of One's Conversion," Charles Wesley, 1739

Music: *Azmon*, 8686; melody by Carl G. Gläser (1784–1829); adapted and harmonized by Lowell Mason, 1829

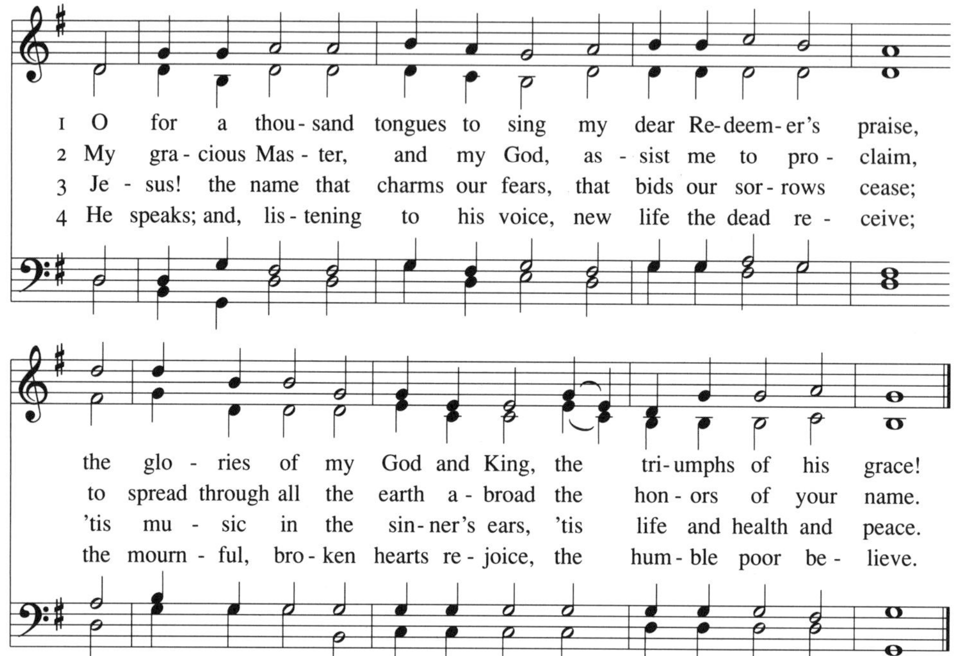
1 O for a thou - sand tongues to sing my dear Re-deem-er's praise,
2 My gra - cious Mas - ter, and my God, as - sist me to pro - claim,
3 Je - sus! the name that charms our fears, that bids our sor - rows cease;
4 He speaks; and, lis - tening to his voice, new life the dead re - ceive;
the glo - ries of my God and King, the tri-umphs of his grace!
to spread through all the earth a - broad the hon - ors of your name.
'tis mu - sic in the sin-ner's ears, 'tis life and health and peace.
the mourn - ful, bro - ken hearts re - joice, the hum - ble poor be - lieve.

5 Hear him, ye deaf; his praise, ye dumb,
your loosened tongues employ;
ye blind, behold your Savior come;
and leap, ye lame, for joy.

6 Glory to God, and praise and love
be now and ever given
by saints below and saints above,
the Church in earth and heaven.

12 Yigdal elohim chai

The living God be praised

Yigdal, medieval Jewish; versification attributed to Daniel ben Judah, c. 1400 or earlier; translated by Max Landsberg and Newton Mann, 1884–85, and others

Music: *Leoni*, 6684D; traditional Yigdal melody, transcribed by Meyer Lyon, c. 1770; harmony by Russell Schulz-Widmar, 1990

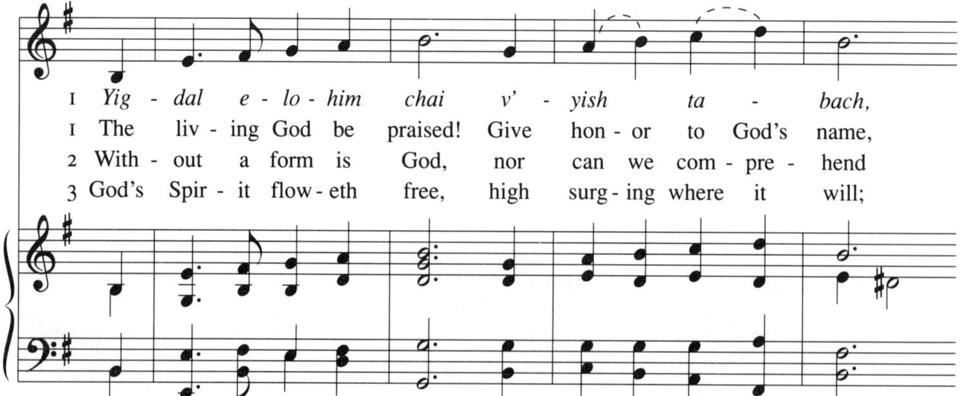
1 *Yig - dal e - lo - him chai v' - yish ta - bach,*
1 The liv - ing God be praised! Give hon - or to God's name,
2 With - out a form is God, nor can we com - pre - hend
3 God's Spir - it flow-eth free, high surg - ing where it will;

nim - tza v' - ein eit el m' - tzi - u - to.
who was, and is, and is to be, for e'er the same;
the mea - sure of God's love for us with - out an end.
in pro - phet's word God spoke of old and speak - eth still.
E - chad v' - ein ya - chid k' - yi - chu - do,
the one e - ter - nal God ere aught that now ap - pears,
For God is Lord of all, cre - a - tion speaks God's praise;
Es - tab - lished is God's law and change - less it shall stand,
ne - lam v' - gam ein sof l' - ach - du - to.
the First, the Last, be - yond all thought God's time - less years!
the hu - man race and all that lives God's will o - beys.
deep writ up - on the hu - man heart in ev - ery land.

4 Eternal life hath God
implanted in the soul;
God's love shall be our strength and stay
while ages roll.
The living God be praised!
Give honor to God's name,
who was, and is, and is to be,
for e'er the same.

13 God created heaven and earth

Taiwanese traditional hymn; translated by Boris and Clare Anderson, 1983

Music: *Toa-sia*, 7777; Taiwanese traditional melody; harmony by I-to Loh, 1983

Solo
1 God cre - a - ted heaven and earth, all things per - fect
2 Let us praise God's mer - cy great; all our needs by
3 God is one, will ev - er be; i - dols are mere
4 But God's grace be - yond com - pare saves us all from
brought to birth;
love are met;
van - i - ty;
death's de - spair;
All
God's great power made
God, who fash - ions
hand - made gods of
so earth's crea - tures
dark and light, earth re - volv - ing day and night.
all that lives, to each one a bless - ing gives.
wood and clay can - not help us when we pray.
small and great give thanks for that bless - ed state.

14 Crown him with many crowns

Matthew Bridges, 1851

Music: *Diademata*, 6686D; George J. Elvey, 1868

1 Crown him with man - y crowns, the Lamb up - on his throne;
2 Crown him the Lord of love: be - hold his hands and side,
3 Crown him the Lord of peace, whose power a scep - ter sways
4 Crown him the Lord of years, the Po - ten - tate of time,
hark, how the heaven-ly an - them drowns all mu - sic but its own:
rich wounds, yet vis - i - ble a - bove in beau - ty glo - ri - fied:
from pole to pole, that wars may cease, and all be prayer and praise:
Cre - a - tor of the roll - ing spheres, in - ef - fab - ly sub - lime:
a - wake, my soul, and sing of him who died for thee,
no an - gels in the skies can ful - ly bear that sight,
his reign shall know no end; and round his pierc - ed feet
all hail, Re - deem - er, hail! For you have died for me.
and hail him as thy match-less King through all e - ter - ni - ty.
but down - ward bend their burn - ing eyes at mys - ter - ies so bright.
fair flowers of par - a - dise ex - tend their fra - grance ev - er sweet.
Your praise shall nev - er, nev - er fail through - out e - ter - ni - ty.

15 Who is she

Brian Wren, 1983

Music: *Marjorie*, 36566D; Jane Manton Marshall, 1990

1 Who is she, nei - ther male nor fe - male,
2 Who is she, mo - ther - ing her peo - ple,
3 Who is she, spar - kle in the ra - pids,
4 Who is she, mo - ther of all na - ture,
mak - er of all things, on - ly glimpsed or hint - ed,
teach - ing them to walk, lift - ing wea - ry tod - dlers,
cool - ness of the well, liv - ing power of Je - sus
dy - ing to give birth, gasp - ing yet ex - ult - ing,
source of life and gen - der? She is God,
bend - ing down to feed them? She is Love,
flow - ing from the scrip - tures? She is Life,
to a new cre - a - tion? She is Hope,
mo - ther, sis - ter, lov - er; in her love we wake,
cry - ing in a sta - ble, teach - ing from a boat,
wa - ter, wind and laugh - ter, calm, yet nev - er still,
nev - er tired of lov - ing, fill - ing all with worth,

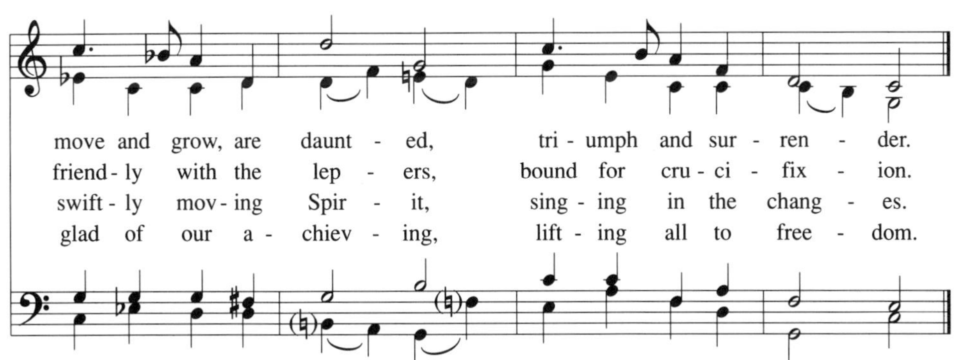
move and grow, are daunt - ed, tri - umph and sur - ren - der.
friend - ly with the lep - ers, bound for cru - ci - fix - ion.
swift - ly mov - ing Spir - it, sing - ing in the chang - es.
glad of our a - chiev - ing, lift - ing all to free - dom.

16 Jesus shall reign

Isaac Watts, 1719, based on Psalm 72

Music: *Duke Street*, 8888; melody in Henry Boyd's *Psalm and Hymn Tunes*, Glasgow, 1793; probably by John Hatton

1 Je - sus shall reign wher - e'er the sun doth its suc -
2 To him shall end - less prayer be made, and prais - es
3 Peo - ple and realms of ev - ery tongue dwell on his
4 Bless - ings a - bound wher - e'er he reigns; the prison - ers

ces - sive jour - neys run; his king - dom stretch from
throng to crown his head; his name like sweet per -
love with sweet - est song; and in - fant voic - es
leap to lose their chains, the wea - ry find e -

shore to shore till moons shall wax and wane no more.
fume shall rise with ev - ery morn - ing sac - ri - fice.
shall pro - claim their ear - ly bless - ings on his name.
ter - nal rest, and all who suf - fer want are blest.

5 Let every creature rise and bring
honors peculiar to our King;
angels descend with songs again,
and earth repeat the loud Amen.

17 Psallite Deo nostro

Music: Canon by Giambattista Martini (1706–1784)

1
Psal - li - te De - o nos - tro,
2
psal - - - li - te,
3
psal - - - li - te.

18 Alleluia! Give thanks to the risen Lord

Donald Fishel, 1971

Music: *Alleluia No. 1*, 88 with refrain; Donald Fishel, 1971, with Betty Pulkingham, Charles Mallory, and George Mims

Refrain
Al - le - lu - ia, al - le - lu - ia! Give thanks to the
ris - en Lord. Al - le - lu - ia, al - le - lu - ia! Give

1–4
5
praise to his name.
name.
1 Je - sus is Lord of all the earth.
2 Spread the good news o'er all the earth:
3 We have been cru - ci - fied with Christ.
4 Come, let us praise the liv - ing God,
D.C.
Je - sus is King of cre - a - tion.
Je - sus has died and has ris - en.
Now we shall live for ev - er.
joy - ful - ly sing to our Sa - vior.
Al- le -
D.C.

19 At the name of Jesus

Caroline M. Noel, 1870

Music: *King's Weston*, 6565D; Ralph Vaughan Williams, 1925

1 At the name of Je - sus ev - ery knee shall bow,
2 At his voice cre - a - tion sprang at once to sight,
3 Hum-bled for a sea - son, to re-ceive a name
4 bore it up tri - umph - ant, with its hu - man light,

ev - ery tongue con - fess him King of glo - ry now;
all the an - gel fac - es, all the hosts of light,
from the lips of sin - ners, un - to whom he came,
through all ranks of crea - tures, to the cen - tral height,

'tis the Fa-ther's plea - sure we should call him Lord,
thrones and dom - in - a - tions, stars up - on their way,
faith - ful - ly he bore it spot - less to the last,
to the throne of God - head, to the Fa-ther's breast;

who from the be - gin - ning was the might - y Word.
all the heaven-ly or - ders in their great ar - ray.
brought it back vic - to - rious, when from death he passed;
filled it with the glo - ry of that per - fect rest.

5 In your hearts enthrone him;
there let him subdue
all that is not holy,
all that is not true;
crown him as your Captain
in temptation's hour;
let his will enfold you
in its light and power.

6 Name him, Christians, name him,
with love strong as death,
name with awe and wonder
and with bated breath;
he is God the Savior,
he is Christ the Lord,
ever to be worshiped,
trusted, and adored.

20 How shall I sing that majesty

John Mason, *Spiritual Songs*, 1683

Music: *Old 22nd*, 8686D; melody of Psalm 16 in the *Anglo-Genevan Psalter*, 1556

These words can also be sung to *Kingsfold*, no. 379.

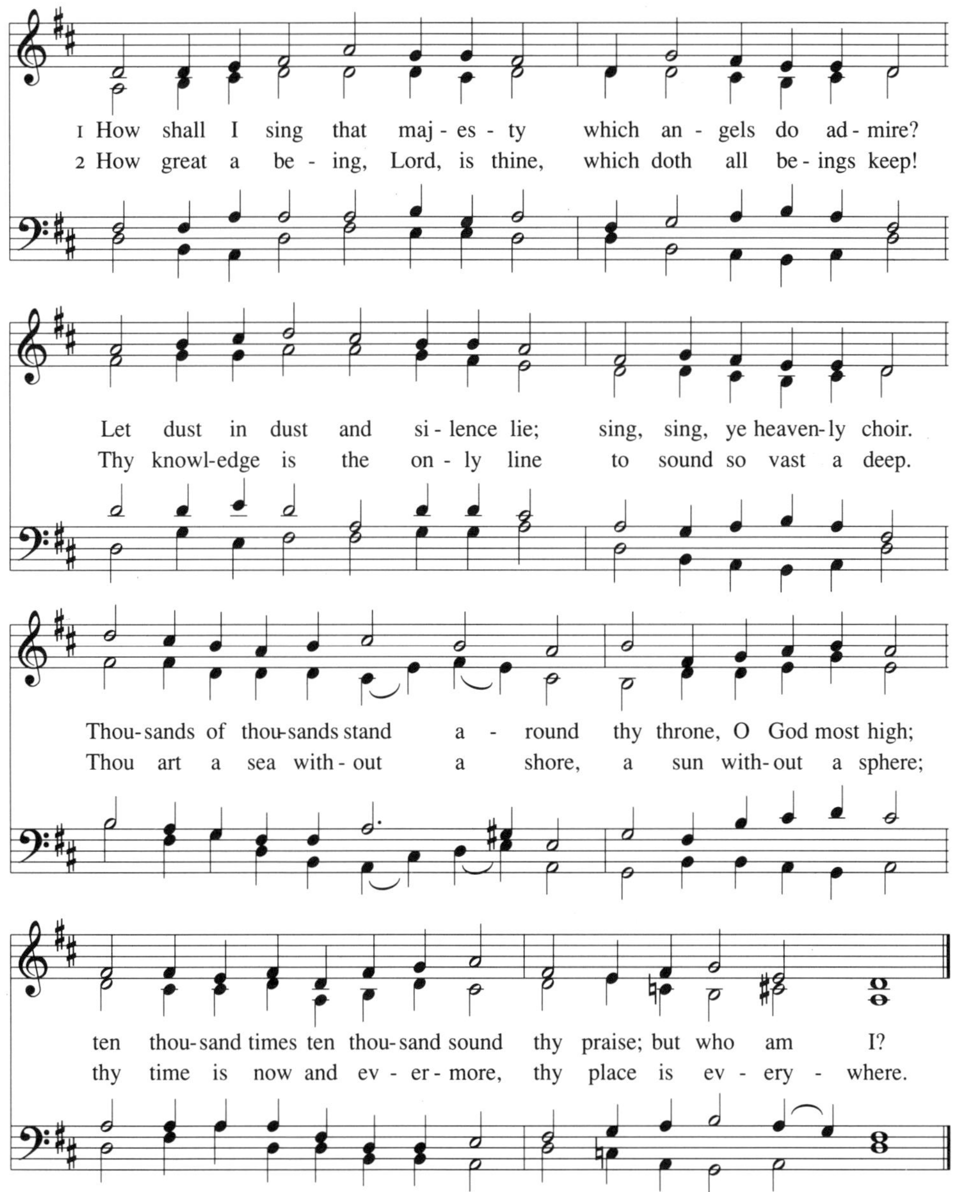
1 How shall I sing that maj - es - ty which an - gels do ad - mire?
2 How great a be - ing, Lord, is thine, which doth all be - ings keep!
Let dust in dust and si - lence lie; sing, sing, ye heaven - ly choir.
Thy knowl - edge is the on - ly line to sound so vast a deep.
Thou - sands of thou - sands stand a - round thy throne, O God most high;
Thou art a sea with - out a shore, a sun with - out a sphere;
ten thou - sand times ten thou - sand sound thy praise; but who am I?
thy time is now and ev - er - more, thy place is ev - ery - where.

21 All hail the power of Jesus' name

Edward Perronet, 1779, 1780, and others

Music: *Coronation*, 8686 extended; melody by Oliver Holden in his *Union Harmony*, 1793

1 All hail the power of Je - sus' name! Let an - gels pros-trate fall;
2 Crown him, ye mar - tyrs of our God, who from his al - tar call;
3 Ye chos - en seed of Is - rael's race, ye ran - somed from the fall,
4 Sin - ners, whose love can ne'er for - get the worm-wood and the gall,
bring forth the roy - al di - a - dem, and crown him Lord of all.
ex - tol the stem of Jes - se's rod, and crown him Lord of all.
hail him who saves you by his grace, and crown him Lord of all.
go spread your tro - phies at his feet, and crown him Lord of all.
Bring forth the roy - al di - a - dem, and crown him Lord of all.
Ex - tol the stem of Jes - se's rod, and crown him Lord of all.
Hail him who saves you by his grace, and crown him Lord of all.
Go spread your tro - phies at his feet, and crown him Lord of all.

5 Let every kindred, every tribe
on this terrestrial ball,
to him all majesty ascribe,
and crown him Lord of all.

6 O that with yonder sacred throng
we at his feet may fall!
We'll join the everlasting song,
and crown him Lord of all.

22 All hail the power of Jesus' name

Edward Perronet, 1779, 1780, and others

Music: *Miles Lane*, 8686 extended; melody by William Shrubsole, 1779

Refrain
1 All hail the power of Je - sus' name! Let an - gels pros-trate fall;
2 Crown him, ye mar - tyrs of our God, who from his al - tar call;
3 Ye chos - en seed of Is - rael's race, ye ran - somed from the fall,
4 Sin - ners, whose love can ne'er for - get the worm-wood and the gall,
bring forth the roy - al di - a - dem,
ex - tol the stem of Jes - se's rod,
hail him who saves you by his grace,
go spread your tro - phies at his feet,
and
crown him, crown him, crown him, crown him Lord of all.

5 Let every kindred, every tribe
on this terrestrial ball,
  to him all majesty ascribe,

Refrain

6 O that with yonder sacred throng
we at his feet may fall!
  We'll join the everlasting song,

Refrain

23 I greet thee, who my sure Redeemer art

Je te salue, mon certain Redempteur

Attributed to John Calvin, 1545; translated by Elizabeth Lee Smith, 1869, and others

Music: *Sheldonian*, 10.10.10.10; Cyril V. Taylor, 1943

These words can also be sung to *Toulon*, no. 431.

1 I greet thee, who my sure Re - deem - er art,
2 Thou art the source of mer - cy and of grace,
3 Thou art the Life, by which a - lone we live,
4 Thou hast the true and per - fect gen - tle - ness,
my on - ly trust and Sa - vior of my heart,
rul - ing om - ni - po - tent in ev - ery place;
and all our sub - stance and our strength re - ceive;
no harsh - ness hast thou and no bit - ter - ness:
who pain didst un - der - go for my poor sake;
so reign in us and our whole be - ing sway;
sus - tain us by thy faith and by thy power,
O grant to us the grace we find in thee,
I pray thee from our hearts all cares to take.
shine on us with the light of thy pure day.
and give us strength in ev - ery try - ing hour.
that we may dwell in per - fect u - ni - ty.

5 Our hope is in no other save in thee;
our faith is built upon thy promise free;
Lord, give us peace, and make us calm and sure,
that in thy strength we evermore endure.

24 Holy, holy, holy! Lord God Almighty

Reginald Heber, 1826

Music: *Nicaea*, 11.12.12.10; John Bacchus Dykes, 1861

1 Ho - ly, ho - ly, ho - ly! Lord God Al - might - y!
2 Ho - ly, ho - ly, ho - ly! All the saints a - dore thee,
3 Ho - ly, ho - ly, ho - ly! Though the dark - ness hide thee,
4 Ho - ly, ho - ly, ho - ly! Lord God Al - might - y!
Ear - ly in the morn - ing our song shall rise to thee:
cast - ing down their gold - en crowns a - round the glass - y sea;
though the eye made blind by sin thy glo - ry may not see,
All thy works shall praise thy name in earth, and sky, and sea;
ho - ly, ho - ly, ho - ly! Mer - ci - ful and might - y,
cher - u - bim and ser - a - phim fall - ing down be - fore thee,
on - ly thou art ho - ly; there is none be - side thee,
Ho - ly, ho - ly, ho - ly! Mer - ci - ful and might - y,
God in three per - sons, bless - ed Trin - i - ty.
God ev - er - last - ing through e - ter - ni - ty.
per - fect in power, in love, and pur - i - ty.
God in three per - sons, bless - ed Trin - i - ty.

25 Joyful, joyful we adore thee

Henry Van Dyke, 1907

Music: *Hymn to Joy*, 8787D; melody taken from Beethoven's Ninth Symphony by Elam Ives in *The Mozart Collection*, New York, 1846

1 Joy - ful, joy - ful we a - dore thee, God of glo - ry, Lord of love;
2 All thy works with joy sur - round thee, earth and heaven re - flect thy rays,
3 Mor- tals, join the might - y cho - rus which the morn - ing stars be - gan;
hearts un - fold like flowers be - fore thee, o - pening to the sun a - bove.
stars and an - gels sing a - round thee, cen - ter of un - brok - en praise.
love di - vine is reign - ing o'er us, bind - ing all with - in its span.
Melt the clouds of sin and sad - ness; drive the dark of doubt a - way;
Field and for - est, vale and moun-tain, flow - ery mea - dow, flash - ing sea,
Ev - er sing - ing, march we on - ward, vic - tors in the midst of strife;
Giv - er of im - mor - tal glad - ness, fill us with the light of day.
chant - ing bird and flow - ing foun - tain, call us to re - joice in thee.
joy - ful mu - sic leads us sun - ward in the tri - umph song of life.

26 O God, beneath thy guiding hand

Leonard Bacon, for the bicentenary of New Haven, Connecticut, 1838

Music: *Duke Street*, 8888; melody from Henry Boyd's *Psalm and Hymn Tunes*, 1793; probably by John Hatton

1 O God, be - neath thy guid - ing hand
2 Thou heard'st, well pleased, the song, the prayer:
3 Laws, free - dom, truth, and faith in God
4 And here thy name, O God of love,
our ex - iled fore - bears crossed the sea;
thy bless - ing came; and still its power
came with those ex - iles o'er the waves;
their chil - dren's chil - dren shall a - dore,
and when they trod the win - try strand,
shall on - ward, through all a - ges, bear
and where their pil - grim feet have trod,
till these e - ter - nal hills re - move,
with prayer and psalm they wor - shiped thee.
the mem - ory of that ho - ly hour.
the God they trust - ed guards their graves.
and spring a - dorns the earth no more.

27 Let all the world in every corner sing

George Herbert, 1633 (posth.)

Music: *MacDougall*, 6666 with refrain; Calvin Hampton, 1974

Let all the world in ev - ery cor - ner sing, my
God and King. Let all the world in
ev - ery cor - ner sing, my God and King.
1 The
2 The

heavens are not too high, God's prais - es there may fly; the
Church with psalms must shout, no door can keep them out; but,
earth is not too low, God's prais - es there may grow.
a - bove all, the heart must bear the long - est part.
Let all the world in ev - ery cor - ner sing, my
God and King. King. A - men.
1
2

28 Let all the world in every corner sing

George Herbert, 1633 (posth.)

Music: *Augustine*, 6666 with refrain; Erik Routley, 1960

Let all the world in ev-ery cor-ner sing, my God and King.
1 The heavens are not too high, God's prais-es there may fly;
the
the earth is not too low, God's prais-es there may grow.
(accomp.)
Let all the world in ev-ery cor-ner sing, my God and King.
2 The Church with psalms must shout, no door can keep them out;
but,

but, a - bove all, the heart must bear the long - est part.
(accomp.)
Let all the world in every cor- ner sing, my God and King.

29 Morning glory, starlit sky

W. H. Vanstone, 1980

Music: *Bingham*, 7777; Dorothy Howell Sheets, 1985

1 Morn- ing glo - ry, star- lit sky, soar - ing mu- sic, schol-ar's truth,
2 o - pen are the gifts of God, gifts of love to mind and sense;
3 Love that gives, gives ev - er- more, gives with zeal, with ea - ger hands,
4 Drained is love in mak-ing full, bound in set- ting o- thers free,

flight of swal-lows, au- tumn leaves, mem- ory's trea - sure, grace of youth:
hid - den is love's a - go - ny, love's en - deav - or, love's ex - pense.
spares not, keeps not, all out - pours, ven- tures all, its all ex - pends.
poor in mak - ing man - y rich, weak in giv - ing power to be.

5 Therefore he who shows us God
helpless hangs upon the tree;
and the nails and crown of thorns
tell of what God's love must be.

6 Here is God: no monarch he,
throned in easy state to reign;
here is God, whose arms of love
aching, spent, the world sustain.

30 Lift up your heads

Macht hoch die Tür

Georg Weissel, 1642 (posth.), based on Psalm 24;
translation adapted from Catherine Winkworth, 1855

Music: *Macht hoch die Tür*, 88888866; melody by J. A. Freylinghausen, 1704; harmony by Rudolf Mauersberger (1889–1971) for the Dresden Kreuzchor

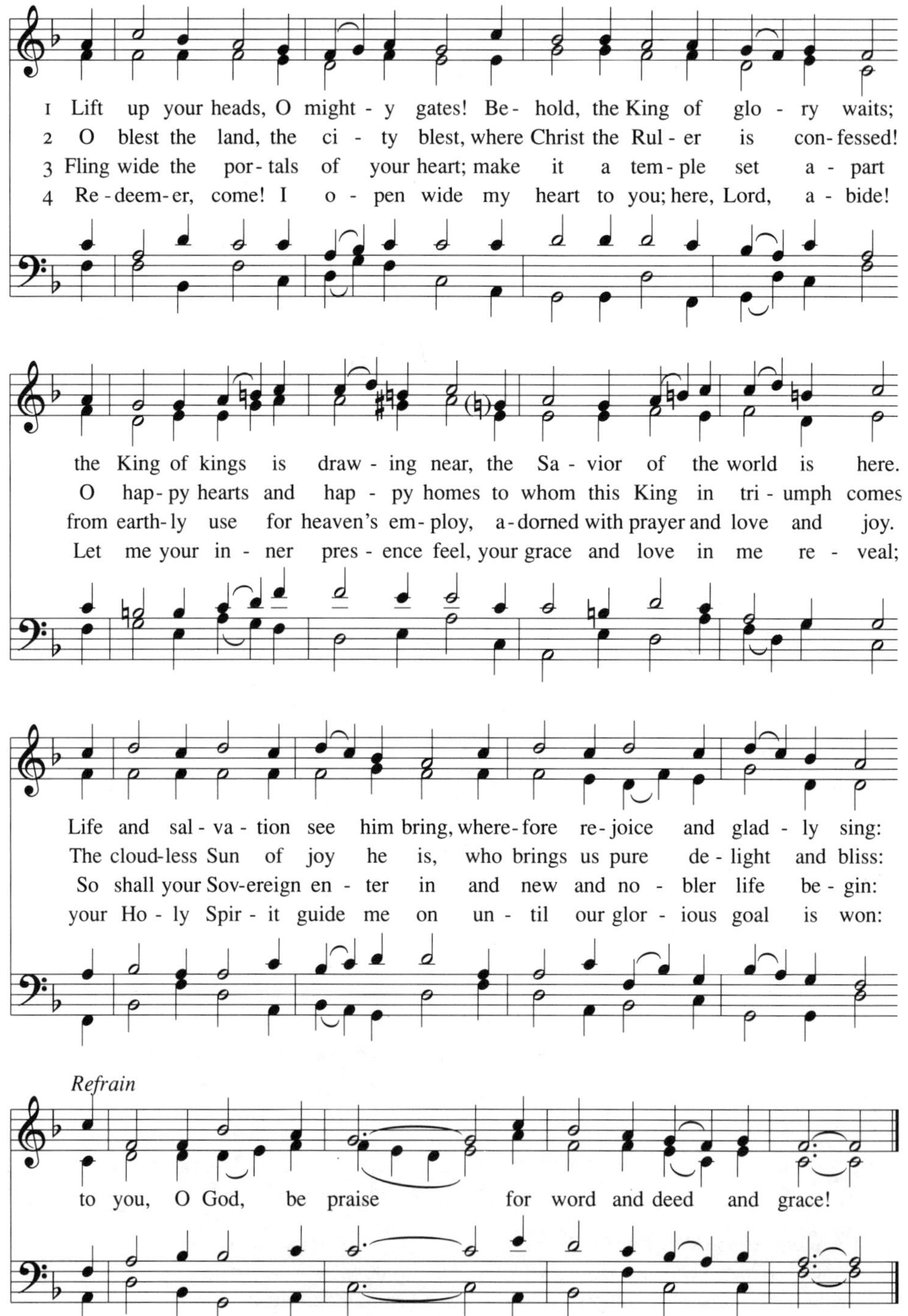
1 Lift up your heads, O might - y gates! Be- hold, the King of glo - ry waits;
2 O blest the land, the ci - ty blest, where Christ the Rul - er is con- fessed!
3 Fling wide the por- tals of your heart; make it a tem- ple set a - part
4 Re - deem- er, come! I o - pen wide my heart to you; here, Lord, a - bide!
the King of kings is draw - ing near, the Sa - vior of the world is here.
O hap- py hearts and hap - py homes to whom this King in tri - umph comes
from earth- ly use for heaven's em- ploy, a - dorned with prayer and love and joy.
Let me your in - ner pres - ence feel, your grace and love in me re - veal;
Life and sal - va - tion see him bring, where- fore re- joice and glad - ly sing:
The cloud-less Sun of joy he is, who brings us pure de - light and bliss:
So shall your Sov-ereign en - ter in and new and no - bler life be - gin:
your Ho - ly Spir - it guide me on un - til our glor - ious goal is won:
Refrain
to you, O God, be praise for word and deed and grace!

31 My song is love unknown

Samuel Crossman, 1664

Music: *Love Unknown*, 66664444; John Ireland, 1918

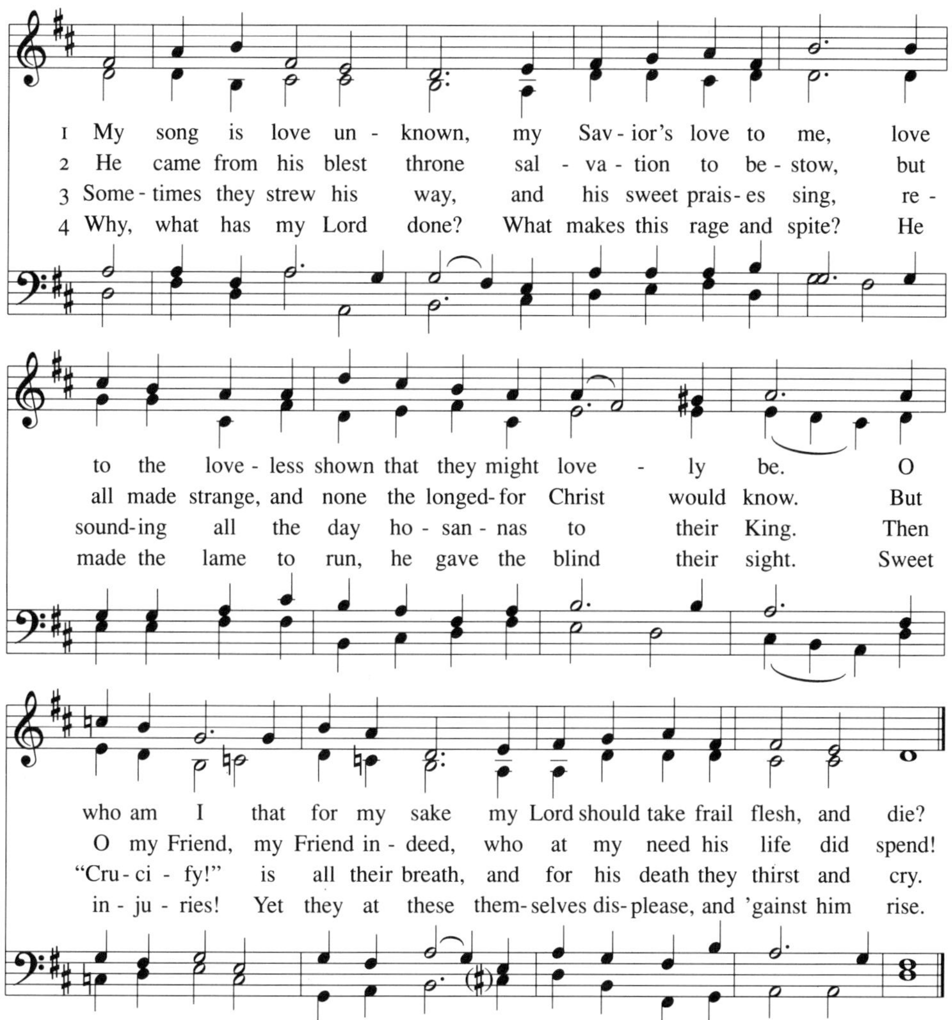
1 My song is love un - known, my Sav - ior's love to me, love
2 He came from his blest throne sal - va - tion to be - stow, but
3 Some - times they strew his way, and his sweet prais - es sing, re -
4 Why, what has my Lord done? What makes this rage and spite? He
to the love - less shown that they might love - ly be. O
all made strange, and none the longed - for Christ would know. But
sound - ing all the day ho - san - nas to their King. Then
made the lame to run, he gave the blind their sight. Sweet
who am I that for my sake my Lord should take frail flesh, and die?
O my Friend, my Friend in - deed, who at my need his life did spend!
"Cru - ci - fy!" is all their breath, and for his death they thirst and cry.
in - ju - ries! Yet they at these them - selves dis - please, and 'gainst him rise.
(♮)

5 They rise, and needs will have
my dear Lord made away;
a murderer they save,
the Prince of life they slay.
Yet cheerful he
to suffering goes,
that he his foes
from thence might free.

6 In life no house, no home
my Lord on earth might have;
in death no friendly tomb
but what a stranger gave.
What may I say?
Heaven was his home;
but mine the tomb
wherein he lay.

7 Here might I stay and sing,
no story so divine:
never was love, dear King,
never was grief like thine.
This is my Friend,
in whose sweet praise
I all my days
could gladly spend.

32 Let folly praise what fancy loves

Robert Southwell (1561–1595)

Music: *Tye (Acts)*, 8686D; Christopher Tye, 1553

1 Let fol - ly praise what fan - cy loves, I praise and love that child
2 Love's sweet- est mark, laud's high- est theme, our most de- sired for light,
3 Though young yet wise, though small yet strong, though Man, yet God he is;
whose heart no thought, whose tongue no word, whose hand no deed de - filed.
to love him life, to leave him death, to live in him de - light.
as wise he knows, as strong he can, as God he loves to bless.
I praise him most, I love him best, all praise and love is his;
He mine by gift, I his by debt, thus each to oth - er due,
His knowl-edge rules, his strength de - fends, his love doth cher-ish all;
while him I love, in him I live, and can - not live a - miss.
first friend he was, best friend he is, all times will find him true.
his birth our joy, his life our light, his death our end of thrall.

33 O Trinity, O Trinity

Michael Saward (b. 1932); from the Lenten *Triodion* of the Orthodox Church

Music: *Trinity*, 86867788; Kenneth W. Coates (b. 1917)

1 O Trin - i - ty, O Trin - i - ty, the un - cre - at - ed One;
2 O Maj - es - ty, O Maj - es - ty, Cre - a - tor of our race;
3 O Vir - gin - born, O Vir - gin - born, of hu - man - kind the least;
4 O Wind of God, O Wind of God, in - vig - or - ate the dead;
O U - ni - ty, O U - ni - ty, of Fa - ther, Spir - it, Son:
O Mys - ter - y, O Mys - ter - y, we can - not see your face:
O Vic - tim torn, O Vic - tim torn, both spot - less lamb and priest:
O Fire of God, O Fire of God, your burn - ing rad - iance spread:
you are with - out be - gin - ning, your life is nev - er end - ing;
your jus - tice is un - swerv - ing, your love is o - ver - pow - ering;
you died and rose vic - to - rious, you reign a - bove all - glo - rious;
your fruit our lives re - new - ing, your gifts the Church trans - form - ing;
Refrain
and though our tongues are earth - bound clay, light them with flam - ing fire to - day.

5 O Trinity, O Trinity,
the uncreated One;
O Unity, O Unity
of Father, Spirit, Son:
you are without beginning,
your life is never ending;

Refrain

34 Nature with open volume stands

Isaac Watts, 1707

Music: *Eltham*, 8888; melody in Nathaniel Gawthorn's *Harmonia Perfecta*, London, 1730; harmony by Samuel Sebastian Wesley, 1872

1 Na - ture with o - pen vol - ume stands
2 But in the grace that res - cued us
3 Here God's whole name ap - pears com - plete;
4 O the sweet won - ders of that cross
to spread her Mak - er's praise a - broad
God's bright - est form of glo - ry shines;
nor wit can guess, nor rea - son prove
where God the Sa - vior loved and died!
and ev - ery la - bor of his hands
'tis fair - est drawn here on the cross
which of the let - ters best is writ,
Its nob - lest life my spir - it draws
shows some - thing wor - thy of a God.
in pre - cious blood and crim - son lines.
the power, the wis - dom, or the love.
from his dear wounds and bleed - ing side.

5 I would for ever speak his name
in sounds to mortal ears unknown,
with angels join to praise the Lamb
and worship at his Father's throne!

35 Now thank we all our God

Nun danket alle Gott

Martin Rinkart, c. 1636; translated by Catherine Winkworth, 1858

Music: *Nun danket alle Gott*, 67676666; melody by Johann Crüger, 1647; harmony adapted from Mendelssohn's *Lobgesang*, 1840

1 Now thank we all our God with heart and hands and voic - es,
2 O may this boun-teous God through all our life be near us,
3 All praise and thanks to God the Fa - ther now be giv - en,
who won-drous things hath done, in whom this world re - joic - es;
with ev - er joy - ful hearts and bless - ed peace to cheer us;
the Son, and Spir - it blest, who reign in high-est hea - ven,
who from our mo - ther's arms hath blessed us on our way
and keep us strong in grace, and guide us when per - plexed,
the one e - ter - nal God, whom earth and heaven a - dore;
with count-less gifts of love, and still is ours to - day.
and free us from all ills in this world and the next.
for thus it was, is now, and shall be ev - er - more.

36 O Morning Star, how fair and bright

Wie schön leuchtet der Morgenstern

Philipp Nicolai, 1599; stanzas 1–2 based on Catherine Winkworth, 1863;
stanza 3 from *Lutheran Book of Worship*, 1978

Music: *Wie schön leuchtet der Morgenstern*, 8878874848; Philipp Nicolai, 1598;
harmony by Johann Herman Schein, 1627

1 O Morn-ing Star, how fair and bright! You shine with God's own truth and light,
2 Come, heaven-ly bright-ness, light di - vine, and deep with - in our hearts now shine;
3 What joy to know, when life is past, that you, O Lord, are first and last,
a - glow with grace and mer - cy! Of Ja-cob's race, King Da-vid's Son,
there light a flame un - dy - ing! In your one bo - dy let us be
the end and the be - gin - ning! You will one day, O glo-rious grace,
our Lord and Mas - ter, you have won our hearts to serve you on - ly!
as liv - ing branch-es of a tree, your life our lives sup-ply - ing.
trans-port us to that hap - py place be - yond all tears and sin - ning!
Low - ly, ho - ly! Great and glo-rious, all vic - to-rious, rich in bless-ing!
Now, though dai - ly earth's deep sad-ness may per-plex us and dis-tress us,
A - men! A - men! Come, Lord Je - sus! Crown of glad-ness! We are yearn-ing

Rule and might o'er all pos - sess - ing!
yet with heaven - ly joy you bless us.
for the day of your re - turn - ing.

37 Praise, my soul, the King of heaven

Henry Francis Lyte, 1834, based on Psalm 103

Music: *Lauda anima*, 878787; John Goss, 1869

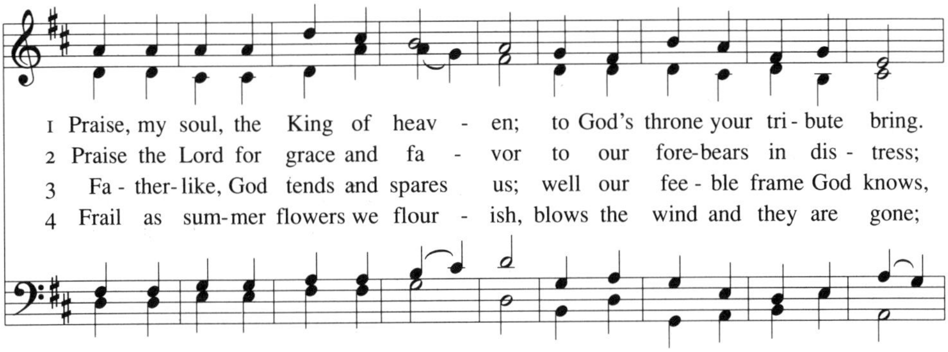

1 Praise, my soul, the King of heav - en; to God's throne your tri - bute bring.
2 Praise the Lord for grace and fa - vor to our fore-bears in dis - tress;
3 Fa - ther-like, God tends and spares us; well our fee - ble frame God knows,
4 Frail as sum-mer flowers we flour - ish, blows the wind and they are gone;

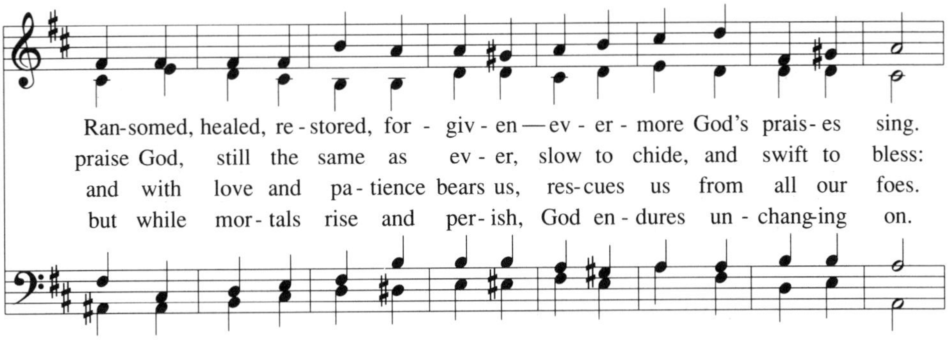

Ran-somed, healed, re - stored, for - giv - en — ev - er - more God's prais - es sing.
praise God, still the same as ev - er, slow to chide, and swift to bless:
and with love and pa - tience bears us, res-cues us from all our foes.
but while mor - tals rise and per - ish, God en - dures un - chang-ing on.

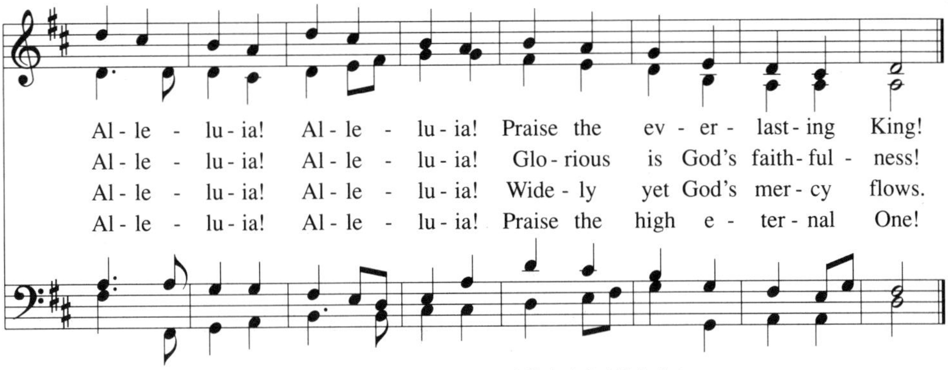

Al - le - lu - ia! Al - le - lu - ia! Praise the ev - er - last - ing King!
Al - le - lu - ia! Al - le - lu - ia! Glo - rious is God's faith - ful - ness!
Al - le - lu - ia! Al - le - lu - ia! Wide - ly yet God's mer - cy flows.
Al - le - lu - ia! Al - le - lu - ia! Praise the high e - ter - nal One!

5 Angels, songs of joy outpouring,
who behold God face to face,
sun and moon, who bow adoring,
all who dwell in time and space:
Alleluia! Alleluia!
Praise with us the God of grace!

38 Praise to the Holiest in the height

From "The Dream of Gerontius," John Henry Newman, 1865

Music: *Newman*, 8686; Richard R. Terry, 1912

1 Praise to the Ho - liest in the height, and in the
2 O lov - ing wis - dom of our God, when all was
3 O wis - est love, that flesh and blood, which did in
4 and that a high - er gift than grace should flesh and
depth be praise; in all his words most
sin and shame, a sec - ond A - dam
A - dam fail, should strive a - fresh a -
blood re - fine: God's pres - ence and his
won - der - ful, most sure in all his ways!
to the fight and to the res - cue came.
gainst the foe, should strive, and should pre - vail;
ve - ry self, and es - sence all di - vine.

5 O generous love! that Christ who smote
in man for man the foe,
the double agony in man
for man should undergo;

6 and in the garden secretly,
and on the cross on high,
should teach us all, and should inspire
to suffer and to die.

7 Praise to the Holiest in the height,
and in the depth be praise;
in all his words most wonderful,
most sure in all his ways!

39 Praise to the Lord, the Almighty

Lobe den Herren

Joachim Neander, 1680; based on Psalms 103 and 150; translated by Catherine Winkworth, 1863, and others

Music: *Lobe den Herren*, 14.14.4.7.8; melody in *Stralsund Gesangbuch*, 1665; harmony from Johannes Zahn's *Psalter und Harfe*, Gütersloh, 1886

1 Praise to the Lord, the Al - might - y, who rules all cre - a - tion!
2 Praise to the Lord, a - bove all things so might - i - ly reign - ing,
3 Praise to the Lord, who will pros - per our work and de - fend us;
4 Praise to the Lord, O let all that is in me a - dore him!
O my soul, praise him, at all times your health and sal - va - tion!
keep - ing us safe at his side, and so gent - ly sus - tain - ing.
sure - ly his good - ness and mer - cy will dai - ly at - tend us.
All that has life and breath come now with prais - es be - fore him!
Come, all who hear: bro - thers and sis - ters, draw near,
Have you not seen how all you need - ed has been
Pon - der a - new what the Al - might - y can do,
Let the A - men! sound from God's peo - ple a - gain;
join - ing in glad a - dor - a - tion!
met by God's gra - cious or - dain - ing?
who out of love will be - friend us.
glad - ly with praise we a - dore him!

40 Tell out, my soul

Timothy Dudley-Smith, 1961, based on *Magnificat*

Music: *Woodlands*, 10.10.10.10; Walter Greatorex, 1919

1 Tell out, my soul, the great - ness of the Lord!
2 Tell out, my soul, the great - ness of his name!
3 Tell out, my soul, the great - ness of his might!
4 Tell out, my soul, the glo - ries of his word!
Un - num - bered bless - ings give my spir - it voice;
Make known his might, the deeds his arm has done;
Powers and do - min - ions lay their glo - ry by.
Firm is his prom - ise, and his mer - cy sure.
ten - der to me the prom - ise of his word;
his mer - cy sure, from age to age the same;
Proud hearts and stub - born wills are put to flight,
Tell out, my soul, the great - ness of the Lord

in God my Sa - vior shall my heart re - joice.
his ho - ly name — the Lord, the Might - y One.
the hun - gry fed, the hum - ble lift - ed high.
to chil - dren's chil - dren and for ev - er - more!

41 Holy God, we praise your name

Großer Gott, wir loben dich

Attributed to Ignaz Franz, c. 1770, based on *Te Deum laudamus*; translated by Clarence Walworth, 1853

Music: *Großer Gott, wir loben dich*, 787877;
melody in *Katholisches Gesangbuch*, Vienna, 1774

1 Ho - ly God, we praise your name, Lord of all, we bow be - fore you;
2 Hark, the glad ce - les - tial hymn an - gel choirs a - bove are rais - ing;
3 Lo, the a - pos - to - lic train joins your sa - cred name to hal - low;
4 Ho - ly Fa - ther, Ho - ly Son, Ho - ly Spir - it, Three we name you,

all on earth your rule ac - claim, all in heaven a - bove a - dore you;
cher - u - bim and ser - a - phim, in un - ceas - ing cho - rus prais - ing,
pro - phets swell the glad re - frain, and the white - robed mar - tyrs fol - low;
through in es - sence on - ly one, un - di - vid - ed God we claim you;

in - fin - ite your vast do - main, ev - er - last - ing is your reign.
fill the heavens with sweet ac - cord: ho - ly, ho - ly, ho - ly Lord!
and, from morn till set of sun, through the Church the song goes on.
and, a - dor - ing, bend the knee while we own the mys - ter - y.

42 Praise the Lord! O heavens, adore him

Anonymous, based on Psalm 148; from a leaflet pasted in the back of *Psalms, Hymns and Anthems of the Foundling Hospital*, London, 1796–1801

Music: *Rustington*, 8787D; C. Hubert H. Parry, 1897

These words can also be sung to *Austria*, no. 291.

1 Praise the Lord! O heavens, a - dore him; praise God, an - gels in the height;
2 Praise the Lord, for he is glo- rious, nev - er shall God's pro-mise fail;
sun and moon, re - joice be - fore him; praise God, gleam- ing stars and light.
God has made his saints vic - to- rious, sin and death shall not pre - vail.
Praise the Lord, for he has spok-en; worlds his might- y voice o - beyed;
Praise the God of our sal - va- tion; hosts on high, his power pro - claim;
laws which nev - er shall be brok- en for their guid- ance God has made.
heaven and earth, and all cre - a- tion, laud and mag - ni - fy God's name!

43 Sing praise to God who reigns above

Sei Lob und Ehr' dem höchsten Gut

Johann Jakob Schütz, 1675; translated by Frances Elizabeth Cox, 1864

Music: *Mit Freuden zart*, 8787887; melody in *Kirchengesang*, Berlin, 1566; harmony by Russell Schulz-Widmar, 1990

1 Sing praise to God who reigns a - bove, the God of all cre - a - tion,
2 The Lord is nev - er far a - way, but, through all grief dis - tress - ing,
3 Thus, all my glad - some way a - long, I sing a - loud your prais - es,
4 Let all who name Christ's ho - ly name give God all praise and glo - ry;
the God of power, the God of love, the God of our sal - va - tion.
an ev - er pres - ent help and stay, our peace and joy and bless - ing.
that all may hear the grate - ful song my voice un - wea - ried rais - es.
let all who own his power pro - claim a - loud the won - drous sto - ry!
With heal - ing balm my soul is filled and ev - ery faith - less mur - mur stilled:
As with a moth - er's ten - der hand, God gent - ly leads the cho - sen band:
Be joy - ful in the Lord, my heart, both soul and bod - y bear your part:
Cast each false i - dol from its throne, for Christ is Lord, and Christ a - lone:
to God all praise and glo - ry.
to God all praise and glo - ry.
to God all praise and glo - ry.
to God all praise and glo - ry.

44 Rejoice, the Lord is King

Charles Wesley, 1746

Music: *Gopsal*, 666688; melody and bass by G. F. Handel (1685–1759); edited and arranged by John Wilson (b. 1905)

These words can also be sung to *Darwall's 148th*, no. 300.

1 Re - joice, the Lord is King! Your Lord and King a - dore!
2 Je - sus the Sa - vior reigns, the God of truth and love;
3 His king-dom can - not fail, he rules o'er earth and heaven;
4 Re - joice in glo - rious hope; Je - sus the Judge shall come,
Mor - tals, give thanks and sing, and tri - umph ev - er - more:
when he had purged our stains he took his seat a - bove:
the keys of death and hell are to our Je - sus given:
and take his ser - vants up to their e - ter - nal home:
Refrain
Lift up your heart, lift up your voice; Re-joice! A-gain I say: Re-joice!

45 We sing the praise of him who died

Thomas Kelly, 1815

Music: *Breslau*, 8888; German traditional melody;
arranged and harmonized by Felix Mendelssohn in his *St. Paul*, 1836

1 We sing the praise of him who died,
2 In - scribed up - on the cross we see
3 The cross! It takes our guilt a - way,
4 It makes the cow - ard spir - it brave,
of him who died up - on the cross;
in shin - ing let - ters, "God is love";
and holds the faint - ing spir - it up;
and nerves the fee - ble arm for fight;
the sin - ner's hope let sin de - ride;
he bears our sins up - on the tree:
it cheers with hope the gloom - y day,
it takes all ter - ror from the grave,
for this we count the world but loss.
he brings us mer - cy from a - bove.
and sweet - ens ev - ery bit - ter cup.
and gilds the bed of death with light;

5 the balm of life, the cure of woe,
the measure and the pledge of love,
the sinners' refuge here below,
the angels' theme in heaven above.

46 Sing praise to the Lord

Henry W. Baker, 1875, and others; based on Psalm 150

Music: *Laudate Dominum*, 10.10.11.11;
arranged in 1916 by C. Hubert H. Parry from his anthem "Hear my words," 1897

1 Sing praise to the Lord! Sing praise in the height; re - joice in God's word, you an - gels of light; O heav - ens, a - dore him by whom you were made, and wor - ship be - fore him, in bright - ness ar - rayed.
2 Sing praise to the Lord! Sing praise up - on earth, in tune - ful ac - cord, all you of new birth; O praise him who brought you his grace from a - bove; O praise him who taught you to sing of his love.
3 Sing praise to the Lord, all things that give sound; each ju - bi - lant chord, re - ech - o a - round; loud or - gans, his glo - ry tell out in deep tone, and trum - pets, the sto - ry of what God has done.
4 Sing praise to the Lord! Thanks - giv - ing and song to God be out - poured all ag - es a - long: for love in cre - a - tion, for heav - en re - stored, for grace and sal - va - tion, sing praise to the Lord!

47 Thou wast, O God, and thou wast blest

John Mason, 1683

Music: *The Third Tune*, 8686D; Thomas Tallis, c. 1557

1 Thou wast, O God, and thou wast blest, be - fore the world be - gan;
2 Great and good God, it pleas - ed thee thy God - head to de - clare;
3 To whom, Lord, should I sing, but thee, the Mak - er of my tongue?
of thine e - ter - ni - ty pos - sessed be - fore time's hour glass ran.
and what thy good - ness did de - cree thy great - ness did pre - pare:
Lo, oth - er lords would seize on me, but I to thee be - long.
Thou need - est none thy praise to sing, as if thy joy could fade;
thou spak'st, and heaven and earth ap - peared, and an - swered to thy call;
As wa - ters haste in - to their sea, and earth in - to its earth,
could'st thou have need - ed an - y - thing, thou could'st have no - thing made.
as if their Mak - er's voice they heard, which is the crea - ture's all.
so let my soul re - turn to thee, from whom it had its birth.

48 Of God's very heart begotten

Corde natus ex Parentis

Marcus Aurelius Clemens Prudentius (348–413);
translated by John M. Neale, 1851, Henry W. Baker, 1859, and others

Music: *Divinum mysterium*, 8787877; melody adapted from a medieval Sanctus trope in Petri's *Piae Cantiones*, 1582; accompaniment by Bruce Neswick, 1984

1 Of God's ve - ry heart be - got - ten, ere the worlds be - gan to be,
2 O that birth for ev - er bless - ed, when the Vir - gin, full of grace,
3 O ye heights of heaven a - dore him; an - gel hosts his prais - es sing;
4 Christ, to thee with God most bless - ed, and, O Ho - ly Ghost, to thee,
he is Al - pha and O - me - ga, he the source, the end - ing he,
by the Ho - ly Ghost con - ceiv - ing, bore the Sa - vior of our race;
powers, do - min - ions, bow be - fore him and ex - tol our God and King;
hymn and chant and high thanks-giv - ing, and un - wear - ied prais - es be:
of the things that are, that have been,
and the babe, the world's Re - deem - - - - er,
let no tongue on earth be si - - - - lent,
hon - or, glo - ry, and do - min - - - - ion,

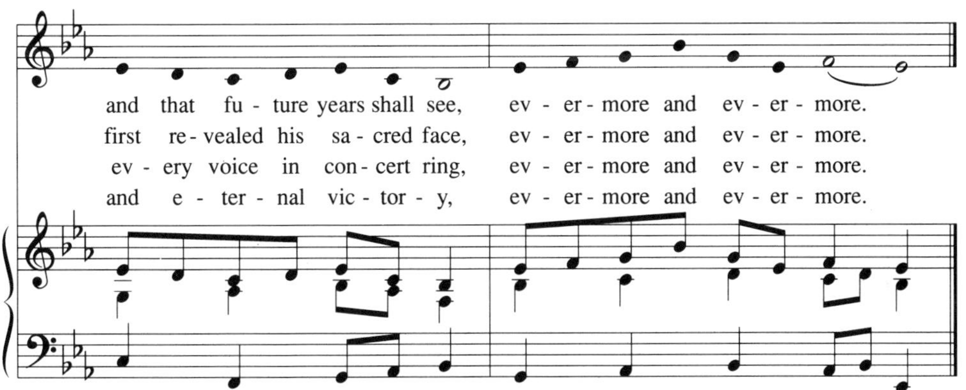
and that fu - ture years shall see, ev - er - more and ev - er - more.
first re - vealed his sa - cred face, ev - er - more and ev - er - more.
ev - ery voice in con - cert ring, ev - er - more and ev - er - more.
and e - ter - nal vic - tor - y, ev - er - more and ev - er - more.

49 Come now, Almighty King

"Hymn to the Trinity," anon. English, c. 1757

Music: *Italian Hymn*, 6646664; melody by Felice de Giardini, 1769; harmony by Russell Schulz-Widmar, 1990

1 Come now, Al - might - y King, help us your name to sing,
2 Come now, In - car - nate Word, by heaven and earth a - dored,
3 Come, Ho - ly Com - fort - er, your sa - cred wit - ness bear
4 To you, great One in Three, e - ter - nal prais - es be

help us to praise: Sov - ereign all glo - ri - ous, o'er all vic -
our prayer at - tend; come, and your peo - ple bless, and give your
in this glad hour. Your grace to us im - part, now rule in
for ev - er - more. Your sov - ereign maj - es - ty may we in

to - ri - ous, come, and reign o - ver us, An - cient of Days!
word suc - cess; grant us your ho - li - ness, Sa - vior and Friend!
ev - ery heart, nev - er from us de - part, Spir - it of power!
glo - ry see, and to e - ter - ni - ty love and a - dore.

50 Name of all majesty

Timothy Dudley-Smith, 1979

Music: *Majesty*, 6.6.10.6.6.6.4; Carl Schalk, 1989

1 Name of all maj - es - ty, fath - om - less mys - ter - y,
2 Child of our des - ti - ny, God from e - ter - ni - ty,
3 Sa - vior of Cal - va - ry, cost - li - est vic - to - ry,
4 Source of all sov - ereign - ty, light, im - mor - tal - i - ty,
King of the ag - es by an - gels a - dored;
love of the Fa - ther on sin - ners out - poured;
dark - ness de - feat - ed and E - den re - stored;
life ev - er - last - ing and heav - en as - sured;
power and au - thor - i - ty, splen - dor and dig - ni - ty,
see now what God has done send - ing his on - ly Son,
born as a man to die, nailed to a cross on high,
so with the ran - somed, we praise him e - ter - nal - ly,

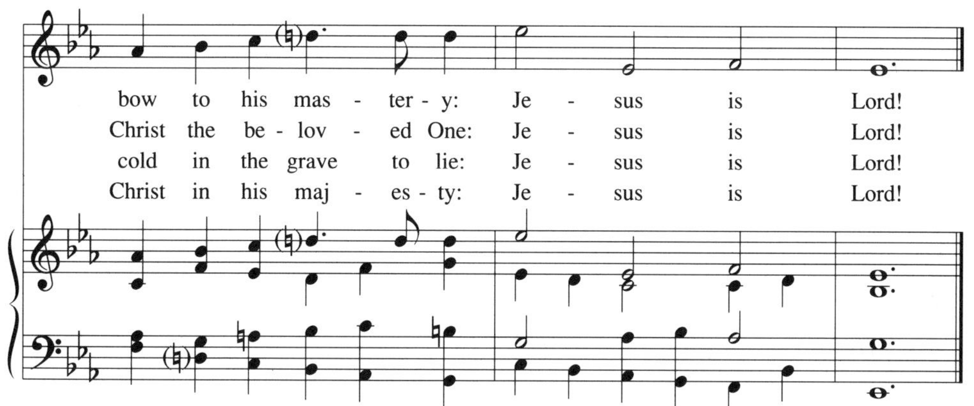
bow to his mas - ter - y: Je - sus is Lord!
Christ the be - lov - ed One: Je - sus is Lord!
cold in the grave to lie: Je - sus is Lord!
Christ in his maj - es - ty: Je - sus is Lord!

51 Creating God, your fingers trace

Jeffery Rowthorn, 1974, based on Psalm 148

Music: *Kedron*, 8888; melody in Amos Pilsbury's *United States Sacred Harmony*, 1799

These words can also be sung to *Mendon*, no. 497.

1 Cre - at - ing God, your fin - gers trace the
2 Sus - tain - ing God, your hand up - hold earth's
3 Re - deem - ing God, your arms em - brace all
4 In - dwell - ing God, your gos - pel claims one

bold de - signs of farth - est space; let sun and moon and
mys - teries known or yet un - told; let wa - ter's fra - gile
now de - spised for creed or race; let peace, de - scend - ing
fam - ily with a bil - lion names; let ev - ery life be

stars and light and what lies hid - den praise your might.
blend with air, en - a - bling life, pro - claim your care.
like a dove, make known on earth your heal - ing love.
touched by grace un - til we praise you face to face.

52 O love, how deep, how broad, how high

O amor quam ecstaticus

Attributed to Thomas à Kempis (c. 1380–1471);
translation by Benjamin Webb, 1854, and others

Music: *Deo Gracias* (*Agincourt Song*), 8888; "Owre kynge went forth to normandy,"
ballad celebrating the victory of Henry V at Agincourt, 1415;
harmony by Ralph Vaughan Williams (1872–1958)

1 O love, how deep, how broad, how high,
2 For us bap - tized, for us he bore
3 For us he prayed; for us he taught;
4 For us to wick - ed powers be - trayed,
how pass - ing thought and fan - ta - sy,
his ho - ly fast and hun - gered sore;
for us his dai - ly works he wrought;
scourged, mocked, in pur - ple robe ar - rayed,
that God, the Son of God, should take
for us temp - ta - tions sharp he knew,
by words and signs and ac - tions, thus
he bore the shame - ful cross and death;

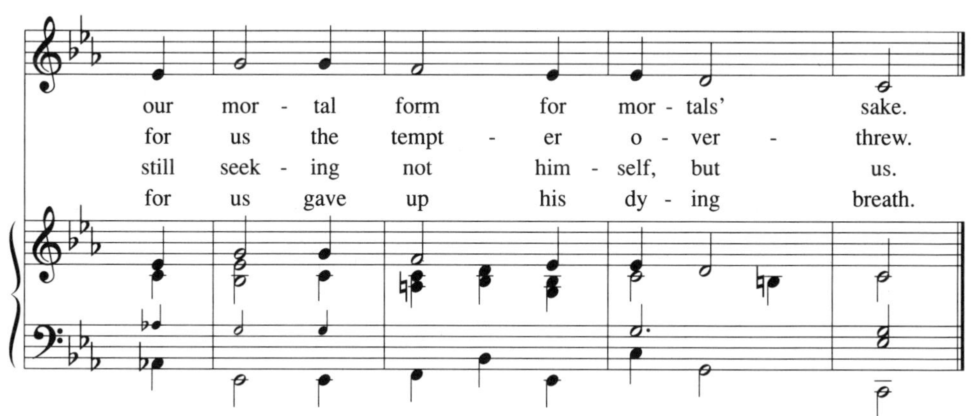
our mor - tal form for mor - tals' sake.
for us the tempt - er o - ver - threw.
still seek - ing not him - self, but us.
for us gave up his dy - ing breath.

5 For us he rose from death again,
for us he went on high to reign;
for us he sent his Spirit here
to guide, to strengthen, and to cheer.

6 All glory to our Lord and God
for love so deep, so high, so broad;
the Trinity whom we adore
for ever and for evermore.

53 There's a spirit in the air

"Praise the Holy Spirit," Brian Wren, 1969

Music: *Lauds*, 7777; John Wilson, 1969

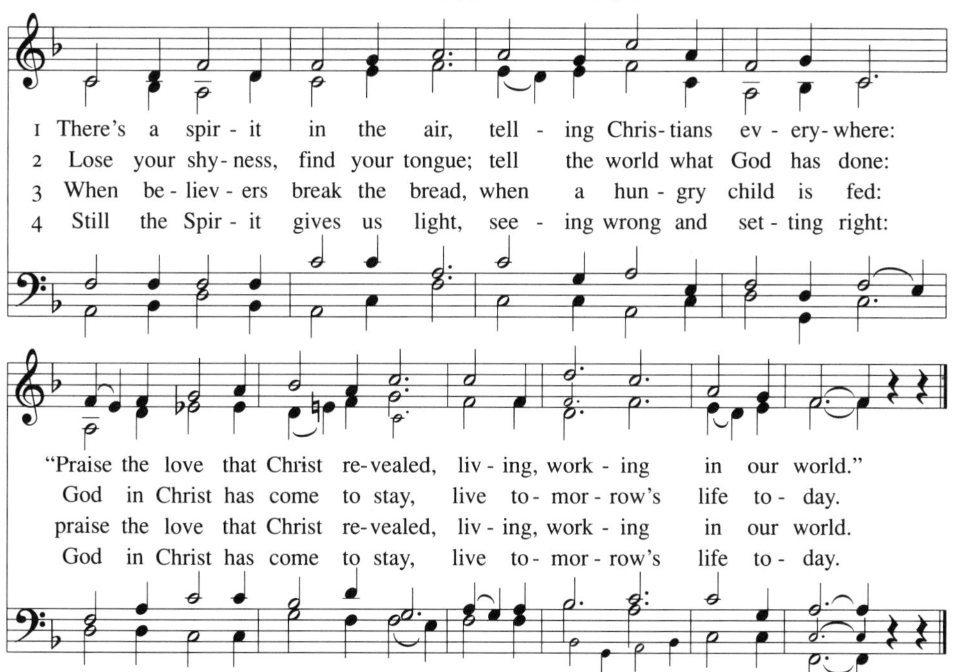
1 There's a spir - it in the air, tell - ing Chris- tians ev - ery- where:
2 Lose your shy- ness, find your tongue; tell the world what God has done:
3 When be - liev - ers break the bread, when a hun - gry child is fed:
4 Still the Spir - it gives us light, see - ing wrong and set - ting right:
"Praise the love that Christ re- vealed, liv - ing, work - ing in our world."
God in Christ has come to stay, live to- mor - row's life to - day.
praise the love that Christ re- vealed, liv - ing, work - ing in our world.
God in Christ has come to stay, live to- mor - row's life to - day.

5 When a stranger's not alone
where the homeless find a home,
praise the love that Christ revealed,
living, working in our world.

6 May the Spirit fill our praise,
guide our thoughts and change our ways.
God in Christ has come to stay,
live tomorrow's life today.

7 There's a Spirit in the air,
calling people everywhere:
praise the love that Christ revealed,
living, working in our world.

54 Retell what Christ's great love has done

Jeffery Rowthorn, 1986

Music: *Wichmann*, 888888; Gerre Hancock, 1986

1 Re - tell what Christ's great love has done, how crib and
2 Re - call the cov - e - nant of grace in which you
3 Re - view the tap - es - try of saints, that can - vas
4 Re - hearse the chor - us of the heart, let all earth's
cross the vic - tory won: God's call o - beyed, temp - ta - tions faced,
free - ly find your place: with wa - ter washed, at ta - ble fed,
which the Spir - it paints: a pro - phet scorned, a teach - er famed,
hopes and fears take part: the shouts of youth, the cries of age,
the good news preached, then death em - braced. Let us who
in Christ a - live, to self now dead. Then with your
a host un - known and un - ac - claimed, yet one and
the pris - oners' groans, the vic - tims' rage. And may each
(♭)

share his Eas - ter light sing praise to God, our chief de - light.
lives, by day and night, sing praise to God, your chief de - light.
all who fought the fight sing praise to God, their chief de - light.
voice which seeks the right sing praise to God, its chief de - light.

5 Rejoice at what Christ yet will do,
intent on making all things new:
the hungry filled, the peaceful blessed,
the wounded healed, each heart at rest.
Then sing, till faith gives way to sight,
in praise of God, our chief delight.

55 Many and great, O God, are your works

Native American hymn from *Dakota Odowan*, 1879; paraphrased by Philip Frazier, 1930

Music: *Lacquiparle*, 969996; Native American melody

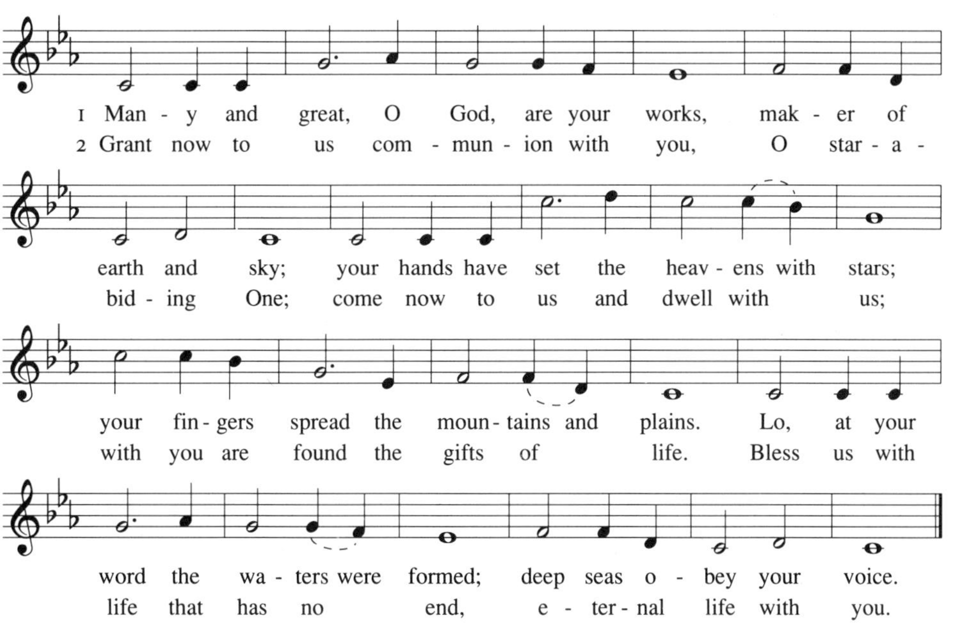
1 Man - y and great, O God, are your works, mak - er of
2 Grant now to us com - mun - ion with you, O star - a -
earth and sky; your hands have set the heav - ens with stars;
bid - ing One; come now to us and dwell with us;
your fin - gers spread the moun - tains and plains. Lo, at your
with you are found the gifts of life. Bless us with
word the wa - ters were formed; deep seas o - bey your voice.
life that has no end, e - ter - nal life with you.

Suggested percussion part for hand drum or tom-tom:

56 Mountains are all aglow

Ok In Lim, 1967; translated by Hae Jong Kim, 1988; versified by Hope Kawashima

Music: *Kahm-sah*, 13.13.13.15; Jae Hoon Park, 1967

1 Moun-tains are all a - glow with au - tumn col - ors so bright;
2 Ev - ery land so a - bun - dant - ly rich the har - vest bears;
3 Ear - ly spring is the time to sow all God's rich seeds of life,
4 Praise the Lord as we're plant - ing God's word deep in each heart;
riv - ers are filled with wa - ter, giv - ing life to our days.
ev - ery or - chard is filled with sweet - ly rip - ened new fruit.
work - ing hard, till - ing God's earth, mak - ing pre - par - a - tion.
God has sent sun - shine and the rain so the seed - lings may grow.
Gold - en fields wave in praise of God's boun - ti - ful har - vest;
Sun and rain by the Lord's de - sign shall come all in due time;
Look - ing for - ward to re - wards of har - vest so plen - ti - ful,
Des - ert lands which seem bar - ren, flow - ers there still bloom;
grate - ful - ly, with hearts up - lift - ed, hear our joy - ous songs of praise!
work - ing hard, God has giv - en us rea - sons for deep grat - i - tude.
prom - ised bless - ings will soon be ours in each re - ve - la - tion.
trust - ing in God's prom - is - es, our thanks to God we will show!

57 God of the sparrow God of the whale

Jaroslav J. Vajda, 1983

Music: *Roeder*, 54677; Carl F. Schalk, 1983

Unison
1 God of the spar - row God of the whale
2 God of the earth - quake God of the storm
3 God of the rain - bow God of the cross
4 God of the hun - gry God of the sick
God of the swirl - ing stars
God of the trum - pet blast
God of the emp - ty grave
God of the prod - i - gal
How does the crea - ture say Awe
How does the crea - ture cry Woe
How does the crea - ture say Grace
How does the crea - ture say Care
How does the crea - ture say Praise
How does the crea - ture cry Save
How does the crea - ture say Thanks
How does the crea - ture say Life
1–5
6
*

* *Last time.*

5 God of the neighbor
God of the foe
God of the pruning hook
How does the creature say Love
How does the creature say Peace

6 God of the ages
God near at hand
God of the loving heart
How do your children say Joy
How do your children say Home

58 All creatures of our God and King

Altissimo, omnipotente bon Signore

Francis of Assisi (1182–1226), "Canticle of the Sun";
paraphrase by William H. Draper, 1926, and others

Music: *Lasst uns erfreuen*, 8888 with refrains; later form of a melody in *Auserlesene Catholische Geistliche Kirchengesänge*, Cologne, 1623; harmony by Ralph Vaughan Williams, 1906

Unison
1 All crea - tures of our God and King,
2 O rush - ing wind and breez - es soft,
3 O flow - ing wa - ter, pure and clear,
4 Dear mo - ther earth, who day by day
lift up your voice and with us sing:
O clouds that ride the winds a - loft,
make mu - sic for your Lord to hear:
un - folds rich bless - ings on our way,
Harmony
O praise ye! Al - le - lu - ia!
O praise ye! Al - le - lu - ia!
O praise ye! Al - le - lu - ia!
O praise ye! Al - le - lu - ia!
Unison
O burn - ing sun with gold - en beam,
O ris - ing morn, in praise re - joice,
O fire so mas - ter - ful and bright,
The flowers and fruits that ver - dant grow,

O sil - ver moon with soft - er gleam:
O lights of eve - ning, find a voice:
pro - vid - ing us with warmth and light:
let them his glo - ry al - so show:
Harmony
O praise ye! O praise ye! Al - le - lu - ia!
O praise ye! O praise ye! Al - le - lu - ia!
O praise ye! O praise ye! Al - le - lu - ia!
O praise ye! O praise ye! Al - le - lu - ia!
Unison
Al - le - lu - ia! Al - le - lu - ia!
Al - le - lu - ia! Al - le - lu - ia!
Al - le - lu - ia! Al - le - lu - ia!
Al - le - lu - ia! Al - le - lu - ia!

5 O everyone of tender heart,
forgiving others, take your part,
O praise ye! Alleluia!
All you who pain and sorrow bear,
praise God and on him cast your care:
O praise ye! O praise ye!
Alleluia! Alleluia! Alleluia!

6 And you, most kind and gentle death,
waiting to hush our final breath,
O praise ye! Alleluia!
You lead to heaven the child of God,
where Christ our Lord the way has trod:
O praise ye! O praise ye!
Alleluia! Alleluia! Alleluia!

7 Let all things their Creator bless,
and worship God in humbleness,
O praise ye! Alleluia!
Praise, praise your Maker and your King,
lift up your voice and with us sing:
O praise ye! O praise ye!
Alleluia! Alleluia! Alleluia!

59 Let the whole creation cry

Stopford A. Brooke, 1881, based on Psalm 148

Music: *Jouissance*, 7777 with refrains; melody and bass by Pierre Bonnet (1638–1708); inner voices by Russell Schulz-Widmar, 1990

1 Let the whole cre - a - tion cry,
2 Praise, you an - gel hosts a - bove,
3 All who teach and all who learn,
4 Men and wo - men, young and old,
Al - le - lu - ia!
"Glo - ry to the Lord on high!"
ev - er bright and fair in love;
to your God with praise re - turn;
raise the an - them loud and bold:
Al - le - lu - ia!
Heaven and earth, a - wake and sing, "Praise to you, al - might - y King!"
sun and moon, lift up your voice; night and stars, in God re - joice.
you to whom the arts be - long, add your voi - ces to the song.
from the north to south - ern pole let the might - y cho - rus roll.

60 Let the whole creation cry

Stopford A. Brooke, 1881, based on Psalm 148

Music: *Llanfair*, 7777 with refrains; Robert Williams, 1817; harmony by John Roberts, 1837

1 Let the whole cre - a - tion cry,
2 Praise, you an - gel hosts a - bove,
3 All who teach and all who learn,
4 Men and wo - men, young and old,
Al - le - lu - ia!
"Glo - ry to the Lord on high!"
ev - er bright and fair in love;
to your God with praise re - turn;
raise the an - them loud and bold:
Al - le - lu - ia!
Heaven and earth, a - wake and sing,
sun and moon, lift up your voice;
you to whom the arts be - long,
from the north to south - ern pole,
Al - le - lu - ia!
Unison
"Praise to you, al - might - y King!"
night and stars, in God re - joice.
add your voi - ces to the song.
let the might - y cho - rus roll:
Al - le - lu - ia!

61 God out of love for us lent us this planet

"The Stewardship of Earth," Fred Pratt Green, 1973

Music: *Ecology*, 11.10.11.10; Austin C. Lovelace, 1974, 1990

Unison
1 God out of love for us lent us this plan - et,
2 Thanks be to God for its boun - ty and beau - ty,
3 Long have our hu - man wars ru - ined its har - vest;
4 Cas - ual de - spoil - ers, or high priests of Mam - mon
gave it a pur - pose in time and in space;
life that sus - tains us in bod - y and mind:
long has earth bowed to the ter - ror of force.
sell - ing the fu - ture for pres - ent re - wards,
small as a spark from the fire of cre - a - tion,
plen - ty for all, if we learn how to share it,
Now we pol - lute it, in cyn - i - cal si - lence,
care - less of life and con - temp - tuous of beau - ty:
cra - dle of life and the home of our race.
rich - es un - dreamed of to fath - om and find.
pois - on the foun - tain of life at its source.
bid them re - mem - ber: the Earth is the Lord's.

5 Earth is the Lord's: it is ours to enjoy it,
ours, as God's stewards, to farm and defend.
From its pollution, misuse and destruction,
good Lord, deliver us, world without end!

62 I sing the mighty power of God

"Praise for Creation and Providence," Isaac Watts, 1715, and others

Music: *Forest Green*, 8686D; English folksong melody, "The Ploughboy's Dream," arranged and harmonized by Ralph Vaughan Williams, 1906

1 I sing the might-y power of God, that made the moun-tains rise;
2 I sing the good-ness of the Lord, who filled the earth with food,
3 There's not a plant or flower be-low but makes your glo-ries known;
that spread the flow-ing seas a-broad, and built the lof-ty skies.
who formed cre-a-tion with a word, and then pro-nounced it good.
and clouds a-rise and tem-pests blow by or-der from your throne;
I sing the wis-dom that or-dained the sun to rule the day;
Lord, how your won-ders are dis-played, wher-e'er I turn my eye:
while all that bor-rows life from you is ev-er in your care,
the moon shines full at God's com-mand, and all the stars o-bey.
if I sur-vey the ground I tread, or gaze up-on the sky!
and ev-ery-where that I may be, you, God, are pres-ent there.

63 The spacious firmament on high

Joseph Addison, 1712, based on Psalm 19:1–6

Music: *Creation*, 8888D; adapted from a chorus in Haydn's *The Creation*, 1798, by Isaac B. Woodbury in *The Sacred Choir*, New York, 1838

1 The spa - cious fir - ma - ment on high,
2 Soon as the even - ing shades pre - vail,
3 What though in sol - emn si - lence all
with all the blue e - ther - eal sky,
the moon takes up the won - drous tale,
move round the dark ter - res - trial ball?
and spang - led heavens, a shin - ing frame,
and night - ly to the listen - ing earth
What though no re - al voice, no sound,
their great O - rig - i - nal pro - claim.
re - peats the sto - ry of her birth;
a - mid their ra - diant orbs be found?

The un - wea - ried sun from day to day
whilst all the stars that round her burn,
In rea - son's ear they all re - joice,
does his Cre - a - tor's power dis - play,
and all the plan - ets in their turn,
and ut - ter forth a glo - rious voice,
and pub - lish - es to ev - ery land
con - firm the tid - ings, as they roll,
for - ev - er sing - ing as they shine,
the work of an al - might - y hand.
and spread the truth from pole to pole.
"The hand that made us is di - vine."

64 The stars declare his glory

Timothy Dudley-Smith, 1970, based on Psalm 19

Music: *Aldine*, 768686; Richard Proulx, 1985

1 The stars de - clare his glo - ry; the vault of heav - en springs,
2 The dawn re - turns in splen - dor, the heav - ens burn and blaze,
3 So shine the Lord's com-mand- ments to make the sim - ple wise;
4 So or - der too this life of mine, di - rect it all my days;
mute wit - ness of the Mas-ter's hand in all cre - at - ed things,
the ris - ing sun re - news the race that mea - sures all our days,
more sweet than hon-ey to the taste, more rich than an - y prize,
the med - i - ta-tions of my heart be in - no-cence and praise,
and through the si - lenc - es of space
and writes in fire a - cross the skies
a law of love with - in our hearts,
my Rock, and my re - deem - ing Lord,

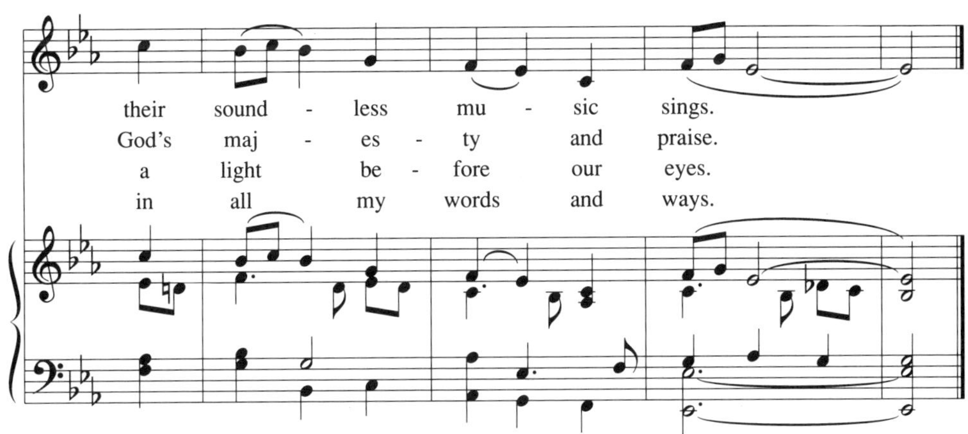
their sound - less mu - sic sings.
God's maj - es - ty and praise.
a light be - fore our eyes.
in all my words and ways.

65 How wonderful this world of thine

Fred Pratt Green, c. 1947

Music: *Willoughby New*, 886886; based on a melody in *Southern Harmony*, 1835; harmony by Jeffrey H. Rickard, 1990

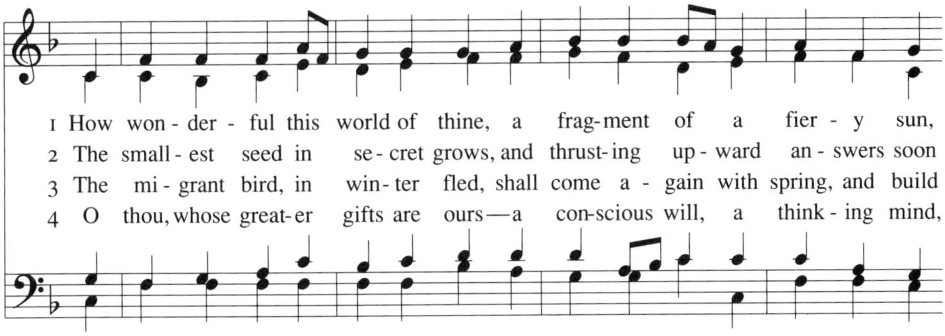

1 How won - der - ful this world of thine, a frag-ment of a fier - y sun,
2 The small - est seed in se - cret grows, and thrust-ing up - ward an - swers soon
3 The mi - grant bird, in win - ter fled, shall come a - gain with spring, and build
4 O thou, whose great-er gifts are ours — a con-scious will, a think - ing mind,

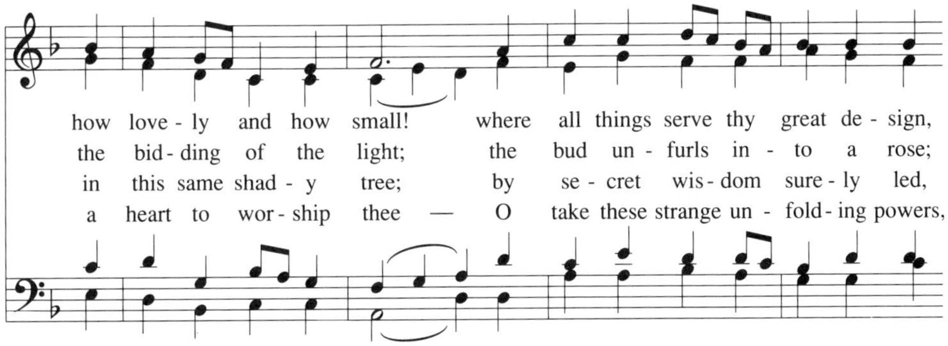

how love - ly and how small! where all things serve thy great de - sign,
the bid - ding of the light; the bud un - furls in - to a rose;
in this same shad - y tree; by se - cret wis - dom sure - ly led,
a heart to wor - ship thee — O take these strange un - fold - ing powers,

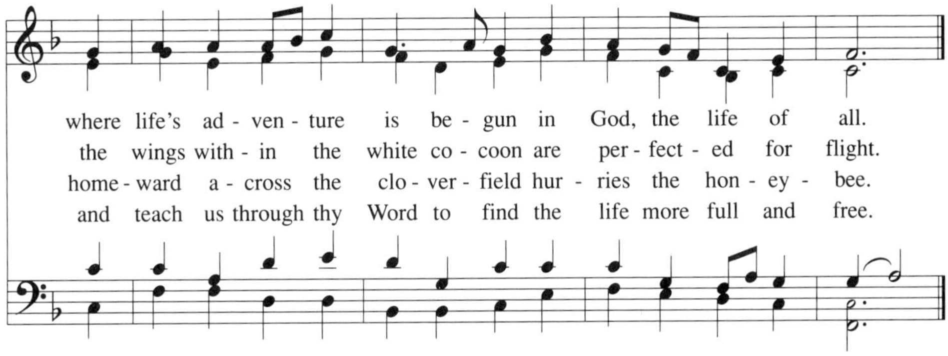

where life's ad - ven - ture is be - gun in God, the life of all.
the wings with - in the white co - coon are per - fect - ed for flight.
home - ward a - cross the clo - ver - field hur - ries the hon - ey - bee.
and teach us through thy Word to find the life more full and free.

66 God, who stretched the spangled heavens

Catherine Cameron, 1969

Music: *Beach Spring*, 8787D; melody in *The Sacred Harp*, 1844; attributed to Benjamin F. White; harmony by Ronald A. Nelson, 1978

1 God, who stretched the span-gled heav - ens in - fi - nite in
2 Proud - ly rise our mod - ern cit - ies, state - ly build - ings,
3 We have ven - tured worlds un - dreamed of since the child - hood
4 As each far hor - i - zon beck - ons, may it chal - lenge
time and place, flung the suns in burn - ing ra - diance
row on row; yet their win - dows, blank, un - feel - ing,
of our race; known the ec - sta - sy of wing - ing
us a - new, shar - ing your cre - a - tive pur - pose,
through the si - lent fields of space: we, your chil - dren in your
stare on can - yoned streets be - low, where the lone - ly drift un -
through un - trav - eled realms of space; probed the se - crets of the
serv - ing oth - ers, honor - ing you. May our dreams prove rich with
like - ness, share in - ven - tive powers with you; Great Cre - a - tor,
no - ticed in the cit - y's ebb and flow, lost to pur - pose
at - om, yield - ing un - i - mag - ined power, fac - ing us with
prom - ise, each en - deav - or well be - gun. Great Cre - a - tor,

still cre - at - ing, show us what we yet may do.
and to mean - ing, scarce - ly car - ing where they go.
life's de - struc - tion or our most tri - um - phant hour.
give us guid - ance till our goals and yours are one.

67 For the beauty of the earth

"The Sacrifice of Praise," Folliott Sandford Pierpont, 1864

Music: *Dix*, 777777; melody by Conrad Kocher, 1838; abridged and arranged by William H. Monk, 1861

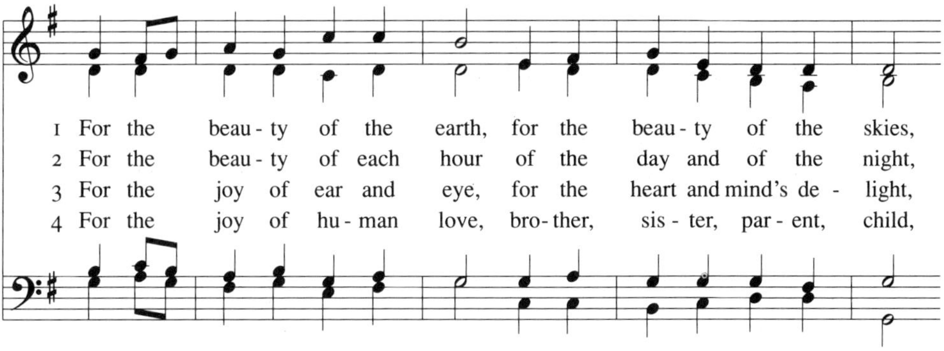

1 For the beau - ty of the earth, for the beau - ty of the skies,
2 For the beau - ty of each hour of the day and of the night,
3 For the joy of ear and eye, for the heart and mind's de - light,
4 For the joy of hu - man love, bro - ther, sis - ter, par - ent, child,

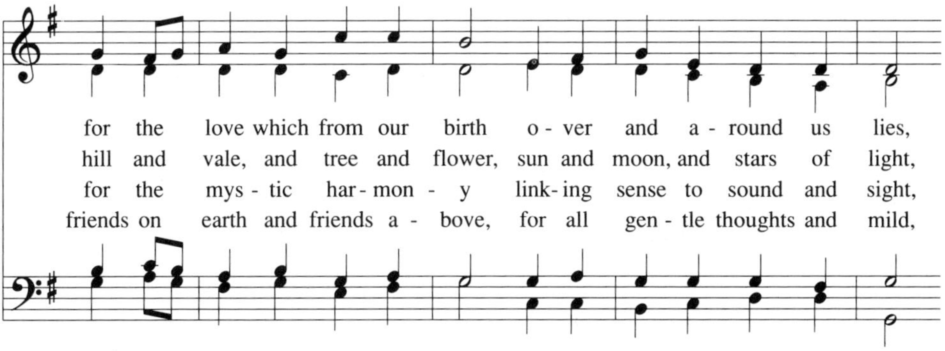

for the love which from our birth o - ver and a - round us lies,
hill and vale, and tree and flower, sun and moon, and stars of light,
for the mys - tic har - mon - y link - ing sense to sound and sight,
friends on earth and friends a - bove, for all gen - tle thoughts and mild,

Refrain

Lord of all, to thee we raise this our sac - ri - fice of praise.

5 For each perfect gift of thine
unto us so freely given,
faith and hope and love divine,
peace on earth and joy in heaven,

Refrain

68 Praise the Lord of heaven

Thomas Browne, 1844

Music: *Nous allons*, 6565D; French carol melody; harmony by Martin Shaw, 1928

1 Praise the Lord of heav - en! Praise God in the height;
2 Praise the Lord, you foun - tains of the depths and seas,
3 Praise God, fowl and cat - tle, rul - ers and all kings;
praise God, all you an - gels; praise now, stars and light!
rocks and hills and moun - tains, ce - dars and all trees!
praise now, men and wo - men, all cre - at - ed things;
And you clouds and wa - ters which, a - bove the skies,
Praise now, clouds and va - pors, snow and hail and fire,
glo - ri - ous and might - y is God's name a - lone;
when God first com - mand - ed, did es - tab - lished rise!
storm - y wind ful - fill - ing God's all - wise de - sire!
all the earth God's foot - stool, heav - en God's great throne.

69 Immortal, invisible, God only wise

W. Chalmers Smith, 1867

Music: *St. Denio*, 11.11.11.11; melody in John Robert's *Caniadaeth y Cysegr*, 1839; adapted from a Welsh ballad

1 Im - mor - tal, in - vis - i - ble, God on - ly wise,
2 Un - rest - ing, un - hast - ing, and si - lent as light,
3 To all life thou giv - est, to both great and small;
4 O Sov - ereign of glo - ry, O source of all light,
in light in - ac - ces - si - ble hid from our eyes,
nor want - ing, nor wast - ing, thou rul - est in might;
in all life thou liv - est, the true life of all;
thine an - gels a - dore thee, all veil - ing their sight;
most bless - ed, most glo - rious, the An - cient of Days,
thy jus - tice like moun - tains high soar - ing a - bove
we blos - som and flour - ish like leaves on the tree,
all praise we would ren - der; O help us to see
al - might - y, vic - to - rious, thy great name we praise.
thy clouds, which are foun - tains of good - ness and love.
then with - er and per - ish; but naught chang - eth thee.
'tis on - ly the splen - dor of light hid - eth thee.

70 Come, ye thankful people, come

Henry Alford, 1844

Music: *St. George's, Windsor*, 7777D; George J. Elvey, 1858

1 Come, ye thank - ful peo - ple, come, raise the song of har - vest - home:
2 All the world is God's own field, fruit un - to God's praise to yield;
3 For the Lord our God shall come, and shall take this har - vest home;
4 Ev - en so, Lord, quick - ly come to your fi - nal har - vest - home;
all is safe - ly gath - ered in, ere the win - ter storms be - gin;
wheat and tares to - geth - er sown, un - to joy or sor - row grown:
from this field shall in that day all of - fens - es purge a - way;
gath - er all your peo - ple in, free from sor - row, free from sin;
God, our Mak - er, does pro - vide for our wants to be sup - plied;
first the blade, and then the ear, then the full corn shall ap - pear:
give the an - gels charge at last in the fire the tares to cast,
there, for ev - er pur - i - fied, in your pres - ence to a - bide:
come to God's own tem - ple, come, raise the song of har - vest - home.
grant, O har - vest Lord, that we whole - some grain and pure may be.
but the fruit - ful ears to store in God's gar - ner ev - er - more.
come, with all your an - gels, come, raise the glo - rious har - vest - home.

71 For the fruit of all creation

Fred Pratt Green, 1970

Music: *Santa Barbara*, 84848884; Emma Lou Diemer, 1978

1 For the fruit of all cre - a - tion, thanks be to God.
2 In the just re - ward of la - bor, God's will is done.
3 For the har - vests of the Spir - it, thanks be to God.
For God's gifts to ev - ery na - tion, thanks be to God.
In the help we give our neigh - bor, God's will is done.
For the good we all in - her - it, thanks be to God.
For the plow - ing, sow - ing, reap - ing, si - lent growth while we are sleep - ing,
In our world - wide task of car - ing for the hun - gry and de - spair - ing,
For the won - ders that a - stound us, for the truths that still con - found us,
fu - ture needs in earth's safe - keep - ing, thanks be to God.
in the har - vests we are shar - ing, God's will is done.
most of all that love has found us, thanks be to God.

72 We gather together to ask the Lord's blessing

Wilt heden nu treden voor God den Heere

From Adrian Valerius's *Nederlandtsch Gedenckclanck*, 1626; translated by Theodore Baker, 1917

Music: *Wilt heden nu treden*, 12.11.12.11; from the same book; arranged by Edward Kremser, 1895

1 We ga - ther to - geth - er to ask the Lord's bless - ing,
2 Be - side us to guide us, our God with us join - ing,
3 We all do ex - tol thee, thou Lord of cre - a - tion,
who chast - ens and hast - ens his will to make known;
or - dain - ing, main - tain - ing the king - dom di - vine;
and pray that thou still our de - fend - er wilt be.
the wick - ed op - press - ing now cease from dis - tress - ing:
so from the be - gin - ning the fight we were win - ning:
Let thy con - gre - ga - tion es - cape tri - bu - la - tion;
sing praise - es to his name, who for - gets not his own.
thou, Lord, wast at our side: all glo - ry be thine!
thy name be ev - er praised! O Lord, make us free!

73 As those of old their first fruits brought

Frank von Christierson, 1961

Music: *Forest Green*, 8686D; English folksong melody, "The Ploughboy's Dream," arranged and harmonized by Ralph Vaughan Williams, 1906

1 As those of old their first fruits brought of vine-yard, flock, and field
2 A world in need now sum-mons us to la - bor, love, and give;
3 With gra - ti - tude and hum - ble trust we bring our best to - day
to God, the giv - er of all good, the source of boun-teous yield;
to make our life an of - fer - ing to God that all may live;
to serve your cause and share your love with all a - long life's way.
so we to - day our first fruits bring, the wealth of this good land,
the Church of Christ is call - ing us to make the dream come true;
O God who gave your - self to us in Je - sus Christ your Son,
of farm and mar - ket, shop and home, of mind, and heart, and hand.
a world re-deemed by Christ-like love; all life in Christ made new.
help us to give our - selves each day un - til life's work is done.

HOW TO SING PSALMS

Psalm tones are simple melodic formulae that expand or contract to accommodate the singing of psalm verses of varying lengths. Since each psalm verse consists of two parts, each psalm tone also has two parts. The dividing point is signaled by an asterisk.

The first note in each half of the psalm tone is a reciting note to which one or more syllables are sung. The point (•) in the text indicates the syllable where the singer moves from the reciting note to the next note. Usually there are three syllables after this point—one for each of the three remaining notes. When there are more than three syllables, the additional syllables are sung to the last note.

Antiphons add richness to the psalmody, either interspersed between groups of verses or sung at the beginning and ending of the psalm.

Some possible methods of singing psalms:

With antiphons:

1. The congregation sings only the antiphon; the choir (or soloist) sings the verses. When the congregation is to sing the antiphon, a soloist usually sings it through once and then the congregation immediately repeats it.
2. The reverse of the above.
3. The congregation sings both the antiphon and the verses, the antiphon having been lined out initially by a soloist.

Without antiphons:

1. The choir (or soloist) and congregation sing alternate verses.
2. Everyone sings throughout.
3. The congregation is divided into two groups who alternate in singing the verses of the psalm.

The publisher extends to groups who have purchased multiple copies of this book the right to duplicate the following antiphons in service leaflets. They may not be duplicated under other circumstances without permission of the publisher.

PSALM TONES

74

Mark Bangert
A
*
Mark Bangert
B
*
Paul G. Bunjes
C
*
Paul G. Bunjes
D
*
Paul G. Bunjes
E
*

PSALM ANTIPHONS

75

Advent

Richard Proulx

To you, O God, I lift up my soul.

Use with tone A.

76

Christmas and Epiphany

Richard Proulx

All the ends of the earth have seen the
sav - ing pow- er of God.

Use with tone B.

77

Lent

Richard Proulx

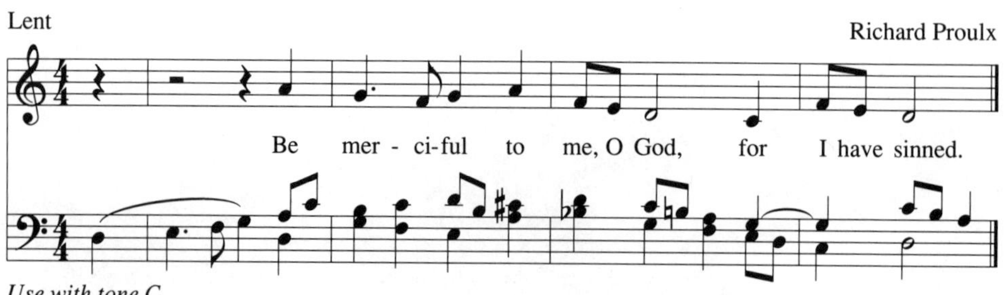
Be mer - ci-ful to me, O God, for I have sinned.

Use with tone C.

78
Eastertide
Richard Proulx
This day was made by God; let us re- joice and be glad.
Use with tone D.
79
Richard Proulx
Blessed be the God of Is - ra - el.
Use with tone E.
80
Richard Proulx
O God, you have the words of ev- er- last- ing life.
Use with tone A.
81
Richard Proulx
I will praise your name for - ev - er, O God.
Use with tone B.
82
Richard Proulx
Show me your ways; teach me your paths.

Use with tone C.

83 Psalm 1

אשרי האיש אשר לא הלך

1 Blessed are those who do not walk in the counsel • of the wicked;*
or stand in the way of sinners, or sit in the • seat of scoffers;
2 but their delight is in the law • of the Lord,*
and on God's law they meditate • day and night.
3 They are like trees planted by streams of water, that yield their fruit in season, and their leaves • do not wither:*
in all that they • do, they prosper.
4 The wicked • are not so,*
but are like chaff which the wind • drives away.
5 Therefore the wicked will not stand • in the judgment;*
nor sinners in the congregation • of the righteous;
6 for the Lord knows the way • of the righteous;*
but the way of the wick•ed will perish.

84 Psalm 2

למה רגשו גוים

1 Why do the na•tions conspire,*
and the people • plot in vain?
2 The kings of the earth rise up, and the rulers take coun•sel together*
against God and • God's anointed.
3 "Let us burst their • bonds," they say,*
"and cast their • cords from us."
4 The One who sits in the • heavens laughs,*
and holds them • in derision.
5 Then God will speak to • them in anger,*
and terrify them in • fury, saying,
6 "I have set the one who • rules for me*
on Zion, my • holy hill."
7 I will tell of the decree • of the Lord,*
who said to me: "You are my child, today I have be•gotten you.
8 Ask of me, and I will make the nations your • heritage,*
and the ends of the earth • your possession.
9 You shall break them with a • rod of iron,*
and dash them in pieces like a • potter's vessel."
10 Now therefore, O • kings, be wise;*
be warned, O rulers • of the earth.
11 Serve the Lord with • fear and trembling;*
humble yourselves be•fore the Lord
12 lest God be angry, and you perish • in the way;*
for God's wrath is • quickly kindled.
13 Blessed • are all they*
who take refuge • in the Lord.

85 Psalm 3

יהוה מה רבו צרי

1 O Lord, how many • are my foes!*
Many are ris•ing against me;
2 many are say•ing of me,*
"There is no • help in God."
3 But you, O Lord, are a • shield about me,*
my glory, and the lifter • of my head.
4 I cry aloud • to the Lord,*
who answers me from God's • holy hill.
5 I lie • down and sleep;*
I wake again, for the • Lord sustains me.
6 I am not afraid of ten • thousand people*
who have set themselves against me on • every side.
7 Arise, O Lord! Deliver me; • O my God!*
For you strike all my enemies on the cheek,
you break the teeth • of the wicked.
8 Deliverance belongs • to the Lord;*
your blessing be up•on your people!

86 Psalm 4

בקראי ענני

1 Answer me when I call, O God • of my right!*
You have given me room when I was in distress;
be gracious to me, and • hear my prayer.
2 How long, O people, shall my honor • suffer shame?*
How long will you love vain words, and seek • after lies?

3 But know that the Lord has set apart the
righteous • as God's own;*
the Lord hears • when I call.
4 Be angry, but • do not sin;*
commune with your own hearts in your beds, •
and be silent.
5 Offer right • sacrifices,*
and put your trust • in the Lord.
6 There are many who say, "O that we might • see
some good!*
Lift up the light of your countenance upon •
us, O Lord!"
7 You have put more joy • in my heart*
than they have when their grain and • wine
abound.
8 In peace I will both lie • down and sleep;*
for you alone, O Lord, make me lie • down in
safety.

87 Psalm 5:1–8

אמרי האזינה יהוה

1 Give ear to my • words, O Lord;*
give heed • to my groaning.
2 Hearken to the sound of my cry, my Ruler • and
my God,*
for to • you I pray.
3 O Lord, in the morning you • hear my voice;*
in the morning I prepare a sacrifice for • you,
and watch.
4 For you are not a God who de•lights in
wickedness;*
evil may not • dwell with you.
5 The boastful may not stand be•fore your eyes;*
you hate all • evildoers.
6 You destroy those • who speak lies;*
the Lord abhors the bloodthirsty • and
deceitful.
7 But, through the abundance of your steadfast
love, I will en•ter your house;*
toward your holy temple I will worship • you
in awe.
8 Lead me, O Lord, in your righteousness
because • of my enemies;*
make your way • straight before me.

88 Psalm 8

יהוה אדנינו מה אדיר שמך

1 O • Lord, our Lord,*
how majestic is your name in • all the earth!
2 Your glory is chanted a•bove the heavens*
by the mouth of • babes and infants:
3 you have set up a defense a•gainst your foes,*
to still the enemy and • the avenger.
4 When I look at your heavens, the work • of
your fingers,*
the moon and the stars which you • have
established,
5 what are human beings that you are mind•ful
of them,*
and mortals that you • care for them?
6 Yet you have made them little • less than God,*
and crowned them with glo•ry and honor.
7 You have given them dominion over the works •
of your hands;*
you have put all things un•der their feet,
8 all • sheep and oxen,*
and also the beasts • of the field,
9 the birds of the air, and the fish • of the sea,*
whatever passes along the paths • of the seas.
10 O • Lord, our Lord,*
how majestic is your name in • all the earth!

89 Psalm 9:11–20

זמרו ליהוה ישב ציון

11 Sing praises to the Lord, who • dwells in Zion!*
Tell among the peo•ples God's deeds!
12 The Lord who avenges blood is mind•ful of
them,*
and does not forget the cry of • the afflicted.
13 Be gracious to • me, O Lord,*
see what I suffer from those who hate me;
you are the One who lifts me up from the •
gates of death;
14 that I may recount • all your praises,*
and in the gates of the daughter of Zion
rejoice in • your deliverance.

[15] The nations have sunk in the pit • which they made;*
their own foot has been caught in the net • which they hid.
[16] The Lord is made known! The Lord has exe•cuted judgment!*
The wicked are snared in the work of • their own hands.
[17] The wicked shall depart • to Sheol,*
all the nations that • forget God.
[18] For the needy shall not always • be forgotten,*
and the hope of the poor shall not per•ish for ever.
[19] Arise, O Lord! Let not mor•tals prevail;*
let the nations be • judged before you!
[20] Put them in • fear, O Lord;*
let the nations know that • they are mortal!

90 Psalm 10:12–19

קומה יהוה אל נשא ידך

[12] Arise, O Lord; O God, lift • up your hand;*
forget not • the afflicted.
[13] Why do the wicked • renounce God,*
and say in their hearts, "You will not call • to account"?
[14] You indeed see, you note trouble • and vexation,*
that you may take it in•to your hands;
[15] the unfortunate commit them•selves to you;*
you have been the helper • of the orphan.
[16] Break the arm of the wicked and • evildoers;*
seek out their wickedness till • you find none.
[17] The Lord is Ruler for ev•er and ever;*
the nations shall perish • from God's land.
[18] O Lord, you will hear the desire • of the meek,*
you will strength•en their hearts;
[19] you will incline your ear to do justice to the orphan and • the oppressed,*
so that people on earth may strike ter•ror no more.

91 Psalm 13

עד אנה יהוה תשכחני נצח

[1] How long, O Lord? Will you forget • me for ever?*
How long will you hide your • face from me?
[2] How long must I bear pain in my soul, and have sorrow in my heart • all the day?*
How long shall my enemy be exalted • over me?
[3] Consider and answer me, O • Lord my God;*
lighten my eyes, lest I sleep the • sleep of death;
[4] lest my enemy say, "I have prevailed • over you";*
lest my foes rejoice because • I am shaken.
[5] But I trusted in your • steadfast love;*
my heart shall rejoice in • your salvation.
[6] I will sing • to the Lord,*
for the Lord has dealt bountiful•ly with me.

92 Psalm 14

אמר נבל בלבו

[1] Fools say in their hearts, "There • is no God."*
They are corrupt, they do abominable deeds, there is none • that does good.
[2] The Lord looks down from heaven • on all people,*
to see if there are any that are wise, who seek • after God.
[3] They have all gone astray, they are all a•like perverse;*
there is none that does good, • no, not one.
[4] Have they no knowledge, the • evildoers*
who eat up my people as they eat bread, and do not call up•on the Lord?
[5] There they shall be • in great terror,*
for God is with the generation • of the righteous.
[6] You would confound the plans • of the poor,*
but the Lord • is their refuge.

7 O that deliverance for Israel would • come from Zion!*
When the Lord restores their fortunes, Jacob shall rejoice and Israel • shall be glad!

10 For you do not give me up • to Sheol,*
or let your godly one • see the pit.
11 You show me the • path of life;*
in your presence there is fullness of joy, in your right hand are pleasures for • evermore.

93 Psalm 15

יהוה מי יגור באהלך

1 O Lord, who shall abide • in your tent?*
Who shall dwell in your • holy hill?
2 Whoever walks blamelessly, and does • what is right,*
and speaks truth • from the heart;
3 who does not slander with the tongue, and does no evil • to a friend,*
nor takes up a reproach a•gainst a neighbor;
4 in whose eyes a reproach • is despised,*
but who honors those who • fear the Lord;
5 who has sworn to • do no wrong,*
and does not take • back that promise;
6 who does not put out mon•ey at interest,*
and does not take a bribe a•gainst the innocent.
7 Whoever • does these things*
shall nev•er be moved.

94 Psalm 16:5–11

יהוה מנת חלקי

5 The Lord is my chosen portion • and my cup;*
you up•hold my lot.
6 The lines have fallen for me in • pleasant places;*
I have a • glorious heritage.
7 I bless the Lord who • gives me counsel;*
even at night my • heart instructs me.
8 I have set the Lord al•ways before me;*
the Lord is at my right hand, I shall • not be moved.
9 Therefore my heart is glad, and my • soul rejoices;*
my body also • dwells secure.

95 Psalm 17:1–7, 15

שמעה יהוה צדק

1 Hear a just cause, O Lord; attend • to my cry!*
Give ear to my prayer from lips free • of deceit!
2 From you let my vindi•cation come!*
Let your eyes • see the right!
3 If you try my heart, if you visit • me by night,*
if you test me, you will find no wicked•ness in me;
4 I do not transgress with my mouth as • others do;*
I have avoided the ways of the violent by follow•ing your word.
5 My steps have held fast • to your paths,*
my feet • have not slipped.
6 I call upon you, for you will answer • me, O God;*
incline your ear to me, • hear my words.
7 Wondrously show your • steadfast love,*
O Savior of those who seek refuge from their adversaries at • your right hand.
15 As for me, I shall behold your • face in righteousness;*
when I awake I shall be satisfied with behold•ing your presence.

96 Psalm 19

השמים מספרים כבוד אל

1 The heavens are telling the glo•ry of God;*
and the firmament proclaims God's • handiwork.
2 Day to day • pours forth speech,*
and night to night • declares knowledge.

3 There is no speech, nor • are there words;*
their voice • is not heard;
4 yet their voice goes out through • all the earth,*
and their words to the end • of the world.
5 In them God has set a tent • for the sun,*
which comes forth like a bridegroom leaving his chamber, and runs its course with joy like • a strong man.
6 Its rising is from the end of the heavens, and its circuit to the • end of them;*
and there is nothing hid • from its heat.
7 The law of the Lord is perfect, reviv•ing the soul;*
the testimony of the Lord is sure, making • wise the simple;
8 the precepts of the Lord are right, rejoic•ing the heart;*
the commandment of the Lord is pure, enlighten•ing the eyes;
9 the fear of the Lord is clean, endur•ing for ever;*
the ordinances of the Lord are true, and righteous • altogether.
10 More to be desired are they than gold, even • much fine gold;*
sweeter also than honey and drippings of the • honeycomb.
11 Moreover by them is your • servant warned;*
in keeping them there is • great reward.
12 But who can under•stand one's errors?*
Clear me from • hidden faults.
13 Also keep your servant from the insolent; let them not have dominion • over me!*
Then I shall be blameless, and innocent of • great transgression.
14 Let the words of my mouth and the meditation of my heart be acceptable • in your sight,*
O Lord, my rock and • my redeemer.

97 Psalm 20

יענך יהוה ביום צרה

1 May the Lord answer you in the • day of trouble!*
The name of the God of Ja•cob protect you!
2 May God send you help from the • sanctuary,*
and give you sup•port from Zion,
3 remembering • all your offerings,*
and regarding with favor your burnt • sacrifices!
4 May God grant you your • heart's desire,*
and fulfill • all your plans!
5 May we shout for joy over your victory, and in the name of our God set • up our banners!*
May God fulfill all • your petitions!
6 Now I know that God will help the a•nointed one,*
and will answer from God's holy heaven with mighty victories by • God's right hand.
7 Some boast of chariots, and • some of horses;*
but we boast of the name of the • Lord our God.
8 They will col•lapse and fall;*
but we shall rise and • stand upright.
9 Give victory to the one who • rules, O God;*
answer us • when we call.

98 Psalm 21:1–7

יהוה בעזך ישמח מלך

1 In your strength the king rejoic•es, O God,*
and in your help how greatly • he exults!
2 You have satisfied the desire • of his heart,*
and have not withheld the request • of his lips.
3 For with goodly blessings you • meet the one*
upon whose head you set a crown • of fine gold.
4 The king asked life of • you; you gave it,*
length of days for ev•er and ever.
5 Through your help, great is the glory • of the ruler,*
upon whom you bestow splendor and • majesty.
6 You make him most bless•ed for ever,*
glad with the joy • of your presence.
7 For the king • trusts in God,*
and through the steadfast love of the Most High will • not be moved.

99 Psalm 22:1–17, 24–30

אלי אלי למה עזבתני

1 My God, my God, why have you for•saken me?*
Why are you so far from helping me, from the words • of my groaning?
2 O my God, I cry by day, but you • do not answer;*
and by night, but • find no rest.
3 Yet • you are holy,*
enthroned on the prais•es of Israel.
4 In you our an•cestors trusted;*
they trusted, and you de•livered them.
5 To you they cried, • and were saved;*
in you they trusted, and were not • disappointed.
6 But I am a worm, • and not human,*
scorned by everyone, and despised • by the people.
7 All who see me • mock at me,*
they make mouths at me, they wag their • heads and say,
8 "You trusted in the Lord; let God de•liver you,*
let God rescue you, for God de•lights in you!"
9 Yet you, O God, are the one who took me • from the womb;*
you kept me safe upon my • mother's breasts.
10 Upon you I was cast • from my birth,*
and since my mother bore me you have • been my God.
11 Be not far from me, for trou•ble is near,*
and there is • none to help.
12 Many bulls en•compass me,*
strong bulls of Ba•shan surround me;
13 they open wide their • mouths at me,*
like a ravening and • roaring lion.
14 I am poured out like water, and all my bones are • out of joint;*
my heart is like wax, it is melted with•in my breast;
15 my strength is dried up like a potsherd, and my tongue cleaves • to my jaws;*
you lay me in the • dust of death.
16 Even dogs are round about me; a company of evildoers en•circle me;*
they have pierced my hands and feet—I can count • all my bones.
17 They stare and gloat • over me;*
they divide my garments among them, and for my raiment • they cast lots.
24 From you comes my praise in the great • congregation;*
my vows I shall pay before those • who fear God.
25 The afflicted shall eat and be satisfied; those who seek God shall • praise the Lord:*
"May your hearts • live forever!"
26 All the ends of the earth shall remember and turn • to the Lord;*
and all the families of the nations shall worship • before God.
27 For dominion belongs • to the Lord,*
who rules o•ver the nations.
28 Indeed, to God shall all the proud of the • earth bow down;*
before God shall bow all who go down to the dust, and those who cannot keep them•selves alive.
29 Posterity shall • serve the Lord;*
people shall tell of the Lord to the coming • generation.
30 They shall proclaim God's deliverance to a people • yet unborn,*
that • God has wrought it.

100 Psalm 23

יהוה רעי

1 The Lord • is my shepherd;*
I • shall not want.
2 God makes me lie down • in green pastures,*
and leads me be•side still waters;
3 God re•stores my soul,*
and leads me in paths of righteousness for the sake • of God's name.

[4] Even though I walk through the valley of the shadow of death, I • fear no evil;*
for you are with me; your rod and your staff, they • comfort me.
[5] You prepare a table before me in the presence of my • enemies;*
you anoint my head with oil, my cup • overflows.
[6] Surely goodness and mercy shall follow me all the days • of my life;*
and I shall dwell in the house of the • Lord for ever.

101 Psalm 24

ליהוה הארץ ומלואה

[1] The earth is the Lord's and the full•ness thereof,*
the world and those who • dwell therein;
[2] for God has founded it up•on the seas,*
and established it up•on the rivers.
[3] Who shall ascend the hill • of the Lord?*
And who shall stand in God's • holy place?
[4] Those who have clean hands • and pure hearts,*
who do not lift up their souls to what is false, and do not • swear deceitfully.
[5] They will receive blessing • from the Lord,*
and vindication from the God of • their salvation.
[6] Such is the generation of those who • seek the Lord,*
who seek the face of the • God of Jacob.
[7] Lift up your heads, O gates! and be lifted up, O • ancient doors!*
that the Ruler of glory • may come in.
[8] Who is the Rul•er of glory?*
The Lord, strong and mighty, the Lord, might•y in battle!
[9] Lift up your heads, O gates! and be lifted up, O • ancient doors!*
that the Ruler of glory • may come in.
[10] Who is this Rul•er of glory?*
The Lord of hosts, the Lord is the Rul•er of glory!

102 Psalm 25:1–9

אליך יהוה נפשי אשא

[1] To you, O Lord, I lift up my soul. O my God, in • you I trust,*
let me not be put to shame; let not my enemies exult • over me.
[2] Let none that wait for you be • put to shame;*
let them be ashamed who are • clothed with treachery.
[3] Make me to know your • ways, O Lord;*
teach • me your paths.
[4] Lead me in your • truth, and teach me,*
for you are the God of my salvation; for you I wait all • the day long.
[5] Be mindful of your mercy, O Lord, and of your • steadfast love,*
for they have been • from of old.
[6] Remember not the sins of my youth or • my transgressions;*
according to your steadfast love remember me, for the sake of your good•ness, O Lord.
[7] Good and upright • is the Lord;*
therefore the Lord instructs sinners • in the way,
[8] and leads the humble in • what is right,*
and teaches • them their way.
[9] All the paths of the Lord are steadfast love and • faithfulness*
for those who keep the Lord's covenant and • testimonies.

103 Psalm 26

שפטני יהוה

[1] Vindicate me, O God, for I have walked with in•tegrity,*
and I have trusted in you • without wavering.
[2] Prove me, O • God, and try me;*
test my heart • and my mind.
[3] For your steadfast love is be•fore my eyes,*
and I walk in faithful•ness to you.
[4] I do not sit with those • who are false,*
nor do I consort • with dissemblers;
[5] I hate the company of • evildoers,*
and I will not sit • with the wicked.

6 I wash my • hands in innocence,*
and go about your al•tar, O God,
7 singing aloud a song • of thanksgiving,*
and telling all your • wondrous deeds.
8 O God, I love the habitation • of your house,*
and the place where your • glory dwells.
9 Sweep me not a•way with sinners,*
nor my life with those • who are bloodthirsty,
10 in whose hands are e•vil devices,*
and whose right hands are • full of bribes.
11 But as for me, I walk in my in•tegrity;*
redeem me, and be gra•cious to me.
12 My foot stands on • level ground;*
in the great congregation I • will bless God.

104 Psalm 27

יהוה אורי וישעי

1 The Lord is my light and my salvation; whom • shall I fear?*
The Lord is the stronghold of my life; of whom shall I • be afraid?
2 When evildoers assail me, to de•vour my flesh,*
my adversaries and foes shall stum•ble and fall.
3 Though a host en•camp against me,*
my heart • shall not fear;
4 though war a•rise against me,*
yet I • will be confident.
5 One thing I asked of the Lord, that will • I seek after:*
that I may dwell in the house of the Lord all the days • of my life,
6 to behold the beauty • of the Lord,*
and to inquire in • the Lord's temple.
7 The Lord will hide me in a safe shelter in the • day of trouble,*
will conceal me under the cover of the Lord's tent, and will set me high up•on a rock.
8 And now my head shall be • lifted up*
above my enemies • round about me;
9 and I will offer sacrifices in the Lord's tent with • shouts of joy;*
I will sing and make melody • to the Lord.
10 Hear, O Lord, when I • cry aloud,*
be gracious to me and • answer me!
11 "Come," my heart said, "seek • the Lord's face."*
Your face, O • Lord, I seek.
12 Hide not your • face from me;*
turn not your servant away in anger, for you have • been my help.
13 Cast me not off, for•sake me not,*
O God of • my salvation!
14 If my father and mother • should forsake me,*
the Lord would • take me up.
15 Teach me your • way, O Lord,*
and lead me on a level path because • of my enemies.
16 Give me not up to the will of my • adversaries,*
for false witnesses have risen against me, and they • breathe out violence.
17 I believe that I shall see the goodness • of the Lord*
in the land • of the living!
18 Wait for the Lord; be strong, and let your • heart take courage.*
Wait • for the Lord!

105 Psalm 28

אליך יהוה אקרא

1 To you, O Lord, I call; my rock, be not • deaf to me,*
lest, if you are silent to me, I become like those who go down • to the pit.
2 Hear the voice of my supplication, as I cry to • you for help,*
as I lift up my hands toward your most • holy sanctuary.
3 Take me not away with the wicked, with those who are work•ers of evil,*
who speak peace with their neighbors, while mischief is • in their hearts.
4 Repay them according • to their work,*
and according to the evil • of their deeds;
5 repay them according to the work • of their hands;*
render them their • due reward.

[6] The Lord will break them down and build them • up no more,*
because they do not regard the deeds of the Lord or the work • of the Lord's hands.
[7] Blessed • be the Lord,*
who has heard the voice of my • supplications!
[8] The Lord is my • strength and shield,*
in whom • my heart trusts;
[9] so I am helped, and my • heart exults,*
and with my song I give thanks • to the Lord.
[10] The Lord is the strength • of the people,*
the saving refuge of • the anointed.
[11] O save your people, and • bless your heritage;*
be their shepherd, and carry • them for ever.

106 Psalm 29

הבו ליהוה בני אלים

[1] Ascribe to the Lord, O heav•enly beings,*
ascribe to the Lord glo•ry and strength.
[2] Ascribe to the Lord the glory • of the Lord's name;*
worship the Lord in • holy splendor.
[3] The voice of the Lord is up•on the waters;*
the God of glory thunders, the Lord, upon • many waters.
[4] The voice of the • Lord is powerful,*
the voice of the Lord is • full of majesty.
[5] The voice of the Lord • breaks the cedars,*
the Lord breaks the ce•dars of Lebanon.
[6] The Lord makes Lebanon to skip • like a calf,*
and Sirion like a • young wild ox.
[7] The voice of the Lord flashes forth flames of fire, the voice of the Lord • shakes the wilderness;*
the Lord shakes the wilder•ness of Kadesh.
[8] The voice of the Lord makes the oaks to whirl, and strips the • forests bare;*
and in the temple • all cry, "Glory!"
[9] The Lord sits enthroned o•ver the flood;*
the Lord sits enthroned as Rul•er for ever.
[10] May the Lord give strength • to the people!*
May the Lord bless the peo•ple with peace!

107 Psalm 30:4–13

זמרו ליהוה חסידיו

[4] Sing praises to the Lord, O you • faithful ones,*
and give thanks to God's • holy name.
[5] Surely the Lord's anger is but • for a moment;*
the Lord's favor is • for a lifetime.
[6] Weeping may tarry • for the night,*
but joy comes • with the morning.
[7] As for me, I said in • my prosperity,*
"I shall nev•er be moved."
[8] By your favor, O Lord, you had established me as • a strong mountain;*
then you hid your face, and I • was dismayed.
[9] To you, O • Lord, I cried,*
and to the Lord I made • supplication:
[10] "What profit is there in my death, if I go down • to the pit?*
Will the dust praise you? Will it tell • of your faithfulness?
[11] Hear, O Lord, and be gra•cious to me!*
O Lord, • be my helper!"
[12] You have turned my mourning • into dancing;*
you have loosed my sackcloth and girded • me with gladness,
[13] that my soul may praise you and • not be silent.*
O Lord, my God, I will give thanks to • you for ever.

108 Psalm 31:1–16

בך יהוה חסיתי

[1] In you, O Lord, I seek refuge; let me never be • put to shame;*
in your righteousness de•liver me!
[2] Incline your ear to me, rescue me • speedily!*
Be a rock of refuge for me, a strong for•tress to save me!*
[3] You are indeed my rock • and my fortress,*
for your name's sake lead • me and guide me.
[4] Take me out of the net which is hid•den for me,*
for you • are my refuge.
[5] Into your hand I com•mit my spirit;*
you have redeemed me, O Lord, • faithful God.

6 I hate those who pay regard • to vain idols;*
but I trust • in the Lord.
7 I will rejoice and be glad in your • steadfast love,*
because you have seen my affliction, and have taken heed of • my adversities.
8 You have not delivered me into the hand • of the enemy;*
you have set my feet in • a broad place.
9 Be gracious to me, O Lord, for I am • in distress,*
my eye is wasted from grief, my soul and • body also.
10 For my life is spent with sorrow, and my • years with sighing;*
my strength fails because of my misery, and my bones • waste away.
11 I am the scorn of all my adversaries, a horror to my neighbors, an object of dread to • my acquaintances;*
those who see me in the street • flee from me.
12 I have passed out of mind like one • who is dead;*
I have become like a • broken vessel.
13 For I hear the whispering of many—terror • all around!—*
as they scheme together against me, as they plot to • take my life.
14 But I trust in • you, O Lord,*
I say, "You • are my God."
15 My times are • in your hand;*
deliver me from the hand of my enemies and • persecutors.
16 Let your face shine • on your servant;*
save me through your • steadfast love!

109 Psalm 32

אשרי נשוי פשע

1 Blessed are those whose transgression • is forgiven,*
whose • sin is covered.
2 Blessed are those whom the Lord does • not hold guilty,*
and in whose spirit there is • no deceit.
3 When I did not declare my sin, my body wast•ed away,*
through my groaning • all day long.
4 For day and night your hand was heav•y upon me;*
my strength was dried up as by the • heat of summer.
5 I acknowledged my • sin to you,*
and I did not hide • my iniquity.
6 I said, "I will confess my transgressions • to the Lord";*
then you forgave the guilt • of my sin.
7 Therefore let those who are godly offer • prayer to you;*
in a time of distress the rush of great waters • shall not reach them.
8 You are a hiding place for me, you preserve • me from trouble;*
you encompass me • with deliverance.
9 I will instruct you and teach you the way • you should go;*
I will counsel you with my • eye upon you.
10 Do not be like an unruly horse or a mule, without • understanding,*
whose temper must be curbed with • bit and bridle.
11 Many are the pangs • of the wicked;*
but steadfast love surrounds those who trust • in the Lord.
12 Be glad in the Lord, and re•joice, O righteous;*
shout for joy, all you up•right in heart!

110 Psalm 33

רננו צדיקים ביהוה

1 Rejoice in the Lord, • O you righteous!*
Delight in praise, • O you upright!
2 Praise the Lord • with the lyre,*
make melody to the Lord with the harp • of ten strings!
3 Sing to the Lord • a new song,*
play skillfully on the strings, • with loud shouts.

4 Upright is the word • of the Lord,*
whose work is • done in faithfulness.
5 The Lord loves righteous•ness and justice;*
the earth is full of the steadfast love • of the Lord.
6 By the word of the Lord the heav•ens were made,*
and all their host by the breath • of God's mouth.
7 The Lord gathered the waters of the sea as • in a bottle*
and put the • deeps in storehouses.
8 Let all the earth • fear the Lord,*
let all the inhabitants of the world • stand in awe!
9 For the Lord spoke, and it • came to be;*
the Lord commanded, and • it stood forth.
10 The Lord brings the counsel of the na•tions to nothing*
and frustrates the plans • of the peoples.
11 The counsel of the Lord • stands for ever,*
the thoughts of God's heart to all • generations.
12 Blessed is the nation whose God • is the Lord,*
the people whom the Lord has chosen • as a heritage!
13 The Lord looks • down from heaven,*
and • sees all peoples;
14 the Lord sits enthroned • and looks forth*
on all the inhabitants • of the earth,
15 fashioning the hearts • of them all,*
and observing • all their deeds.
16 A king is not saved by • his great army;*
a warrior is not delivered by • his great strength.
17 The war-horse is a vain • hope for victory,*
and despite its great might it • cannot save.
18 Behold, the eye of the Lord is on those • who are faithful*
and hope for God's • steadfast love
19 to deliver their • soul from death,*
and to keep them a•live in famine.
20 Our soul waits • for the Lord,*
who is our • help and shield.
21 Our heart is glad • in the Lord,*
because we trust in God's • holy name.
22 Let your steadfast love, O Lord, • be upon us,*
even as we • hope in you.

III Psalm 34

אברכה את יהוה

1 I will bless the Lord • at all times;*
God's praise shall continually be • in my mouth.
2 My soul makes its boast • in the Lord;*
let the afflicted hear • and be glad.
3 O magnify the • Lord with me,*
and let us exalt God's • name together!
4 I sought the Lord, who • answered me,*
and delivered me from • all my fears.
5 Look to God • and be radiant,*
so your faces shall never • be ashamed.
6 The poor cried out, and • the Lord heard,*
and saved them out of • all their troubles.
7 The angel of the Lord encamps around • those who fear God,*
the angel of the Lord de•livers them.
8 O taste and see that the • Lord is good!*
Happy are those who take ref•uge in God!
9 O fear the Lord, you • holy ones,*
for those who fear God • have no want!
10 The young lions suffer • want and hunger,*
but those who seek the Lord lack • no good thing.
11 Come, O children, lis•ten to me,*
I will teach you the fear • of the Lord.
12 Which of • you desires life*
and covets many days • to enjoy good?
13 Keep your • tongue from evil,*
and your lips from speak•ing deceit.
14 Depart from evil, • and do good;*
seek peace, • and pursue it.
15 The eyes of the Lord are to•ward the righteous,*
the ears of the Lord • hear their cry.
16 The face of the Lord is against • evildoers,*
to cut off the remembrance of them • from the earth.
17 When the righteous cry for help, • the Lord hears,*
and delivers them out of • all their troubles.
18 The Lord is near to the • brokenhearted,*
and saves the • crushed in spirit.
19 Many are the afflictions • of the righteous;*
but the Lord de•livers them.

20 The Lord keeps • all their bones;*
not one of • them is broken.
21 Evil shall • slay the wicked;*
and those who hate the righteous will • be condemned.
22 God redeems the life • of God's servants;*
none of those who take refuge in God will • be condemned.

112 Psalm 35:17–28

אדני כמה תראה

17 How long, O God, will • you look on?*
Rescue me from their ravages, my life • from the lions!
18 Then I will thank you in the great • congregation;*
in the mighty throng • I will praise you.
19 Let not those rejoice over me who are wrongful•ly my foes,*
and let not those wink the eye who hate me • without cause.
20 For they do • not speak peace,*
but against those who are quiet in the land they conceive words • of deceit.
21 They open wide their • mouths against me;*
they say, "Aha! Aha! our • eyes have seen it!"
22 You have seen, O God, • be not silent!*
O God, be not • far from me!
23 Bestir yourself, and awake • for my right,*
for my cause, my God • and my Lord!
24 Vindicate me, O Lord my God, according to your • righteousness;*
and let them not rejoice • over me!
25 Let them not say to themselves, "Aha, we have our • heart's desire!"*
Let them not say, "We have swallowed • that one up."
26 Let them be put to shame and confusion altogether who rejoice at • my calamity!*
Let them be clothed with shame and dishonor who magnify them•selves against me!
27 Let those who desire my vindication shout for joy • and be glad,*
and say evermore, "Great is God, who delights in the welfare • of God's servant!"
28 Then my tongue shall tell of your • righteousness*
and of your praise all • the day long.

113 Psalm 36:5–10

יהוה בהשמים חסדך

5 Your steadfast love, O Lord, extends • to the heavens,*
your faithfulness • to the clouds.
6 Your righteousness is like the mighty mountains, your judgments are like • the great deep;*
O Lord, humans and ani•mals you save!
7 O God, how precious is your • steadfast love!*
All people may take refuge in the shadow • of your wings.
8 They feast on the abundance • of your house,*
and you give them drink from the river of • your delights.
9 For with you is the foun•tain of life;*
in your light do • we see light.
10 O continue your steadfast love to • those who know you,*
and your salvation to the up•right of heart!

114 Psalm 37:1–11

אל תתחר במרעים

1 Do not be angry because • of the wicked,*
do not be envious • of wrongdoers!
2 For they will soon fade • like the grass,*
and wither like • the green herb.
3 Trust in the Lord, • and do good;*
so you will dwell in the land, and en•joy security.
4 Take delight • in the Lord,*
who will give you the desires • of your heart.

5 Commit your way • to the Lord,*
trust in God, • who will act;
6 bringing forth your vindication • as the light,*
and your right • as the noonday.
7 Be still and wait patiently be•fore the Lord;*
do not be angry because of those who prosper
in their way, because of those who carry out
e•vil devices!
8 Refrain from anger, • and forsake wrath!*
Do not be angry; it leads on•ly to evil.
9 For the wicked shall • be cut off;*
but those who wait for the Lord shall
pos•sess the land.
10 Yet a little while, and the wicked will • be no
more;*
though you look at their place, they will •
not be there.
11 But the meek shall pos•sess the land,*
and delight in abun•dant prosperity.

115 Psalm 39

אמרתי אשמרה דרכי

1 I said, "I will • guard my ways,*
that I may not sin • with my tongue;
2 I will keep a muzzle • on my mouth,*
so long as the wicked are • in my presence."
3 I was mute and silent, I held my peace to • no
avail;*
my distress grew worse, my heart became •
hot within me.
4 As I mused • the fire burned;*
then I spoke • with my tongue:
5 "Lord, let me know my end, and what is the
measure • of my days;*
let me know how fleet•ing my life is!
6 You have made my days a few handbreadths,
and my lifetime is as nothing • in your sight,*
surely every human being is an • empty
breath!
7 Surely everyone goes about as a shadow!
Surely they are in tur•moil for nothing;*
they heap up, and do not know • who will
gather!
8 "And now, Lord, for what • do I wait?*
My hope • is in you.
9 Deliver me from all • my transgressions.*
Make me not the scorn • of the fool!
10 I am mute, I do not o•pen my mouth;*
for it is you • who have done it.
11 Remove your • stroke from me;*
I am spent by the blows • of your hand.
12 When you chasten people with rebukes for sin,
you consume like a moth what is • dear to them;*
surely every human being is an • empty
breath!
13 Hear my prayer, O Lord, and give ear • to my
cry;*
hold not your peace • at my tears!
14 For I am your • passing guest,*
a sojourner, like • all my forebears.
15 Look away from me, that I • may know
gladness,*
before I depart and • am no more!"

116 Psalm 40:1–12

קוה קויתי יהוה

1 I waited patiently • for the Lord,*
who inclined to me and • heard my cry.
2 The Lord drew me up from the desolate pit, out
of the • miry bog,*
setting my feet upon a rock, and making my •
steps secure.
3 The Lord put a new song in my mouth, a song
of praise • to our God.*
Many will see and be in awe, and put their
trust • in the Lord.
4 Blessed are those who make the • Lord their
trust,*
who do not turn to the proud, to those who
go astray af•ter false gods!
5 O Lord my God, you have multiplied your
wondrous deeds and your • thoughts toward us;*
none can com•pare with you!
6 Were I to proclaim and • tell of them,*
they would be more than • can be numbered.
7 Sacrifice and offering you do • not desire,*
but you have given me an • open ear.

8 Burnt offering and sin offering you have • not required.*
Then I said, "Lo, I come; in the roll of the book it is writ•ten of me:
9 I delight to do your will, • O my God;*
your law is with•in my heart."
10 I have told the glad news of deliverance in the great • congregation;*
lo, I have not restrained my lips, as you • know, O Lord.
11 I have not hid your saving help within my heart, I have spoken of your faithfulness and • your salvation;*
I have not concealed your steadfast love and faithfulness from the great • congregation.
12 O Lord, do not withhold your • mercy from me,*
let your steadfast love and faithfulness ev•er preserve me!

117 Psalm 41

אשרי משכיל אל דל

1 Blessed are those who consid•er the poor!*
The Lord delivers them in the • day of trouble;
2 the Lord protects them and keeps them alive; they are called blessed • in the land;*
you do not give them up to the will • of their enemies.
3 The Lord sustains them • on their sickbed;*
in their illness you heal all • their infirmities.
4 As for me, I said, "O Lord, be • gracious to me;*
heal me, for I have • sinned against you!"
5 My enemies say of • me in malice:*
"When will that person die, and • that name perish?"
6 Those who come to see me utter empty words, while their hearts • gather mischief;*
when they go out, they tell • it abroad.
7 All who hate me whisper togeth•er about me;*
they imagine the • worst for me.
8 They say, "A deadly thing has fastened up•on that person,*
who has lain down never to • rise again."
9 Even my bosom friend in whom I trusted, who ate • of my bread,*
has lifted a • heel against me.
10 But you, O Lord, be gracious to me and • raise me up*
that I • may repay them!
11 By this I know that you are • pleased with me,*
in that my enemy has not triumphed • over me.
12 But you have upheld me because of • my integrity,*
and set me in your pres•ence for ever.
13 Blessed be the Lord, the • God of Israel,*
from everlasting to everlasting!
A•men. Amen.

118 Psalm 42

כאיל תערג

1 As a deer longs for • flowing streams,*
so longs my soul for • you, O God.
2 My soul thirsts for God, for the • living God.*
When shall I come and behold the • face of God?
3 My tears have been my food • day and night,*
while people say to me continually, "Where • is your God?"
4 These things I remember as I pour • out my soul:*
how I went with the throng, and led them in procession to the • house of God,
5 with glad shouts and songs • of thanksgiving,*
a multitude • keeping festival.
6 Why are you cast down, • O my soul,*
and why are you disquiet•ed within me?
7 Hope in God whom again • I shall praise,*
my help • and my God.
8 My soul is cast • down within me,*
therefore I remember you from the land of Jordan and of Hermon, • from Mount Mizar.
9 Deep calls to deep at the thunder • of your cataracts;*
all your waves and your billows have gone • over me.
10 By day the Lord commands God's • steadfast love;*
and at night God's song is with me, a prayer to the God • of my life.

11 I say to God, my rock: "Why have you for•gotten me?*
Why do I mourn because of the oppression • of the enemy?"
12 Like a deadly wound in my body, my adver•saries taunt me,*
they say to me continually, "Where • is your God?"
13 Why are you cast down, • O my soul,*
and why are you disquiet•ed within me?
14 Hope in God whom again • I shall praise,*
my help • and my God.

119 Psalm 43

שפטני אלהים

1 Vindicate me, O God, and defend my cause against an un•godly people;*
from the deceitful and un•just deliver me!
2 For you are the God in whom I take refuge; why have you • cast me off?*
Why must I mourn because of the oppression • of the enemy?
3 O send out your light and your truth; • let them lead me,*
let them bring me to your holy hill and • to your dwelling!
4 Then I will go to the altar of God, to God my • exceeding joy;*
and I will praise you with the lyre, O • God, my God.
5 Why are you cast down, • O my soul,*
and why are you disquiet•ed within me?
6 Hope in God whom again • I shall praise,*
my help • and my God.

120 Psalm 44:1–8

אלהים באזנינו שמענו

1 We have heard with our ears, O God, our ances•tors have told us,*
what deeds you performed in their days, in the • days of old:
2 you with your own hand drove out the nations, but • them you planted;*
you afflicted the peoples, but them • you set free;
3 for not by their own sword did they win the land, nor did their own arm • give them victory;*
but by your right hand, and your arm, and the light of your countenance; for you de•lighted in the
4 You are my Ruler • and my God,*
who ordains victo•ries for Jacob.
5 Through you we push • down our foes;*
through your name we tread down • our assailants.
6 For not in my bow • do I trust,*
nor can • my sword save me.
7 But you have saved us • from our foes,*
and have put to confusion • those who hate us.
8 In God we have boasted con•tinually,*
and we will give thanks to your • name forever.

121 Psalm 46

אלהים לנו מחסה

1 God is our ref•uge and strength,*
a very present • help in trouble.
2 Therefore we will not fear though the • earth should change,*
though the mountains shake in the heart • of the sea;
3 though its waters • roar and foam,*
though the mountains tremble • with its tumult.
4 The Lord of • hosts is with us;*
the God of Jacob • is our refuge.
5 There is a river whose streams make glad the cit•y of God,*
the holy habitation of • the Most High.
6 God is in the midst of the city which shall • not be moved,*
God will help it at the dawn • of the day.
7 The nations rage, the • kingdoms totter;*
God speaks and • the earth melts.
8 The Lord of • hosts is with us;*
the God of Jacob • is our refuge.
9 Come, behold the works • of the Lord,*
who has wrought desolations • in the earth;

10 who makes wars cease to the end • of the earth;*
who breaks the bow, shatters the spear, and burns the • shields with fire!
11 "Be still, and know that • I am God;*
I am exalted among the nations, I am exalted • in the earth!"
12 The Lord of • hosts is with us;*
the God of Jacob • is our refuge.

122 Psalm 47

כל העמים תקעו כף

1 Clap your • hands, all peoples!*
Shout to God with loud • songs of joy!
2 For the Lord, the Most High, is • to be feared,*
a great Ruler over • all the earth,
3 who subdued peoples • under us,*
and nations un•der our feet,
4 who chose our heri•tage for us,*
the pride of Jacob • whom God loves.
5 God has gone up • with a shout,*
the Lord with the sound • of a trumpet.
6 Sing praises to • God, sing praises!*
Sing praises to our Rul•er, sing praises!
7 For God is the Ruler of • all the earth;*
sing praises • with a psalm!
8 God reigns o•ver the nations;*
God sits on the • holy throne.
9 The princes of the • people gather*
with the people of the • God of Abraham.
10 For the shields of the earth be•long to God,*
who is high•ly exalted!

123 Psalm 48

גדול יהוה

1 Great is the Lord and greatly • to be praised*
in the city • of our God;
2 whose holy mountain, beautiful in elevation, is the joy of • all the earth,*
Mount Zion, in the far north, the city of • the great Ruler.
3 God is with•in its citadels,*
and has proven a • sure defense.
4 For lo, the rul•ers assembled,*
they • marched together.
5 As soon as they saw it, they • were astounded,*
they were in panic, they • took to flight;
6 trembling took hold of them there, anguish as of a wom•an in travail,*
as when an east wind shatters the • ships of Tarshish.
7 As we have heard, so have we seen in the city of the • Lord of hosts,*
in the city of our God, which God establish•es for ever.
8 We have thought on your steadfast • love, O God,*
in the midst • of your temple.
9 As your name, O God, so your praise reaches to the ends • of the earth;*
your right hand is • filled with victory.
10 Let Mount Zion be glad! Let the daughters of Ju•dah rejoice*
because • of your judgments!
11 Walk about Zion, go • round about it,*
num•ber its towers.
12 Consider well its ramparts, go • through its citadels,*
that you may tell the next • generation,
13 "This is God, our God for ev•er and ever.*
God will be our • guide for ever."

124 Psalm 50:1–15

אל אלהים יהוה דבר

1 The Mighty One, God the Lord, speaks and sum•mons the earth*
from the rising of the sun • to its setting.
2 Out of Zion, the perfec•tion of beauty,*
our • God shines forth.
3 Our God comes, and does • not keep silence,*
before whom is a devouring fire, round about whom is a • mighty storm.
4 God calls to the heavens above and • to the earth*
that the people • may be judged:
5 "Gather to me my • faithful ones,*
who made a covenant with • me by sacrifice!"

[6] The heavens de•clare God's righteousness,*
for God a•lone is judge!
[7] "Hear, O my people, and I will speak; O Israel,
I will testi•fy against you;*
for I am • God, your God.
[8] I do not reprove you • for your sacrifices;*
your burnt offerings are continual•ly before
me.
[9] But I will not accept a bull • from your house,*
nor a he-goat • from your folds.
[10] For every beast of the for•est is mine,*
the cattle on a • thousand hills.
[11] I know all the birds • of the air,*
and all that moves in the • field is mine.
[12] If I were hungry, I • would not tell you;*
for the world and all that is in • it is mine.
[13] Do I eat the • flesh of bulls,*
or drink the • blood of goats?
[14] Offer to God a sacrifice • of thanksgiving,*
and pay your vows to • the Most High.
[15] Call upon me in the • day of trouble;*
I will deliver you, and you shall • glorify me."

125 Psalm 51:1–18

חנני אלהים כחסדך

[1] Have mercy on me, O God, according to your •
steadfast love;*
according to your abundant mercy blot out •
my transgressions.
[2] Wash me thoroughly from • my iniquity,*
and cleanse me • from my sin!
[3] For I know • my transgressions,*
and my sin is ev•er before me.
[4] Against you, you only, • have I sinned,*
and done that which is evil • in your sight,
[5] so that you are justified • in your sentence,*
and blameless • in your judgment.
[6] Behold, I was born in•to iniquity,*
and I have been sinful since my moth•er
conceived me.
[7] Behold, you desire truth in the • inward being;*
therefore teach me wisdom in my • secret
heart.
[8] Purge me with hyssop, and I • shall be clean;*
wash me, and I shall be whit•er than snow;
[9] Make me hear with • joy and gladness;*
let the bones which you have bro•ken
rejoice.
[10] Hide your face • from my sins,*
and blot out all • my iniquities.
[11] Create in me a clean • heart, O God,*
and put a new and right spir•it within me.
[12] Cast me not away • from your presence,*
and take not your holy • Spirit from me.
[13] Restore to me the joy of • your salvation,*
and sustain in me a • willing spirit.
[14] Then I will teach transgres•sors your ways,*
and sinners will re•turn to you.
[15] Deliver me from death, O God, God of • my
salvation,*
and my tongue will sing aloud of • your
deliverance.
[16] O Lord, o•pen my lips,*
and my mouth shall show • forth your praise.
[17] For you have no de•light in sacrifice;*
were I to give a burnt offering, you would •
not be pleased.
[18] The sacrifice acceptable to God is a • broken
spirit;*
a broken and contrite heart, O God, you will •
not despise.

126 Psalm 53

אמר נבל בלבו

[1] Fools say in their heart, "There • is no God."*
They are corrupt, doing abominable iniquity;
there is none • that does good.
[2] God looks down from heaven upon • human
beings*
to see if there are any that are wise, that seek •
after God.
[3] They have all fallen away; they are all a•like
depraved;*
there is none that does good, • no, not one.
[4] Have those who work evil no • understanding,*
who eat up my people as they eat bread, and
do not call • upon God?

5 There they are, in great terror, in terror such as • has not been!*
For God will scatter the bones of the ungodly; they will be put to shame, for God has re•jected them.
6 O that deliverance for Israel would • come from Zion!*
When God restores the fortunes of God's people, Jacob will rejoice and Isra•el be glad.

127 Psalm 57

חנני אלהים חנני

1 Be merciful to me, O God, be merciful to me, for in you my • soul takes refuge;*
in the shadow of your wings I will take refuge, till the storms of destruc•tion pass by.
2 I cry to • God Most High,*
to God who fulfills God's pur•pose for me.
3 God will send from heaven and save me, putting to shame those who tram•ple upon me.*
God will send forth God's steadfast love and • faithfulness!
4 I lie in the midst of lions that greedily devour their • human prey;*
their teeth are spears and arrows, their • tongues sharp swords.
5 Be exalted, O God, a•bove the heavens!*
Let your glory be over • all the earth!
6 They set a net for my steps, my soul • was bowed down;*
they dug a pit in my way, but they have fallen into • it themselves.
7 My heart is steadfast, O God, my • heart is steadfast!*
I will sing • and make melody!
8 Awake, my soul! Awake, O • harp and lyre!*
I will a•wake the dawn!
9 I will give thanks to you, O God, a•mong the peoples;*
I will sing praises to you a•mong the nations.
10 For your steadfast love is greater • than the heavens,*
your faithfulness reaches • to the clouds.
11 Be exalted, O God, a•bove the heavens!*
Let your glory be over • all the earth!

128 Psalm 62:6–14

אך לאלהים דומי נפשי

6 For God alone my soul • waits in silence,*
for my hope • is from God,
7 who alone is my rock and • my salvation,*
my fortress, so that I shall • not be shaken.
8 On God rests my deliverance • and my honor;*
my mighty rock, my ref•uge is God.
9 Trust in God at all • times, O people;*
pour out your heart before God who is a ref•uge for us.
10 Those of low estate are • but a breath,*
those of high estate are • a delusion;
11 in the balances • they go up;*
they are together lighter • than a breath.
12 Put no confidence in extortion, set no vain • hopes on robbery;*
if riches increase, set not your • heart on them.
13 Once God has spoken, twice • have I heard this:*
power be•longs to God;
14 and to you, O Lord, belongs • steadfast love,*
for you repay all according • to their work.

129 Psalm 63:1–8

אלהים אלי אתה

1 O God, you are my God, I seek you, my soul • thirsts for you;*
my flesh faints for you, as in a dry and weary land where no • water is.
2 So I have looked upon you in the • sanctuary,*
beholding your • power and glory.
3 Because your steadfast love is bet•ter than life,*
my • lips will praise you.
4 So I will bless you as long • as I live;*
I will lift up my hands and call • on your name.
5 My soul is feasted as with mar•row and fat,*
and my mouth praises you with • joyful lips,
6 when I think of you up•on my bed,*
and meditate on you in the watches • of the night;
7 for you have • been my help,*
and in the shadow of your wings I • sing for joy.
8 My soul • clings to you;*
your right • hand upholds me.

130 Psalm 65

לך דמיה תהלה

[1] Praise is due to you, O • God, in Zion;*
and to you shall vows • be performed.
[2] To • you who hear prayer*
all flesh shall come because • of their sins.
[3] When our transgressions prevail • over us,*
you, O • God, forgive them.
[4] Blessed are those whom you choose and bring
near, to dwell • in your courts!*
We shall be satisfied with the goodness of
your house, your • holy temple!
[5] By dread deeds you answer us with deliverance,
O God of • our salvation,*
who is the hope of all the ends of the earth,
and of the • farthest seas;
[6] who by your strength estab•lished the
mountains,*
being gird•ed with might;
[7] who stills the roaring • of the seas,*
the roaring of their waves, the tumult • of the
peoples;
[8] so that those who dwell at earth's farthest
bounds are afraid • at your signs;*
you make the morning and the evening
re•sound with joy.
[9] You visit the earth and water it, you great•ly
enrich it;*
the river of God is • full of water.
[10] You pro•vide its grain,*
for so you • have prepared it.
[11] You water its furrows abundantly, set•tling its
ridges,*
softening it with showers, and bless•ing its
growth.
[12] You crown the year • with your bounty;*
the tracks of your chariot • drip with fatness.
[13] The pastures of the wil•derness drip,*
the hills gird them•selves with joy,
[14] the meadows clothe themselves with flocks,
the valleys deck them•selves with grain,*
they shout and sing togeth•er for joy.

131 Psalm 66:7–18

ברכו עמים אלהינו

[7] Bless our • God, O peoples,*
let the sound of God's • praise be heard,
[8] who has kept us a•mong the living,*
and has not • let our feet slip.
[9] For you, O God, have • tested us;*
you have tried us as sil•ver is tried.
[10] You brought us in•to the net;*
you laid affliction • on our loins;
[11] you let people ride over our heads; we went
through • fire and water;*
yet you have brought us forth to a • spacious
place.
[12] I will come into your house with burnt offerings;
I will pay • you my vows,*
that which my lips uttered and my mouth
promised when I • was in trouble.
[13] I will offer to you burnt offerings of fatlings,
with the smoke of the sacri•fice of rams;*
I will make an offering of • bulls and goats.
[14] Come and hear, all you who • worship God,*
and I will tell what God has • done for me.
[15] I cried a•loud to God,*
who was highly praised • with my tongue.
[16] If I had cherished iniquity • in my heart,*
the Lord would • not have listened.
[17] But truly • God has listened,*
and has given heed to the voice • of my prayer.
[18] Blessed be God, who has not reject•ed my
prayer,*
or removed steadfast • love from me.

132 Psalm 67

אלהים יחננו

[1] O God, be gracious to • us and bless us,*
and make your face to • shine upon us,
[2] that your way may be known • upon earth,*
your saving power a•mong all nations.
[3] Let the peoples praise • you, O God;*
let all the • peoples praise you!

4 Let the nations be glad and • sing for joy,*
for you judge the peoples with equity and guide the nations • upon earth.
5 Let the peoples praise • you, O God;*
let all the • peoples praise you!
6 The earth has yield•ed its increase;*
God, our • God, has blessed us.
7 God • has blessed us;*
let all the ends of the • earth fear God!

133 Psalm 68:1–10

יקום אלהים

1 Let God arise, let God's ene•mies be scattered;*
let those who • hate God flee!
2 As smoke is driven away, so drive • them away;*
as wax melts before fire, let the wicked per•ish before God!
3 But let the righteous be joyful, let them ex•ult before God;*
let them be jubi•lant with joy!
4 Sing to God, sing praises to God's name, lift up a song to the One who rides up•on the clouds;*
exult before the One whose • name is Lord!
5 In the holy habitation God is par•ent of orphans,*
and protec•tor of widows.
6 God gives the desolate a home to dwell in, and leads out the prisoners • to prosperity;*
but the rebellious dwell in • a parched land.
7 O God, when you went forth be•fore your people,*
when you marched through the • wilderness,
8 the earth quaked, the heavens poured down water, at the presence of God, the • God of Sinai,*
at the presence of God, the • God of Israel.
9 Rain in abundance, O God, you • shed abroad;*
you restored your heritage • as it languished;
10 your flock found a • dwelling in it;*
in your goodness, O God, you provided • for the needy.

134 Psalm 69:7–17

אל יבשו בי קויך

7 Let not those who hope in you be put to shame through me, O Lord • God of hosts;*
let not those who seek you be brought to dishonor through me, O • God of Israel.
8 For it is for your sake that I have • borne reproach,*
that shame has cov•ered my face.
9 I have become a stranger • to my family,*
an alien to my • mother's children.
10 For zeal for your house • has consumed me,*
and the insults of those who insult you have fal•len on me.
11 When I humbled my • soul with fasting,*
it became • my reproach.
12 When I made sack•cloth my clothing,*
I became a by•word to them.
13 I am the talk of those who sit • in the gate,*
and the drunkards make • songs about me.
14 But as for me, my prayer is to • you, O God;*
at an acceptable time, O God, in the abundance of your steadfast love • answer me.
15 With your faithful help • rescue me*
from sinking • in the mire;
16 let me be delivered • from my enemies*
and from • the deep waters.
17 Let not the flood sweep over me, or the deep swal•low me up,*
or the pit close its mouth • over me.

135 Psalm 70

אלהים להצילני

1 Be pleased, O God, to de•liver me!*
O God, make • haste to help me!
2 Let them be put to shame and confusion who • seek my life!*
Let them be turned back and brought to dishonor who de•sire my hurt!
3 Let them be appalled because • of their shame*
who say, "A•ha! Aha!"

4 May all who seek you rejoice and be • glad in you!*
May those who love your salvation say evermore, • "God is great!"
5 But I am • poor and needy;*
hasten to • me, O God!
6 You are my help and • my deliverer;*
O God, • do not tarry!

136 Psalm 71:1–12

בך יהוה חסיתי

1 In you, O God, do • I take refuge;*
let me never be • put to shame!
2 In your righteousness deliver me and • rescue me;*
incline your ear to • me, and save me!
3 Be to me a rock of refuge, a strong for•tress, to save me,*
for you are my rock • and my fortress.
4 Rescue me, O my God, from the hand • of the wicked,*
from the grasp of the unjust • and the cruel.
5 For you, O God, • are my hope,*
my trust, O God, • from my youth.
6 Upon you I have leaned • from my birth;*
you are the one who took me from my mother's womb; my praise is continual•ly of you.
7 I have been as a por•tent to many;*
but you are • my strong refuge.
8 My mouth is filled • with your praise,*
and with your glory • all the day.
9 Do not cast me off in the time • of old age;*
forsake me not when my • strength is spent.
10 For my enemies speak con•cerning me,*
those who watch for my life con•sult together.
11 They say, "God has forsaken the • one who trusted;*
pursue and seize the forsaken one, for there is no one to • give deliverance."
12 O God, be not • far from me;*
O my God, make • haste to help me!

137 Psalm 72:1–14

אלהים משפטיך למלך תן

1 Give the ruler your jus•tice, O God,*
and your righteousness to the • royal heir!
2 May the ruler judge your people with • righteousness,*
and your • poor with justice!
3 Let the mountains bear prosperity • for the people,*
and the hills, in • righteousness!
4 May the ruler defend the cause of the poor • of the people,*
give deliverance to the needy, and crush • the oppressor!
5 May the ruler live while the • sun endures,*
and as long as the moon, throughout all • generations!
6 May the ruler be like rain that falls on • the mown grass,*
like showers that wa•ter the earth!
7 In the ruler's days may righ•teousness flourish,*
and peace abound, till the moon • be no more!
8 May the ruler have dominion from • sea to sea,*
and from the River to the ends • of the earth!
9 May the foes of the rul•er bow down,*
and the enemies • lick the dust!
10 May the kings of Tarshish and of the isles • render tribute,*
may the kings of Sheba and Se•ba bring gifts!
11 May all • kings bow down*
and all nations • serve the ruler!
12 For the ruler delivers the needy • when they call,*
the poor and those who • have no helper,
13 and has pity on the weak • and the needy,*
and saves the lives • of the needy.
14 The ruler redeems their lives from oppres•sion and violence,*
and their blood is precious in the • ruler's sight.

138 Psalm 74

למה אלהים זנחת לנצח

1 O God, why do you cast us • off for ever?*
Why does your anger smoke against the sheep • of your pasture?
2 Remember your congregation, which you have gotten of old, and redeemed to be the tribe • of your heritage!*
Remember Mount Zion, where • you have dwelt.
3 Direct your steps to the per•petual ruins,*
for the enemy has destroyed everything • in the sanctuary.
4 Your foes roared in the midst of your • holy place;*
they set up their own banners for • signs of victory.
5 At the upper entrance they hacked the wooden trel•lis with axes;*
all its carved wood they broke down with hatch•ets and hammers
6 They set your sanctuar•y on fire;*
to the ground they desecrated the dwelling place • of your name.
7 They said to themselves, "We will utter•ly subdue them";*
they burned all the meeting places of God • in the land.
8 We do not • see our signs;*
there is no longer any prophet, nor any among us who • knows how long.
9 How long, O God, is the • foe to scoff?*
Is the enemy to revile your • name for ever?
10 Why do you hold • back your hand,*
why do you keep your right hand • in your bosom?
11 Yet God my Ruler is • from of old,*
working salvation in the midst • of the earth.
12 You divided the sea • by your might;*
you broke the heads of the dragons • on the waters.
13 You crushed the heads of Le•viathan,*
you gave him as food for the creatures of the • wilderness.
14 You cleaved open • springs and brooks;*
you dried up ever • flowing streams.
15 Yours is the day, yours al•so the night;*
you established the luminaries • and the sun.
16 You have fixed all the bounds • of the earth;*
you have made sum•mer and winter.
17 Remember this, O Lord, how the en•emy scoffs,*
and an impious people re•viles your name.
18 Do not deliver the soul of your dove to • the wild beasts;*
do not forget the life of your • poor for ever.
19 Have regard • for your covenant;*
for the dark places of the land are the habita•tion of violence.
20 Let not the downtrodden be • put to shame;*
let the poor and needy • praise your name.
21 Arise, O God, • plead your cause;*
remember how the impious scoff at you • all the day!
22 Do not forget the clamor • of your foes,*
the uproar of your adversaries which goes • up continually!

139 Psalm 76

נודע ביהודה אלהים

1 In Judah • God is known,*
whose name is • great in Israel,
2 whose abode has been estab•lished in Salem,*
whose dwelling place • is in Zion.
3 There God broke the • flashing arrows,*
the shield, the sword, and the weap•ons of war.
4 How glo•rious you are!*
more majestic than the ever•lasting mountains.
5 The stout-hearted were stripped of their spoil; they sank • into sleep;*
all the soldiers were unable to • use their hands.
6 At your rebuke, O • God of Jacob,*
both rider and • horse lay stunned.
7 You indeed are • to be feared!*
Who can stand before you when once your an•ger is roused?
8 From the heavens you • uttered judgment;*
the earth feared • and was still,

9 when God arose to es•tablish judgment*
and to save all the oppressed • of the earth.
10 Surely human • wrath shall praise you;*
the residue of wrath you will • gird upon you.
11 Make vows to the Lord your • God, and keep them;*
let those who surround God bring gifts to the One • to be feared,
12 who cuts off the spir•it of monarchs,*
and makes the rulers of the • earth afraid.

140 Psalm 77:11–20

אזכיר מעללי יה

11 I will call to mind the deeds • of the Lord;*
I will remember your won•ders of old.
12 I will meditate on • all your work,*
and muse on your • mighty deeds.
13 Your way, O • God, is holy.*
What god is • great like our God?
14 You are the God • who works wonders,*
you manifested your might a•mong the peoples.
15 You redeemed with your • arm your people,*
the descendants of Ja•cob and Joseph.
16 When the waters saw you, O God, when the waters saw you, they • were afraid;*
the ver•y deeps trembled.
17 The clouds • poured out water,*
the skies gave forth thunder; your arrows flashed on • every side.
18 The crash of your thunder was in the whirlwind, your lightnings illu•mined the world;*
the earth trem•bled and shook.
19 Your way was through the sea, your path through • the great waters;*
yet your footprints • were unseen.
20 You led your people • like a flock*
by the hand of Mo•ses and Aaron.

141 Psalm 78:1–4, 9–20, 33–38

האזינה עמי תורתי

1 Give ear, O my people, • to my teaching;*
incline your ears to the words • of my mouth!
2 I will open my mouth • in a parable;*
I will utter dark sayings • from of old;
3 things that we have heard and known, that our fore•bears have told us,*
we will not hide them from their children, but tell to the coming • generation
4 the glorious deeds • of the Lord,*
the might and wonders • God has wrought.
9 The Ephraimites, armed • with the bow,*
turned back on the • day of battle.
10 They did not • keep God's covenant,*
and refused to walk according • to God's law.
11 They forgot the deeds • of the Lord,*
the miracles that • God had shown them.
12 The Lord wrought marvels in the sight • of their forebears,*
in the land of Egypt, in the • fields of Zoan,
13 the Lord divided the sea and let • them pass through it,*
and made the waters stand • like a heap,
14 led them with a cloud • in the daytime,*
and all the night with a • fiery light,
15 cleft rocks • in the wilderness,*
and gave them drink abundantly as • from the deep,
16 made streams come out • of the rock,*
and caused waters to flow • down like rivers.
17 Yet they sinned still • more against God,*
rebelling against the Most High • in the desert.
18 They tested God • in their heart,*
demanding the • food they craved.
19 They spoke a•gainst God, saying,*
"Can God spread a table • in the wilderness?
20 Indeed God struck the rock so that water gushed out and streams • overflowed;*
but can God also give bread, or provide meat • for the people?"
33 They did not believe • in God's wonders,*
so God made their days like a breath and turned their years • into terror.

34 Whenever God slew them, they would inquire • after God,*
repent, and seek God • earnestly.
35 They remembered that God • was their rock,*
the Most High God • their redeemer,
36 whom they flattered • with their mouths,*
yet lied to • with their tongues.
37 Their heart was not steadfast • toward God;*
they were not true • to God's covenant.
38 Yet God, being compassionate, forgave • their iniquity*
and did • not destroy them.

142 Psalm 80

רעה ישראל האזינה

1 Give ear, O Shepherd of Israel, you who lead Joseph • like a flock!*
You who are enthroned upon the cheru•bim, shine forth!
2 In the presence of Ephraim and Benjamin • and Manasseh,*
stir up your might, and • come to save us!
3 Restore us, O • God of hosts;*
let your face shine, that we • may be saved!
4 O Lord • God of hosts,*
how long will you be angry with your • people's prayers?
5 You have fed them with the • bread of tears,*
and given them tears to drink • in full measure.
6 You make us the scorn • of our neighbors;*
and our enemies laugh a•mong themselves.
7 Restore us, O • God of hosts;*
let your face shine, that we • may be saved!
8 You brought a vine • out of Egypt;*
you drove out the nations and • planted it.
9 You cleared the • ground for it;*
it took deep root and • filled the land.
10 The mountains were covered • with its shade,*
the mighty cedars • with its branches;
11 it sent out its branches • to the sea,*
and its shoots • to the river.
12 Why then have you broken • down its walls,*
so that all who pass along the way • pluck its fruit?
13 The boar from the forest rav•ages it,*
and all that move in the field • feed on it.
14 Turn again, O God of hosts! Look down from heav•en, and see;*
have regard for this vine, the stock which your • right hand planted.
15 They have burned it with fire, they have • cut it down;*
may they perish at the rebuke • of your countenance!
16 But let your hand be upon those of • your right hand,*
the ones whom you have made strong • for yourself!
17 Then we will never turn • back from you;*
give us life, and we will call • on your name!
18 Restore us, O Lord • God of hosts;*
let your face shine, that we • may be saved!

143 Psalm 81:1–10

הרנינו לאלהים עוזנו

1 Sing aloud to • God our strength;*
shout for joy to the • God of Jacob!
2 Raise a song, • sound the tambourine,*
the sweet lyre • with the harp.
3 Blow the trumpet at • the new moon,*
at the full moon, • on our feast day.
4 For it is a stat•ute for Israel,*
an ordinance of the • God of Jacob,
5 who made it a de•cree in Joseph,*
when God went out over the • land of Egypt.
6 I hear a voice I do • not know, saying,*
"I relieved your shoulder of the burden;
your hands were freed • from the basket.
7 In distress you called, and I de•livered you;*
I answered you in the secret place of thunder,
and tested you at the wa•ters of Meribah.
8 Hear, O my people, while I ad•monish you!*
O Israel, if you would but lis•ten to me!
9 There shall be no strange • god among you;*
you shall not bow down to a • foreign god.
10 I am the Lord your God, who brought you up out of the • land of Egypt;*
open wide your mouth, and • I will fill it."

144 Psalm 82

אלהים נצב בעדת אל

1 God stands up in the • divine council;*
in the midst of the gods, • God holds judgment:
2 "How long will you • judge unjustly,*
and show partiality • to the wicked?
3 Give justice to the weak • and the orphan;*
maintain the right of the afflicted • and the destitute.
4 Rescue the weak • and the needy,*
deliver them from the hand • of the wicked."
5 They have neither knowledge nor understanding,
they walk about • in confusion;*
all the foundations of the • earth are shaken.
6 I say, • "You are gods,*
offspring of the Most High, • all of you;
7 nevertheless, you shall • die like mortals,*
and fall like • any ruler."
8 Arise, O God, • judge the earth;*
for to you belong • all the nations!

145 Psalm 84

מה ידידות משכנותיך

1 How lovely is your • dwelling place,*
O • Lord of hosts!
2 My soul longs, indeed faints for the courts •
of the Lord;*
my heart and flesh sing for joy to the • living God.
3 O Lord of hosts, my Ruler and my God, at
your altars even the sparrow • finds a home,*
and the swallow a nest for herself, where she may • lay her young.
4 Blessed are those who dwell • in your house,*
ever sing•ing your praise!
5 Blessed are those whose strength • is in you,*
in whose heart are the high•ways to Zion.
6 As they go through the valley of tears, they
make it a • place of springs;*
the early rain also covers • it with pools.
7 They go from • strength to strength;*
the God of gods will be • seen in Zion.
8 O Lord God of hosts, • hear my prayer;*
give ear, O • God of Jacob!
9 Behold our • shield, O God;*
look upon the face of • your anointed!
10 For a day in your courts is better than a •
thousand elsewhere;*
I would rather be a doorkeeper in the house of my God than dwell in the • tents of wickedness.
11 For the Lord God is a • sun and shield,*
and bestows fa•vor and honor.
12 No good thing does the Lord withhold from
those who • walk uprightly;*
O Lord of hosts, blessed are those who • trust in you!

146 Psalm 85

רצית יהוה ארצך

1 Lord, you showed favor • to your land;*
you restored the for•tunes of Jacob.
2 You forgave the iniquity • of your people;*
you pardoned • all their sin.
3 You withdrew • all your wrath;*
you turned from • your hot anger.
4 Restore us again, O God of • our salvation,*
and put away your indig•nation toward us!
5 Will you be angry with • us for ever?*
Will you prolong your anger to all • generations?
6 Will you not revive • us again,*
that your people may re•joice in you?
7 Show us your steadfast • love, O Lord,*
and grant us • your salvation.
8 Let me hear what • God will speak,*
for the Lord will speak peace to those who are faithful, to those who turn to the Lord • in their hearts.
9 Surely salvation is at hand for those who • fear
the Lord,*
that God's glory may dwell • in our land.
10 Steadfast love and faithful•ness will meet;*
righteousness and peace will • kiss each other.
11 Faithfulness will spring up • from the ground,*
and righteousness will look down • from the sky.

12 The Lord will give • what is good,*
and our land will • yield its increase.
13 Righteousness will go be•fore the Lord,*
and make a way • for God's footsteps.

147 Psalm 86

הטה יהוה אזנך

1 Incline your ear, O Lord, and • answer me,*
for I am • poor and needy.
2 Preserve my life, for • I am godly;*
save your servant who trusts in you, for
you • are my God,
3 Be gracious to • me, O Lord,*
for I cry to you all • the day long.
4 Gladden the soul • of your servant,*
for to you, O Lord, do I lift • up my soul.
5 For you, O Lord, are good • and forgiving,*
abounding in steadfast love to all who • call
on you.
6 Give ear, O Lord, • to my prayer,*
hearken to my cry of • supplication.
7 In the day of my trouble I will • call on you,*
for you will • answer me.
8 There is none like you among the • gods,
O Lord,*
nor are there any • works like yours.
9 All the nations you have made will come and
bow down before • you, O Lord,*
and will glori•fy your name.
10 For you are great and do • wondrous things,*
you a•lone are God.
11 Teach me your way, O Lord, that I may walk •
in your truth;*
knit my heart to you that I may • fear your
name.
12 I give thanks to you, O Lord my God, with •
my whole heart,*
and I will glorify your • name for ever.
13 For great is your steadfast • love toward me;*
you have delivered my soul from the • depths
of Sheol.
14 O God, insolent people have risen up against
me, and a band of ruthless ones • seeks my life,*
they do not set you be•fore their eyes.
15 But you, O Lord, are a God merci•ful and
gracious,*
slow to anger and abounding in steadfast •
love and faithfulness.
16 Turn to me and take pit•y on me;*
give your strength to your servant and save
the child • of your handmaid.
17 Show me a sign of your favor, that those who
hate me may see and be • put to shame,*
because you, Lord, have helped and
com•forted me.

148 Psalm 89:1–4, 19–37

חסדי יהוה עולם אשירה

1 I will sing of your steadfast love, O • Lord,
for ever;*
with my mouth I will proclaim your
faithfulness to all • generations.
2 Your steadfast love is estab•lished for ever,*
your faithfulness is firm • as the heavens.
3 You have said, "I have made a covenant with
my • chosen one,*
I have sworn to Da•vid my servant:
4 'I will establish your descend•ants for ever,*
and build your throne for all • generations.' "
19 Then you spoke in a vision to your faithful • one,
and said:*
"I have set the crown upon one who is
mighty, I have exalted one chosen • from the
people.
20 I have found Da•vid, my servant;*
with my holy oil I have a•nointed him,
21 so that my hand shall ever a•bide with him,*
my arm also shall • strengthen him.
22 The enemy shall • not outwit him,*
the wicked shall not • humble him.
23 I will crush his • foes before him*
and strike down • those who hate him.
24 My faithfulness and my steadfast love shall •
be with him,*
and in my name shall his horn • be exalted.
25 I will set his hand • on the sea,*
and his right hand • on the rivers.
26 He shall cry to me, 'You • are my Father,*
my God, and the Rock of • my salvation.'

27 And I will make • him the first-born,*
the highest of the kings • of the earth.
28 My steadfast love I will keep for • him for ever,*
and my covenant will stand • firm for him.
29 I will establish his • line for ever*
and his throne as the days • of the heavens.
30 If his children for•sake my law*
and do not walk according • to my ordinances,
31 if they vio•late my statutes*
and do not keep • my commandments,
32 then I will punish their transgression • with the rod*
and their iniqui•ty with scourges;
33 but I will not remove from him my • steadfast love,*
or be false • to my faithfulness.
34 I will not vio•late my covenant,*
or alter the word that went forth • from my lips.
35 Once for all I have sworn • by my holiness:*
I will not • lie to David.
36 His line shall en•dure for ever,*
his throne as long as the • sun before me.
37 Like the moon it shall be estab•lished for ever;*
it shall stand firm while the • skies endure."

149 Psalm 90

אדני מעון אתה היית לנו

1 Lord, you have been our • dwelling place*
in every • generation.
2 Before the mountains were brought forth, or ever you had formed the earth • and the world,*
from everlasting to everlasting • you are God.
3 You turn people • back to dust,*
and say, "Go • back, O mortals."
4 For a thousand years in your sight are but as yesterday when • it is past,*
or as a watch • in the night.
5 You sweep us away • like a dream,*
like grass which is renewed • in the morning.
6 In the morning it flourishes and • is renewed;*
in the evening it • fades and withers.
7 For we are consumed • by your anger;*
by your wrath we are • overwhelmed.
8 You have set our iniqui•ties before you,*
our secret sins in the light • of your countenance.
9 For all our days pass away un•der your wrath,*
our years come to an end • like a sigh.
10 The years of our life are threescore and ten,
or even by reason of • strength fourscore;*
yet their span is but toil and trouble; they are soon gone, and we • fly away.
11 Who considers the power • of your anger,*
the awesomeness • of your wrath?
12 So teach us to num•ber our days*
that we may receive a • heart of wisdom.
13 Return, O • Lord! How long?*
Have pity • on your servants!
14 Satisfy us in the morning with your • steadfast love,*
that we may rejoice and be glad • all our days.
15 Make us glad for as many days as you have af•flicted us,*
for as many years as we • have seen evil.
16 Let your work be manifest • to your servants,*
and your glorious power • to their children.
17 Let the favor of the Lord our God • be upon us,*
establish the work of our hands; yes, establish
the work • of our hands.

150 Psalm 91

ישב בסתר עליון

1 Those who dwell in the shelter of • the Most High,*
who abide in the shadow of the Almighty, will say • to the Lord,
2 "My refuge • and my fortress;*
my God, in • whom I trust."
3 For the Lord will deliver you from the snare of the fowler and from the deadly • pestilence;*
the Lord will cover • you with pinions.
4 Under the Lord's wings you • will find refuge;*
God's faithfulness is a • shield and buckler.
5 You will not fear the ter•ror of the night,*
nor the arrow that • flies by day,
6 nor the pestilence that • stalks in darkness,*
nor the destruction that • wastes at noonday.

7 A thousand may fall at your side, ten thousand at • your right hand,*
but it will • not come near you.
8 You only have to look • with your eyes*
to see the recompense • of the wicked.
9 Because you have made the • Lord your refuge,*
the Most High your • habitation,
10 no evil • shall befall you,*
no scourge come • near your tent.
11 For God will give angels charge • over you*
to guard you in • all your ways.
12 They will bear you up • on their hands*
lest you dash your foot a•gainst a stone.
13 You will tread on the lion • and the adder;*
the young lion and the serpent you will trample • under foot.
14 Because they cleave to me in love, I will de•liver them,*
I will protect them, because they • know my name.
15 When they call to me, I will • answer them;*
I will be with them in trouble, I will rescue them and • honor them.
16 I will satisfy them • with long life,*
and show them • my salvation.

151 Psalm 92:1–4, 11–14

טוב להדות ליהוה

1 It is good to give thanks • to the Lord,*
to sing praises to your name, • O Most High;
2 to declare your steadfast love • in the morning,*
and your faithful•ness by night,
3 to the music of the lute • and the harp,*
to the melody • of the lyre.
4 For you, O Lord, have made me glad • by your work;*
at the works of your hands I • sing for joy.
11 The righteous flourish • like the palm tree,*
and grow like a ce•dar in Lebanon.
12 They are planted in the house • of the Lord,*
they flourish in the courts • of our God.
13 They still bring forth fruit • in old age,*
they are ever full of • sap and green,
14 to show that the • Lord is upright,*
the Lord who is my rock, in whom there is • no unrighteousness.

152 Psalm 93

יהוה מלך גאות לבש

1 The Lord reigns and is • robed in majesty;*
the Lord is robed and is gird•ed with strength.
2 The Lord has estab•lished the world;*
it shall nev•er be moved.
3 Your throne has been established • from of old;*
you are from • everlasting!
4 The floods have lifted up, O Lord, the floods have lifted • up their voice,*
the floods lift • up their roaring.
5 Mightier than the thunders of many waters, mightier than the waves • of the sea,*
the Lord on • high is mighty!
6 Your decrees are • very sure;*
holiness befits your house, O Lord, for • evermore.

153 Psalm 94:12–22

אשרי הגבר אשר תיסרנו

12 Blessed are those whom you chas•ten, O God,*
and whom you teach out • of your law
13 to give them respite from • days of trouble,*
until a pit is dug • for the wicked.
14 For God will not for•sake God's people,*
and will not aban•don God's heritage;
15 for justice will return • to the righteous,*
and all the upright in heart will • follow it.
16 Who rises up for me a•gainst the wicked?*
Who stands up for me against the • evildoers?
17 If God had not • been my help,*
my soul would soon have dwelt in the • land of silence.
18 When I thought, • "My foot slips,"*
your steadfast love, O God, • held me up.

19 When the cares of my • heart are many,*
your consolations • cheer my soul.
20 Can wicked rulers be al•lied with you,*
who frame mis•chief by statute?
21 They band together against the life • of the righteous,*
and condemn the inno•cent to death.
22 But the Lord has be•come my stronghold,*
and my God the rock • of my refuge.

154 Psalm 95

לכו נרננה ליהוה

1 O come, let us sing • to the Lord;*
let us make a joyful noise to the rock of • our salvation!
2 Let us come into God's presence • with thanksgiving;*
let us make a joyful noise with • songs of praise!
3 For the Lord • is a great God,*
and a great Ruler a•bove all gods,
4 in whose hands are the depths • of the earth,*
and also the heights • of the mountains.
5 The sea belongs to • God who made it,*
and the dry land, be•cause God formed it.
6 O come, let us wor•ship and bow down,*
let us kneel before the • Lord, our Maker!
7 For the Lord • is our God,*
we are the people of God's pasture, the sheep • of God's hand.
8 Hear the voice of the • Lord today!*
Harden not your hearts, as at Meribah, as on the day at Massah • in the wilderness,
9 when your forebears • tested me,*
and put me to the proof, though they had • seen my work.
10 For forty years I loathed that genera•tion and said,*
"They are a people who err in heart, who do not re•gard my ways."
11 Therefore I swore • in my anger*
that they should not en•ter my rest.

155 Psalm 96

שירו ליהוה שיר חדש

1 O sing to the Lord • a new song;*
sing to the Lord, • all the earth!
2 Sing to the Lord, • bless God's name;*
proclaim God's salvation from • day to day.
3 Declare the Lord's glory a•mong the nations,*
the Lord's marvelous works among • all the peoples!
4 For great is the Lord and greatly • to be praised,*
to be feared a•bove all gods.
5 For all the gods of the peo•ples are idols;*
but the Lord • made the heavens.
6 Honor and majesty are be•fore the Lord,*
in whose sanctuary are • strength and beauty.
7 Ascribe to the Lord, O families • of the peoples,*
ascribe to the Lord glo•ry and strength!
8 Ascribe to the Lord the glory • of the Lord's name!*
Bring an offering, and come into the courts • of the Lord!
9 Worship the Lord in • holy splendor;*
tremble before the Lord, • all the earth!
10 Say among the nations, • "The Lord reigns!*
The Lord has established the world, it shall never be moved. The Lord will judge the peo•ples with equity."
11 Let the heavens be glad, and let the • earth rejoice,*
let the sea roar, and • all that fills it.
12 Let the field exult, and every•thing in it!*
Then shall all the trees of the wood sing for joy before the Lord, who comes to • judge the earth.
13 The Lord will judge the world with • righteousness,*
and the peo•ples with truth.

156 Psalm 97

יהוה מלך תגל הארץ

1 The Lord reigns; let the • earth rejoice;*
let the many coast•lands be glad!

2 Clouds and thick darkness sur•round the Lord;*
righteousness and justice are the foundation •
of God's throne.
3 Fire goes be•fore the Lord,*
and burns up adversaries • round about.
4 The Lord's lightnings illu•mine the world;*
the earth • sees and trembles.
5 The mountains melt like wax be•fore the Lord,*
before the Lord of • all the earth.
6 The heavens pro•claim God's righteousness*
and all the peoples be•hold God's glory.
7 All worshipers of images are put to shame, who
make their boast in • worthless idols;*
all gods bow down be•fore the Lord.
8 Zion hears and is glad, and the daughters of
Ju•dah rejoice,*
because of your judg•ments, O God.
9 For you, O Lord, are most high over • all the
earth;*
you are exalted far a•bove all gods.
10 The Lord loves those • who hate evil,*
the Lord preserves the lives of the faithful,
and delivers them from the hand • of the
wicked.
11 Light dawns • for the righteous,*
and joy for the up•right in heart.
12 Rejoice in the Lord, • O you righteous,*
and give thanks to God's • holy name!

157 Psalm 98

שירו ליהוה שיר חדש

1 O sing to the Lord • a new song,*
for the Lord has done • marvelous things!
2 God's right hand and • holy arm*
have got•ten the victory.
3 God has declared • victory,*
and has revealed God's vindication in the
sight • of the nations.
4 The Lord has remembered to show steadfast
love and faithfulness to the • house of Israel;*
all the ends of the earth have seen the
victory • of our God.
5 Make a joyful noise to the Lord, • all the earth;*
break forth into joyous song • and sing
praises!
6 Sing praises to the Lord • with the lyre,*
with the lyre and the • sound of melody!
7 With trumpets and the sound • of the horn*
make a joyful noise before the Rul•er, the
Lord!
8 Let the sea roar, and • all that fills it,*
the world and those who • dwell in it!
9 Let the floods • clap their hands;*
let the hills sing for joy together before the
Lord, who comes to • judge the earth.
10 The Lord will judge the • world with
righteousness,*
and the peo•ples with equity.

158 Psalm 99

יהוה מלך ירגזו עמים

1 The Lord reigns; let the • peoples tremble!*
The Lord sits enthroned upon the cherubim;
let • the earth quake!
2 The Lord is • great in Zion,*
and is exalted over • all the peoples.
3 Let them praise your great and • wondrous
name!*
Holy • is the Lord!
4 Mighty Ruler, lover of justice, you have
es•tablished equity;*
you have executed justice and
righteous•ness in Jacob.
5 Extol the Lord our God, worship at • the Lord's
footstool!*
Holy • is the Lord!
6 Moses and Aaron were a•mong God's priests,*
Samuel also was among those who called • on
God's name.
7 They cried to the Lord, who answered them,
who spoke to them in the pil•lar of cloud;*
they kept God's testimonies, and the statutes •
God gave them.
8 O Lord, our God, you • answered them;*
you were a forgiving God to them, but an
avenger of • their wrongdoings.
9 Extol the Lord our God, and worship at God's •
holy mountain.*
Surely the Lord our • God is holy!

159 Psalm 100

הריעו ליהוה כל הארץ

1 Make a joyful noise to the Lord, • all the lands!*
Serve the Lord with gladness and come into
God's pres•ence with singing!
2 Know that the Lord, who made • us, is God.*
We are the Lord's, we are God's people and
the sheep • of God's pasture.
3 Enter God's gates with thanksgiving, and
God's • courts with praise!*
Give thanks and • bless God's name!
4 For the • Lord is good;*
God's steadfast love endures for ever, God's
faithfulness to all • generations.

160 Psalm 101

חסד ומשפט אשירה

1 I will sing of loyalty • and of justice;*
to you, O God, • I will sing.
2 I will give heed to the way that is blameless.
O when will you • come to me?*
I will walk with integrity of heart with•in
my house;
3 I will not set before my eyes anything • that is
base.*
I hate the work of those who fall away; it
shall not • cleave to me.
4 Perverseness of heart shall be • far from me;*
I will know noth•ing of evil.
5 The one who slanders a neighbor secretly I •
will destroy;*
the one of haughty looks and arrogant heart I
will • not endure.
6 I will look with favor on the faithful in the land,
that they may • dwell with me;*
one who walks in the way that is blameless
shall minis•ter to me.
7 No one who practices deceit shall dwell • in my
house;*
no one who utters lies shall continue • in my
presence.
8 Morning by morning I will destroy all the
wicked • in the land,*
cutting off all the evildoers from the city •
of the Lord.

161 Psalm 102:1–12

יהוה שמעה תפלתי

1 Hear my prayer, O Lord, and let my cry • come
to you!*
Do not hide your face from me in the day
of • my distress!
2 Incline your • ear to me;*
answer me speedily in the day • when I call!
3 For my days pass a•way like smoke,*
and my bones burn • like a furnace.
4 My heart is smitten like • grass, and withered;*
I am too wasted to • eat my bread.
5 Because of • my loud groaning*
my bones cleave • to my flesh.
6 I am like an owl • of the wilderness,*
like a little owl of • the waste places;
7 I lie a•wake and groan;*
I am like a lonely bird • on the housetop.
8 All the day my ene•mies taunt me,*
those who deride me use my name • for a
curse.
9 For I eat ash•es like bread,*
and mingle tears • with my drink.
10 Because of your indigna•tion and anger*
you have taken me up and thrown • me away.
11 My days are like an • evening shadow;*
I wither a•way like grass.
12 But you, O Lord, are en•throned for ever;*
and your name endures to all • generations.

162 Psalm 103:1–18

ברכי נפשי את יהוה

1 Bless the Lord, • O my soul,*
and all that is within me, bless God's • holy
name!

[2] Bless the Lord, • O my soul,*
and forget not • all God's benefits,
[3] who forgives all • your iniquity,*
who heals all • your diseases,
[4] who redeems your life • from the pit,*
who crowns you with steadfast • love and mercy,
[5] who satisfies you with good as long • as you live,*
so that your youth is renewed • like the eagle's.
[6] The Lord, who works • vindication*
and justice for all who • are oppressed,
[7] has made known God's • ways to Moses,*
God's acts to the peo•ple of Israel.
[8] The Lord is merci•ful and gracious,*
slow to anger and abounding in • steadfast love.
[9] The Lord will not • always chide,*
not harbor an•ger for ever.
[10] The Lord does not deal with us according • to our sins,*
nor repay us according to • our iniquities.
[11] For as the heavens are high a•bove the earth,*
so great is the Lord's steadfast love • toward the faithful.
[12] As far as the east is • from the west,*
so far does the Lord remove our transgres•sions from us.
[13] As parents show compassion • to their children,*
so the Lord shows compassion • to the faithful.
[14] For the Lord • knows our frame,*
and remembers that • we are dust.
[15] As for mortals, their days • are like grass;*
they flourish like a flower • of the field;
[16] for the wind passes over it, and • it is gone,*
and its place knows • it no more.
[17] But the steadfast love of the Lord is from everlasting to everlasting up•on the faithful,*
and the righteousness of the Lord to • children's children,
[18] to those who • keep God's covenant*
and remember to do • God's commandments.

163 Psalm 104:1–13, 25–37

ברכי נפשי את יהוה

[1] Bless the Lord, • O my soul!*
O Lord my God, you are • very great!
[2] You are clothed with honor and • majesty,*
and cover yourself with light as • with a garment;
[3] you have stretched out the heavens • like a tent,*
and have laid the beams of your chambers • on the waters;
[4] you make the clouds your chariot and ride on the wings • of the wind;*
you make the winds your messengers, fire and • flame your ministers.
[5] You set the earth on • its foundations,*
so that it should nev•er be shaken.
[6] You covered it with the deep as • with a garment;*
the waters stood a•bove the mountains.
[7] At your re•buke they fled;*
at the sound of your thunder they • took to flight.
[8] They rose up to the mountains, ran down • to the valleys,*
to the place which you appoint•ed for them.
[9] You set a bound which they • should not pass,*
so that they might not again cov•er the earth.
[10] You make springs gush forth • in the valleys;*
they flow be•tween the hills;
[11] they give drink to every beast • of the field;*
the wild asses • quench their thirst.
[12] Above the springs the birds of the air • have their nests;*
they sing a•mong the branches.
[13] From your lofty place you wa•ter the mountains;*
with the fruit of your work the earth is • satisfied.
[25] O Lord, how manifold • are your works!*
In wisdom you have made them all; the earth is full • of your creatures.
[26] Yonder is the sea, • great and wide;*
creeping things innumerable are there, living things both • small and great.

27 There • go the ships,*
and Leviathan which you formed to • play in it.
28 These all • look to you,*
to give them their food • in due season.
29 When you give to them, they • gather it;*
when you open your hand, they are filled • with good things.
30 When you hide your face, they • are dismayed;*
when you take away their breath, they die and return • to their dust.
31 When you send forth your spirit, they • are created;*
and you renew the face • of the ground.
32 May the glory of the Lord en•dure for ever,*
may God rejoice • in God's works.
33 God looks on the earth • and it trembles,*
God touches the mountains • and they smoke.
34 I will sing to the Lord as long • as I live;*
I will sing praise to my God while • I have being.
35 May my meditation be pleasing • to the Lord,*
in whom • I rejoice.
36 Let sinners be consumed • from the earth,*
and let the wicked • be no more!
37 Bless the Lord, • O my soul!*
O • praise the Lord!

164 Psalm 105:1–11

הודו ליהוה קראו בשמו

1 O give thanks to the Lord, call • on God's name,*
make known God's deeds a•mong the peoples!
2 Sing to the • Lord, sing praises!*
Tell of all God's won•derful works!
3 Glory in God's • holy name;*
let the hearts of those who seek the • Lord rejoice!
4 Seek the Lord and • the Lord's strength;*
seek the Lord's presence con•tinually!
5 Remember the wonderful works • God has done,*
the miracles and judgments • God has uttered,
6 O offspring of Abra•ham, God's servant,*
children of Jacob, God's • chosen one.
7 The Lord • is our God,*
whose judgments are in • all the earth.
8 The Lord is mindful of the ever•lasting covenant,*
of the word commanded for a thousand • generations,
9 the covenant • made with Abraham,*
the promise • sworn to Isaac,
10 and confirmed to Jacob • as a statute,*
to Israel as an ever•lasting covenant:
11 "To you I will give the • land of Canaan*
as your portion for • an inheritance."

165 Psalm 106:1–12, 19–23, 47–48

הללויה הודו ליהוה כי טוב

1 Praise the Lord! O give thanks to the Lord • who is good;*
whose steadfast love en•dures for ever!
2 Who can utter the mighty doings • of the Lord,*
or show forth • all God's praise?
3 Blessed are they who ob•serve justice,*
who do righteousness • at all times!
4 Remember me, O Lord, when you show favor • to your people;*
help me when • you deliver them,
5 that I may see the prosperity of your chosen ones, and rejoice in the gladness • of your nation,*
that I may glory • with your heritage
6 Both we and our fore•bears have sinned;*
we have committed iniquity, we • have done wickedly.
7 Our forebears, when they were in Egypt, did not consider your won•derful works;*
they did not remember the abundance of your steadfast love, but rebelled against the Most High at • the Red Sea.
8 God saved them for the sake of God's • holy name,*

to make known the mighty • power of God.
9 God rebuked the Red Sea, and • it became dry;*
and led them through the deep as • through a desert.
10 So God saved them from the hand • of the foe,*
and delivered them from the hand • of the enemy.
11 The waters covered their • adversaries;*
not one of • them was left.
12 Then they be•lieved God's words;*
they • sang God's praise.
19 They made a • calf in Horeb*
and worshiped a • molten image.
20 They exchanged the glo•ry of God*
for the image of an ox • that eats grass.
21 They forgot • God, their Savior,*
who had done great • things in Egypt,
22 wondrous works in the • land of Ham,*
and terrible things by • the Red Sea.
23 Therefore the Lord intended to destroy them,
had not Moses, God's chosen one, stood • in the breach,*
to turn away God's wrath from de•stroying them.
47 Save us, O Lord our God, and gather us from a•mong the nations,*
that we may give thanks to your holy name and glory • in your praise.
48 Blessed be the Lord, the God of Israel, from everlasting to • everlasting;*
and let all the people say, "Amen!" • Praise the Lord!

166 Psalm 107:1–9, 33–43

הדו ליהוה כי טוב

1 O give thanks to the Lord, • who is good,*
whose steadfast love en•dures for ever!
2 Let the redeemed of the • Lord say so,*
whom the Lord has re•deemed from trouble
3 and gathered in • from the lands,*
from the east and from the west, from the north and • from the south.
4 Some wandered in the • desert wastes,*
finding no way to a city in • which to dwell;
5 hun•gry and thirsty,*
their soul faint•ed within them.
6 Then in their trouble they cried • to the Lord,*
who delivered them from • their distress,
7 and led them by • a straight way,*
till they reached a city in • which to dwell.
8 Let them thank the Lord for • steadfast love,*
for wonderful works to • humankind.
9 For the Lord satisfies those • who are thirsty,*
and fills the hungry • with good things.
33 The Lord turns rivers in•to a desert,*
springs of water into • thirsty ground,
34 a fruitful land into a • salty waste,*
because of the wickedness of • its inhabitants.
35 The Lord turns a desert into • pools of water,*
a parched land into • springs of water.
36 The Lord lets the • hungry dwell there,*
and they establish a city in • which to live;
37 they sow fields, • and plant vineyards,*
and get a • fruitful yield.
38 They multiply greatly by the blessing • of the Lord,*
who does not let their cat•tle decrease.
39 When they are diminished • and brought low*
through oppression, trou•ble, and sorrow,
40 the Lord pours contempt • upon princes*
and makes them wander in • trackless wastes;
41 but the Lord raises up the needy out • of affliction,*
and makes their fami•lies like flocks.
42 The upright see it • and are glad;*
and all wickedness • stops its mouth.
43 Whoever is wise, give heed • to these things,*
consider the steadfast love • of the Lord.

167 Psalm 111

הללו יה אודה יהוה בכל לבב

1 Praise the Lord! I will give thanks to the Lord with • my whole heart,*
in the company of the upright, in the • congregation.

2 Great are the works • of the Lord,*
studied by all who have pleas•ure in them.
3 Full of honor and majesty • is God's work,*
and God's righteousness en•dures forever.
4 God has caused wonderful works to • be
remembered,*
and is gracious and • merciful,
5 providing food for • those who fear God,*
and being ever mindful • of the covenant.
6 God has shown the people the power • of God's
works*
in giving them the heritage • of the nations.
7 The works of God's hands are faith•ful and
just;*
all God's pre•cepts are trustworthy,
8 they are established for • ever and ever,*
to be performed with faithful•ness and
uprightness.
9 God sent redemption to God's people, and
commanded the cove•nant for ever.*
Holy and terrible • is God's name!
10 The fear of the Lord is the begin•ning of
wisdom;*
a good understanding have all those who
practice it; God's praise en•dures for ever!

168 Psalm 112

הללו יה אשרי איש ירא את יהוה

1 Praise the Lord! Blessed are those who • fear
the Lord,*
who greatly delight in • God's
commandments!
2 Their descendants will be mighty • in the land;*
the generation of the upright • will be blessed.
3 Wealth and riches are • in their house,*
and their righteousness en•dures for ever.
4 They rise in the darkness as a light • for the
upright,*
they are gracious, merci•ful and righteous.
5 It is well with those who deal generous•ly and
lend,*
who conduct their af•fairs with justice.
6 For the righteous shall nev•er be moved;*
they will be remem•bered for ever.
7 They are not afraid of • evil tidings;*
their hearts are firm, trusting • in the Lord.
8 When they see their • adversaries,*
their hearts are steady, they will not • be
afraid.
9 They have distributed freely and given • to the
poor;*
their righteousness endures for ever, their
horn is exalt•ed in honor.
10 The wicked see it and are angry; they gnash
their teeth and • melt away;*
the desire of the wicked • comes to nothing.

169 Psalm 113

הללו יה הללו עבדי יהוה

1 Praise the Lord! Praise, O servants • of the
Lord,*
praise the name • of the Lord!
2 Blessed be the name • of the Lord*
from this time forth and for • evermore!
3 From the rising of the sun • to its setting*
the name of the Lord is • to be praised!
4 The Lord is high a•bove all nations,*
God's glory a•bove the heavens!
5 Who is like the Lord our God, who is seat•ed
on high,*
who looks far down upon the heavens • and
the earth?
6 God raises the poor • from the dust,*
and lifts the needy • from the ash heap,
7 to make them • sit with nobles,*
with the nobles a•mong God's people.
8 God gives the barren wom•an a home,*
making her the joyous mother of children. •
Praise the Lord!

170 Psalm 114

בצאת ישראל ממצרים

1 When Israel went • forth from Egypt,*
the house of Jacob from a people • of strange
language,

[2] Judah became God's • sanctuary,*
Israel • God's dominion.
[3] The sea • looked and fled,*
Jor•dan turned back.
[4] The mountains • skipped like rams,*
the • hills like lambs.
[5] What ails you, O sea, • that you flee?*
O Jordan, that • you turn back?
[6] O mountains, that you • skip like rams?*
O • hills, like lambs?
[7] Tremble, O earth, at the presence • of the Lord,*
at the presence of the • God of Jacob,
[8] who turns the rock into a • pool of water,*
the flint into a • spring of water.

171 Psalm 115:1–11

לא לנו יהוה

[1] Not to us, O Lord, not to us, but to your • name
give glory,*
for the sake of your steadfast • love and
faithfulness!
[2] Why should the • nations say,*
"Where • is their God?"
[3] Our God is • in the heavens;*
whatever God pleas•es, God does.
[4] Their idols are sil•ver and gold,*
the work of • human hands.
[5] They have mouths, but • do not speak;*
eyes, but • do not see.
[6] They have ears, but • do not hear;*
noses, but • do not smell.
[7] They have hands, but do not feel, and feet,
but • do not walk;*
they have throats, but • make no sound.
[8] Those who make i•dols are like them;*
so are all who • trust in them.
[9] O Israel, trust • in the Lord!*
The Lord is their help • and their shield.
[10] O house of Aaron, trust • in the Lord!*
The Lord is their help • and their shield.
[11] You who fear the Lord, trust • in the Lord!*
The Lord is their help • and their shield.

172 Psalm 116

אהבתי כי ישמע יהוה

[1] I love the Lord, who has heard my voice and
my • supplications,*
and has listened to me whenev•er I called.
[2] The snares of death encompassed me; the
pangs of Sheol laid • hold on me;*
I suffered dis•tress and anguish.
[3] Then I called on the name • of the Lord:*
"O Lord, I beseech you, • save my life!"
[4] Gracious is the • Lord, and righteous;*
our God is • merciful.
[5] The Lord pre•serves the simple;*
when I was brought low, • the Lord saved me.
[6] Return, O my soul, • to your rest;*
for the Lord has dealt bounti•fully with you.
[7] For you have delivered my • soul from death,*
my eyes from tears, my • feet from stumbling;
[8] I walk be•fore the Lord*
in the land • of the living.
[9] I kept my faith, even when I said, "I am
great•ly afflicted."*
I said in my consternation, "All humans are •
a vain hope."
[10] What shall I return • to the Lord*
for • all my benefits?
[11] I will lift up the cup • of salvation*
and call on the name • of the Lord,
[12] I will pay my vows • to the Lord*
in the presence of • all God's people.
[13] Precious in the sight • of the Lord*
is the death of • faithful ones.
[14] O Lord, I • am your servant;*
I am your servant, and the child of your
handmaid; you have • loosed my bonds.
[15] I will offer to you the sacrifice • of
thanksgiving*
and call on the name • of the Lord.
[16] I will pay my vows • to the Lord*
in the presence of • all God's people,
[17] in the courts of the house • of the Lord,*
in your midst, O Jerusalem. • Praise the Lord!

173 Psalm 118:14–29

עזי וזמרת יה

14 The Lord is my strength • and my power;*
the Lord has become • my salvation.
15 There are joyous • songs of victory*
in the tents • of the righteous:
16 "The right hand of the • Lord does valiantly,*
the right hand of the Lord is exalted, the
right hand of the • Lord does valiantly!"
17 I shall not die, but • I shall live,*
and recount the deeds • of the Lord.
18 The Lord has chas•tened me sorely,*
but has not given me o•ver to death.
19 Open to me the • gates of righteousness,*
that I may enter through them and give
thanks • to the Lord.
20 This is the gate • of the Lord;*
the righteous shall • enter through it.
21 I thank you that • you have answered me*
and have become • my salvation.
22 The stone which the build•ers rejected*
has become the • cornerstone.
23 This is • the Lord's doing;*
it is marvelous • in our eyes.
24 This is the day which the • Lord has made;*
let us rejoice and be • glad in it.
25 Save us, we beseech • you, O Lord!*
O Lord, we beseech you, give • us success!
26 Blessed is the one who comes in the name • of
the Lord!*
We bless you from the house • of the Lord.
27 The Lord is God, who has giv•en us light;*
lead the festal procession with branches, up
to the horns • of the altar!
28 You are my God, and I will give • thanks to
you;*
you are my God, I • will extol you.
29 O give thanks to the Lord, • who is good;*
for God's steadfast love en•dures for ever!

174 Psalm 119:1–8, 33–48, 129–144

אשרי תמימי דרך

1 Blessed are those whose • way is blameless,*
who walk in the law • of the Lord!
2 Blessed are those who keep God's •
testimonies,*
who seek God with • their whole heart,
3 who also • do no wrong,*
but walk • in God's ways!
4 You have command•ed your precepts*
to • be kept diligently.
5 O that my ways • may be steadfast*
in keep•ing your statutes!
6 Then I shall not be • put to shame,*
having my eyes fixed on all • your
commandments.
7 I will praise you with an • upright heart,*
when I learn your • righteous ordinances.
8 I will ob•serve your statutes;*
O forsake • me not utterly!
33 Teach me, O Lord, the way • of your statutes,*
and I will keep it • to the end.
34 Give me understanding, that I may • keep your
law,*
and observe it with • my whole heart.
35 Lead me in the path of • your commandments,*
for I de•light in it.
36 Incline my heart • to your testimonies,*
and • not to gain!
37 Turn my eyes from looking at • vanities,*
and give me life • in your ways.
38 Confirm to your serv•ant your promise,*
which is for • those who fear you.
39 Turn away the reproach • which I dread,*
for your ordinan•ces are good.
40 Behold, I long • for your precepts;*
in your righteousness • give me life!
41 Let your steadfast love come to • me, O Lord,*
your salvation according • to your promise;
42 then shall I have an answer for • those who
taunt me,*
for I trust • in your word.
43 Do not take not the word of truth utterly out •
of my mouth,*
for my hope is • in your ordinances.

44 I will keep your law con•tinually,*
for ev•er and ever;
45 and I shall • walk at liberty,*
for I have • sought your precepts.
46 I will also speak of your testimonies • before rulers,*
and shall not be • put to shame;
47 for I find my delight in • your commandments,*
which I have • always loved.
48 I revere your commandments, • which I love,*
and I will meditate • on your statutes.
129 Your testimonies are • wonderful;*
therefore • my soul keeps them.
130 The unfolding of your • words gives light;*
it imparts understanding • to the simple.
131 With open • mouth I pant,*
because I long for • your commandments.
132 Turn to me and be gra•cious to me,*
for you are just to those who • love your name.
133 Keep steady my steps according • to your promise,*
and let no iniquity get dominion • over me.
134 Rescue me from those • who oppress me,*
that I may • keep your precepts.
135 Make your face shine up•on your servant,*
and teach • me your statutes.
136 My eyes shed • streams of tears,*
because your law • is not kept.
137 Righteous are • you, O Lord,*
and right • are your judgments.
138 You have appointed your testimonies in • righteousness*
and • in all faithfulness.
139 My • zeal consumes me,*
because my foes for•get your words.
140 Your promise • is well tried,*
and your • servant loves it.
141 I am small • and despised,*
yet I do not for•get your precepts.
142 Your righteousness is righ•teous for ever,*
and your • law is true.
143 Trouble and anguish have • come upon me,*
but your commandments are • my delight.
144 Your testimonies are righ•teous for ever;*
give me understanding that • I may live.

175 Psalm 121

אשא עיני אל ההרים

1 I lift up my eyes • to the hills;*
from whence does • my help come?
2 My help comes • from the Lord,*
who made heav•en and earth.
3 The Lord will not let your • foot be moved,*
the Lord who keeps you • will not slumber.
4 Behold, the One • who keeps Israel*
will neither slum•ber nor sleep.
5 The Lord • is your keeper;*
the Lord is your shade on • your right hand.
6 The sun shall not smite • you by day,*
nor the • moon by night.
7 The Lord will keep you • from all evil,*
and will • keep your life.
8 The Lord will keep your going out and your • coming in,*
from this time forth and for • evermore.

176 Psalm 122

שמחתי באמרים לי

1 I was glad when they • said to me,*
"Let us go to the house • of the Lord!"
2 Our • feet were standing*
within your gates, • O Jerusalem.
3 Jerusalem is built • as a city*
and is bound firm•ly together,
4 to which the tribes go up, the tribes • of the Lord,*
to give thanks to the name of the Lord, as was de•creed for Israel.
5 Thrones for judgment • were set there,*
the thrones of the • house of David.
6 Pray for the peace • of Jerusalem:*
"May they pros•per who love you!
7 Peace be with • in your walls,*
and security with•in your towers!"
8 For the sake of my rela•tives and friends*
I will say, "Peace • be within you!"
9 For the sake of the house of the • Lord our God,*
I will • seek your good.

177 Psalm 124

לולי יהוה שהיה לנו

1 If it had not been the Lord who was • on our
side—*
let Isra•el now say—
2 if it had not been the Lord who was • on our
side,*
when foes rose • up against us,
3 then they would have swallowed us • up alive,*
when their anger was kin•dled against us;
4 then the flood would have swept • us away,*
the torrent would have gone • over us;
5 then the • raging waters*
would have gone • over us.
6 Blessed • be the Lord,*
who has not given us as prey • to their teeth!
7 We have escaped as a bird from the snare • of
the fowlers;*
the snare is broken, and we • have escaped!
8 Our help is in the name • of the Lord,*
who made heav•en and earth.

178 Psalm 125

הבטחים ביהוה כהר ציון

1 Those who trust in God are • like Mount Zion,*
which cannot be moved, but a•bides forever.
2 As the mountains stand a•bout Jerusalem,*
so God stands about God's people, from this
time forth and for • evermore.
3 For the scepter of wickedness shall not rest upon
the land allotted • to the righteous,*
lest the righteous put forth their hands • to do
wrong.
4 Do good, O God, to those • who are good,*
and to those who are upright • in their hearts.
5 But those who turn aside upon their crooked
ways God will lead away with the • evildoers.*
May peace be up•on Israel!

179 Psalm 126

בשוב יהוה את שיבת ציון

1 When the Lord restored the for•tunes of
Zion,*
we were like • those who dream.
2 Then our mouth was • filled with laughter,*
and our tongue with • shouts of joy.
3 Then they said a•mong the nations,*
"The Lord has done great • things for
them."
4 The Lord has done great • things for us;*
and we are • glad indeed.
5 Restore our for•tunes, O Lord,*
like the watercourses • in the Negeb!
6 May those who • sow in tears*
reap with • shouts of joy!
7 Those who go forth weeping, bearing the •
seed for sowing,*
shall come home with shouts of joy,
carry•ing their sheaves.

180 Psalm 127

אם יהוה לא יבנה בית

1 Unless the Lord • builds the house,*
those who build it la•bor in vain.
2 Unless the Lord watches o•ver the city,*
the watcher stays a•wake in vain.
3 It is in vain that you rise up early and go late
to rest, eating the bread of • anxious toil;*
for God gives sleep to • God's beloved.
4 Children are a heritage • from the Lord,*
the fruit of the womb • a reward.
5 Like arrows in the hand • of a warrior*
are the children • of one's youth.
6 Happy are those who have a quiver • full of
them!*
They shall not be put to shame when
speaking with enemies • in the gate.

181 Psalm 128

אשרי כל ירא יהוה

1 Blessed is everyone • who fears God,*
who walks • in God's ways!
2 You shall eat the fruit of the labor • of your hands;*
you shall be happy, and it shall be • well with you.
3 Your beloved will be like a fruitful vine with•in your house;*
your children will be like olive shoots a•round your table.
4 Thus shall the • one be blessed*
who holds • God in awe.
5 God bless • you from Zion!*
May you see the prosperity of Jerusalem all the days • of your life!
6 May you live to see your • children's children!*
May peace be • upon Israel!

182 Psalm 130

ממעמקים קראתיך יהוה

1 Out of the depths I cry to you, O Lord; Lord, • hear my voice!*
Let your ears be attentive to the voice of my • supplications!
2 If you, O Lord, should • mark iniquities,*
Lord, • who could stand?
3 But there is forgive•ness with you,*
that you • may be worshiped.
4 I wait for the Lord, • my soul waits,*
in the Lord's • word I hope;
5 my soul waits for the Lord, more than those who watch • for the morning,*
more than those who watch • for the morning.
6 O Israel, hope • in the Lord!*
For with the Lord there is • steadfast love.
7 With the Lord is plen•teous redemption,*
and the Lord will redeem Israel from • all iniquities.

183 Psalm 132:1–5, 11–19

זכור יהוה לדוד

1 O Lord, in • David's favor*
remember all the hardships • he endured;
2 how he swore • to the Lord*
and vowed to the Mighty • One of Jacob,
3 "I will not en•ter my house,*
or get in•to my bed;
4 I will not give sleep • to my eyes*
or slumber • to my eyelids,
5 until I find a place • for the Lord,*
a dwelling place for the Mighty • One of Jacob."
11 The Lord swore to Da•vid a sure oath*
and from it will • not turn back:
12 "One of the fruit • of your body*
I will set • on your throne.
13 If your children keep my covenant and my testimonies which • I shall teach them,*
their children also for ever shall sit up•on your throne."
14 For the Lord has • chosen Zion,*
and has desired it for God's • habitation:
15 "This is my resting • place for ever;*
here I will dwell, for I • have desired it.
16 I will abundantly bless • its provisions;*
I will satisfy its • poor with bread.
17 Its priests I will clothe • with salvation,*
and its faithful will • shout for joy.
18 There I will make a horn to • sprout for David;*
I have prepared a lamp for • my anointed.
19 His enemies I will • clothe with shame,*
but his crown will • shine upon him."

184 Psalm 133

הנה מה טוב

1 Behold, how good and pleas•ant it is*
when we live togeth•er in unity!
2 It is like precious oil up•on the head,*
running down up•on the beard,
3 upon the • beard of Aaron,*
running down on the collar • of his robes.

4 It is like the • dew of Hermon*
which falls on the moun•tains of Zion.
5 For there the Lord has command•ed the blessing,*
life for • evermore.

185 Psalm 134

הנה ברכו את יהוה

1 Come, bless the Lord, all you servants • of the Lord,*
who stand by night in the house • of the Lord.
2 Lift up your hands in the • holy place,
and • bless the Lord;*
3 may the Lord who made heav•en and earth*
bless • you from Zion.

186 Psalm 135:1–14

הללו יה הללו את שם יהוה

1 Praise the Lord! Praise the name • of the Lord;*
give praise, O servants • of the Lord,
2 you that stand in the house • of the Lord,*
in the courts of the house • of our God!
3 Praise the Lord, for the • Lord is good;*
sing to the Lord's name, for the • Lord is gracious!
4 For the Lord has chosen Jacob • as God's own,*
Israel as God's • own possession.
5 For I know that the • Lord is great,*
and that our Lord is a•bove all gods.
6 Whatever the Lord pleases, the Lord does, in heaven • and on earth,*
in the seas • and all deeps.
7 It is the Lord who makes the clouds rise at the end • of the earth,*
makes lightnings for the rain and brings wind from the store•house of God.
8 It was the Lord who struck the first • born of Egypt,*
both of animals and of • humankind;
9 who in your midst, O Egypt, sent • signs and wonders*
against Pharaoh and • all his servants;
10 who struck • many nations*
and slew • mighty kings,
11 Sihon, king of the Amorites, and Og, • king of Bashan,*
and all the king•doms of Canaan,
12 and gave their land • as a heritage,*
a heritage to God's • people Israel.
13 Your name, O Lord, en•dures for ever,*
your renown, O Lord, through•out all ages.
14 For God will vindi•cate God's people,*
and have compassion • on God's servants.

187 Psalm 137:1–6

על נהרות בבל

1 By the rivers of Babylon, there we sat • down and wept,*
when we re•membered Zion.
2 On the • willows there*
we hung • up our lyres.
3 For there our captors required of us songs, and our tormentors • mirth, saying,*
"Sing us one of the • songs of Zion."
4 How shall we • sing the Lord's song*
in a • foreign land?
5 If I forget you, • O Jerusalem,*
let my • right hand wither!
6 Let my tongue cleave to the roof of my mouth, if I do not re•member you,*
if I do not set Jerusalem above my • highest joy.

188 Psalm 138

אודך בכל לבי

1 I give you thanks, O Lord, with • my whole heart;*
before the gods I • sing your praise.
2 I bow down toward your • holy temple*
and give thanks to your name for your steadfast • love and faithfulness;

[3] for you have exalt•ed your name*
and your word above • everything.
[4] On the day I called, you • answered me,*
you strength•ened my life.
[5] All the rulers of the earth shall praise • you,
O Lord,*
for they have heard the words • of your mouth;
[6] and they shall sing of the ways • of the Lord,*
for great is the glory • of the Lord.
[7] For the Lord is high, but re•gards the lowly;*
yet knows the haughty • from afar.
[8] Though I walk in the midst of trouble, you
pre•serve my life;*
you stretch out your hand against the wrath
of my enemies, and your right • hand delivers
me.
[9] O Lord, fulfill your pur•pose for me;*
O Lord, may your steadfast love endure for
ever; do not forsake the work • of your hands.

189 Psalm 139:1–17, 22–23

יהוה חקרתני ותדע

[1] O Lord, you have searched • me and known
me!*
You know when I sit down and when I rise
up; you discern my thoughts • from afar.
[2] You search out my path and my • lying down,*
and are acquainted with • all my ways.
[3] Even before a word is on my • tongue,
O Lord,*
you know it • altogether.
[4] You pursue me behind • and before,*
and lay your • hand upon me.
[5] Such knowledge is too wonder•ful for me;*
it is high, I can•not attain it.
[6] Whither shall I go • from your spirit?*
Or whither shall I flee • from your presence?
[7] If I ascend to heaven, • you are there.*
If I make my bed in Sheol, • you are there.
[8] If I take the wings • of the morning*
and dwell in the uttermost parts • of the sea,
[9] even there your • hand shall lead me,*
and your right • hand shall hold me.
[10] If I say, "Let only • darkness cover me,*
and the light about • me be night,"
[11] even the darkness is not dark to you, for the
night is bright • as the day;*
for darkness is as • light with you.
[12] For it was you who formed my • inward parts,*
you knit me together in my • mother's womb.
[13] I praise you, for you are fearful and •
wonderful;*
wonderful • are your works!
[14] You know me very well, and my frame was not
hid•den from you,*
when I was being made in secret, intricately
wrought in the depths • of the earth.
[15] Your eyes beheld my • unformed substance;*
in your book were written the days that were
formed for me, every day, before they came •
into being.
[16] How profound to me are your • thoughts,
O God!*
How vast is the • sum of them!
[17] I could no more count them than I • could the
sand;*
and suppose I could, you would • still be
with me.
[22] Search me, O God, and • know my heart;*
try me and • know my thoughts.
[23] See if there be any wicked • way in me,*
and lead me in the way • everlasting!

190 Psalm 143:1–10

יהוה שמע תפלתי

[1] Hear my prayer, O Lord; in your faithfulness
give ear to my • supplications;*
in your righteousness • answer me!
[2] Enter not into judgment • with your servant;*
for no one living is righ•teous before you.
[3] For enemies have pursued me; they have
crushed my life • to the ground;*
they have made me sit in darkness like • those
long dead.

4 Therefore my spirit • faints within me;*
my heart within me • is appalled.
5 I remember the days of old, I meditate on all
that • you have done;*
I muse on what your • hands have wrought.
6 I stretch out my • hands to you;*
my soul thirsts for you like • a parched land.
7 Make haste to answer me, O Lord! My • spirit
fails!*
Hide not your face from me, lest I be like
those who go down • to the pit.
8 In the morning let me hear of your steadfast
love, for in you I • put my trust.*
Teach me the way I should go, for to you I
lift • up my soul.
9 Deliver me, O Lord, from my • enemies!*
I have fled to • you for refuge.
10 Teach me to do your will, for you • are my
God;*
let your good Spirit lead me on a • level path.

191 Psalm 145:8–22

חנון ורחום יהוה

8 God is gracious and • merciful,*
slow to anger and abounding in • steadfast
love.
9 God is • good to all,*
and has compassion over all that • God has
made.
10 All your works shall give thanks to • you,
O Lord,*
and all your • saints shall bless you.
11 They shall speak of the glory • of your realm,*
and tell • of your power,
12 to make known to all people your • mighty
deeds,*
and the glorious splendor • of your realm.
13 Your realm is an ever•lasting realm,*
and your dominion endures throughout all •
generations.
14 God is faithful in • every word,*
and gracious in • every deed.
15 God upholds all • who are falling,*
and raises up all who • are bowed down.
16 The eyes of all • look to you,*
and you give them their food • in due season.
17 You o•pen your hand,*
and satisfy the desire of every • living thing.
18 God is just in • all God's ways,*
and kind in • every act.
19 God is near to all who call • upon God,*
to all who call upon • God in truth.
20 God fulfills the desire of • all who fear God,*
and hears their • cry, and saves them.
21 God preserves • all who love God,*
but will destroy • all the wicked.
22 My mouth will speak the • praise of God,*
and let all flesh bless God's holy name
for • ever and ever.

192 Psalm 146

הללו יה הללי נפשי את יהוה

1 Praise the Lord! Praise the Lord, • O my soul!*
I will praise the Lord as long as I live; I will
sing praises to my God while • I have being.
2 Put not your • trust in rulers,*
in mortals, in whom there • is no help.
3 Their breath departs, they return • to the earth;*
on that very day • their plans perish.
4 Happy are those whose help is in the • God of
Jacob,*
whose hope is in the • Lord, their God,
5 who made heaven and earth, the sea, and all
that • is in them;*
who keeps • faith for ever;
6 who executes justice for • the oppressed,*
and gives food • to the hungry.
7 The Lord sets the prisoners free, the Lord opens
the eyes • of the blind;*
the Lord lifts up those who are bowed down,
the Lord • loves the righteous.
8 The Lord watches over the sojourners, and
upholds the widow • and the orphan;*
but the Lord brings the way of the wick•ed
to ruin.
9 The Lord will • reign for ever,*
your God, O Zion, from generation to
generation. • Praise the Lord!

193 Psalm 147

הללו יה כי טוב זמרה אלהינו

1 Praise the Lord! For it is good to sing praises • to our God;*
a song of • praise is fitting.
2 The Lord builds • up Jerusalem,*
and gathers the out•casts of Israel.
3 The Lord heals the • brokenhearted,*
and binds • up their wounds.
4 The Lord determines the number • of the stars,*
and gives to all of • them their names.
5 Great is our Lord, and abun•dant in power,*
whose understanding is • beyond measure.
6 The Lord lifts up • the downtrodden,*
but casts the wicked • to the ground.
7 Sing to the Lord • with thanksgiving;*
make melody upon the lyre • to our God,
8 who covers the heav•ens with clouds,*
and prepares rain • for the earth;
9 who makes grass to grow up•on the hills,*
and green plants to • meet our needs.
10 The Lord gives to the • beasts their food,*
and to the young ra•vens that cry.
11 The Lord takes no delight in the might • of a horse,*
nor pleasure in the strength • of a runner,
12 but the Lord takes pleasure • in the faithful,*
in those whose hope in the Lord's • steadfast love.
13 Praise the Lord, • O Jerusalem!*
Praise your • God, O Zion!
14 The Lord strengthens the bars • of your gates,*
and blesses your children • in your midst;
15 makes peace • in your borders,*
and fills you with the • finest wheat.
16 The Lord sends forth commands • to the earth;*
the • word runs swiftly.
17 The Lord gives • snow like wool,*
and scatters hoar • frost like ashes,
18 The Lord casts forth • ice like morsels;
who can with•stand its cold?
19 The Lord sends forth the • word and melts them,*
makes the wind blow, and the • waters flow.
20 The Lord declares the • word to Jacob,*
the statutes and ordinan•ces to Israel.
21 The Lord has not dealt thus with any • other nation;*
they do not know God's ordinances. • Praise the Lord!

194 Psalm 148

הללו יה הללו את יהוה מן השמים

1 Praise the Lord! Praise the Lord • from the heavens,*
praise the Lord, • in the heights!
2 Praise the • Lord, all angels,*
praise the • Lord, all hosts!
3 Praise the Lord, • sun and moon,*
praise the Lord, all • shining stars!
4 Praise the Lord, • highest heavens,*
and all waters a•bove the heavens!
5 Let them praise the name • of the Lord,*
who commanded and they • were created,
6 who established them for ev•er and ever,*
and fixed their bounds which can•not be passed.
7 Praise the Lord • from the earth,*
sea monsters • and all deeps,
8 fire and hail, • snow and smoke,*
stormy wind fulfilling • God's command;
9 mountains • and all hills,*
fruit trees • and all cedars;*
10 beasts • and all cattle,*
creeping things and • flying birds;
11 monarchs of the earth • and all peoples,*
princes and all rulers • of the earth;
12 young men and maid•ens together,*
old • men and children;
13 let them praise the name • of the Lord,*
whose name alone is exalted, whose glory is above • earth and heaven.
14 God has raised up a horn for the people, and praise for all the • faithful ones,*
for the people of Israel who are near their God. • Praise the Lord!

195 Psalm 149

הללו יה שירו ליהוה שיר חדש

[1] Praise the Lord! Sing to the Lord • a new song,*
God's praise in the assembly • of the faithful!
[2] Let Israel be glad • in its Maker,*
let the children of Zion rejoice • in their Ruler.
[3] Let them praise God's • name with dancing,*
making melody with tim•brel and lyre.
[4] For God takes pleasure • in God's people,*
and adorns the hum•ble with victory.
[5] Let the faithful ex•ult in glory;*
let them sing for joy • on their couches.
[6] Let the high praises of God be • in their throats*
and two-edged swords • in their hands,
[7] to wreak vengeance • on the nations*
and chastisement • on the peoples,
[8] to bind their rulers with chains and their nobles with fet•ters of iron,*
to execute on them the • judgment written.
[9] This is glory for all God's • faithful ones.*
O • praise the Lord!

196 Psalm 150

הללו יה הללו אל בקדשו

[1] Praise the Lord! Praise God in the • sanctuary;*
praise God in the • mighty firmament!
[2] Praise God for • mighty deeds;*
praise God for ex•ceeding greatness!
[3] Praise God with • trumpet sound;*
praise God with • lute and harp!
[4] Praise God with tambou•rine and dance;*
praise God with • strings and pipe!
[5] Praise God with • sounding cymbals;*
praise God with loud • clashing cymbals!
[6] Let everything that breathes • praise the Lord!*
O • praise the Lord!

197 The Lord's my shepherd

Psalm 23

From the *Scottish Psalter*, 1650

Music: *Crimond*, 8686; melody by Jessie S. Irvine, 1872;
harmony by T. C. L. Pritchard, 1929

1 The Lord's my shep - herd, I'll not want,
2 My soul thou dost re - store a - gain;
3 Yea, though I walk in death's dark vale,
4 My ta - ble thou hast fur - nish - ed
God makes me down to lie in pas - tures green;
and me to walk doth make with - in the paths
yet will I fear none ill; for thou art with
in pres - ence of my foes; my head thou dost
God lead - eth me the qui - et wa - ters by.
of righ - teous - ness, e'en for thine own name's sake.
me, and thy rod and staff me com - fort still.
with oil a - noint, and my cup o - ver - flows.

5 Goodness and mercy all my life
shall surely follow me;
and in God's house for evermore
my dwelling place shall be.

198 My Shepherd, you supply my need

Psalm 23

Isaac Watts, 1719, and others

Music: *Resignation*, 8686D; melody from *Southern Harmony*, 1835; harmony by Virgil Thomson, 1959

1 My Shep - herd, you sup - ply my need; Je - ho - vah is your
2 When I walk through the shades of death, your pres - ence is my
3 The sure pro - vi - sions of my God at - tend me all my
name. In pas - tures fresh you make me feed, be - side the
stay; one word of your sup - port - ing breath drives all my
days; O may your house be my a - bode, and all my
liv - ing stream. You bring my wan-dering spir - it back, when
fears a - way. Your hand, in sight of all my foes, does
work be praise! There would I find a set - tled rest, while

I for - sake your ways; and lead me, for your
still my ta - ble spread; my cup with bless - ings
oth - ers go and come; no more a stran - ger,
mer - cy's sake, in paths of truth and grace.
o - ver - flows, your oil a - noints my head.
nor a guest, but like a child at home.

199 The Lord is a light to my pathway

Psalm 27:1–4, 6

Keith Landis, 1988

Music: *Harvest*, 9898; Geoffrey Laycock, 1971

1 The Lord is a light to my path - way, a strong - hold no powers can in - vade; the source of my life and my Sa - vior! Of whom then shall I be a - fraid?
2 A host may sur - round and be - siege me; a - lone my de - fens - es will fail, but al - lied with God my pro - tect - or, our forc - es will sure - ly pre - vail!
3 This bless - ing of bless - ings I ask for: to dwell in the house of the Lord! In God is all beau - ty em - bod - ied, be - side whom my soul is re - stored!
4 Make mel - o - dy, sing and be joy - ful, a - dorn - ing God's al - tar with praise! Your - self un - re - serv - ed - ly giv - ing, ex - alt God in num - ber - less ways!

200 Through all the changing scenes of life

Psalm 34:1–9

From *New Version of the Psalms*, 1696, by Nahum Tate and Nicholas Brady

Music: *Fiducia*, 8686D; J. Robertson, in *The Good Old Songs*, Thornton, Arkansas, 1913

1 Through all the chang-ing scenes of life, in trou-ble and in joy,
2 Of his de-liv-erance I will boast, till all that are dis-tressed
3 The hosts of God en-camp a-round the dwell-ings of the just;
4 O make but tri-al of his love; ex-per-ience will de-cide
the prais-es of my God shall still my heart and tongue em-ploy.
from my ex-am-ple com-fort take and soothe their griefs to rest.
de-liv-erance he af-fords to all who on his suc-cor trust.
how blest are they, and on-ly they, who in his truth con-fide.
Refrain
O mag-ni-fy the Lord with me, with me ex-alt his name;
when in dis-tress to him I called, he to my res-cue came.

5 Fear him, ye saints, and you will then
have nothing else to fear;
make you his service your delight,
he'll make your wants his care.

Refrain

201 La palabra del Señor es recta

Righteous and just is the word of our Lord
Psalm 33:4–11

Juan Luis Garcia (b. 1935); translated by George Lockwood, 1987

Music: *Nelson*, 8888D with refrain; Juan Luis Garcia

Refrain
La pa-la-bra del Se-ñor es rec-ta y sus o-bras son ma-ra-vi-llo-sas.
Righ-teous and just is the word of our Lord; faith-ful and mar-vel-ous are the Lord's works.
La jus-ti-cia y el de-re-cho tie-nen tro-nos a su dies-tra
Jus-tice and right are what God loves, they sit on thrones at God's right hand.
y de su mi-se-ri-cor-dia lle-na es-tá to-da la tie-rra.
And from the Lord's lov-ing kind-ness all the earth is filled with mer-cy,
Y de su mi-se-ri-cor-dia lle-na es-tá to-da la tie-rra.
and from the Lord's lov-ing kind-ness all the earth is filled with mer-cy!
1–2
3
tie-rra.
mer-cy!

1 Con su di- vi - na pa - la-bra fue - ron cre - a - dos los cie - los.
2 Té - ma- le to - da la tie-rra. Pós - tren- se to - dos los pue- blos;
1 By the di- vine word from heav-en thus were the heav-ens cre - at - ed;
2 Fear God, all earth and all peo-ple! Bow down to God, all you na- tions!
Del a - lien - to de su bo - ca se for - ma - ron los lu - ce - ros.
o - bras tan gran - des y ex- cel - sas, a su man - da - to sur- gie - ron.
then from God's mouth came great breath- ing, form-ing the stars of the morn-ing.
Mas- ter- piece works, grand and won- drous, at God's com-mand sprang to be - ing.
Él co- mo en o - dre re - co - ge del in- quie - to mar las a - guas.
Frus- tra el Se - ñor los de - sig - nios de los que en el mal se em - bria- gan.
God gath-ered up, as in wine-skins, all the wa - ters of the o- ceans;
But those ad - dict- ed to e - vil find their plans by God frus - tra - ted.
D.C.
Del a - bis- mo ha- ce un es- tan- que; de los ri - os las ca - ña - das.
Só - lo sus pla - nes y jui - cios se con - fir - man y pro - cla- man.
God put the deeps in their cham- bers and made val - leys from the riv - ers.
On - ly God's judg-ments and God's plans are con-firmed, pro-claimed for ev - er.

202 El Señor es mi fuerza

God is my rock
Psalm 46

Juan Antonio Espinosa, 1978; translation from *Celebremos, Segunda Parte*, 1983

Music: *Perú*, 11.6.11.6 with refrain; Juan Antonio Espinosa, 1978

Refrain
1–4
5
Fine
El Se - ñor es mi fuer-za, mi ro - ca y sal-va-ción. ción.
God is my rock and my sal- va-tion, the strength of my life. life.
1 Tú me guí - as por sen - das de jus - ti - cia, me en - se - ñas la ver - dad. Tú me das el va - lor pa - ra la lu-cha, sin mie-do a-van-za - ré.
2 I - lu - mi - nas las som - bras de mi vi - da, al mun - do das la luz; aun - que pa - se por va - lles de ti - nie-blas yo nun - ca te - me - ré.
1 You still call us to walk in paths of jus - tice, you help us see the way. As you give us the cour - age for life's tri - als, we shall not be a - fraid.
2 In the midst of our fears and darken - ing shad - ows you bring us hope and light. In your pres - ence we go through death's dark val-leys, we shall not be a - fraid.
D.C.

3 *Yo confío el destino de mi vida*
al Dios de mi salud;
a los pobres enseñas el camino,
su escudo eres Tú.

Refrain

4 *El Señor es la fuerza de su pueblo,*
su gran libertador;
tú le haces vivir en la confianza,
seguro en tu poder.

Refrain

3 We entrust you, the God of our salvation,
with all the future holds.
Guide, protect and defend the poor and helpless,
you are their rock and shield.

Refrain

4 Lord Almighty, the strength of all your people,
our strong Deliverer;
Liberator, secure us in your power,
we trust in you alone.

Refrain

203 Thy praise alone, O Lord, doth reign

Psalm 65:1,2,5,8

John Hopkins, 1561

Music: *York (The Stilt)*, 8686; melody from *Scottish Psalter*, 1615; harmony by John Milton, Sr., in *Ravenscroft's Psalter*, 1621 (the soprano and tenor are interchanged)

1 Thy praise a - lone, O Lord, doth reign in Zi - on, thine own hill: their vows to thee they do main - tain, and ev - er - more ful - fill.
2 For that thou dost their prayers still hear and dost there - to a - gree, thy peo - ple all, both far and near, with trust shall come to thee.
3 Of thy great jus - tice hear, O God, our health of thee doth rise; the hope of all the earth a - broad, and the sea - coasts like - wise.
4 The folk that dwell through - out the earth shall dread thy signs to see, which morn and even - ing with great mirth send prais - es up to thee.

204 How lovely is thy dwelling place

Psalm 84

Stanzas 1 and 2 from *Scottish Psalter*, 1650; stanzas 3 and 4 by Carl P. Daw, Jr., 1982

Music: *Brother James' Air*, 868686; melody by James Leith Macbeth Bain (c. 1840–1925); harmony adapted from an anthem by Gordon Jacob, 1934

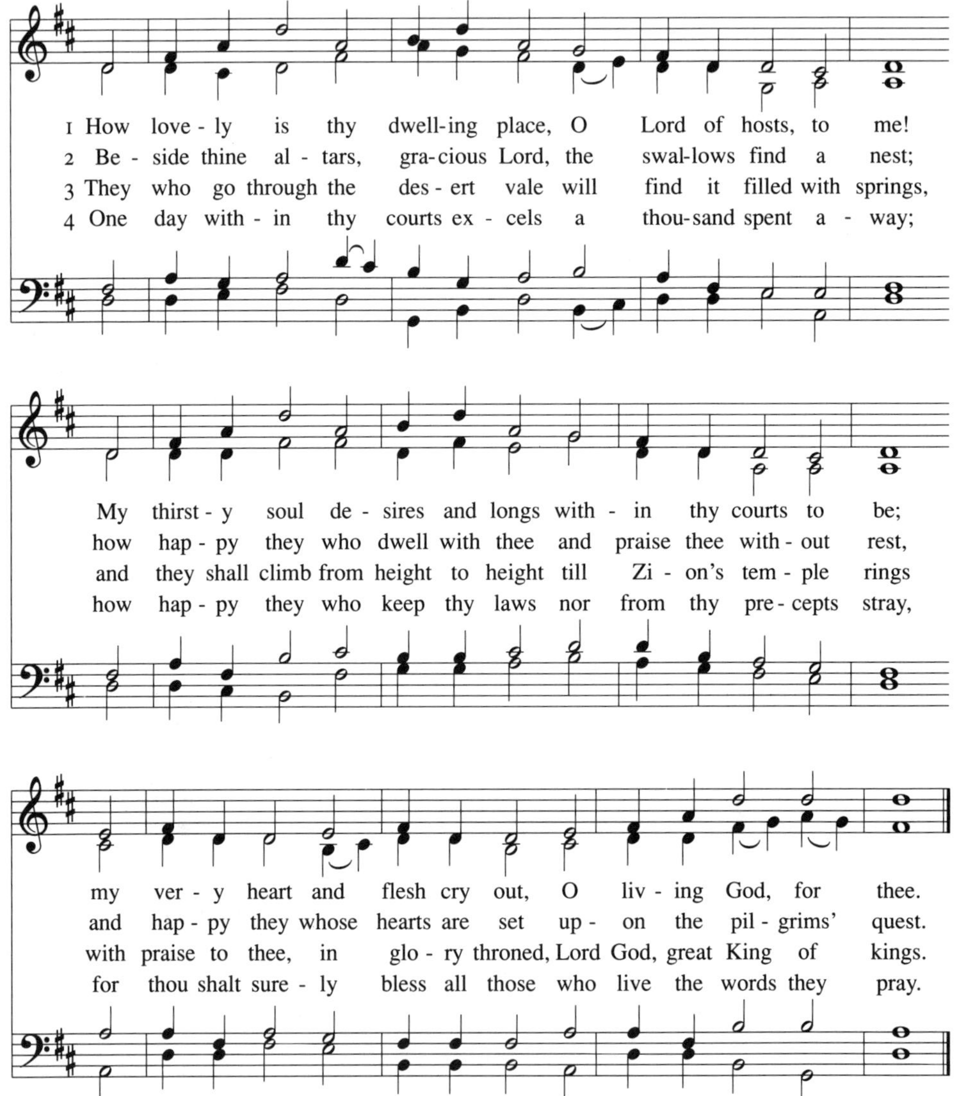
1 How love - ly is thy dwell-ing place, O Lord of hosts, to me!
2 Be - side thine al - tars, gra-cious Lord, the swal-lows find a nest;
3 They who go through the des - ert vale will find it filled with springs,
4 One day with - in thy courts ex - cels a thou-sand spent a - way;
My thirst - y soul de - sires and longs with - in thy courts to be;
how hap - py they who dwell with thee and praise thee with - out rest,
and they shall climb from height to height till Zi - on's tem - ple rings
how hap - py they who keep thy laws nor from thy pre - cepts stray,
my ver - y heart and flesh cry out, O liv - ing God, for thee.
and hap - py they whose hearts are set up - on the pil - grims' quest.
with praise to thee, in glo - ry throned, Lord God, great King of kings.
for thou shalt sure - ly bless all those who live the words they pray.

205 O God, our help in ages past

Psalm 90:1,2,4,5

Isaac Watts, 1719

Music: *St. Anne*, 8686; melody in *A Supplement to the New Version*, London, 1708; probably by William Croft

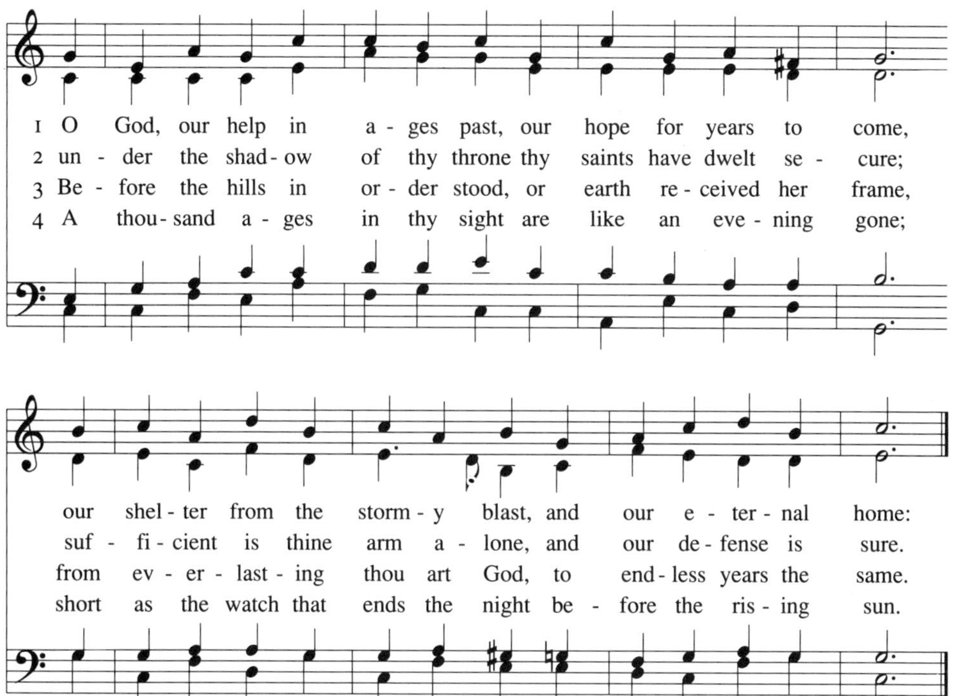
1 O God, our help in a - ges past, our hope for years to come,
2 un - der the shad - ow of thy throne thy saints have dwelt se - cure;
3 Be - fore the hills in or - der stood, or earth re - ceived her frame,
4 A thou - sand a - ges in thy sight are like an eve - ning gone;
our shel - ter from the storm - y blast, and our e - ter - nal home:
suf - fi - cient is thine arm a - lone, and our de - fense is sure.
from ev - er - last - ing thou art God, to end - less years the same.
short as the watch that ends the night be - fore the ris - ing sun.

5 Time, like an ever-rolling stream,
bears all our years away;
they fly, forgotten, as a dream
dies at the opening day.

6 O God, our help in ages past,
our hope for years to come,
be thou our guard while life shall last,
and our eternal home.

206 New songs of celebration

Psalm 98

Erik Routley, 1972

Music: *Rendez à Dieu*, 9898D; melody in *Strasbourg Psalter*, 1545; revised in *Genevan Psalter*, 1551; harmony by John Wilson, 1979

1 New songs of cel - e - bra - tion ren - der to God who has great won - ders done; awed by your love, your foes sur - ren - der and fall be - fore you, Might - y One. You have made known your great sal - va - tion which all your friends with joy con - fess; you have re -
2 Joy - ful - ly, heart - i - ly re - sound - ing, let ev - ery in - stru - ment and voice peal out the praise of grace a - bound - ing, call - ing the whole world to re - joice. Trum - pets and or - gans, set in mo - tion such sounds as make the heav - ens ring: all things that
3 Riv - ers and seas and tor - rents roar - ing, hon - or the Lord with wild ac - claim; moun - tains and stones, look up a - dor - ing and find a voice to praise God's name. Righ - teous, com - mand - ing, ev - er glo - rious, our praise of God will nev - er cease; just is our

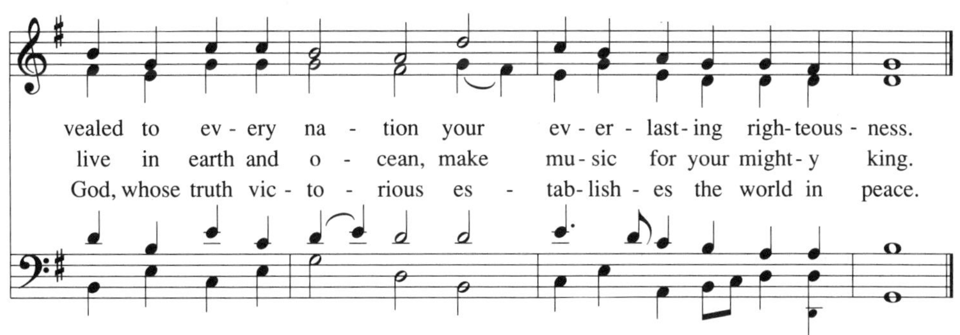
vealed to ev - ery na - tion your ev - er - last - ing righ - teous - ness.
live in earth and o - cean, make mu - sic for your might - y king.
God, whose truth vic - to - rious es - tab - lish - es the world in peace.

207 I to the hills lift up mine eyes

Psalm 121:1–8

From the *Bay Psalm Book*, Cambridge, Massachusetts, 1640

Music: *Dundee*, 8686; melody in *Scottish Psalter*, 1615; harmony adapted from *Ravenscroft's Psalter*, 1621

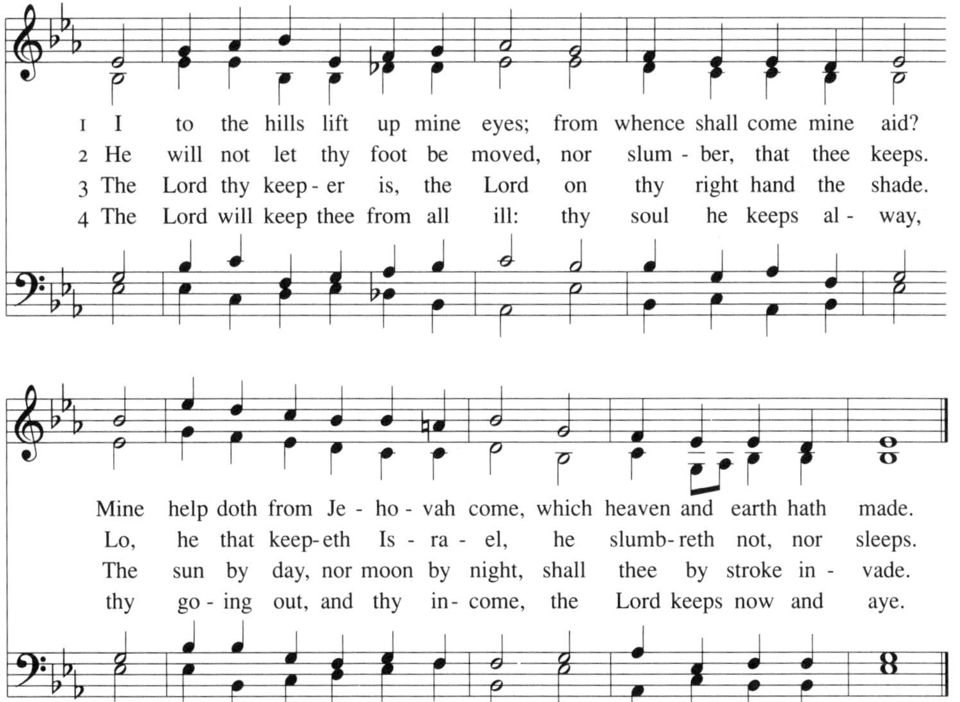
1 I to the hills lift up mine eyes; from whence shall come mine aid?
2 He will not let thy foot be moved, nor slum - ber, that thee keeps.
3 The Lord thy keep - er is, the Lord on thy right hand the shade.
4 The Lord will keep thee from all ill: thy soul he keeps al - way,
Mine help doth from Je - ho - vah come, which heaven and earth hath made.
Lo, he that keep - eth Is - ra - el, he slumb - reth not, nor sleeps.
The sun by day, nor moon by night, shall thee by stroke in - vade.
thy go - ing out, and thy in - come, the Lord keeps now and aye.

208 Lord, thou hast searched me

Psalm 139:1–11

From *The Psalter Hymnal*, 1927

Music: *Tender Thought*, 8888; melody from Ananias Davisson's *Kentucky Harmony*, 1816

1 Lord, thou hast searched me and dost know wher - e'er I rest, wher- e'er I go; thou know - est all that I have planned, and all my ways are in thy hand.
2 My words from thee I can - not hide; I feel thy power on ev - ery side; O won - drous knowl- edge, awe - ful might, un - fath - omed depth, un - mea - sured height!
3 Where can I go a - part from thee, or whith - er from thy pre - sence flee? In heaven? It is thy dwell- ing fair; in death's a - bode? Lo, thou art there.
4 If I the wings of morn - ing take, and far a - way my dwell - ing make, the hand that lead - eth me is thine, and my sup - port thy power di - vine.

5 If deepest darkness cover me,
the darkness hideth not from thee;
to thee both night and day are bright,
the darkness shineth as the light.

209 Hal'luhu, hal'luhu

Praise the Lord with trumpet and drum
Psalm 150

Jewish traditional folksong; translation adapted from *Union Songster*, New York, 1960

Music: *Hal'luhu*, 86868888; Jewish traditional melody; harmony by Abraham W. Binder, 1960

1 Ha - l' - lu - hu, ha - l' - lu - hu, b' - tzil - tz' - lei sha - ma,
1 Praise the Lord with trum-pet and drum, with strings and winds and voice;
ha - l' - lu - hu, ha - l' - lu - hu, b' - tzil - tz' - lei t'ru- ah,
praise the Lord with song and with prayer, with joy and dance and love.
kol han'-sha - mah t' - ha - leil Yah, ha - l' - lu- yah, ha - l' - lu- yah,
Let all who breathe sing praise to the Lord, Hal - le - lu- yah! Hal- le- lu- yah!
kol han'-sha - mah t' - ha - leil Yah, ha - l' - lu - yah, ha- l' - lu-yah.
Let all who breathe sing praise to the Lord, Hal - le - lu - yah! Hal-le- lu-yah!

Hymns Based on Psalms

Psalm	*Hymn*
5	Lord, as we wake, no. 353
19	The spacious firmament, no. 63
19	The stars declare his glory, no. 64
23	The King of love my shepherd is, no. 400
24	Lift up your heads, no. 30
46	A mighty fortress is our God, no. 460
72	Hail to the Lord's Anointed, no. 563
72	Jesus shall reign, no. 16
82/85/86	The Lord will come and not be slow, no. 557
97	Earth's scattered isles, no. 476
98	Joy to the world, no. 245
100	All people that on earth do dwell, nos. 1, 2
103	Praise, my soul, the King, no. 37
103	Praise to the Lord, the Almighty, no. 39
104	O worship the King, no. 6
117	From all that dwell below the skies, no. 327
130	Out of the depths I cry to thee, no. 376
139	There is no moment in my life, no. 488
146	I'll praise my Maker while I've breath, no. 3
148	Creating God, your fingers trace, no. 51
148	Let the whole creation cry, nos. 59, 60
148	Praise the Lord, no. 42
150	Praise to the Lord, the Almighty, no. 39
150	Sing praise to the Lord, no. 46

210 Bendito el Rey

Blest be the King

Federico J. Pagura, 1960; translated by Fred Pratt Green, 1974

Music: *Valet will ich dir geben*, 7676D; melody by Melchior Teschner, 1615; adapted and harmonized by J. S. Bach in his *St. John Passion*, 1724

1 *¡Ben - di - to el Rey que vie - ne en el nom - bre del Se - ñor!*
2 *¡Ben - di - to el Rey que vie - ne en el nom - bre del Se - ñor!*
1 Blest be the King whose com - ing is in the name of God!
2 Blest be the King whose com - ing is in the name of God!

¡Al - zad, al - zad las puer - tas del du - ro co - ra - zón!
¡A - ten - tos los o - í - dos, a - ten - tos a su voz!
For him let doors be o - pened, no hearts a - gainst him barred!
By those who tru - ly lis - ten his voice is tru - ly heard.
No vie - ne re - ves - ti - do de su ro - pa - je real:
¡Pues ay del que or - gu - llo - so no quie - re per - ci - bir
Not robed in roy - al splen - dor, in power and pomp, comes he,
Pi - ty the proud and haugh - ty, who have not learned to heed
su tú - ni - ca es de sier - vo, tal es su hu - mil - dad.
al Cri - sto pro - me - ti - do que vie - ne a re - di - mir!
but clad as are the poor - est, such his hu - mil - i - ty!
the Christ who is the Prom - ise, who has a - tone - ment made.

3 *¡Bendito el Rey que viene en el nombre del Señor!*
Que muestre a los humildes la faz del santo Dios;
a quien le han sido dadas la gloria y el poder,
que al fin de las edades los pueblos han de ver.

4 *¡Bendito el Rey que viene en el nombre del Señor!*
Que ofrece a los cansados descanso y salvación.
Es manso y es humilde y en su servicio está
el yugo que nos lleva a eterna libertad.

3 Blest be the King whose coming is in the name of God!
He only to the humble reveals the face of God.
All power is his, all glory! All things are in his hand,
all ages and all peoples, till time itself shall end!

4 Blest be the King whose coming is in the name of God!
He offers to the burdened the rest and grace they need.
Gentle is he and humble! And light his yoke shall be,
for he would have us bear it so he can make us free!

211 Wake, awake, for night is flying

Wachet auf, ruft uns die Stimme

Philipp Nicolai, 1599; translation adapted from Catherine Winkworth, 1858

Music: *Wachet auf*, 898898664448; Philipp Nicolai, 1599; arranged and harmonized by J. S. Bach in Cantata no. 140, 1731

1 Wake, a-wake, for night is fly - ing; the watch-men on the
2 Zi - on hears the watch-men sing - ing, and all her heart with
3 Now let all the heavens a - dore you, and saints and an - gels
heights are cry - ing: A - wake, Je - ru - sa - lem, at last!
joy is spring - ing; she wakes, she ris - es from her gloom;
sing be - fore you, with harp and cym-bal's clear - est tone;
Mid-night hears the wel-come voic - es and at the thrill-ing
for her Lord comes down all - glo - rious, the strong in grace, in
of one pearl each shin - ing por - tal, where we are with the
cry re - joic - es; come forth, O vir - gins, night is past;
truth vic - to - rious. Her star is risen; her light is come.
choir im - mor - tal of an - gels round your daz - zling throne;

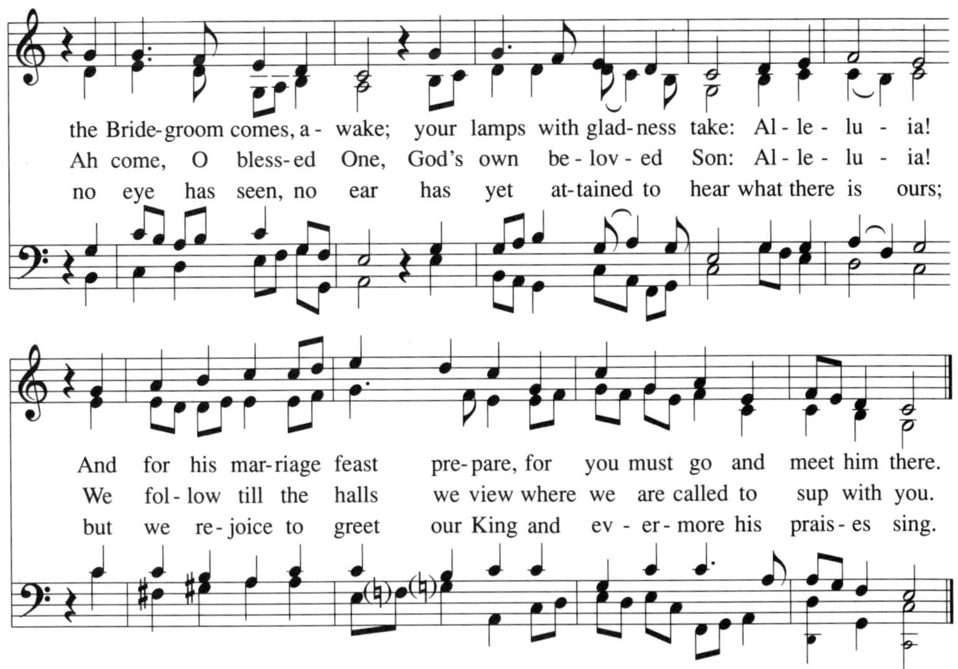
the Bride-groom comes, a - wake; your lamps with glad-ness take: Al - le - lu - ia!
Ah come, O bless-ed One, God's own be - lov - ed Son: Al - le - lu - ia!
no eye has seen, no ear has yet at-tained to hear what there is ours;
And for his mar-riage feast pre-pare, for you must go and meet him there.
We fol - low till the halls we view where we are called to sup with you.
but we re - joice to greet our King and ev - er - more his prais - es sing.

212

Come, thou long-expected Jesus

Charles Wesley, 1744

Music: *Stuttgart*, 8787; adapted by Henry J. Gauntlett, 1861, from a melody in C. F. Witt's *Harmonia Sacra*, Gotha, 1715

1 Come, thou long - ex - pect - ed Je - sus, born to set thy peo - ple free;
2 Is - rael's strength and con - so - la - tion, hope of all the earth thou art;
3 Born thy peo - ple to de - liv - er, born a child, and yet a king,
4 By thine own e - ter - nal Spir - it rule in all our hearts a - lone:
from our fears and sins re - lease us, let us find our rest in thee.
dear de - sire of ev - ery na - tion, joy of ev - ery long - ing heart.
born to reign in us for ev - er, now thy gra - cious king-dom bring.
by thine all - suf - fi - cient mer - it raise us to thy glo - rious throne.

213 "Comfort, comfort now my people"

Tröstet, tröstet meine Lieben

Johann Olearius, 1671; translated by Catherine Winkworth, 1863, and others

Music: *Geneva 42 (Freu dich sehr)*, 87877788; melody in *Genevan Psalter*, 1551; harmony adapted from Claude Goudimel, 1565

1 "Com- fort, com - fort now my peo- ple, speak of peace," thus says our God.
2 Hark, the voice of one who's cry - ing in the des - ert far and near,
3 O make straight what long was crook-ed, make the rough - er plac - es plain;
"Com- fort those who sit in dark- ness, mourn- ing 'neath their sor- rows' load.
bid - ding all to full re- pent- ance since the King- dom now is here.
let your hearts be true and hum - ble, as be - fits God's ho - ly reign.
Speak un - to Je - ru - sa - lem of the peace that waits for them;
O that warn - ing cry o - bey! Now pre - pare for God a way;
For the glo - ry of the Lord now o'er earth is shed a- broad,
tell them that their sins I cov - er, and their war - fare now is o - ver."
let the val - leys rise to meet him and the hills bow down to greet him.
and all flesh shall see the to - ken that God's word is nev - er bro - ken.

214 Prepare the way, O Zion

Bereden väg för Herran

Frans Mikael Franzén, 1812, 1817; translated by various authors and adapted by Charles P. Price, 1982

Music: *Bereden väg för Herran*, 767677 with refrain; melody in *Then Swenska Psalmboken*, 1697; harmony adapted from *Koralbok för Svenska Kyrkan*, 1939

1 Pre - pare the way, O Zi - on, your Christ is draw - ing near!
2 He brings God's rule, O Zi - on; he comes from heaven a - bove.
3 Fling wide your gates, O Zi - on; your Sa - vior's rule em- brace.
Let ev - ery hill and val - ley a lev - el way ap - pear.
His rule is peace and free - dom, and jus - tice, truth, and love.
His tid - ings of sal - va - tion pro - claim in ev - ery place.
Greet One who comes in glo - ry, fore - told in sa - cred stor - ry.
Lift high your praise re - sound - ing, with grace and joy a - bound - ing.
All lands will bow be - fore him, their voic - es will a - dore him.
Refrain
Oh, blest is Christ who came in God's most ho - ly name.

215 There's a voice in the wilderness crying

James Lewis Milligan, 1925

Music: *Ascension*, irregular meter; Henry Hugh Bancroft, 1938

1 There's a voice in the wil-der-ness cry-ing, a call from the way un-trod: Pre-pare in the des-ert a high-way, a high-way for our God! The val-leys shall be ex-alt-ed, the loft-y hills brought low; make
2 O Zi-on, that bring-est good tid-ings, get thee up to the heights and sing! Pro-claim to a des-o-late peo-ple the com-ing of their King. Like the flowers of the field they per-ish, like grass our works de-cay, the
3 but the word of our God en-dur-eth, the arm of the Lord is strong; God stands in the midst of na-tions, and soon will right the wrong. He shall feed the flock like a shep-herd, the lambs so gen-tly hold, to

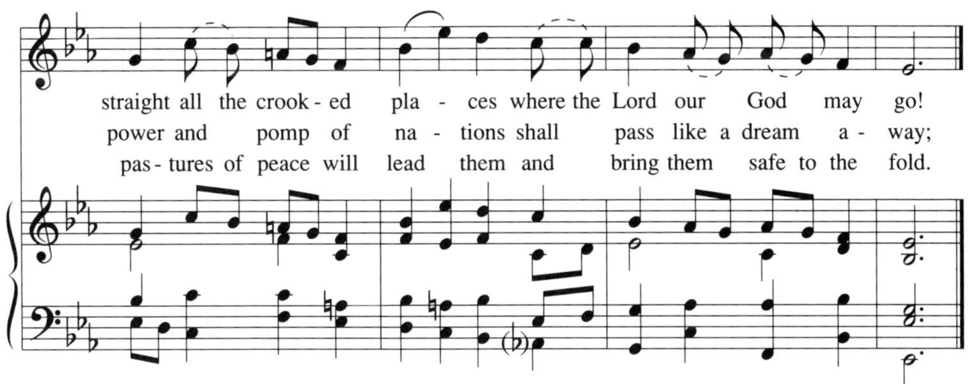
straight all the crook - ed pla - ces where the Lord our God may go!
power and pomp of na - tions shall pass like a dream a - way;
pas - tures of peace will lead them and bring them safe to the fold.
(♭)

216 Creator of the stars of night

Conditor alme siderum

Ninth century; translation adapted from John Mason Neale (1818–1866) and *The Hymnal 1940*

Music: *Conditor alme siderum*, 8888; plainsong; accompaniment by Bruce Neswick, 1985

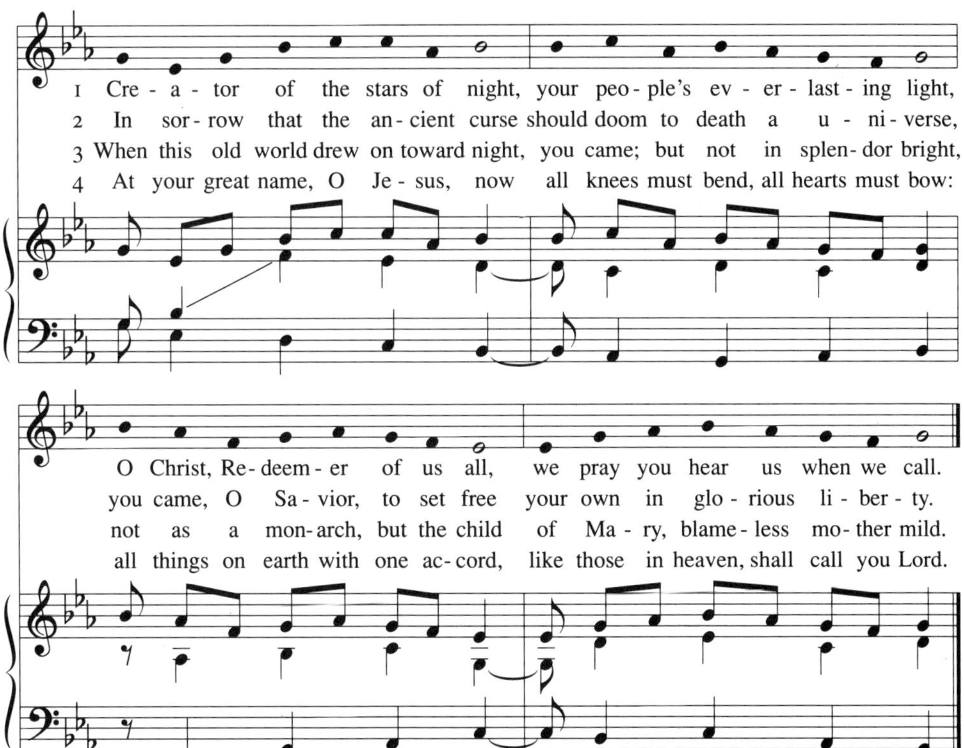
1 Cre - a - tor of the stars of night, your peo - ple's ev - er - last - ing light,
2 In sor - row that the an - cient curse should doom to death a u - ni - verse,
3 When this old world drew on toward night, you came; but not in splen - dor bright,
4 At your great name, O Je - sus, now all knees must bend, all hearts must bow:
O Christ, Re - deem - er of us all, we pray you hear us when we call.
you came, O Sa - vior, to set free your own in glo - rious li - ber - ty.
not as a mon - arch, but the child of Ma - ry, blame - less mo - ther mild.
all things on earth with one ac - cord, like those in heaven, shall call you Lord.

This rhythm may be used throughout: ♪♩ ♪♩

5 Come in your holy might, we pray,
redeem us for eternal day;
defend us while we dwell below
from all assaults of our dread foe.

6 To God Creator, God the Son,
and God the Spirit, Three in One,
praise, honor, might, and glory be
from age to age eternally.

217 O Lord, how shall I meet you

Wie soll ich dich empfangen

Paul Gerhardt, 1653; translation adapted from Catherine Winkworth, 1863; from *Lutheran Book of Worship*, 1978

Music: *Wie soll ich dich empfangen*, 7676D; melody by Johann Crüger, 1653

1 O Lord, how shall I meet you, how wel - come you a - right?
2 Your Zi - on strews be - fore you green boughs and fair - est palms;
3 Love caused your in - car - na - tion; love brought you down to me.
4 Re - joice, then, you sad - heart - ed, who sit in deep - est gloom,
Your peo - ple long to greet you, our hope, our hearts' de - light!
and I, too, will a - dore you with joy - ous songs and psalms.
Your thirst for my sal - va - tion pro - cured my lib - er - ty.
who mourn your joys de - part - ed and trem - ble at your doom.
O kin - dle, Lord most ho - ly, your lamp with - in each breast
My heart shall bloom for ev - er for you with prais - es new
O love be - yond all tell - ing, that led you to em - brace
De - spair not; Christ is near you, there, stand - ing at the door,
to do in spir - it low - ly all that may please you best.
and from your name shall nev - er with - hold the hon - or due.
in love, all love ex - cell - ing, our lost and fall - en race.
who best can help and cheer you and bids you weep no more.

5 He comes to judge the nations,
a terror to his foes,
a light of consolations
and blessed hope to those
who love the Lord's appearing.
O glorious Sun, now come,
send forth your beams so cheering
and guide us safely home.

218 O come, O come, Emmanuel

Veni, veni, Emmanuel

From *Psalteriolum Cantionum Catholicarum*, Cologne, 1710; based on the ancient "O Antiphons" of Advent Vespers; translation adapted from *The Hymnal 1982*

Music: *Veni Emmanuel*, 8888 with refrain; melody from a 15th-century French *Processional*; harmony by Richard Proulx, 1975

1 O come, O come, Em-man - u - el, and ran-som cap-tive Is - ra - el
2 O come, O Wis-dom from on high, who or-ders all things might - i - ly;
3 O come, O come, great Lord of might, who to your tribes on Si - nai's height
4 O come, O Rod of Jes - se's stem, from ev-ery foe de - liv - er them
that mourns in lone-ly ex - ile here un-til the Son of God ap-pear.
to us the path of knowl - edge show, and teach us in her ways to go.
in an-cient times once gave the law in cloud, and ma-jes-ty, and awe.
that trust your might-y power to save, and give them vic-tory o'er the grave.
Refrain
Re-joice! Re-joice! Em-man - u-el shall come to thee, O Is - ra-el.

5 O come, O Key of David, come,
and open wide our heavenly home;
make safe the way that leads on high,
and close the path to misery.

Refrain

6 O come, O Dayspring, from on high,
and cheer us by your drawing nigh;
disperse the gloomy clouds of night,
and death's dark shadows put to flight.

Refrain

7 O come, Desire of nations, bind
all peoples in one heart and mind;
O bid our sad divisions cease,
and be for us the Prince of Peace.

Refrain

219

Selected stanzas of no. 218, for singing in two parts; melody and harmonizing voice from a 15th-century French *Processional*; edited by Mary Berry, 1983:

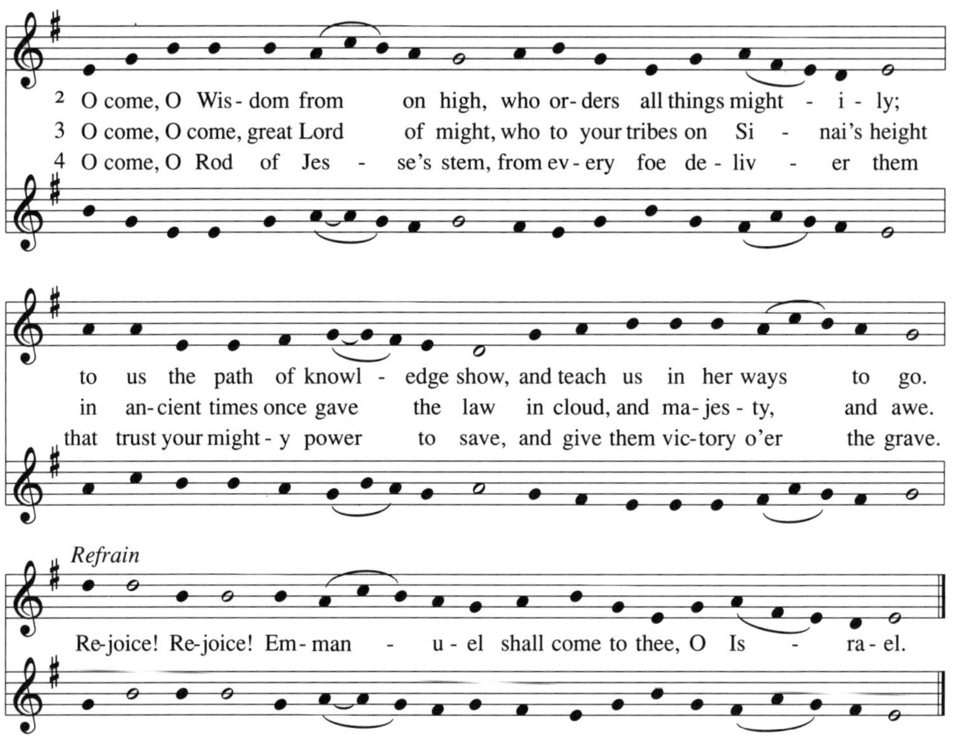
2 O come, O Wis-dom from on high, who or-ders all things might - i - ly;
3 O come, O come, great Lord of might, who to your tribes on Si - nai's height
4 O come, O Rod of Jes - se's stem, from ev-ery foe de-liv - er them
to us the path of knowl - edge show, and teach us in her ways to go.
in an-cient times once gave the law in cloud, and ma-jes-ty, and awe.
that trust your might-y power to save, and give them vic-tory o'er the grave.
Refrain
Re-joice! Re-joice! Em-man - u-el shall come to thee, O Is - ra-el.

220 On Jordan's bank the Baptist's cry

Jordanis oras praevia

Charles Coffin, 1736; translated by John Chandler, 1837

Music: *Winchester New*, 8888; melody adapted by W. H. Havergal in *Old Church Psalmody*, 1847; from a chorale in Wittwe's *Musikalisches Hand-buch*, 1690

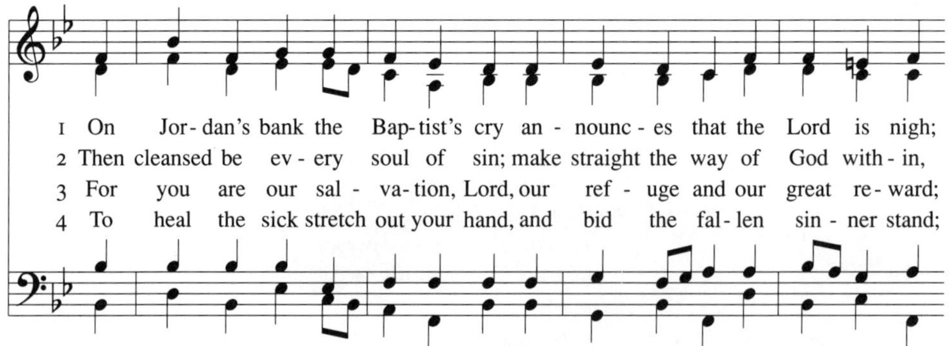
1 On Jor-dan's bank the Bap-tist's cry an - nounc-es that the Lord is nigh;
2 Then cleansed be ev - ery soul of sin; make straight the way of God with-in,
3 For you are our sal - va-tion, Lord, our ref - uge and our great re-ward;
4 To heal the sick stretch out your hand, and bid the fal-len sin - ner stand;

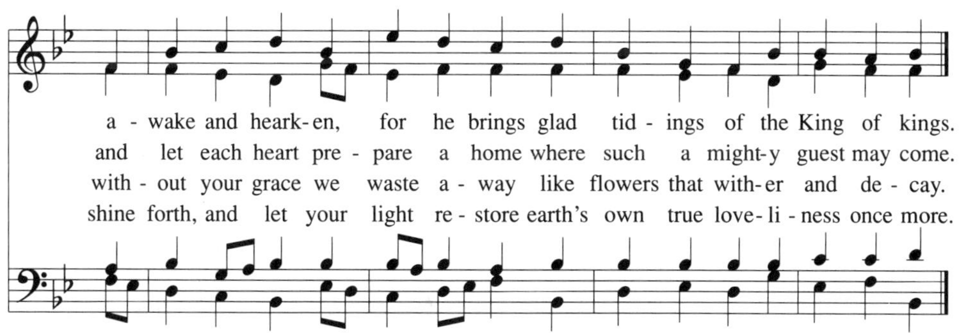
a - wake and heark-en, for he brings glad tid - ings of the King of kings.
and let each heart pre - pare a home where such a might-y guest may come.
with - out your grace we waste a - way like flowers that with-er and de - cay.
shine forth, and let your light re - store earth's own true love-li - ness once more.

5 We praise you, Lord, eternally,
whose advent sets your people free;
whom with the Father we adore
and Spirit blest for evermore.

221 Savior of the nations, come

Veni Redemptor gentium

Nun komm, der Heiden Heiland

Latin by Ambrose of Milan (d. 397); German paraphrase by Martin Luther, 1523;
translation from various sources

Music: *Nun komm, der Heiden Heiland*, 7777; melody based on *Veni Redemptor gentium*;
from Erfurt *Enchiridia*, 1524; harmony by Melchior Vulpius (c. 1560–1616)

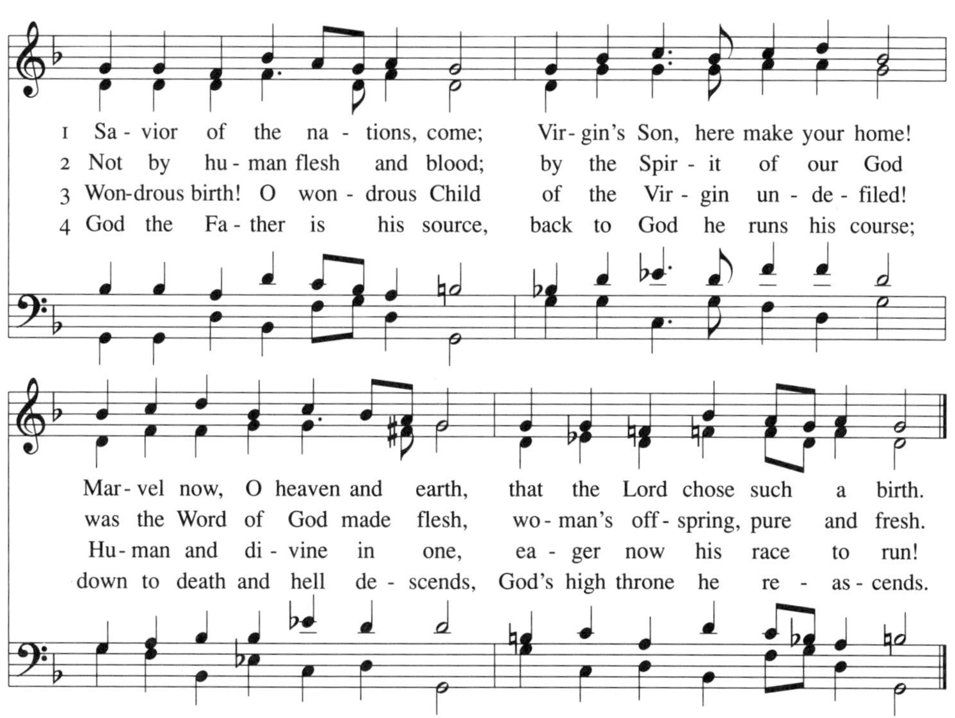
1 Sa - vior of the na - tions, come; Vir- gin's Son, here make your home!
2 Not by hu - man flesh and blood; by the Spir - it of our God
3 Won-drous birth! O won - drous Child of the Vir - gin un - de - filed!
4 God the Fa - ther is his source, back to God he runs his course;
Mar- vel now, O heaven and earth, that the Lord chose such a birth.
was the Word of God made flesh, wo - man's off - spring, pure and fresh.
Hu- man and di - vine in one, ea - ger now his race to run!
down to death and hell de - scends, God's high throne he re - as - cends.

5 God the Father's precious Son
girds himself in flesh to run
for the trophies of our souls,
longer than this round earth rolls.

222 People, look East

Eleanor Farjeon, 1928

Music: *Besançon*, 879887; French traditional melody; harmony by Barry Rose, 1986

1 Peo - ple, look East. The time is near of the crown-ing of the year.
2 Fur - rows, be glad. Though earth is bare, one more seed is plant - ed there.
3 Birds, though you long have ceased to build, guard the nest that must be filled.
4 Stars, keep the watch. When night is dim, one more light the bowl shall brim,
Make your house fair as you are a - ble, trim the hearth and set the ta - ble.
Give up your strength the seed to nour-ish, that in course the flower may flour-ish.
E - ven the hour when wings are froz - en now for fledg - ing - time is chos - en.
shin - ing be - yond the frost - y weath-er, bright as sun and moon to - geth - er.
Peo-ple, look East, and sing to - day: Love the Guest is on the way.
Peo-ple, look East, and sing to - day: Love the Rose is on the way.
Peo-ple, look East, and sing to - day: Love the Bird is on the way.
Peo-ple, look East, and sing to - day: Love the Star is on the way.

5 Angels, announce with shouts of mirth
Christ who brings new life to earth.
Set every peak and valley humming
with the word, the Lord is coming.
People, look East, and sing today:
Love the Lord is on the way.

Promise and Fulfillment

See also:

Hail to the Lord's Anointed, no. 563
Lift up your heads, no. 30
Lo, he comes with clouds descending, no. 558
Tell out, my soul, no. 40

223 Go tell it on the mountain

African American 19th-century spiritual; the present stanzas are by John Wesley Work, Jr., 1940

Music: *Go tell it*, 7676 with refrain; African American spiritual, 19th century; arranged by Hugh Porter, 1958

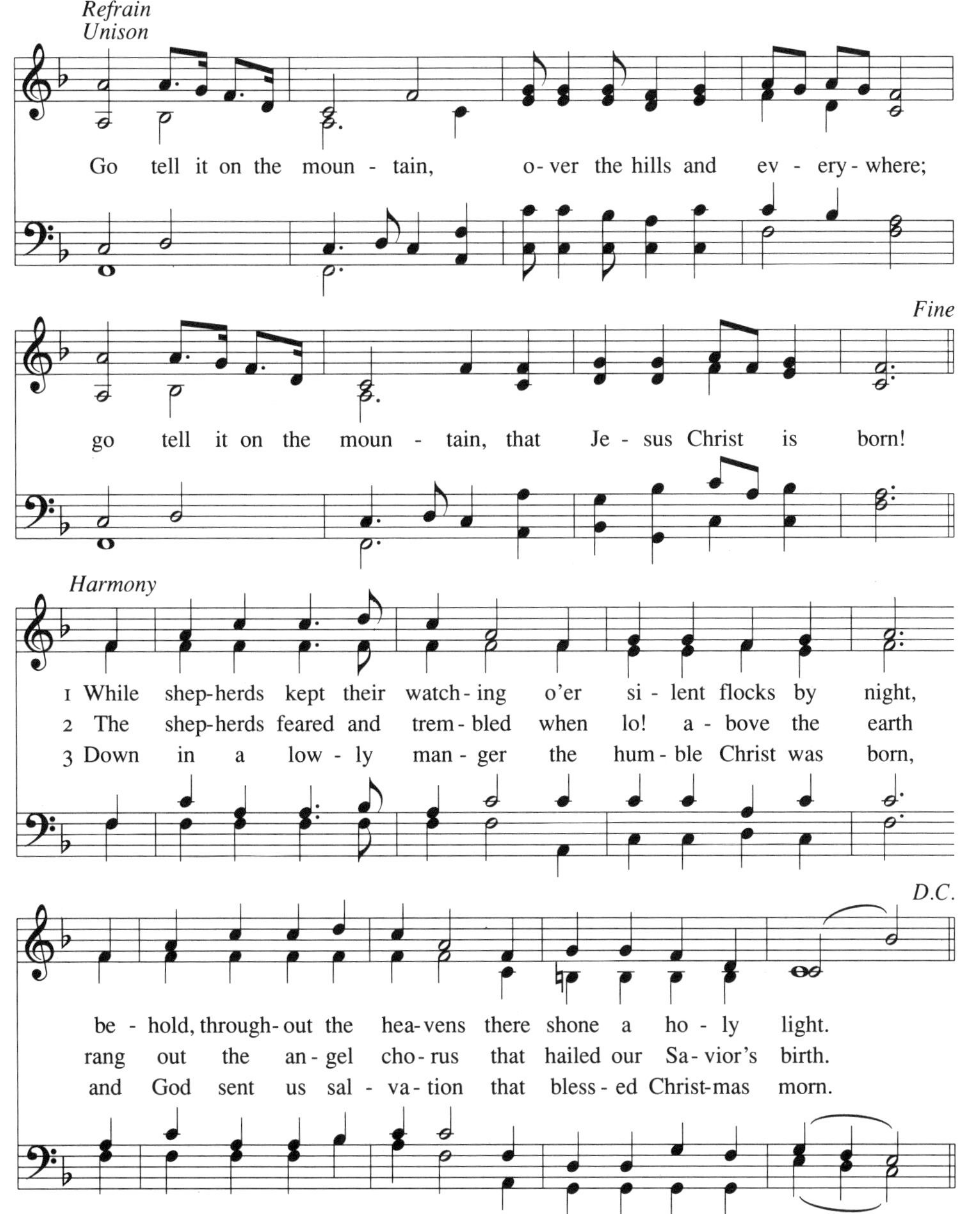
Refrain
Unison
Go tell it on the moun - tain, o- ver the hills and ev - ery - where;
go tell it on the moun - tain, that Je - sus Christ is born!
Fine
Harmony
1 While shep-herds kept their watch - ing o'er si - lent flocks by night,
2 The shep-herds feared and trem - bled when lo! a - bove the earth
3 Down in a low - ly man - ger the hum - ble Christ was born,
be - hold, through- out the hea- vens there shone a ho - ly light.
rang out the an - gel cho - rus that hailed our Sa - vior's birth.
and God sent us sal - va - tion that bless - ed Christ-mas morn.
D.C.

224 A stable lamp is lighted

Richard Wilbur, 1959

Music: *Andújar*, 76766676; David Hurd, 1983

1 A stable lamp is lighted whose glow shall wake the sky; the stars shall bend their voices, and every stone shall cry. And every stone shall
2 (This) child through David's city shall ride in triumph by; the palm shall strew its branches, and every stone shall cry. And every stone shall
3 (Yet) he shall be forsaken, and yielded up to die; the sky shall groan and darken, and every stone shall cry. And every stone shall
4 (But) now, as at the ending, the low is lifted high; the stars shall bend their voices, and every stone shall cry. And every stone shall

cry, and straw like gold shall shine; a barn shall har - bor
cry, though hea - vy, dull, and dumb, and lie with - in the
cry, for hearts made hard by sin: God's blood up - on the
cry, in prais - es of the Child by whose de - scent a -
hea - ven, a stall be - come a shrine.
road - way to pave his king - dom come.
spear - head, God's love re - fused a - gain.
mong us the worlds are re - con - ciled.
1–3
4
2 This
3 Yet
4 But

225 O come, all ye faithful

Adeste, fideles

Latin, 18th century; translation by Frederick Oakeley, 1841, and others

Music: *Adeste, fideles*, 6.6.10.5.6 with refrain; English 18th-century melody, probably by J. F. Wade (1711–1786); harmony from *The English Hymnal*, 1906

1 A - des - te, fi - de - les, lae - ti tri - um - phan - tes; ve - ni - te, ve - ni - te in Beth - le - hem.
Na - tum vi - de - te Re - gem an - ge - lo - rum.
1 O come, all ye faith - ful, joy - ful and tri - umph - ant, O come ye, O come ye to Beth - le - hem;
come, and be - hold him, born the King of an - gels;
2 God from God, Light from Light e - ter - nal, lo! he re - jects not the Vir - gin's womb;
our ver - y God, be - got - ten not cre - at - ed;
3 Sing, choirs of an - gels, sing in ex - ul - ta - tion, sing, all ye ci - ti - zens of heaven a - bove;
glo - ry to God, glo - ry in the high - est;
Refrain
Ve - ni - te a - do - re - mus, ve - ni - te a - do - re - mus, ve -
O come, let us a - dore him, O come, let us a - dore him, O

ni - te a - do - re - mus, Do - mi - num.
come, let us a - dore him, Christ the Lord.

4 See how the shepherds,
summoned to his cradle,
leaving their flocks, draw nigh to gaze;
we too will thither
bend our joyful footsteps;

Refrain

5 Child, for us sinners
poor and in the manger,
we would embrace thee, with love and awe;
who would not love thee,
loving us so dearly?

Refrain

226 From heaven above to earth I come

Vom Himmel hoch da komm' ich her

Martin Luther, 1535, for his family's Christmas Eve celebration;
translation adapted from Catherine Winkworth, 1855

Music: *Vom Himmel hoch*, 8888; attributed to Luther; melody in Valentin Schumann's
Geistliche Lieder, 1539; harmony by Hans Leo Hassler, 1608

1 From heaven a - bove to earth I come to bring good news to ev - ery - one!
2 to you this night is born a child of Ma - ry, cho - sen vir - gin mild;
3 This is the Christ, God's Son most high, who hears your sad and bit - ter cry;
4 These are the signs which you will see to let you know that it is he:
Glad tid - ings of great joy I bring to all the world, and glad - ly sing:
this new-born child of low - ly birth shall be the joy of all the earth.
he will him - self your Sa - vior be and from all sin will set you free.
in man - ger bed, in swad - dling clothes the child who all the earth up-holds.

5 Our hearts for very joy now leap,
our voices cannot silence keep;
we too must join the angel throng
to sing with joy his cradle song:

6 "Glory to God in highest heaven,
who unto us the Son has given."
With angels sing in pious mirth:
a glad new year to all the earth!

227 Silent night, holy night

Stille Nacht, heilige Nacht

Joseph Mohr, 1818; translation attributed to John Freeman Young, c. 1863

Music: *Stille Nacht*, 668866; Franz Grüber, 1818; harmony by Carl Reinecke (1824–1910)

1 *Stil - le Nacht, hei - li - ge Nacht! Al - les schläft,*
ein - sam wacht nur das trau - te hoch - hei - li - ge Paar,
hold - er Kna - be mit lock - i - gem Haar, schlaf in himm - li - scher
Ruh, schlaf in himm - li - scher
1 Si - lent night, ho - ly night, all is calm,
all is bright round yon vir - gin mo - ther and child.
Ho - ly in - fant so ten - der and mild,
sleep in heav - en - ly peace, sleep in heav - en - ly peace.
2 Si - lent night, ho - ly night, shep - herds quake
at the sight, glo - ries stream from heav - en a - far,
heaven - ly hosts sing al - le - lu - ia;
Christ the Sa - vior is born, Christ the Sa - vior is born!
3 Si - lent night, ho - ly night, Son of God,
love's pure light ra - diant beams from thy ho - ly face,
with the dawn of re - deem - ing grace,
Je - sus, Lord, at thy birth, Je - sus, Lord, at thy birth.

4 Silent night, holy night,
wondrous star, lend thy light;
with the angels let us sing
alleluia to our King;
Christ the Savior is born,
Christ the Savior is born!

228 Good Christian friends, rejoice

John Mason Neale, 1853

Music: *In dulci jubilo*, 66777855; German medieval carol; harmony by Winfred Douglas, 1918

1 Good Chris-tian friends, re - joice with heart, and soul, and voice;
2 Good Chris-tian friends, re - joice with heart, and soul, and voice;
3 Good Chris-tian friends, re - joice with heart, and soul, and voice;
now give heed to what we say: Je - sus Christ is born to - day;
now you hear of end - less bliss: Je - sus Christ was born for this!
now you need not fear the grave: Je - sus Christ was born to save!
ox and ass be - fore him bow, and he is in the man - ger now.
He has o - pened heav - en's door, and all are blest for ev - er - more.
Calls you one and calls you all to gain his ev - er - last - ing hall.
Christ is born to - day! Christ is born to - day!
Christ was born for this! Christ was born for this!
Christ was born to save! Christ was born to save!

229 It came upon the midnight clear

Edmund H. Sears, 1849

Music: *Carol*, 8686D; Richard S. Willis, 1850, 1860

1 It came up - on the mid-night clear, that glo - rious song of old,
2 Still through the clov - en skies they come with peace - ful wings un - furled,
3 Yet with the woes of sin and strife the world has suf - fered long;
4 For lo! the days are has-tening on, by pro - phets seen of old,
from an - gels bend - ing near the earth to touch their harps of gold:
and still their heaven - ly mu - sic floats o'er all the wear - y world;
be - neath the heaven - ly hymn have rolled two thou - sand years of wrong;
when with the ev - er - cir - cling years shall come the time fore - told,
"Peace on the earth, good will to all, from heaven's all - gra - cious King."
a - bove its sad and lone - ly plains they bend on hov - ering wing,
and war - ring hu - man-kind hears not the tid - ings which they bring;
when peace shall o - ver all the earth its an - cient splen - dors fling,
The world in sol - emn still - ness lay to hear the an - gels sing.
and ev - er o'er its Ba - bel-sounds the bless - ed an - gels sing.
O hush the noise and cease your strife and hear the an - gels sing!
and all the world give back the song which now the an - gels sing.

230 It came upon the midnight clear

Edmund H. Sears, 1849

Music: *Noel*, 8686D; English traditional melody; adapted and harmonized by Arthur S. Sullivan, 1874

1 It came up - on the mid- night clear, that glo- rious song of old,
2 Still through the clov - en skies they come with peace- ful wings un - furled,
3 Yet with the woes of sin and strife the world has suf - fered long;
4 For lo! the days are has-tening on, by pro- phets seen of old,
from an - gels bend- ing near the earth to touch their harps of gold:
and still their heaven-ly mu - sic floats o'er all the wear - y world;
be - neath the heaven-ly hymn have rolled two thou - sand years of wrong;
when with the ev - er - cir - cling years shall come the time fore - told,
"Peace on the earth, good will to all, from heaven's all - gra - cious King."
a - bove its sad and lone - ly plains they bend on hov - ering wing,
and war - ring hu - man - kind hears not the tid - ings which they bring;
when peace shall o - ver all the earth its an - cient splen - dors fling,
The world in sol - emn still - ness lay to hear the an - gels sing.
and ev - er o'er its Ba - bel- sounds the bless - ed an - gels sing.
O hush the noise and cease your strife and hear the an - gels sing!
and all the world give back the song which now the an - gels sing.

231 Hark! the herald angels sing

Charles Wesley, 1739, and others

Music: *Mendelssohn*, 7777D with refrain; melody from Felix Mendelssohn's *Festgesang*, 1840; arranged by W. H. Cummings, 1856

1 Hark! the her - ald an - gels sing, "Glo - ry to the new - born King;
2 Christ by high - est heaven a - dored, Christ, the ev - er - last - ing Lord,
3 Hail the heaven - born Prince of Peace! Hail the Sun of Righ - teous - ness!
peace on earth, and mer - cy mild, God and sin - ners re - con - ciled!"
late in time be - hold him come, off - spring of a vir - gin's womb.
Light and life to all he brings, risen with heal - ing in his wings.
Joy - ful, all ye na - tions, rise, join the tri - umph of the skies;
Veiled in flesh the God - head see, hail the in - car - nate De - i - ty!
Mild he lays his glo - ry by, born that all no more may die,
with the an - gel - ic host pro - claim, "Christ is born in Beth - le - hem!"
Pleased with us in flesh to dwell, Je - sus, our Em - man - u - el.
born to raise them from the earth, born to give them se - cond birth.

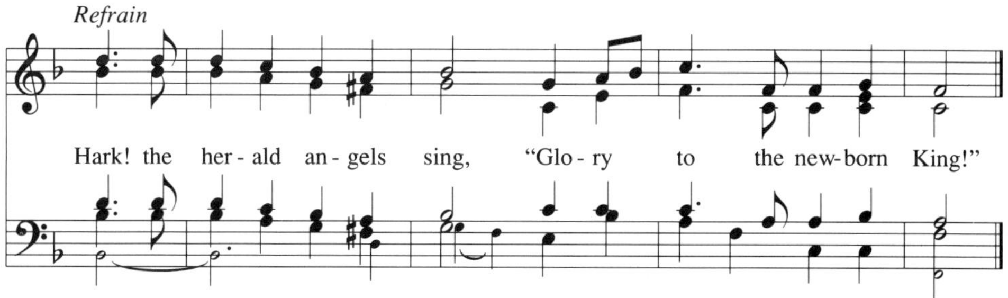
Refrain
Hark! the her - ald an - gels sing, "Glo - ry to the new-born King!"

232 What child is this

William Chatterton Dix, c. 1865

Music: *Greensleeves*, 8787 with refrain; English 16th-century melody; harmony probably by John Stainer, 1871

1 What child is this, who, laid to rest, on Ma - ry's lap is sleep - ing?
2 Why lies he in such mean es - tate where ox and ass are feed - ing?
3 So bring him in - cense, gold, and myrrh, come, pea - sant, king, to own him;

Whom an - gels greet with an - thems sweet while shep - herds watch are keep - ing?
Good Chris - tian, fear: for sin - ners here the si - lent Word is plead - ing.
the King of kings sal - va - tion brings, let lov - ing hearts en - throne him.

Refrain

This, this is Christ the King, whom shep - herds guard and an - gels sing;
haste, haste to bring him laud, the babe, the son of Ma - ry.

233 En el frio invernal

Cold December flies away

Spanish: Skinner Chavez-Melo, 1987;
English: Catalonian carol translated by Howard Hawhee, 1975

Music: *Lo Desembre congelat*, 76767755666; Catalonian carol;
harmony by Skinner Chavez-Melo, 1987

1 En el fri - o in - ver - nal del mes de di - ciem - bre,
2 Las ti - nie - blas del a - yer hu - yen pron - ta - men - te,
1 Cold De - cem - ber flies a - way at the rose - red splen - dor.
2 In the hope - less time of sin shad - ows deep had fall - en.
un ca - pu - llo del ro - sal bro - ta en un pe - se - bre;
la ma - ña - na de - ja ver sol res - plan - de - cien - te;
A - pril's crown - ing glo - ry breaks while the whole world won - ders
All the world lay un - der death, eyes were closed in sleep - ing.
y el ca - lor pri - ma - ve - ral ha - ce al mun - do des - per - tar, ¡qué fra -
en noc - tur - a os - cu - ri - dad bus - ca el mun - do cla - ri - dad, ¡qué fe -
at the ho - ly un - seen power of the tree which bears the flower. On the
But, when all seemed lost in night, came the sun whose gold - en light brings un -

gan-te o-lor de tan be-lla flor! yo e-sa ro–, yo e-sa ro–, yo e-sa
li-ci-dad es-ta Na-vi-dad! ya la lu–, ya la lu–, ya la
bless-ed tree blooms the red-dest flower, on the tree blooms the rose here in
end-ing joy, brings the end-less joy of our hope, high-est hope, of our
ro-sa an-he-lo del jar-din del cie-lo.
luz di-vi-na al-mun-do i-lu-mi-na.
love's own gar-den, full and strong in glo-ry.
hope's bright dawn-ing, Son be-loved of heav-en.

3 *Va el capullo a florecer rosa blanca y pura,*
su fragancia va a ofrecer a toda criatura;
ese aroma sin igual nueva vida da al mortal,
es de Dios el don, sumo galardón
que al mun-, que al mun-,
que al mundo ha dado, es su Hijo amado.

3 Now the bud has come to bloom, and the world awakens.
In the lily's purest flower dwells a wondrous fragrance.
And it spreads to all the earth from the moment of its birth;
and its beauty lives. In the flower it lives,
in the flower, and it spreads
in its heavenly brightness, sweet perfume delightful.

234 Her baby, newly breathing

"Birthsong," Brian Wren, 1987

Music: *St. Michael's*, 7676D; melody in W. Gawler's *Hymns and Psalms*, 1789

1 Her ba - by, new - ly breath - ing, with wail - ing need - ful cry,
2 The eyes that gaze at Ma - ry have yet to name or trace
3 The milk of life is flow - ing as Ma - ry guides and feeds
4 How mo - ther - like the Wis - dom that car - ried and gave birth
by Ma - ry kissed and cra - dled, is lulled in lull - a - by.
the world of shape and co - lor, or re - cog - nize a face;
her word - less Word, em - bod - ied in in - fant joys and needs.
to all things, seen and un - seen, and nur - tured in - fant earth;
Long months of hope and wait - ing, the thrill and fear of birth,
yet Ho - li - ness E - ter - nal is per - fect - ly ex - pressed
E - nor - mous, form - less striv - ings, and yearn - ings deep and wide,
un - stint - ing, un - pro - tect - ed, pre - pared for nail and thorn,
are crowned with ex - ul - ta - tion, and God is on the earth.
in hands that clutch un - think - ing, and lips that tug the breast.
be - crad - led in com - mun - ion, are fed and sat - is - fied.
con - strict - ed in - to male - ness, and of a wo - man born.

235 Lo, how a Rose e'er blooming

Es ist ein' Ros' entsprungen

German, 15th century; translated by Theodore Baker, 1894

Music: *Es ist ein' Ros'*, 7676676; German traditional melody; harmony by Michael Praetorius, 1609

1 Lo, how a Rose e'er bloom-ing from ten-der stem hath sprung!
2 I - sa - iah 'twas fore - told it, the Rose I have in mind,
Of Jes - se's lin - eage com - ing as seers of old have sung.
with Ma - ry we be - hold it, the vir - gin mo - ther kind.
It came, a blos-som bright, a - mid the cold of win - ter,
To show God's love a - right she bore to us a Sa - vior,
when half spent was the night.
when half spent was the night.

236 O little town of Bethlehem

Phillips Brooks, 1867

Music: *Forest Green*, 8686D; English folksong melody, "The Ploughboy's Dream," arranged and harmonized by Ralph Vaughan Williams, 1906

1 O lit - tle town of Beth - le - hem, how still we see thee lie!
2 For Christ is born of Ma - ry, and gath - ered all a - bove,
3 How si - lent - ly, how si - lent - ly the won - drous gift is given!
4 O ho - ly Child of Beth - le - hem! de - scend to us, we pray;
A - bove thy deep and dream - less sleep the si - lent stars go by;
while mor - tals sleep, the an - gels keep their watch of won-dering love.
So God im - parts to hu - man hearts the bless - ings of his heaven.
cast out our sin and en - ter in, be born in us to - day.
yet in thy dark streets shin - eth the ev - er - last - ing light;
O morn - ing stars, to - geth - er pro - claim the ho - ly birth!
No ear may hear his com - ing, but in this world of sin,
We hear the Christ - mas an - gels the great glad tid - ings tell;
the hopes and fears of all the years are met in thee to - night.
And prais - es sing to God the King, and peace to all on earth.
where meek souls will re - ceive him, still the dear Christ en - ters in.
O come to us, a - bide with us, our Lord Em - man - u - el!

237 On Christmas night all Christians sing

English traditional

Music: *Sussex Carol*, 888888; collected by Ralph Vaughan Williams in 1904 and included in his *Fantasia on Christmas Carols*, 1912; adapted by E. Harold Geer for *Hymnal for Colleges and Schools*, 1956

1 On Christ-mas night all Chris - tians sing, to hear the news the
2 Then why should we on earth be sad, since our Re-deem - er
3 When sin de-parts be - fore his grace, then life and health come
an - gels bring, on Christ-mas night all Chris - tians sing, to
made us glad, then why should we on earth be sad, since
in its place, when sin de-parts be - fore his grace, then
hear the news the an-gels bring: news of great joy, news of great
our Re-deem - er made us glad, when from our sin he set us
life and health come in its place; heav - en and earth with joy may
mirth, news of our mer - ci - ful King's birth.
free, all for to gain our lib - er - ty?
sing, all for to see the new - born King.

238 The angel Gabriel from heaven came

Birjina gaztettobat zegoen

Basque carol; paraphrased by Sabine Baring-Gould, 1922

Music: *Gabriel's Message*, 10.10.12.7.3; Basque carol; arranged by C. Edgar Pettman, 1922

1 The an - gel Ga - bri - el from heav - en came,
2 "For know a bless - ed Mo - ther thou shalt be,
3 Then gen - tle Ma - ry meek - ly bowed her head,
4 Of her, Em - man - u - el, the Christ, was born
with wings as drift - ed snow, with eyes as flame;
all gen - er - a - tions laud and hon - or thee,
"To me be as it pleas - eth God," she said,
in Beth - le - hem, all on a Christ - mas morn,
"All hail to thee, thou low - ly maid - en Ma - ry,
thy Son shall be Em - man - u - el, by seers fore - told,
"my soul shall laud and mag - ni - fy God's ho - ly name."
and Chris - tian folk through - out the world will ev - er say,
most high - ly fa - vored la - dy," Glo - - - ri - a!
most high - ly fa - vored la - dy," Glo - - - ri - a!
Most high - ly fa - vored la - dy, Glo - - - ri - a!
"Most high - ly fa - vored la - dy," Glo - - - ri - a!

239 'Twas in the moon of wintertime

Estennialon de tsonue Jesus ahatonnia

Jesse Edgar Middleton (1872–1960), and others, based on a Canadian Huron carol attributed to Jean de Brébeuf (1593–1649)

Music: *Une jeune pucelle*, 868688 with refrain; French 16th-century folk melody; harmony by Frederick Jackisch, 1978

1 'Twas in the moon of win-ter-time, when all the birds had fled,
2 With-in a lodge of brok-en bark the ten-der babe was found,
3 The ear-liest moon of win-ter-time is not so round and fair
4 O chil-dren of the for-est free, the an-gel song is true;
that God the Lord of all the earth sent an-gel choirs in-stead;
a rag-ged robe of rab-bit skin en-wrapped his beau-ty round;
as was the ring of glo-ry on the help-less in-fant there.
the ho-ly child of earth and heaven is born to-day for you.
be-fore their light the stars grew dim, and wan-dering hun-ters heard the hymn:
but as the hun-ter braves drew nigh, the an-gel song rang loud and high:
The chiefs from far be-fore him knelt with gifts of fox and bea-ver pelt.
Come, kneel be-fore the ra-diant boy, who brings you beau-ty, peace, and joy.
Refrain
Je-sus your King is born, Je-sus is born, in ex-cel-sis glo-ri-a.

240 Angels we have heard on high

Les anges dans nos campagnes

French traditional, probably 19th century; translation by James Chadwick (1813–1882)

Music: *Gloria*, 7777 with refrain; French carol melody; arranged by Edward Shippen Barnes, 1937

1 An - gels we have heard on high sweet - ly sing- ing o'er the plains,
2 Shep-herds, why this ju - bi - lee? Why your joy - ous strains pro - long?
3 Come to Beth - le - hem and see Christ whose birth the an - gels sing;
4 See him in a man - ger laid, whom the choirs of an - gels praise;
and the moun-tains in re - ply e - cho - ing their joy - ous strains.
What the glad-some tid - ings be which in - spire your heaven - ly song?
come, a - dore on bend - ed knee Christ, the Lord, the new - born King.
Ma - ry, Jo - seph, lend your aid, while our hearts in love we raise.
Refrain
Glo - - - ri- a, in ex-cel- sis De- o!
Glo - - - ri- a, in ex-cel-sis De - o!

241

The preceding carol, in French:

1 Les an - ges dans nos cam-pag- nes ont en - ton- né l'hym - ne des cieux,
2 Ber- gers, pour qui cet - te fê - te? Quel est l'ob-jet de tous ces chants?
3 Cher-chons tous l'heur- eux vil - la - ge qui l'a vu naî - tre sous ses toits;

Refrain is at no. 240.

et l'é - cho de nos mon - tag - nes re - dit ce chant mé - lo - di - eux.
Quel vain-queur, quel - le con - quê - te mé - ri - te ces cris tri - om- phants?
of - frons - lui le ten-dre hom-ma - ge et de nos cœurs et de nos voix!

242 While shepherds watched their flocks

Nahum Tate, 1700; paraphrase of Luke 2:8–14

Music: *Winchester Old*, 8686; melody in *Est(e)'s Psalmes*, 1592

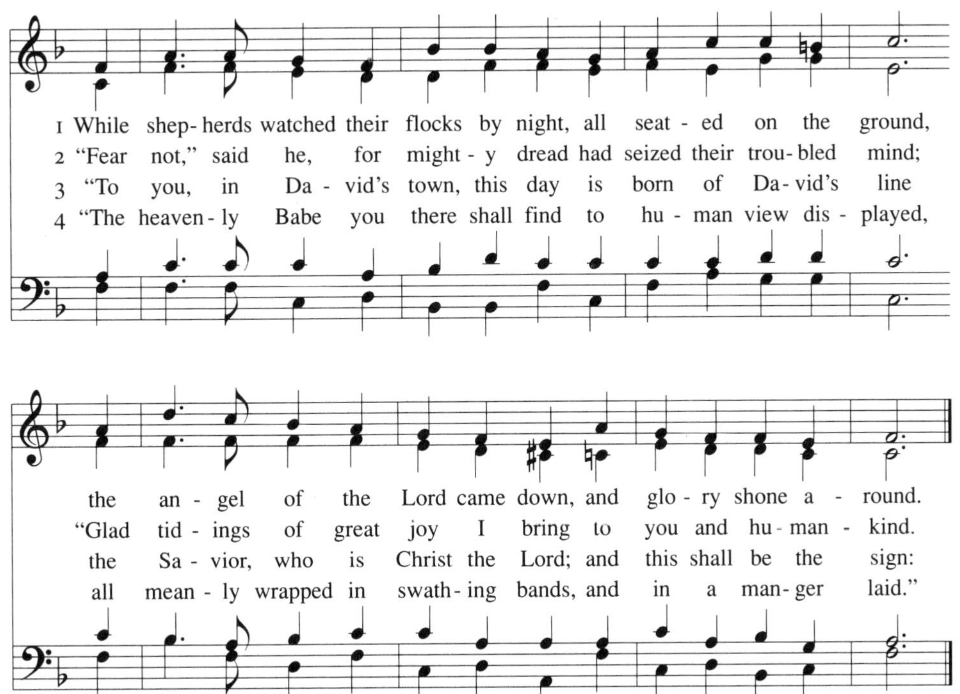
1 While shep- herds watched their flocks by night, all seat - ed on the ground,
2 "Fear not," said he, for might - y dread had seized their trou- bled mind;
3 "To you, in Da - vid's town, this day is born of Da- vid's line
4 "The heaven - ly Babe you there shall find to hu - man view dis - played,
the an - gel of the Lord came down, and glo - ry shone a - round.
"Glad tid - ings of great joy I bring to you and hu - man - kind.
the Sa - vior, who is Christ the Lord; and this shall be the sign:
all mean - ly wrapped in swath - ing bands, and in a man- ger laid."

5 Thus spake the seraph, and forthwith
appeared a shining throng
of angels praising God, who thus
addressed their joyful song:

6 "All glory be to God on high
and on the earth be peace;
good will henceforth from heaven to earth
begin and never cease."

243 **Another harmonization of no. 242; from *Ravenscroft's Psalter*, 1621:**

The melody is in the tenor.

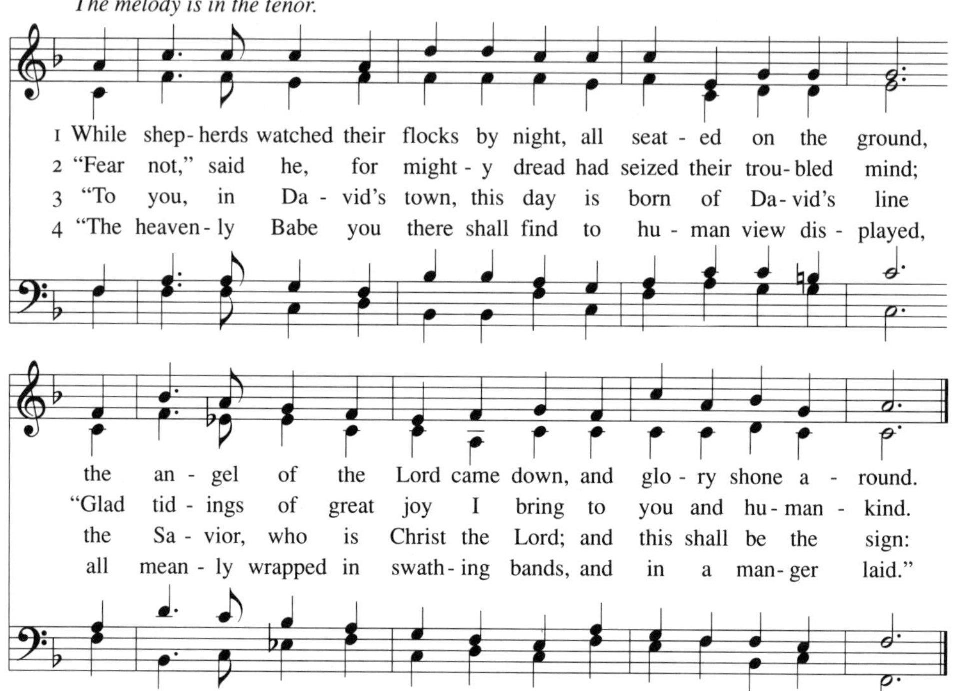
1 While shep-herds watched their flocks by night, all seat - ed on the ground,
2 "Fear not," said he, for might - y dread had seized their trou-bled mind;
3 "To you, in Da - vid's town, this day is born of Da-vid's line
4 "The heaven-ly Babe you there shall find to hu - man view dis - played,
the an - gel of the Lord came down, and glo - ry shone a - round.
"Glad tid - ings of great joy I bring to you and hu-man - kind.
the Sa - vior, who is Christ the Lord; and this shall be the sign:
all mean - ly wrapped in swath-ing bands, and in a man-ger laid."

5 Thus spake the seraph, and forthwith
appeared a shining throng
of angels praising God, who thus
addressed their joyful song:

6 "All glory be to God on high
and on the earth be peace;
good will henceforth from heaven to earth
begin and never cease."

244 On this day earth shall ring

Personent hodie

Theodoric Petri's *Piae Cantiones*, 1582; translated by Jane M. Joseph, 1924

Music: *Personent hodie*, 66666 with refrain; from the same book; accompaniment by Gustav Holst, 1925

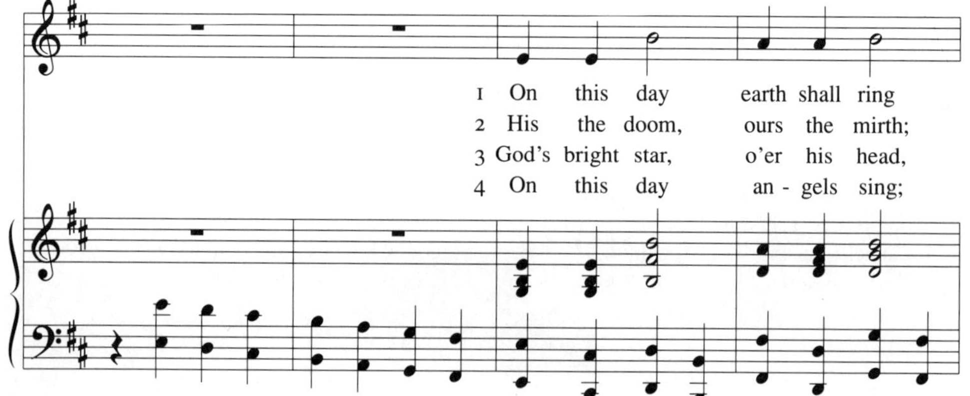
1 On this day earth shall ring
2 His the doom, ours the mirth;
3 God's bright star, o'er his head,
4 On this day an - gels sing;

with the song chil-dren sing to the Lord, Christ our King,
when he came down to earth, Beth-le-hem saw his birth;
wise men three to him led, kneel they low by his bed,
with their song earth shall ring, prais-ing Christ, heav-en's King,
born on earth to save us; God in him for-gave us.
ox and ass be-side him from the cold would hide him.
lay their gifts be-fore him, praise him and a-dore him.
born on earth to save us; peace and love he gave us.
Refrain
I-de-o-o-o, i-de-o-o-o,
i-de-o glo-ri-a in ex-cel-sis De-o!

245 Joy to the world

Isaac Watts, 1719; based on Psalm 98:4–9

Music: *Antioch*, 8686 extended; Lowell Mason, 1848, "arranged from Handel" (probably *Messiah*)

1 Joy to the world! the Lord is come: let earth re - ceive her
2 Joy to the world! the Sa - vior reigns: let all their songs em -
3 No more let sins and sor - rows grow, nor thorns in - fest the
4 He rules the world with truth and grace, and makes the na - tions
King; let ev - ery heart pre - pare him room, and
ploy, while fields and floods, rocks, hills and plains, re -
ground; he comes to make his bless - ings flow far
prove the glo - ries of his righ - teous - ness, and
heaven and na - ture sing, and heaven and na - ture
peat the sound - ing joy, re - peat the sound - ing
as the curse is found, far as the curse is
won - ders of his love, and won - ders of his
1 and heaven and na - ture sing, and
2 re - peat the sound - ing joy, re -
3 far as the curse is found, far
4 and won - ders of his love, and

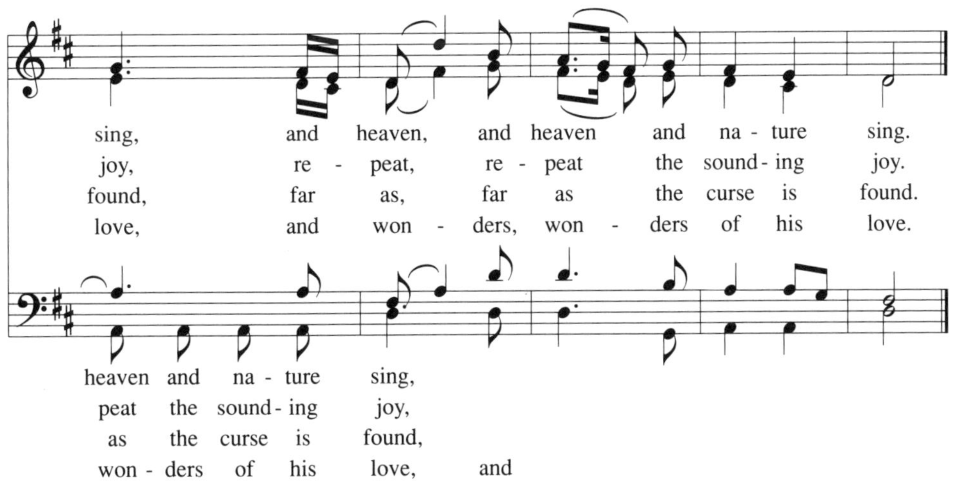
sing, and heaven, and heaven and na - ture sing.
joy, re - peat, re - peat the sound - ing joy.
found, far as, far as the curse is found.
love, and won - ders, won - ders of his love.
heaven and na - ture sing,
peat the sound - ing joy,
as the curse is found,
won - ders of his love, and

246 Angels, from the realms of glory

James Montgomery, 1816, 1825

Music: *Regent Square*, 878787; Henry Smart, 1867

1 An - gels, from the realms of glo - ry, wing your flight o'er all the earth;
2 Shep-herds in the field a - bid - ing, watch - ing o'er your flocks by night,
3 Sag - es, leave your con - tem - pla - tions; bright - er vi - sions beam a - far:
4 Saints be - fore the al - tar bend - ing, watch - ing long in hope and fear,

ye, who sang cre - a - tion's sto - ry, now pro - claim Mes - si - ah's birth:
God on earth is now re - sid - ing; yon - der shines the in - fant light:
seek the great de - sire of na - tions; ye have seen his na - tal star:
sud - den - ly the Lord, de - scend - ing, in his tem - ple shall ap - pear:

Refrain

Come and wor - ship, come and wor - ship, wor - ship Christ, the new - born King.

5 Though an infant now we view him,
Christ shall reign from heaven's throne,
gather all the nations to him;
every knee shall then bow down.
Refrain

The Birth of Jesus

See also:

All glory be to God on high, no. 312
In Bethlehem a new-born boy, no. 528
Let all mortal flesh keep silence, no. 408
Mine eyes have seen the glory, no. 573
Of God's very heart begotten, no. 48
The King of glory comes to earth, no. 574
The tree of life my soul hath seen, nos. 461, 462

247 As with gladness men of old

William Chatterton Dix, c. 1858

Music: *Dix*, 777777; Conrad Kocher, 1838; abridged and arranged by William H. Monk, 1861

1 As with glad-ness men of old did the guid-ing star be-hold;
2 As with joy-ful steps they sped to that low-ly man-ger-bed;
3 As they of-fered gifts most rare at that man-ger crude and bare;
4 Ho-ly Je-sus, ev-ery day keep us in the nar-row way;
as with joy they hailed its light, lead-ing on-ward, beam-ing bright;
there to bend the knee be-fore Christ whom heaven and earth a-dore;
so may we with ho-ly joy, pure and free from sin's al-loy,
and, when earth-ly things are past, bring our ran-somed souls at last
so, most gra-cious Lord, may we ev-er-more your splen-dor see.
so may we with ea-ger pace ev-er seek your throne of grace.
all our cost-liest trea-sures bring, Christ, to you, our heav-enly King.
where they need no star to guide, where no clouds your glo-ry hide.

5 In the heavenly country bright
none shall need created light;
you, its light, its joy, its crown,
you, its sun which goes not down;
there upon you may we gaze,
offering you eternal praise.

248 The first Nowell

English traditional carol

Music: *The First Nowell*, irregular meter, with refrain; English traditional melody; harmony probably by John Stainer, 1871

1 The first No - well the an - gel did say was to cer - tain poor
2 They look - ed up and saw a star shin-ing in the
3 And by the light of that same star three wise men
4 This star drew nigh to the north - west, o'er Beth - le -
shep-herds, in fields as they lay, in fields where they lay a - keep-ing their
east, be - yond them far; and to the earth it gave great
came from coun - try far; to seek for a king was their in -
hem it took its rest; and there it did both stop and
sheep, on a cold win-ter's night that was so deep.
light, and so it con - tin - ued both day and night.
tent, and to fol - low the star wher - ev - er it went.
stay right o - ver the place where Je - sus lay.
Refrain
No - well, No - well, No - well, No - well,
born is the King of Is - ra - el.

5 Then entered in those wise men three
full reverently upon their knee,
and offered there in his presence
their gold, and myrrh, and frankincense.

Refrain

249 Christ, when for us you were baptized

F. Bland Tucker, 1982

Music: *Caithness*, 8686; melody in *Scottish Psalter*, 1635; harmony from *The English Hymnal*, 1906

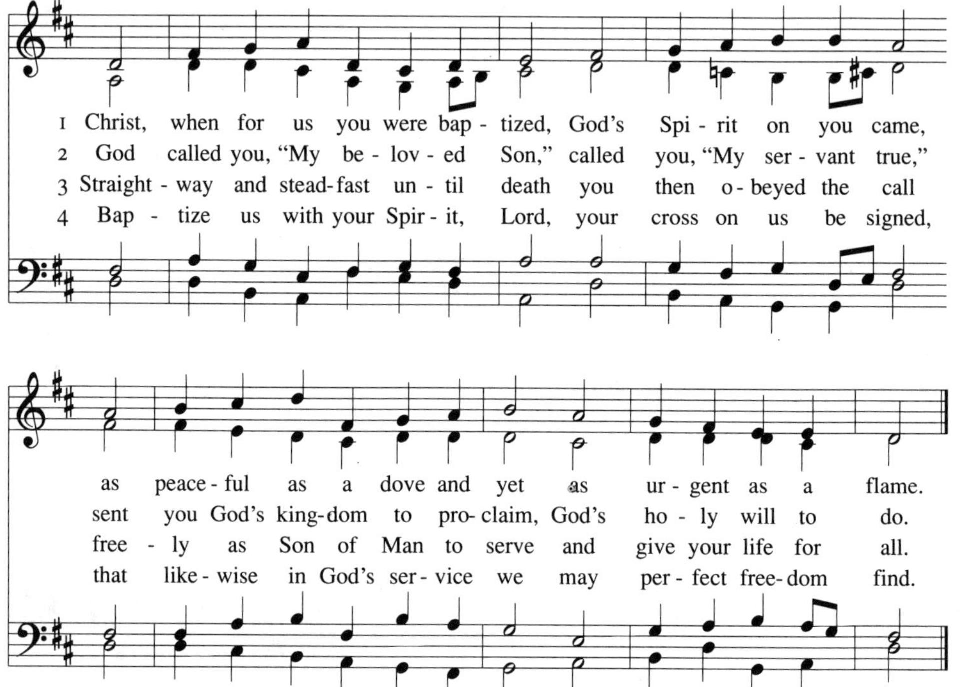
1 Christ, when for us you were bap - tized, God's Spi - rit on you came,
2 God called you, "My be - lov - ed Son," called you, "My ser - vant true,"
3 Straight - way and stead-fast un - til death you then o - beyed the call
4 Bap - tize us with your Spir - it, Lord, your cross on us be signed,
as peace - ful as a dove and yet as ur - gent as a flame.
sent you God's king-dom to pro- claim, God's ho - ly will to do.
free - ly as Son of Man to serve and give your life for all.
that like - wise in God's ser - vice we may per - fect free- dom find.

250 Songs of thankfulness and praise

Christopher Wordsworth, 1862

Music: *Salzburg*, 7777D; melody by Jakob Hintze, 1678; harmony adapted from J. S. Bach (1685–1750)

1 Songs of thank-ful - ness and praise, Je - sus, Lord, to you we raise,
2 Man - i - fest at Jor - dan's stream, Pro-phet, Priest, and King su-preme;
3 Man - i - fest in mak - ing whole pal-sied limbs and faint-ing soul;
4 Grant us grace to see you, Lord, mir-rored in your ho - ly Word;
man - i - fest - ed by the star to the sag - es from a - far;
and at Ca - na, wed - ding guest, in your God-head man - i - fest;
man - i - fest in val - iant fight, quell-ing all the dev - il's might;
with your grace our lives en - dow, grace to im - i - tate you now,
branch of roy - al Da - vid's stem in your birth at Beth - le - hem;
man - i - fest in power di - vine, chang - ing wa - ter in - to wine;
man - i - fest in gra - cious will, ev - er bring - ing good from ill;
that we like to you may be at your great e - pi - pha - ny,
Refrain
an-thems be to you ad-dressed, God in flesh made man - i - fest.

251 Christ upon the mountain peak

"Christ transfigured," Brian Wren, 1962

Music: *Mowsley*, 78784; Cyril V. Taylor, 1962

1 Christ upon the mountain peak stands alone in glory blazing; let us, if we dare to speak, with the saints and angels praise him. Alleluia!

2 Trembling at his feet we saw Moses and Elijah speaking. All the prophets and the Law shout through them their joyful greeting. Alleluia!

3 Swift the cloud of glory came, God proclaiming in its thunder Jesus as the Son by name! Nations cry aloud in wonder! Alleluia!

4 This is God's beloved Son! Law and prophets fade before him; first and last and only One, let creation now adore him! Alleluia!

252 O Lord, throughout these forty days

Gilbert E. Doan, 1978, based on a hymn by Claudia F. Hernaman, 1873

Music: *Caithness*, 8686; melody in *Scottish Psalter*, 1635; harmony from *The English Hymnal*, 1906

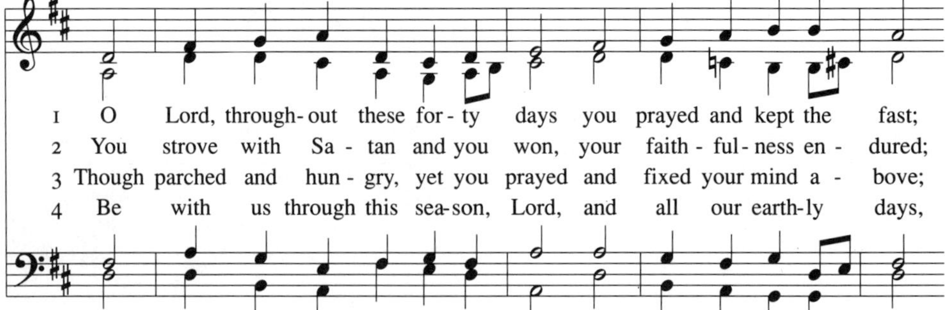
1 O Lord, through-out these for-ty days you prayed and kept the fast;
2 You strove with Sa-tan and you won, your faith-ful-ness en-dured;
3 Though parched and hun-gry, yet you prayed and fixed your mind a-bove;
4 Be with us through this sea-son, Lord, and all our earth-ly days,

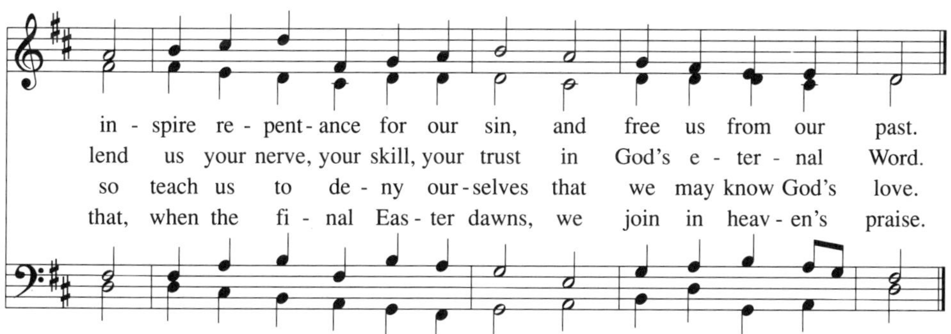
in - spire re - pent - ance for our sin, and free us from our past.
lend us your nerve, your skill, your trust in God's e - ter - nal Word.
so teach us to de - ny our - selves that we may know God's love.
that, when the fi - nal Eas - ter dawns, we join in heav - en's praise.

253 Forty days and forty nights

George H. Smyttan, 1856, and others

Music: *Aus der Tiefe*, 7777; melody attributed to Martin Herbst, 1676 or 1677; harmony adapted from a chorale prelude attributed to J. S. Bach (1685–1750)

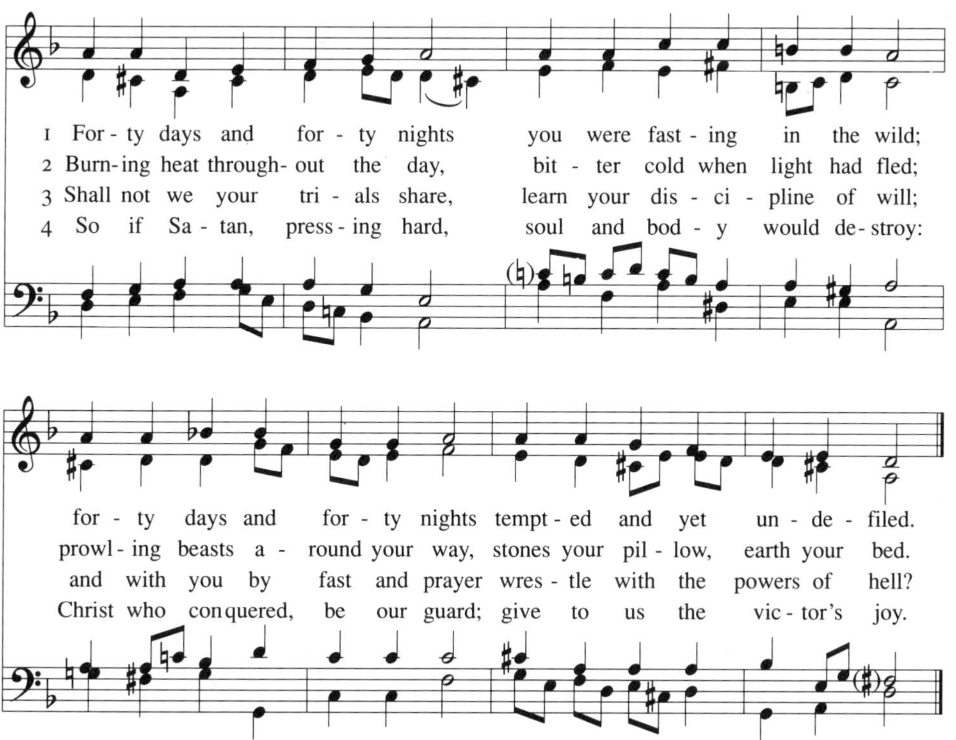
1 For - ty days and for - ty nights you were fast - ing in the wild;
2 Burn - ing heat through - out the day, bit - ter cold when light had fled;
3 Shall not we your tri - als share, learn your dis - ci - pline of will;
4 So if Sa - tan, press - ing hard, soul and bod - y would de - stroy:
for - ty days and for - ty nights tempt - ed and yet un - de - filed.
prowl - ing beasts a - round your way, stones your pil - low, earth your bed.
and with you by fast and prayer wres - tle with the powers of hell?
Christ who con quered, be our guard; give to us the vic - tor's joy.

5 Savior, may we hear your voice;
keep us constant at your side;
and with you we shall rejoice
at the eternal Eastertide.

254 The glory of these forty days

Clarum decus jejunii

Attributed to Gregory the Great (d. 604); translated by Maurice F. Bell, 1906

Music: *Erhalt uns, Herr*, 8888; melody in Klug's *Geistliche Lieder*, 1543; harmony adapted from Hans Leo Hassler, 1608

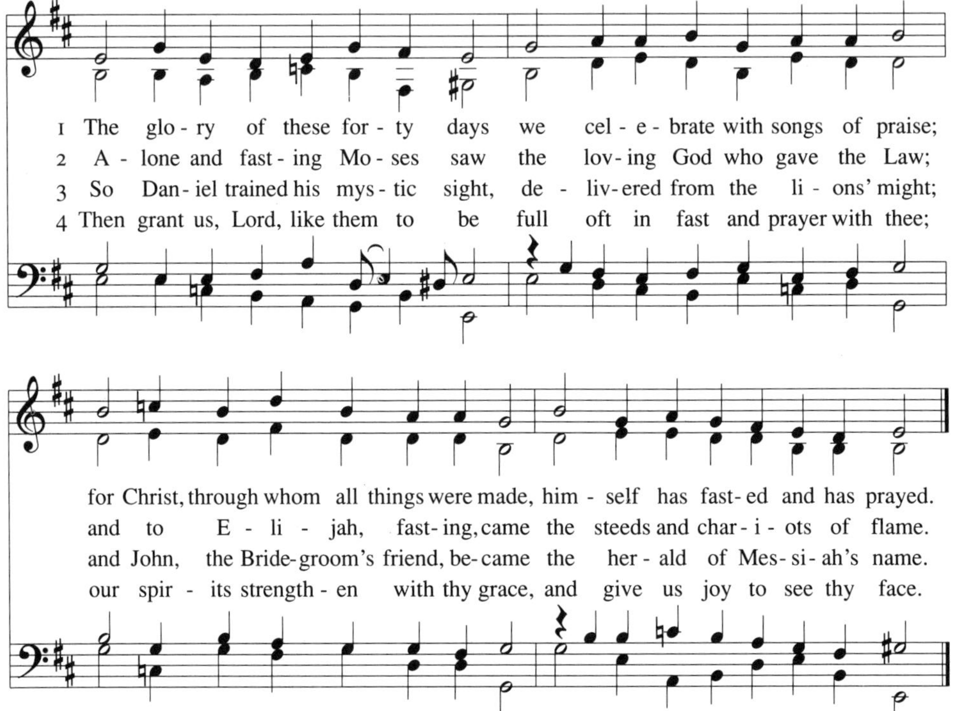
1 The glo - ry of these for - ty days we cel - e - brate with songs of praise;
2 A - lone and fast - ing Mo - ses saw the lov - ing God who gave the Law;
3 So Dan - iel trained his mys - tic sight, de - liv - ered from the li - ons' might;
4 Then grant us, Lord, like them to be full oft in fast and prayer with thee;
for Christ, through whom all things were made, him - self has fast - ed and has prayed.
and to E - li - jah, fast - ing, came the steeds and char - i - ots of flame.
and John, the Bride - groom's friend, be - came the her - ald of Mes - si - ah's name.
our spir - its strength - en with thy grace, and give us joy to see thy face.

Epiphany and Lent

See also:

I danced in the morning, no. 295
Jesu, Jesu, fill us with your love, no. 515
O Christ, the healer, no. 413
O Love, how deep, how broad, how high, no. 52
O Morning Star, how fair and bright, no. 36
"Silence! frenzied, unclean spirit," no. 414
The first one ever, no. 297
When Jesus came preaching, no. 545
Woman in the night, no. 307
Your hands, O Lord, in days of old, no. 416

255 All glory, laud, and honor

Gloria, laus, et honor

Theodulph of Orleans (d. 821); translated by John Mason Neale, 1851

Music: *Valet will ich dir geben*, 7676D; melody by Melchior Teschner, 1615

Refrain
All glo - ry, laud, and hon - or to you Re - deem - er, King,
to whom the lips of chil - dren made sweet ho - san - nas ring.
Fine
1 You are the king of Is - rael and Da - vid's roy - al Son,
2 The com - pa - ny of an - gels are prais - ing you on high;
3 The mul - ti - tude of pil - grims with palms be - fore you went.
4 To you, be - fore your pas - sion, they sang their hymns of praise.
now in the Lord's name com - ing, our King and bless - ed one.
cre - a - tion and all mor - tals in cho - rus make re - ply.
Our praise and prayer and an - thems be - fore you we pre - sent.
To you, now high ex - alt - ed, our mel - o - dy we raise.
D.C.

5 Their praises you accepted;
  accept the prayers we bring,
great author of all goodness,
  O good and gracious King.

Refrain

256 Ride on, ride on in majesty

Henry Hart Milman, 1827

Music: *The King's Majesty*, 8888; Graham George, 1939

1 Ride on, ride on in maj - es - ty! Hark, all the
2 Ride on, ride on in maj - es - ty! In low - ly
3 Ride on, ride on in maj - es - ty! The an - gel
4 Ride on, ride on in maj - es - ty! In low - ly
tribes ho - san - na cry; O Sa - vior meek, your road pur -
pomp ride on to die. O Christ, your tri - umphs now be -
mul - ti - tudes on high look down with sad and wonder - ing
pomp ride on to die, bow your meek head to mor - tal
sue, with palms and scat - tered gar - ments strewed.
gin o'er cap - tive death and con - quered sin.
eyes to see the ap - proach - ing sac - ri - fice.
pain, then take, O Christ, your power and reign!

257 There in God's garden

Paradicsomnak te szép élö fája

Király Imre von Pécselyi (c. 1590–c. 1641); paraphrased by Erik Routley, 1973

Music: *Shades Mountain*, 11.11.11.5; K. Lee Scott, 1987

1 There in God's gar - den stands the Tree of Wis - dom, whose leaves hold
2 Its name is Je - sus, name that says, "Our Sa - vior!" There on its
3 Thorns not its own are tan - gled in its fo - liage; our greed has
4 See how its branch - es reach to us in wel - come; hear what the
forth the heal - ing of the na - tions: Tree of all know - ledge,
branch - es see the scars of suf - fering; see where the ten - drils
starved it, our des - pite has choked it. Yet, look! it lives! its
Voice says, "Come to me, ye wear - y! Give me your sick - ness,
Tree of all com - pas - sion, Tree of all beau - ty.
of our hu - man self - hood feed on its life - blood.
grief has not de - stroyed it nor fire con - sumed it.
give me all your sor - row, I will give bless - ing."

5 This is my ending, this my resurrection;
into your hands, Lord, I commit my spirit.
This have I searched for; now I can possess it.
This ground is holy.

6 All heaven is singing, "Thanks to Christ whose Passion
offers in mercy healing, strength, and pardon.
Peoples and nations, take it, take it freely!"
Amen! Our Savior!

258 Ah, holy Jesus

Herzliebster Jesu

Johann Heermann, 1630, based on a Latin meditation by Jean de Fécamp (d. 1078); translated by Robert Bridges, 1899, and others

Music: *Herzliebster Jesu*, 11.11.11.5; Johann Crüger, 1640

1 Ah, ho - ly Je - sus, how have you of - fend - ed, that we to judge you have in hate pre - tend - ed? By foes de - rid - ed, by your own re - ject - ed, O most af - flict - ed!
2 Who was the guilt - y? Who brought this up - on you? A - las, my trea - son, Je - sus, has un - done you. Yes, I, Lord Je - sus, I it was de - nied you: I cru - ci - fied you.
3 Lo, the Good Shep - herd for the sheep is of - fered; the slave is guilt - y, yet the Son has suf - fered; for our a - tone - ment, while we no - thing heed - ed, God in - ter - ced - ed.
4 For me, kind Je - sus, was your in - car - na - tion, your mor - tal sor - row, and your life's ob - la - tion; your death of an - guish and your bit - ter pas - sion, for my sal - va - tion.

5 Therefore, kind Jesus, since I cannot pay you,
I will adore you, and will ever pray you,
think on your pity and your love unswerving,
not my deserving.

259 O sacred head, sore wounded

Salve caput cruentatum

O Haupt voll Blut und Wunden

Medieval Latin, attributed to Bernard of Clairvaux (1091–1153);
German paraphrase by Paul Gerhardt, 1656; stanzas 1–3 translated by Robert Bridges, 1899;
stanza 4 by James W. Alexander, 1830

Music: *Passion Chorale*, 7676D; Hans Leo Hassler, 1601, based on the love song "Mein G'müt ist mir verwirret"

1 O sa - cred head, sore wound - ed, de - filed and put to scorn;
2 Thy beau - ty, long - de - sir - ed, hath van - ished from our sight;
3 In thy most bit - ter pas - sion my heart to share doth cry,
4 What lan - guage shall I bor - row to thank thee, dear - est friend,
O roy - al head, sur-round - ed with mock - ing crown of thorn:
thy power is all ex - pir - ed, and quenched the Light of light.
with thee for my sal - va - tion up - on the cross to die.
for this thy dy - ing sor - row, thy pi - ty with - out end?
what sor - row mars thy gran - deur? Can death thy bloom de - flower?
Ah me! for whom thou di - est, hide not so far thy grace:
Ah, keep my heart thus mov - ed to stand thy cross be - neath,
O, make me thine for ev - er! and should I faint - ing be,
O count - en - ance whose splen - dor the hosts of heaven a - dore!
show me, O Love most high - est, the bright - ness of thy face.
to mourn thee, well - be - lov - ed, yet thank thee for thy death.
Lord, let me nev - er, nev - er, out - live my love for thee.

260 O sacred head, sore wounded

Salve caput cruentatum

O Haupt voll Blut und Wunden

Medieval Latin, attributed to Bernard of Clairvaux (1091–1153);
German paraphrase by Paul Gerhardt, 1656; stanzas 1–3 translated by Robert Bridges, 1899;
stanza 4 by James W. Alexander, 1830

Music: *Passion Chorale*, 7676D; melody by Hans Leo Hassler, 1601;
adapted and harmonized by J. S. Bach in his *St. Matthew Passion*, 1729

1 O sa - cred head, sore wound - ed, de - filed and put to scorn;
2 Thy beau - ty, long - de - sir - ed, hath van - ished from our sight;
3 In thy most bit - ter pas - sion my heart to share doth cry,
4 What lan-guage shall I bor - row to thank thee, dear - est friend,
O roy - al head, sur - round - ed with mock - ing crown of thorn:
thy power is all ex - pir - ed, and quenched the Light of light.
with thee for my sal - va - tion up - on the cross to die.
for this thy dy - ing sor - row, thy pi - ty with - out end?
what sor - row mars thy gran - deur? Can death thy bloom de - flower?
Ah me! for whom thou di - est, hide not so far thy grace:
Ah, keep my heart thus mov - ed to stand thy cross be - neath,
O, make me thine for ev - er! and should I faint - ing be,
O count - en - ance whose splen - dor the hosts of heaven a - dore!
show me, O Love most high - est, the bright - ness of thy face.
to mourn thee, well - be - lov - ed, yet thank thee for thy death.
Lord, let me nev - er, nev - er, out - live my love for thee.

261 Sing, my tongue, the glorious battle

Pange lingua gloriosi

Venantius Fortunatus, for the transporting of fragments of the True Cross to Poitiers in 569; translation mostly from *The Hymnal 1982*

Music: *Pange lingua*, 878787; plainsong; accompaniment by Ivan Florjanc in *Slavimo Gospoda*, Celje, 1988

1 Sing, my tongue, the glo- rious bat - tle; of the might- y con- flict sing;
2 Thir- ty years a - mong us dwell - ing, his ap- point- ed time ful-filled,
3 He en- dures the nails, the spit - ting, vin - e - gar, and spear, and reed;
4 Faith- ful cross! a - bove all o - ther, one and on - ly no - ble tree!
tell the tri- umph of the Vic- tim, to his cross thy tri - bute bring.
born for this, he meets his pas- sion; this the Sa - vior free - ly willed:
from that ho - ly bod - y brok - en blood and wa - ter forth pro - ceed:
None in fol- iage, none in blos- som, none in fruit thy peer may be:
Je - sus Christ, the world's Re- deem - er, from that cross now reigns as King.
on the cross the Lamb is lift - ed, where his pre - cious blood is spilled.
earth, and stars, and sky, and o - cean, by that flood from stain are freed.
sweet- est wood and sweet- est i - ron! sweet- est weight is hung on thee.

5 Bend thy boughs, O tree of glory!
Thy relaxing sinews bend;
for awhile the ancient rigor
that thy birth bestowed, suspend;
and the King of heavenly beauty
gently on thine arms extend.

6 Now to God be praise and glory
for the victory Christ has won,
and to God by earth and heaven
honor evermore be done;
praise and glory in the highest,
while unending ages run.

262 The flaming banners

Vexilla regis prodeunt

Venantius Fortunatus, for the transporting of fragments of the True Cross to Poitiers in 569; paraphrased by John Webster Grant, 1971

Music: *Vexilla regis*, 8888; plainsong; accompaniment by Russell Schulz-Widmar, 1985

1 The flam - ing ban - ners of our King ad - vance through
2 A Ro - man sol - dier drew a spear to mix his
3 The crowd would have been sat - is - fied to see a
4 With what strange light the rough trunk shone, its pur - ple
his self - of - fer - ing. He lived to rob death of its
blood with wa - ter clear. That blood re - tains its liv - ing
pro - phet cru - ci - fied. They stum - bled on a mys - ter -
limbs a roy - al throne, its load a roy - al trea - sur -
sting; he died e - ter - nal life to bring.
power: the wa - ter cleans - es to this hour.
y: Mes - si - ah reign - ing from a tree.
y: the ran - som of a world set free.

5 The best are shamed before that wood;
the worst gain power to be good.
O grant, most blessed Trinity,
that all may share the victory.

263 To mock your reign, O dearest Lord

Fred Pratt Green, 1972

Music: *The Third Tune*, 8686D; Thomas Tallis, c. 1557

1 To mock your reign, O dear-est Lord, they made a crown of thorns;
2 In mock ac-claim, O gra-cious Lord, they snatched a pur-ple cloak,
3 A scep-tered reed, O pa-tient Lord, they thrust in-to your hand,
set you with taunts a-long the road from which no one re-turns.
your pas-sion turned, for all they cared, in-to a sol-dier's joke.
and act-ed out their grim cha-rade to its ap-point-ed end.
They did not know, as we do now, how glo-rious is that crown;
They did not know, as we do now, that though we mer-it blame
They did not know, as we do now, though em-pires rise and fall,
that thorns would flower up-on your brow, your sor-rows heal our own.
you will your robe of mer-cy throw a-round our na-ked shame.
your King-dom shall not cease to grow till love em-bra-ces all.

264 Three tall trees grew on a windy hill

Herbert O'Driscoll, b. 1928

Music: *Three Tall Trees*; irregular meter; Alfred V. Fedak, 1989

1 Three tall trees grew on a wind-y hill close by a He-brew town; where once a wood had proud-ly stood, now the rest of the trees were down. "A cra-dle," said one, "for a
2 One day there came to that wind-y hill those who were seek-ing wood; their hands reached out to work their will where the last of the trees still stood. From one did they fash-ion a
3 sea-sons passed on that wind-y hill close by a He-brew town. That man-ger cra-dled a ba-by still, and a star in the east looked down. And when as a teach-er he
4 voice cried, "Halt," and a pris-oner stood, bleed-ing and bound and still, while they chose for his cross the last of the wood that had grown on that wind-y hill. It had cra-dled a ba-by a-

child I will be." "As a ship," said a-noth-er, "will I sail the sea." "I will
man-ger stall, from a-noth-er the keel of a fish-boat small, but the
spoke on the shore, that boat was brought and the Lord it bore, and a-
sleep and a-wake, it had held the sail on the storm-y lake: now it
stay," said the third, "I will stand strong and free, still
third they laid by a work-shop wall, so
cross the wa-ters he taught them more of
bore him a-loft for the whole world's sake, the
1, 2, 3
point-ing to God on high."
straight did it stand and high.
love, and a God on high.
2 —
3 The
4 A
4
Son of God most high.

265 Were you there

African American spiritual

Music: *Were You There*, 10.10.10.10 with extensions; African American spiritual; harmony by Winfred Douglas, 1940

1 Were you there when they cru - ci - fied my Lord? Were you there when they cru - ci - fied my Lord? Oh!
2 Were you there when they nailed him to the tree? Were you there when they nailed him to the tree? Oh!
3 Were you there when they pierced him in the side? Were you there when they pierced him in the side? Oh!
4 Were you there when they laid him in the tomb? Were you there when they laid him in the tomb? Oh!
Some-times it caus - es me to trem-ble, trem-ble, trem-ble.
Were you there when they cru - ci - fied my Lord?
Were you there when they nailed him to the tree?
Were you there when they pierced him in the side?
Were you there when they laid him in the tomb?

266 When Jesus wept

Canon by William Billings (1746–1800) in *The New England Psalm Singer*, Boston, 1770

1
2
3
4
When Je - sus wept, the fall - ing tear in mer - cy
flowed be - yond all bound; when Je - sus groaned, a trem - bling
fear seized all the guilt - y world a - round.

Passion and Death

See also:

My song is love unknown, no. 31
Nature with open volume stands, no. 34
O Lamb of God, no. 319
Out of the depths, no. 376
We sing the praise of him who died, no. 45
What wondrous love is this, nos. 448, 449
When I survey the wondrous cross, nos. 454, 455
Where charity and love prevail, nos. 552, 553

267 Jesus Christ is risen today

Stanza 1: *Surrexit Christus hodie*, translated in John Walsh's *Lyra Davidica*, 1708; stanzas 2 and 3 from John Arnold's *Compleat Psalmodist*, 1749; stanzas 4 and 5 by Charles Wesley, 1739

Music: *Easter Hymn*, 7777 with refrains; melody in John Walsh's *Lyra Davidica*, 1708

1 Je - sus Christ is risen to - day, Al - le - lu - ia!
2 Hymns of praise then let us sing, Al - le - lu - ia!
3 But the pains which he en - dured, Al - le - lu - ia!
4 Lives a - gain our glo - rious King; Al - le - lu - ia!
our tri - umph - ant ho - ly day, Al - le - lu - ia!
un - to Christ, our heaven - ly King, Al - le - lu - ia!
our sal - va - tion have pro - cured; Al - le - lu - ia!
where, O death, is now thy sting? Al - le - lu - ia!
who did once up - on the cross, Al - le - lu - ia!
who en - dured the cross and grave, Al - le - lu - ia!
now a - bove the sky he's King. Al - le - lu - ia!
Once he died our souls to save; Al - le - lu - ia!
suf - fer to re - deem our loss. Al - le - lu - ia!
sin - ners to re - deem and save. Al - le - lu - ia!
where the an - gels ev - er sing. Al - le - lu - ia!
where thy vic - to - ry, O grave? Al - le - lu - ia!

5 Soar we now where Christ has led, Alleluia!
following our exalted Head; Alleluia!
made like him, like him we rise, Alleluia!
ours the cross, the grave, the skies. Alleluia!

268 Christ the Lord is risen again

Christ ist erstanden

German, 12th century or earlier, based on *Victimae Paschali laudes*; translation adapted from Catherine Winkworth, 1855

Music: *Christ ist erstanden*, 77774 with refrain; melody in Klug's *Geistliche Lieder*, 1533, based on *Victimae Paschali laudes*; harmony adapted from Hans Leo Hassler, 1608

1 Christ the Lord is risen a - gain! Christ has brok - en ev - ery chain!
2 He who gave for us his life, who for us en - dured the strife,
3 He who bore all pain and loss com - fort - less up - on the cross
Now through all the world it rings that the Lamb is King of kings. Al - le - lu - ia!
takes our sin and guilt a - way that with an - gels we may say: Al - le - lu - ia!
is ex - alt - ed now to save, wrest-ing vic - tory from the grave. Al - le - lu - ia!
Refrain
Al - le - lu - ia, al - le - lu - ia, al - le - lu - ia!
Christ, our Pas - chal Lamb in - deed, Christ, to - day your peo - ple feed. Al - le - lu - ia!

269 Christ Jesus lay in death's strong bands

Christ lag in Todesbanden

Martin Luther, 1524, based on *Victimae Paschali laudes* and *Christ ist erstanden*; translated by Richard Massie, 1858

Music: *Christ lag in Todesbanden*, 87877874; melody probably by Johann Walther, 1524, with incipit from *Victimae Paschali laudes*; harmony adapted from Hans Leo Hassler, 1608

1 Christ Je - sus lay in death's strong bands for our of - fens - es giv - en;
2 It was a strange and dread - ful strife when life and death con - tend - ed;
3 So let us keep the fes - ti - val to which the Lord in - vites us;
4 Then let us feast this ho - ly day on the true Bread of heav - en;
but now at God's right hand he stands and brings us life from heav - en;
the vic - to - ry re - mained with life, the reign of death was end - ed;
Christ is him - self the joy of all, the sun that warms and lights us;
the word of grace has purged a - way the old and wick - ed leav - en;
there - fore let us joy - ful be, and sing to God right thank - ful - ly
stripped of power, no more it reigns, an emp - ty form a - lone re - mains;
by his grace he doth im - part e - ter - nal sun - shine to the heart;
Christ a - lone our souls will feed, he is our meat and drink in - deed;
loud songs of al - le - lu - ia! Al - le - lu - ia!
death's sting is lost for ev - er! Al - le - lu - ia!
the night of sin is end - ed! Al - le - lu - ia!
faith lives up - on no oth - er! Al - le - lu - ia!

270 Now the green blade riseth

John M. C. Crum, 1928

Music: *Noël nouvelet*, 11.10.10.11; later form of a 15th-century French noel; harmony by Martin Shaw, 1928

1 Now the green blade ris - eth from the bur - ied grain,
2 In the grave they laid him, Love whom hate had slain,
3 Forth he came at Eas - ter, like the ris - en grain,
4 When our hearts are win - try, griev - ing, or in pain,
wheat that in dark earth man - y days has lain;
think - ing that nev - er would he wake a - gain,
Je - sus who three days in the grave had lain,
his touch can call us back to life a - gain,
love lives a - gain, that with the dead has been:
laid in the earth like grain that sleeps un - seen:
quick from the dead my ris - en Lord is seen:
fields of our hearts that dead and bare have been:
Refrain
Love is come a - gain like wheat that spring - eth green.

271 Come, you faithful, raise the strain

John of Damascus, c. 750; translated by John Mason Neale, 1859

Music: *St. Kevin*, 7676D; Arthur S. Sullivan, 1872

1 Come, you faith - ful, raise the strain of tri - um - phant glad - ness!
2 'Tis the spring of souls to - day: Christ has burst his pris - on,
3 Now the queen of sea - sons, bright with the day of splen - dor,
4 Nei - ther could the gates of death, nor the tomb's dark por - tal,
God has brought forth Is - ra - el in - to joy from sad - ness,
and from three days' sleep in death as a sun has ris - en;
with the roy - al feast of feasts, comes its joy to ren - der;
nor the watch - ers, nor the seal hold him as a mor - tal:
loosed from Phar - aoh's bit - ter yoke Ja - cob's sons and daugh - ters,
all the win - ter of our sins, long and dark, is fly - ing
comes to glad - den faith - ful hearts, which with true af - fec - tion
for to - day a - mid his own he now stands, be - stow - ing
led them with un - moist - ened foot through the Red Sea wa - ters.
from his light, to whom we give laud and praise un - dy - ing.
wel - come in un - wea - ried strains Je - sus' res - ur - rec - tion!
God's true peace which ev - er - more pass - es hu - man know - ing.

272 Come, you faithful, raise the strain

John of Damascus, c. 750; translated by John Mason Neale, 1859

Music: *Ave virgo virginum*, 7676D; melody in John Horn's *Gesangbuch*, Nuremberg, 1544

1 Come, you faith - ful, raise the strain of tri - um - phant glad - ness!
2 'Tis the spring of souls to - day: Christ has burst his pris - on,
3 Now the queen of sea - sons, bright with the day of splen - dor,
4 Nei - ther could the gates of death, nor the tomb's dark por - tal,
God has brought forth Is - ra - el in - to joy from sad - ness,
and from three days' sleep in death as a sun has ris - en;
with the roy - al feast of feasts, comes its joy to ren - der;
nor the watch - ers, nor the seal hold him as a mor - tal:
loosed from Phar - aoh's bit - ter yoke Ja - cob's sons and daugh - ters,
all the win - ter of our sins, long and dark, is fly - ing
comes to glad - den faith - ful hearts, which with true af - fec - tion
for to - day a - mid his own he now stands, be - stow - ing
led them with un - moist - ened foot through the Red Sea wa - ters.
from his light, to whom we give laud and praise un - dy - ing.
wel - come in un - wea - ried strains Je - sus' res - ur - rec - tion!
God's true peace which ev - er - more pass - es hu - man know - ing.

273 Look there! the Christ

John Bennett, 1980

Music: *Petrus*, 8888 with refrain; William Albright, 1985

f
Look there! the Christ, our Bro-ther, comes re-
Good Je-sus Christ in-side his pain looked
Good Je-sus Christ, our Bro-ther, died in
Look there! the Christ, our Bro-ther, comes re-
splen-dent from the gal-lows tree and what he brings in
down Gol-go-tha's ston-y slope and let the blood flow
dark-est hurt up-on the tree to of-fer us the
splen-dent from the gal-lows tree and what he brings in
his hurt hands is life on life for you and me.
from his flesh to fill the springs of liv-ing hope.
worlds of light that live in-side the Trin-i-ty.
his hurt hands is life on life for you and me.

Refrain

Joy! (joy!) joy! (joy!) joy to the heart and all in this good day's dawn-ing!

ad. lib

Joy! (joy!) joy! (joy!) joy to the heart and all in this good day's dawn - ing!

sfz

f

274 Surrexit Christus hodie

The Lord is risen

Canon by Adam Gumpeltzhaimer (1559–1625)

1
2
3
Sur - re - xit Chris - tus ho - di - e, Al - le - lu -
The Lord is ris - en from the dead, Al - le - lu -
ia, al - le - lu - ia, al - le - lu - ia, al - le - lu - ia.
ia, al - le - lu - ia, al - le - lu - ia, al - le - lu - ia.

275 The strife is o'er

Finita jam sunt praelia

From *Symphonia Sirenum Selectarum*, Cologne, 1695; translation by Francis Pott, 1861

Music: *Victory*, 888 with refrain; William H. Monk, 1861;
adapted from Palestrina's *Magnificat Tertii Toni*, 1591

Al - le - lu - ia, al - le - lu - ia, al - le - lu - ia!
1 The strife is o'er, the bat - tle done, the vic - to - ry of life is won; the song of tri - umph has be - gun. Al - le - lu - ia!
2 The powers of death have done their worst, but Christ their le - gions hath dis - persed: let shouts of ho - ly joy out - burst. Al - le - lu - ia!
3 The three sad days are quick - ly sped, he ris - es glo - rious from the dead: all glo - ry to our ris - en Head! Al - le - lu - ia!
4 He closed the yawn - ing gates of hell, the bars from heaven's high por - tals fell; let hymns of praise his tri - umphs tell! Al - le - lu - ia!

5 Lord, by the stripes which wounded thee,
from death's dread sting thy servants free,
that we may live and sing to thee.
Alleluia!

After last stanza:
Al - le - lu - ia, al - le - lu - ia, al - le - lu - ia!

276 Good Christians all, rejoice and sing

Cyril A. Alington, 1925

Music: *Gelobt sei Gott*, 888 with refrain; Melchior Vulpius, 1609; harmony adapted slightly

1 Good Chris-tians all, re - joice and sing! Now is the
2 The Lord of life is risen this day; bring flowers of
3 Praise we in songs of vic - to - ry that Love, that
4 Your name we bless, O ris - en Lord, and sing to -

tri - umph of our King! To all the world glad news we bring:
song to strew his way; let all the world re - joice and say:
Life which can - not die, and sing with hearts up - lift - ed high:
day with one ac - cord the life laid down, the life re - stored:

Refrain
Al - le - lu - ia, al - le - lu - ia, al - le - lu - ia!
Al - le - lu - ia, al - le - lu - ia, al - le - lu - ia!
Al - le - lu - ia, al - le - lu - ia, al - le - lu - ia!

277 This joyful Eastertide

George R. Woodward, 1902

Music: *Vruechten*, 6767 with refrain;
melody in J. Oudaen's *David's Psalmen*, Amsterdam, 1685;
based on the song "De Liefde Voorgebracht"; harmony by Charles Wood, 1902

1 This joy-ful Eas-ter-tide, a-way with sin and sor-row! My Love, the Cru-ci-fied, has sprung to life this mor-row.
2 Death's flood has lost its chill, since Je-sus crossed the riv-er: Lord of all life, from ill my pass-ing life de-liv-er.
3 My flesh in hope shall rest, and for a sea-son slum-ber, till trump from east to west shall wake the dead in num-ber.
Refrain
Had Christ, who once was slain, ne'er burst his three-day pris-on, our faith had been in vain; but now is Christ a-ris-en, a-ris-en, a-

ris - en, a - ris - en.

278 The day of resurrection

John of Damascus, c. 750; translated by John Mason Neale, 1862; in the Eastern Church this hymn is sung at midnight on Easter Eve, during the lighting of candles.

Music: *Ave Maria, klarer*, 7676D; melody in *Gesangbuch . . . der Herzoglichen Wirtembergischen katholischen Hofkapelle*, 1784; harmony from *Appendix to Hymns Ancient and Modern*, 1868

1 The day of re - sur - rec - tion! Earth, tell it out a - broad!
2 Our hearts be pure from e - vil, that we may see a - right
3 Now let the heavens be joy - ful, let earth her song be - gin!

The Pass - o - ver of glad - ness, the Pass - o - ver of God!
the Lord in rays e - ter - nal of re - sur - rec - tion light;
The round world keep high tri - umph, and all that is there - in;

From death to life e - ter - nal, from earth un - to the sky,
and, listen - ing to his ac - cents, may hear so calm and plain
let all things seen and un - seen their notes in glad - ness blend,

our Christ has brought us o - ver with hymns of vic - to - ry.
his own "All hail!" and, hear - ing, may raise the vic - tor strain.
for Christ the Lord is ris - en, our joy that has no end.

279 Thine is the glory

A toi la gloire

Edmond Budry, 1884; translated by Richard B. Hoyle, 1923

Music: *Maccabaeus*, 10.11.11.11 with refrain; adapted from a chorus in Handel's *Judas Maccabaeus*, 1746, in Thomas Butts's *Harmonia Sacra*, c. 1753; edited by John Wilson, 1983

1 Thine is the glo - ry, ris - en, con - quering Son;
2 Lo, Je - sus meets us, ris - en from the tomb!
3 No more we doubt thee, glo - rious Prince of life;
end - less is the vic - tory thou o'er death hast won!
Lov - ing - ly he greets us, scat - ters fear and gloom;
life is naught with - out thee; aid us in our strife;
An - gels in bright rai - ment rolled the stone a - way,
let the Church with glad - ness hymns of tri - umph sing,
make us more than con - querors, through thy death - less love;
kept the fold - ed grave - clothes where thy bod - y lay.
for the Lord now liv - eth; death hath lost its sting!
bring us safe through Jor - dan to thy home a - bove.

Refrain
Thine is the glo - ry, ris - en, con - quering Son;
end - less is the vic - tory thou o'er death hast won!

280 Awake, arise, lift up your voice

Christopher Smart, 1765

Music: *Richmond*, 8686; melody by Thomas Haweis, 1792; adapted by Samuel Webbe (the younger), 1808

1 A - wake, a - rise, lift up your voice, let Eas - ter mu - sic swell;
2 Oh, with what glad - ness and sur - prise the saints their Sa - vior greet;
3 those hands of lib - eral love in - deed in in - fin - ite de - gree,
4 His en - em - ies had sealed the stone as Pi - late gave them leave,
re - joice in Christ, a - gain re - joice and on his prais - es dwell.
nor will they trust their ears and eyes but by his hands and feet,
those feet still free to move and bleed for mil - lions and for me.
lest dead and friend - less and a - lone he should their skill de - ceive.

5 O Dead, arise! O Friendless, stand
by seraphim adored!
O Solitude, again command
your host from heaven restored!

281 O sons and daughters, let us sing

O filii et filiae

Jean Tisserand (d. 1494); translation by John Mason Neale, 1851

Music: *O filii et filiae*, 888 with refrain; melody in *Airs sur les hymnes sacrez*, Paris, 1523; harmony by Elizabeth Poston, 1967

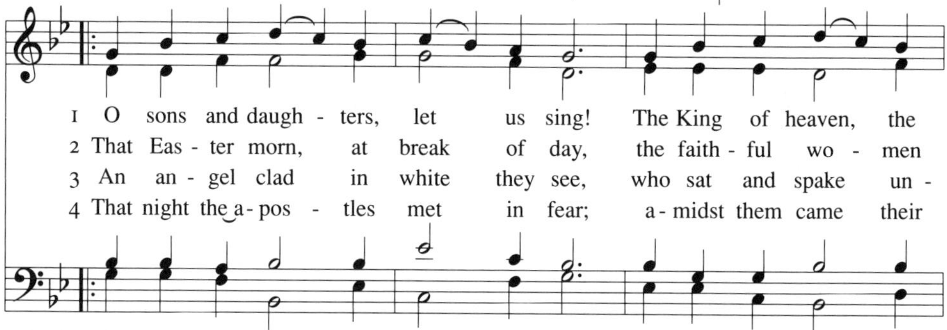

Al - le - lu - ia! Al - le - lu - ia! Al - le - lu - ia!

1 O sons and daugh - ters, let us sing! The King of heaven, the
2 That Eas - ter morn, at break of day, the faith - ful wo - men
3 An an - gel clad in white they see, who sat and spake un -
4 That night the a - pos - tles met in fear; a - midst them came their

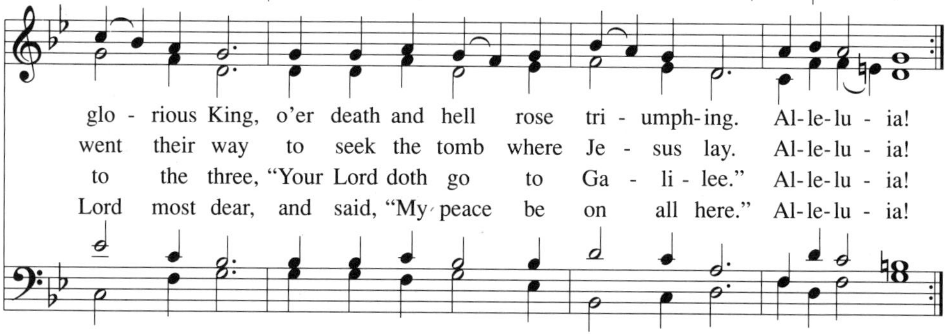

glo - rious King, o'er death and hell rose tri - umph - ing. Al-le-lu - ia!
went their way to seek the tomb where Je - sus lay. Al-le-lu - ia!
to the three, "Your Lord doth go to Ga - li - lee." Al-le-lu - ia!
Lord most dear, and said, "My peace be on all here." Al-le-lu - ia!

5 When Thomas first the tidings heard,
how they had seen the risen Lord,
he doubted the disciples' word.
Alleluia!

6 "My piercéd side, O Thomas, see;
my hands, my feet, I show to thee;
not faithless, but believing be."
Alleluia!

7 No longer Thomas then denied,
he saw the feet, the hands, the side;
"Thou art my Lord and God," he cried.
Alleluia!

8 How blest are they who have not seen,
and yet whose faith has constant been,
for they eternal life shall win.
Alleluia!

9 So, on this holy day of days,
with faith in God your voices raise
in laud and jubilee and praise.
Alleluia!

After last stanza:

Al - le - lu - ia! Al - le - lu - ia! Al - le - lu - ia!

282 Walking in a garden

Hilary Greenwood, b. 1929

Music: *Kaukana Kukkuu*, 65656575; Finnish folksong;
adapted and harmonized by Margaret Irwin-Brandon, 1989

1 Walk - ing in a gar - den at the close of day,
2 Walk - ing in a gar - den where the Lord had gone,
3 Walk - ing in a gar - den at the break of day,
A - dam tried to hide him when he heard God say:
three of the di - sci - ples, Pe - ter, James, and John;
Ma - ry asked the gar - dener where the bod - y lay;
"Why are you so fright - ened, why are you a - fraid?
they were ve - ry wear - y, could not keep a - wake,
but he turned to - wards her, smiled at her and said:
You have brought the win - ter in, made the flow - ers fade."
while the Lord was kneel - ing there, pray - ing for their sake.
"Ma - ry, spring is here to stay, on - ly death is dead."
(♭)

283 Cristo vive

Christ is risen

Nicolas Martinez, 1960; translated by Fred Kaan, 1972

Music: *Argentina (Sosa)*, 8787D; Pablo D. Sosa, 1960

1 ¡Cris-to vi - ve, fue-ra el llan - to, los la - men - tos y el pe - sar!
2 Que si Cris - to no vi - vie - ra va - na fue - ra nues-tra fe;
1 Christ is ris - en, Christ is liv - ing, dry your tears, be un - a - fraid!
2 If the Lord had nev - er ris - en, we'd have noth - ing to be - lieve;
Ni la muer - te ni el se - pul - cro lo han po - di - do su - je - tar.
mas se cum - ple su pro - me - sa: 'Por - que vi - vo, vi - vi - réis.'
Death and dark - ness could not hold him, nor the tomb in which he lay.
but his prom - ise can be trust - ed: "You will live, be - cause I live."
No bus - quéls en - tre los muer - tos al que siem - pre ha de vi - vir,
Si en A - dán en - tró la muer - te, por Je - sús la vi - da en - tró;
Do not look a - mong the dead for one who lives for - ev - er more;
As we share the death of A - dam, so in Christ we live a - gain;
¡Cris - to vi - ve, es - tas nue - vas por do - quier de - jad o - ir.
no te - máis, el triun - fo es vues - tro: ¡El Se - ñor re - su - ci - tó!
tell the world that Christ is ris - en, make it known he goes be - fore.
death has lost its sting and ter - ror, Christ the Lord has come to reign.

3 *Si es verdad que de la muerte*
el pecado es aguijón,
no temáis pues Jesucristo
nos da vida y salvación.
Gracias demos al Dios Padre
que nos da seguridad,
que quien cree en Jesucristo
vive por la eternidad.

3 Death has lost its old dominion,
let the world rejoice and shout!
Christ, the firstborn of the living,
gives us life and leads us out.
Let us thank our God, who causes
hope to spring up from the ground.
Christ is risen, Christ is giving
life eternal, life profound.

284 Look, ye saints, the sight is glorious

Thomas Kelly, 1809

Music: *Victor's Crown*, 878747; Horatio Parker, 1893

1 Look, ye saints, the sight is glo - rious, see the Man of Sor - rows now, from the fight re - turned vic - to - rious, ev - ery knee to him shall bow. Crown him! Crown him! Crowns be - fit the Vic - tor's brow.
2 Crown the Sa - vior, an - gels, crown him, rich the tro - phies Je - sus brings; in the seat of power en - throne him while the vault of heav - en rings. Crown him! Crown him! Crown the Sa - vior King of kings.
3 Sin - ners in de - ri - sion crowned him, mock - ing thus the Sa - vior's claim, saints and an - gels throng a - round him, own his ti - tle, praise his name. Crown him! Crown him! Spread a - broad the Vic - tor's fame.
4 Hark, those bursts of ac - cla - ma - tion, hark, those loud, tri - umph - ant chords; Je - sus takes the high - est sta - tion; O what joy the sight af - fords. Crown him! Crown him! King of kings and Lord of lords!

285 Look, ye saints, the sight is glorious

Thomas Kelly, 1809

Music: *Bryn Calfaria*, 878747 extended; melody by William Owen, 1852; harmony from *Hymns for Church and School*, 1964

1 Look, ye saints, the sight is glo - rious, see the Man of Sor-rows now,
2 Crown the Sa - vior, an-gels, crown him, rich the tro-phies Je - sus brings;
3 Sin - ners in de - ri-sion crowned him, mock-ing thus the Sa-vior's claim,
4 Hark, those bursts of ac - cla - ma - tion, hark, those loud, tri - umph-ant chords;
from the fight re - turned vic - to - rious, ev - ery knee to him shall bow.
in the seat of power en - throne him while the vault of heav - en rings.
saints and an - gels throng a - round him, own his ti - tle, praise his name.
Je - sus takes the high - est sta - tion; O what joy the sight af - fords.
Crown him! Crown him! Crown him! Crown him! Crown him! Crown him!
Crown him! Crown him! Crown him! Crown him! Crown him! Crown him!
Crown him! Crown him! Crown him! Crown him! Crown him! Crown him!
Crown him! Crown him! Crown him! Crown him! Crown him! Crown him!
Crowns be - fit the Vic - tor's brow. Crowns be - fit the Vic - tor's brow.
Crown the Sa - vior King of kings. Crown the Sa - vior King of kings.
Spread a - broad the Vic - tor's fame. Spread a - broad the Vic - tor's fame.
King of kings and Lord of lords! King of kings and Lord of lords!

286 Hail the day that sees him rise

Charles Wesley, 1739

Music: *Llanfair*, 7777 with refrains; melody probably by Robert Williams, 1817; harmony by John Roberts, 1837

1 Hail the day that sees him rise,
2 There the glo - rious tri - umph waits;
3 See! the heaven its Lord re - ceives,
4 See! he lifts his hands a - bove;
Al - le - lu - ia!
glo - rious to his na - tive skies;
lift your heads, e - ter - nal gates!
yet he loves the earth he leaves;
See! he shows the prints of love:
Al - le - lu - ia!
Christ, a - while to mor - tals given,
wide un - fold the ra - diant scene;
though re - turn - ing to his throne,
Hark! his gra - cious lips be - stow,
Al - le - lu - ia!
Unison
en - ters now the high - est heaven!
take the King of glo - ry in!
still he calls the world his own.
bless - ings on his Church be - low.
Al - le - lu - ia!

5 Lord beyond our mortal sight, Alleluia!
raise our hearts to reach thy height, Alleluia!
there thy face unclouded see, Alleluia!
find our heaven of heavens in thee. Alleluia!

Resurrection and Ascension

See also:

Alleluia, alleluia, give thanks to the risen Lord, no. 18
At the Lamb's high feast we sing, no. 395
At the name of Jesus, no. 19
Camina, pueblo de Dios, no. 564
Christ is alive, no. 542
Crown him with many crowns, no. 14
Jesus lives, no. 561
Jesus shall reign, no. 16
Lift high the cross, no. 556
Most glorious Lord of life, no. 369
Name of all majesty, no. 50
Rejoice, the Lord is King, no. 44
The head that once was crowned with thorns, no. 569
We know that Christ is raised, no. 385

287 O Holy Spirit, by whose breath

Veni Creator Spiritus

Medieval, 9th or 10th century; translated by John Webster Grant, 1971

Music: *Komm, Gott Schöpfer*, 8888; adaptation of *Veni Creator Spiritus* in Joseph Klug's *Geistliche Lieder*, 1533; harmony adapted from Seth Calvisius, 1597

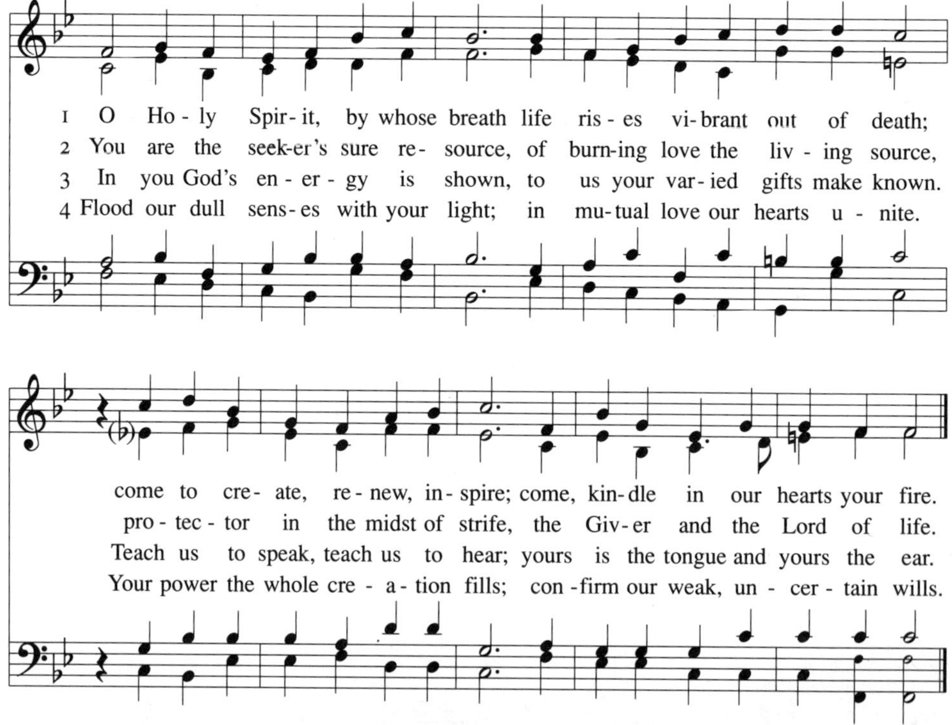
1 O Ho - ly Spir - it, by whose breath life ris - es vi - brant out of death;
2 You are the seek-er's sure re - source, of burn-ing love the liv - ing source,
3 In you God's en - er - gy is shown, to us your var - ied gifts make known.
4 Flood our dull sens - es with your light; in mu - tual love our hearts u - nite.
come to cre - ate, re - new, in - spire; come, kin - dle in our hearts your fire.
pro - tec - tor in the midst of strife, the Giv - er and the Lord of life.
Teach us to speak, teach us to hear; yours is the tongue and yours the ear.
Your power the whole cre - a - tion fills; con - firm our weak, un - cer - tain wills.

5 From inner strife grant us release;
turn nations to the ways of peace.
To fuller life your people bring
that as one body we may sing:

6 Praise to the Father, Christ the Word,
and to the Spirit: God the Lord,
to whom all honor, glory be
both now and for eternity.

288 Like the murmur of the dove's song

Carl P. Daw, Jr., 1982

Music: *Bridegroom*, 8787 with refrain; Peter Cutts, 1969

1 Like the mur - mur of the dove's song, like the chal - lenge of her
2 To the mem - bers of Christ's Bo - dy, to the branch - es of the
3 With the heal - ing of di - vi - sion, with the cease - less voice of
flight, like the vig - or of the wind's rush, like the
vine, to the Church in faith as - sem - bled, to our
prayer, with the power to love and wit - ness, with the
new flame's ea - ger might: come, Ho - ly Spir - it, come.
midst as gift and sign: come, Ho - ly Spir - it, come.
peace be - yond com - pare: come, Ho - ly Spir - it, come.

289 Come, Holy Ghost, our souls inspire

Veni Creator Spiritus

Medieval, 9th or 10th century; translated by John Cosin, 1627, and later included in the 1662 *Book of Common Prayer*; since the 11th century this hymn has been sung at ordinations

Music: *Veni Creator Spiritus*, 8888; plainsong; accompaniment from *Hymnal for Colleges and Schools*, 1956

1 Come, Ho - ly Ghost, our souls in - spire, and light - en with cel - es - tial fire.
2 Thy bless - ed unc - tion from a - bove is com - fort, life, and fire of love.
3 A - noint and cheer our soil - ed face with the a - bun - dance of thy grace.
4 Teach us to know the Fa - ther, Son, and thee, of both, to be but One,
Thou the a - noint - ing Spir - it art, who dost thy seven-fold gifts im - part.
En - a - ble with per - pe - tual light the dull-ness of our blind-ed sight.
Keep far our foes, give peace at home: where thou art guide, no ill can come.
that through the a - ges all a - long, this may be our end - less song:
5 Praise to thy e - ter - nal mer - it, Fa - ther, Son, and Ho - ly Spir - it. A - men.

290 The Church's one foundation

Samuel John Stone, 1866, with revisions by Laurence Hull Stookey, 1983

Music: *Aurelia*, 7676D; Samuel Sebastian Wesley, 1864

1 The Chur-ch's one foun - da - tion is Je - sus Christ our Lord;
2 Called forth from ev - ery na - tion, yet one o'er all the earth;
3 Though with a scorn-ful won - der the world sees us op - pressed,
4 Mid toil and tri - bu - la - tion, and tu - mult of our war,
we are his new cre - a - tion by wa - ter and the Word;
our char - ter of sal - va - tion: one Lord, one faith, one birth.
by schi - sms rent a - sun - der, by her - e - sies dis - tressed,
we wait the con - sum - ma - tion of peace for ev - er - more;
from heaven he came and sought us that we might ev - er be
One ho - ly name pro - fess - ing and at one ta - ble fed,
yet saints their watch are keep - ing; their cry goes up, "How long?"
till with the vi - sion glo - rious our long - ing eyes are blest,
his liv - ing ser - vant peo - ple, by his own death set free.
to one hope al - ways press - ing, by Christ's own Spir - it led.
But soon the night of weep - ing shall be the morn of song.
and the great Church vic - to - rious shall be the Church at rest.

5 We now on earth have union
with God the Three in One,
and share through faith communion
with those whose rest is won.
O happy ones, and holy!
Lord, give us grace that we
like them, the meek and lowly,
on high may dwell with thee.

291 Glorious things of thee are spoken

John Newton, 1779

Music: *Austria*, 8787D; Franz Joseph Haydn, 1797, possibly based on a Croatian folksong; for the national hymn of Austria

These words can also be sung to *Abbot's Leigh*, no. 513.

1 Glor - ious things of thee are spok - en, Zi - on, ci - ty of our God;
2 See! The streams of liv - ing wa - ters, spring - ing from e - ter - nal love,
3 Round each hab - i - ta - tion hov - ering, see the cloud and fire ap - pear
4 Sa - vior, if of Zi - on's ci - ty we through grace a part may claim,
he whose word can - not be brok - en formed thee for his own a - bode:
well sup - ply thy sons and daugh - ters, and all fear of want re - move.
for a glo - ry and a co - vering, show - ing that the Lord is near.
let the world de - ride or pi - ty, we will glo - ry in thy name.
on the Rock of Ag - es found - ed, what can shake thy sure re - pose?
Who can faint, when such a ri - ver e - ver will their thirst as - suage—
Thus de - riv - ing from our ban - ner light by night and shade by day,
Fad - ing is all world - ly plea - sure — all earth's boast - ed pomp and show;
With sal - va - tion's walls sur - round - ed, thou may'st smile at all thy foes.
grace which, like the Lord, the giv - er, ne - ver fails from age to age?
safe we feed up - on the man - na which God gives us when we pray.
sol - id joys and last - ing trea - sure none but Zi - on's chil - dren know.

292 God sends us the Spirit

Tom Colvin, 1969

Music: *Natomah*, 12.9.12.9 with refrain; Gonja folk melody adapted by Tom Colvin, 1969

1 God sends us the Spirit to befriend and help us, recreate and guide us, Spirit-Friend. Spirit who enlivens, sanctifies, enlightens, sets us free, is now our Spirit-Friend.
2 Darkened roads are clearer, heavy burdens lighter, when we're walking with our Spirit-Friend. Now we need not fear the powers of the darkness. None can overcome our Spirit-Friend.
3 Now we are God's people, bonded by your presence, agents of your purpose, Spirit-Friend. Lead us forward ever, slipping backward never, to your remade world, our Spirit-Friend.
Refrain
Spirit of our Father, Spirit-Friend. Spirit of our Jesu, Spirit-Friend. Spirit of God's people, Spirit-Friend.
*Hand claps

293 Holy Spirit, ever dwelling

Timothy Rees, 1922

Music: *Salisbury*, 8787D; Herbert Howells, 1964

These words can also be sung to *Abbot's Leigh*, no. 513.

1 Ho - ly Spir - it, ev - er dwell - ing in the
2 Ho - ly Spir - it, ev - er liv - ing as the
3 Ho - ly Spir - it, ev - er work - ing through the
glo - rious realms of light; Ho - ly Spir - it, ev - er
Chur - ch's ver - y life; Ho - ly Spir - it, ev - er
Chur - ch's min - is - try; quicken - ing, strengthen - ing, and ab -
brood - ing o'er a world of gloom and night;
striv - ing through us in a cease - less strife;
solv - ing, set - ting cap - tive sin - ners free;
Ho - ly Spir - it, ev - er rais - ing those of earth to
Ho - ly Spir - it, ev - er form - ing in the Church the
Ho - ly Spir - it, ev - er bind - ing age to age and

thrones on high;
mind of Christ;
soul to soul,
liv - ing, life - im - part - ing
you we praise with end - less
in com - mu - nion nev - er -
Spir - it, you we praise and mag - ni - fy.
wor - ship for your gifts and fruits un - priced.
end - ing, you we wor - ship and ex - tol.

294 I love thy kingdom, Lord

Timothy Dwight, 1800

Music: *St. Thomas* (*Williams*), 6686; melody in Aaron Williams's *New Universal Psalmodist*, 1770

1 I love thy king - dom, Lord, the house of thine a - bode,
2 I love thy Church, O God: her walls be - fore thee stand,
3 For her my tears shall fall, for her my prayers as - cend;
4 Be - yond my high - est joy I prize her heaven - ly ways,
the Church our blest Re - deem - er saved with his own pre - cious blood.
dear as the ap - ple of thine eye, and grav - en on thy hand.
to her my cares and toils be given, till toils and cares shall end.
her sweet com-mun - ion, sol - emn vows, her hymns of love and praise.

5 Sure as thy truth shall last,
to Zion shall be given
the brightest glories earth can yield,
and brighter bliss of heaven.

295 I danced in the morning

Sydney Carter, 1963, based on "Tomorrow shall be my dancing day"

Music: *Simple Gifts*, irregular meter with refrain; 19th-century American Shaker melody; harmony by Margaret W. Mealy, 1984

1 I danced in the morn - ing when the world was be - gun, and I
2 I danced for the scribe and the phar - i - see, but they
3 I danced on the Sab - bath and I cured the lame; the
4 I danced on a Fri - day when the sky turned black; it's
danced in the moon and the stars and the sun, and I
would not dance, and they would not fol - low me. I
ho - ly peo - ple said it was a shame. They
hard to dance with the dev - il on your back. They
came down from heav - en and I danced on the earth, at
danced for the fish - er - men, for James and John, they
whipped and they stripped and they hung me on high, and they
bur - ied my bod - y and they thought I'd gone, but

Beth - le - hem I had my birth.
came with me and the dance went on.
left me there on a cross to die.
I am the dance and I still go on.
Refrain
Dance, then, wher - ev-er you may be, I am the Lord of the dance, said he, and I'll
lead you all, wher - ev- er you may be, and I'll lead you all in the dance, said he.

Hand claps during refrain:

5 They cut me down and I leapt up high;
I am the dance that'll never, never die:
I'll live in you if you'll live in me —
I am the Lord of the dance, said he.

Refrain

296 For all the saints

William Walsham How, 1864

Music: *Sine nomine*, 10.10.10 with refrain; Ralph Vaughan Williams, 1906

1 For all the saints, who from their la - bors rest,
2 You were their rock, their for - tress, and their might:
3 O may your sol - diers, faith - ful, true, and bold,
4 O blest com - mun - ion, fel - low - ship di - vine!
7 But lo! there breaks a yet more glo - rious day; the
8 From earth's wide bounds, from o - cean's far - thest coast, through
all who by faith be - fore the world con - fessed, your
you, Lord, their cap - tain in the well - fought fight;
fight as the saints who no - bly fought of old, and
We feeb - ly strug - gle, they in glo - ry shine; yet
saints tri - umph - ant rise in bright ar - ray; as
gates of pearl streams in the count - less host,
name, O Je - sus, be for - ev - er blest. Al -
you, in the dark - ness drear, their one true light. Al -
win, with them, the vic - tors' crown of gold. Al -
all are one with - in your great de - sign. Al -
God to glo - ry calls them all a - way. Al -
sing - ing to Fa - ther, Son, and Ho - ly Ghost: Al -

le - lu - ia, al - le - lu - ia!
le - lu - ia, al - le - lu - ia!
le - lu - ia, al - le - lu - ia!
le - lu - ia, al - le - lu - ia!
(Stanzas 5 and 6 follow.)
le - lu - ia, al - le - lu - ia!
le - lu - ia, al - le - lu - ia!
5 And when the strife is fierce, the war- fare long, steals on the ear the dis- tant tri - umph song, and hearts are brave a - gain and arms are strong. Al - le - lu - ia, al - le- lu - ia!
6 The gold - en eve - ning bright - ens in the west; soon, soon to faith - ful war-riors comes their rest; sweet is the calm of par - a - dise the blest. Al - le - lu - ia, al - le- lu - ia!
D.C. for stanzas 7 and 8

297 The first one ever, O ever to know

Linda Willberger Egan, 1980

Music: *Ballad*, irregular meter; Linda Willberger Egan, 1980

Unison
1 The first one ev-er, O ev-er to know of the birth of
2 The first one ev-er, O ev-er to know of Mes - si - ah,
3 The first ones ev-er, O ev-er to know of the ris - ing of
Je-sus was the Maid Ma - ry, was Ma - ry the Maid of
Je-sus, when he said, "I am he," was the Sa - mar - i-tan wo-man who
Je-sus, his glo - ry to be, were Ma - ry, Jo - an - na, and
Gal - i - lee, and bless-ed is she, is she who be- lieves. O
drew from the well, and bless-ed is she, is she who per- ceives. O
Mag - da - lene, and bless-ed are they, are they who see. O
bless-ed is she who be- lieves in the Lord, O bless - ed is she who be -
bless-ed is she who per- ceives the Lord, O bless - ed is she who per -
bless-ed are they who see the Lord, O bless - ed are they who
lieves. She was Ma - ry the Maid of Gal - i -
ceives. 'Twas the Sa - mar - i - tan wo - man who drew from the
see. They were Ma - ry, Jo - an - na, and Mag - da -

lee, and bless - ed is she, is she who be - lieves.
well, and bless - ed is she, is she who per - ceives.
lene, and bless - ed are they, are they who see.

298 Give us the wings of faith

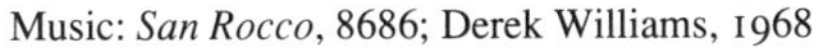

Isaac Watts, 1707

Music: *San Rocco*, 8686; Derek Williams, 1968

1 Give us the wings of faith to rise with - in the veil, and
2 We ask them whence their vic - tory came; they, with u - nit - ed
3 They marked the foot - steps that he trod, his zeal in - spired their
4 Our ris - en Lead - er claims our praise for his own pat - tern

see the saints a - bove, how great their joys, how
breath, as - cribe their con - quest to the Lamb, their
quest; and fol - lowing their in - car - nate God, they
given, while the long cloud of wit - ness - es show

bright their glo - ries be.
tri - umph to his death.
reached the pro - mised rest.
the same path to heaven.

299 Myrrh-bearing Mary

Rae Whitney, 1981

Music: *Myrrhophores*, 10.10.10.10; David Hurd, 1990

1 Myrrh-bear-ing Ma-ry from Mag - da - la came, seek-ing her Je-sus, with
2 Myrrh-bear-ing Ma-ry to Be - tha - ny came, seek-ing her Je - sus who
3 Myrrh-bear-ing Ma-ry to Cal - va - ry came, seek-ing her Je - sus who
4 Myrrh-bear-ing Ma-ry to death's gar-den came, seek-ing her Je - sus who'd
spir - it a - flame; he had com-mand-ed her sick-ness de - part,
called her by name; there she a - noint-ed his feet and his head
hung there in shame; and as the care-less and heed-less passed by,
borne the world's blame; heart-sick, she stood, till she heard the Lord's voice:
she now would thank him for new - ness of heart.
with pre - cious oils that were meant for the dead.
hope-less and help-less she watched her Lord die.
"Ma-ry!" he said, "I am ris - en; re - - -
1–3

4
joice!"

300 Ye holy angels bright

Richard Baxter, 1672, and others

Music: *Darwall's 148th*, 66664444; melody by John Darwall, 1770

1 Ye holy angels bright,
who wait at God's right hand,
or through the realms of light
fly at your Lord's command,
assist our song,
for else the theme
too high doth seem
for mortal tongue.

2 Ye blessed souls at rest,
who ran this earthly race
and now, from sin released,
behold the Savior's face,
God's praises sound,
as in his sight
with sweet delight
ye do abound.

3 Ye saints, who toil below,
adore your heavenly King,
and onward as ye go
some joyful anthem sing;
take what he gives
and praise him still,
through good or ill,
who ever lives!

4 My soul, bear thou thy part,
triumph in God above:
and with a well-tuned heart
sing thou the songs of love!
Let all thy days
till life shall end,
whate'er God send,
be filled with praise.

301 Ye watchers and ye holy ones

Athelstan Riley, 1906

Music: *Lasst uns erfreuen*, 8888 with refrains; later form of a melody in *Auserlesene Catholische Geistliche Kirchengesänge*, Cologne, 1623

Unison
1 Ye watch - ers and ye ho - ly ones, bright ser-aphs, cher - u - bim and thrones, raise the glad strain, Al - le - lu - ia! Cry out, do - min-ions, prince-doms, powers, vir - tues, arch - an - gels, an - gels' choirs,
2 O high - er than the cher - u - bim, more glo-rious than the ser - a - phim, lead their prais - es, Al - le - lu - ia! Thou bear - er of the e - ter - nal Word, most gra-cious, mag - ni - fy the Lord,
3 Re - spond, ye souls in end - less rest, ye pa - tri - archs and pro-phets blest, Al - le - lu - ia, al - le - lu - ia! Ye ho - ly twelve, ye mar - tyrs strong, all saints tri - umph-ant, raise the song,
4 O friends, in glad - ness let us sing, cel - es - tial an-thems e - cho - ing, Al - le - lu - ia, al - le - lu - ia! From now through all e - ter - ni - ty, praise God the bless - ed Tri - ni - ty.
Refrain
Al - le - lu - ia, al - le -

lu - ia, al - le - lu - ia, al - le - lu - ia, al - le - lu - ia!

302 Who are these like stars appearing

Wer sind die vor Gottes Throne

Theobald Heinrich Schenk, 1719; translated by Frances E. Cox, 1841

Music: *All Saints*, 878777; adapted in 1861 by William H. Monk, from a chorale in *Geistreiches Gesangbuch*, Darmstadt, 1698

1 Who are these like stars ap - pear - ing, these, be - fore God's throne who stand?
2 Who are these of daz - zling bright-ness, these in God's own truth ar - rayed,
3 These are they who have con - tend - ed for their Sa - vior's hon - or long,
4 These are they whose hearts were riv - en, sore with woe and an - guish tried,

Each a gold - en crown is wear - ing; who are all this glo - rious band?
clad in robes of pur - est white - ness, robes whose lust - er ne'er shall fade,
wres-tling on till life was end - ed, follow - ing not the sin - ful throng;
who in prayer full oft have striv - en with the God they glo - ri - fied;

Al - le - lu - ia! hark, they sing, prais - ing loud their heaven - ly King.
ne'er be touched by time's rude hand? Whence comes all this glo - rious band?
these, who well the fight sus - tained, tri - umph by the Lamb have gained.
now, their pain - ful con - flict o'er, God has bid them weep no more.

5 These, like priests, have watched and waited,
offering up to Christ their will,
soul and body consecrated,
day and night they serve him still.
Now in God's most holy place,
blest they stand before his face.

303 Woman in the night

"New Disciples," Brian Wren, 1982

Music: *Woman in the Night*, 5555D with refrain; Alfred V. Fedak, 1989

1 Wo-man in the night, spent from giv-ing birth,
2 Wo-man at the well, ques-tion the Mes-siah;
3 Wo-man in the house, nur-tured to be meek,
4 Wo-men on the hill, stand when men have fled!
guard our pre-cious light: peace is on the earth!
find your friends and tell; drink your heart's de-sire!
leave your sec-ond place: lis-ten, think, and speak!
Christ needs lov-ing still, though your hope is dead.
Wo-man in the crowd, creep-ing up be-hind,
Wo-man at the feast, let the righ-teous stare;
Wo-men on the road, wel-comed and re-stored,
Wo-men in the dawn, care and spi-ces bring;

touch-ing is al - lowed: seek and you will find!
come and go in peace; love him with your hair!
trav - el far and wide; wit-ness to the Lord!
ear - li - est to mourn; ear - li - est to sing!
3
3
Refrain
Come and join the song, wom - en, chil - dren, men.
Je - sus makes us free to live a - gain!

304 Rejoice in God's saints

Fred Pratt Green, 1973, 1977

Music: *Laudate Dominum*, 10.10.11.11; arranged in 1916 by C. Hubert H. Parry from his anthem "Hear my words" of 1897

These words can also be sung to *Hanover*, no. 6.

1 Re - joice in God's saints, to - day and all days!
2 Some march with e - vents to turn them God's way;
3 Re - joice in those saints, un - praised and un - known,
4 Re - joice in God's saints, to - day and all days!
A world with - out saints for - gets how to praise.
some need to with - draw, the bet - ter to pray;
who bear some - one's cross, or shoul - der their own:
A world with - out saints for - gets how to praise.
Their faith in ac - quir - ing the hab - it of prayer,
some car - ry the gos - pel through fire and through flood:
they shame our com - plain - ing, our com - forts, our cares:
In lov - ing, in liv - ing, they prove it is true:
their depth of a - dor - ing, Lord, help us to share.
our world is their par - ish: their pur - pose is God.
what pa - tience in car - ing, what cour - age is theirs!
the way of self - giv - ing, Lord, leads us to you.

305 Sing we of the blessed Mother

George B. Timms, 1975

Music: *Rustington*, 8787D; C. Hubert H. Parry, 1897

1 Sing we of the bless - ed Mo-ther who re-ceived the an - gel's word,
2 Sing we, too, of Ma - ry's sor-rows, of the sword that pierced her through,
3 Sing a - gain the joys of Ma - ry when she saw the ris - en Lord,
4 Sing the chief-est joy of Ma - ry when on earth her work was done,
and o - be - dient to the sum-mons bore in love the in - fant Lord;
when be - neath the cross of Je - sus she his weight of suf - fering knew,
and in prayer, with Christ's a - pos - tles, wait - ed on his pro - mised word;
and the Lord of all cre - a - tion brought her to his heav - enly home;
sing we of the joys of Ma - ry at whose breast the child was fed
looked up - on her Son and Sa - vior reign-ing high on Cal - vary's tree,
from on high the blaz-ing glo - ry of the Spir - it's pres - ence came,
Vir - gin Mo - ther, Ma - ry bless-ed, raised on high and crowned with grace,
who is Son of God e - ter - nal and the ev - er - last - ing Bread.
saw the price of our re - demp - tion paid to set the sin - ner free.
heaven - ly breath of God's own be - ing, man - i - fest through wind and flame.
may your Son, the world's Re - deem - er, grant us all to see his face.

306 Sing of Mary

Roland Ford Palmer, 1938

Music: *Raquel*, 8787D; Skinner Chavez-Melo, 1985

1 Sing of Ma - ry, pure and low - ly, maid on whom her God has smiled; sing of God's own Son most ho - ly, who be - came her lit - tle
2 Sing of Je - sus, son of Ma - ry, in the home at Na - za - reth, toil and la - bor can - not wear - y love en - dur - ing un - to
3 Joy - ful mo - ther, full of glad - ness, in your arms your Lord was borne. Mourn - ful mo - ther, full of sad - ness, all your heart with pain was

child. Fair - est child of fair - est mo - ther, God the
death. Con - stant was the love he gave her, though he
torn. Glo - rious mo - ther, now re - ward - ed with a
Lord who came to earth, Word made flesh, our ver - y
went forth from her side, forth to preach, and heal, and
crown at Je - sus' hand, age to age your name re -
bro - ther, takes our na - ture by his birth.
suf - fer, till on Cal - va - ry he died.
cord - ed shall be blest in ev - ery land.

307 Lord, have mercy

Kyrie eleison

Music: Adapted from *Litany of the Saints* by Richard Proulx, 1971

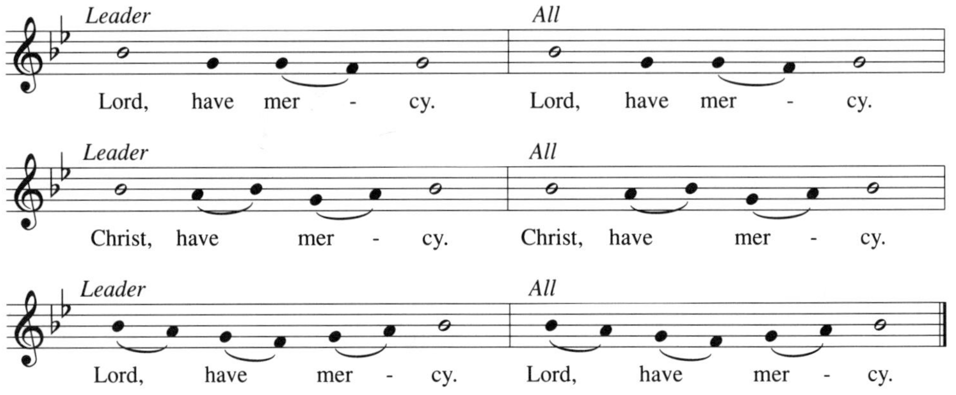
Leader
All
Lord, have mer - cy. Lord, have mer - cy.
Leader
All
Christ, have mer - cy. Christ, have mer - cy.
Leader
All
Lord, have mer - cy. Lord, have mer - cy.

308 Lord, have mercy upon us

Kyrie eleison

Music: Kenneth Leighton, *Communion Service in D*, 1965

Lord, have mer - cy up - on us. Lord, have mer - cy up -

on us. Lord, have mer - cy up - on us.

Christ, have mer - cy up - on us. Christ, have mer - cy up - on us.

Christ, have mer - cy up - on us.

Lord, have mer - cy up - on us. Lord, have mer - cy up - on us.

Lord, have mer - cy up - on us.

309 Kyrie eleison

Music: Canon from Suriname

1
Ky - ri - e, ky - ri - e e - lei - son
2
Chri - ste, Chri - ste e - lei - son
3
Ky - ri - e, ky - ri - e e - lei - son.

310 Kyrie eleison

Music: *Missa orbis factor*

• *Threefold version:*

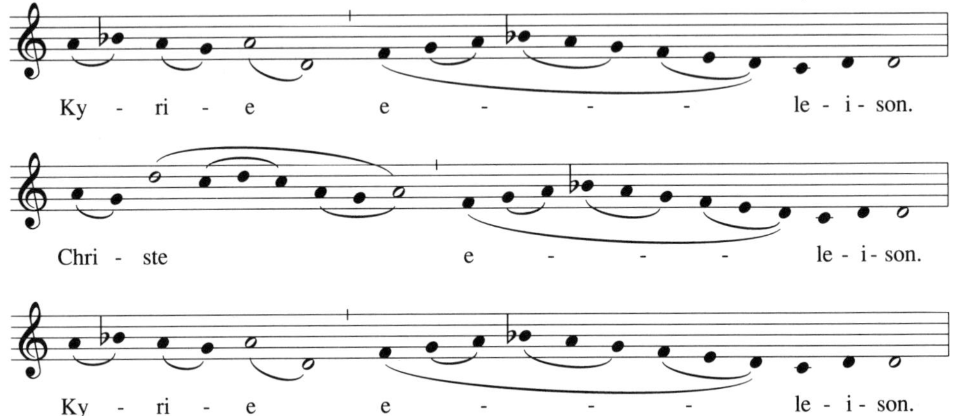
Ky - ri - e e - - - le - i - son.
Chri - ste e - - - le - i - son.
Ky - ri - e e - - - le - i - son.

• *For a sixfold Kyrie, each line is sung first by a leader and then repeated by everyone.*

• *For a ninefold Kyrie, each line is sung three times, but the ninth line is sung as follows:*

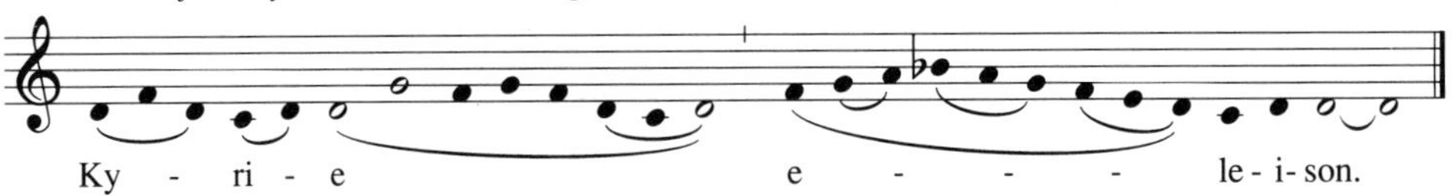
Ky - ri - e e - - - le - i - son.

311 Holy God

Trisagion

Music: Adapted from Alexander Archangelsky (1846–1924), in *The Hymnal 1982*

This may be sung three times.

Ho - ly God, Ho - ly and might - y,
Ho - ly im - mor - tal One, have mer - cy up - on us.

312 All glory be to God on high

Gloria in excelsis Deo

Paraphrased by F. Bland Tucker, 1977

Music: *Allein Gott in der Höh*, 8787887; melody adapted by Nikolaus Decius from an Easter *Gloria in excelsis Deo*, 1539; harmony by Heironymus Praetorius, 1604

1 All glo - ry be to God on high, and
2 O Lamb of God, Lord Je - sus Christ, whom
3 You on - ly are the Ho - ly One, who
peace on earth from heav - en, and God's good will un -
God the Fa - ther gave us, you for the world were
came for our sal - va - tion, and on - ly you are
fail - ing - ly be to all peo - ple giv - en. We
sac - ri - ficed up - on the cross to save us; as
God's true Son, who was be - fore cre - a - tion. You
bless, we wor - ship you, we raise for your great glo - ry
now you sit at God's right hand and we for judg - ment
on - ly, Christ, as Lord we own and, with the Spir - it,
thanks and praise, O God, Al - might - y Fa - ther.
there must stand, have mer - cy, Lord, up - on us.
you a - lone share in the Fa - ther's glo - ry.

313 Glory to God in the highest

Gloria in excelsis Deo

Music: John Rutter, *Communion Service*, 1972

f
Glo-ry to God in the high-est,
and peace to his peo-ple on earth.
mf
Lord God,
heaven-ly King, al-migh-ty God and Fa-ther,
f
we wor-ship
you, we give you thanks, we praise you for your glo-ry.
dim.

p
Lord Je - sus Christ, on - ly Son of the Fa- ther,
p
p
3
Lord God, Lamb of God, you take a - way the sin of the
3
3
3
world: have mer - cy on us; you are seat - ed at the right

hand of the Fa - ther: re - ceive our prayer. For
you a - lone are the Ho - ly One, you a - lone are the
Lord, you a - lone are the Most High,
Je - sus Christ, with the Ho - ly Spi - rit,

f cresc.
broaden
ff
in the glo-ry of God the Fa - ther. A - men.
f cresc.
ff
broaden
f cresc.
ff

314 Holy, holy, holy

Sanctus

Music: Melody adapted by J. S. Bach, 1726, from a medieval Sanctus melody; further adapted by Regina H. Fryxell, 1958, and others; harmony by Russell Schulz-Widmar, 1990

Unison
Ho - ly, ho - ly, ho - ly God of power and might,
heaven and earth are full of your glo - ry. Ho - san - na in the high - est.
Blest is the One who comes in the name of our God. Ho - san-na in the high - est.

315 Holy, holy, holy

Sanctus

Music: Richard Proulx, *Community Mass*, 1971, 1977

Ho-ly, ho-ly, ho - ly Lord, God of pow-er and might, heaven and
earth are full of your glo-ry. Ho - san - na in the high - est, ho -
san-na in the high-est. Blest is he who comes in the name of the
Lord. Ho - san - na in the high - est, ho - san-na in the high-est.

316 Holy, holy, holy

Sanctus

Music: Richard Proulx, *Community Mass*, 1971, 1977

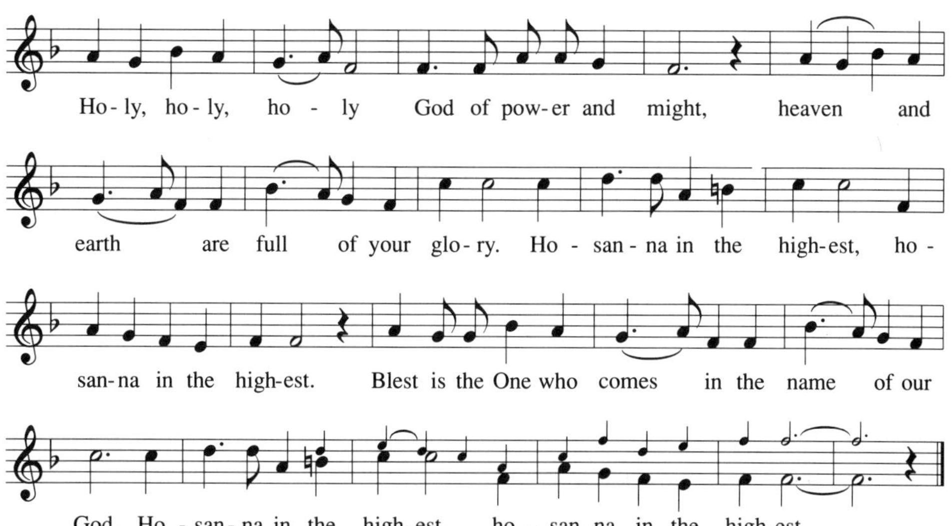
Ho-ly, ho-ly, ho - ly God of pow-er and might, heaven and
earth are full of your glo-ry. Ho - san-na in the high-est, ho -
san-na in the high-est. Blest is the One who comes in the name of our
God. Ho - san-na in the high-est, ho - san-na in the high-est.

The accompaniment is at no. 315.

317 Holy, holy, holy

Sanctus

Music: Ordinarium XVIII

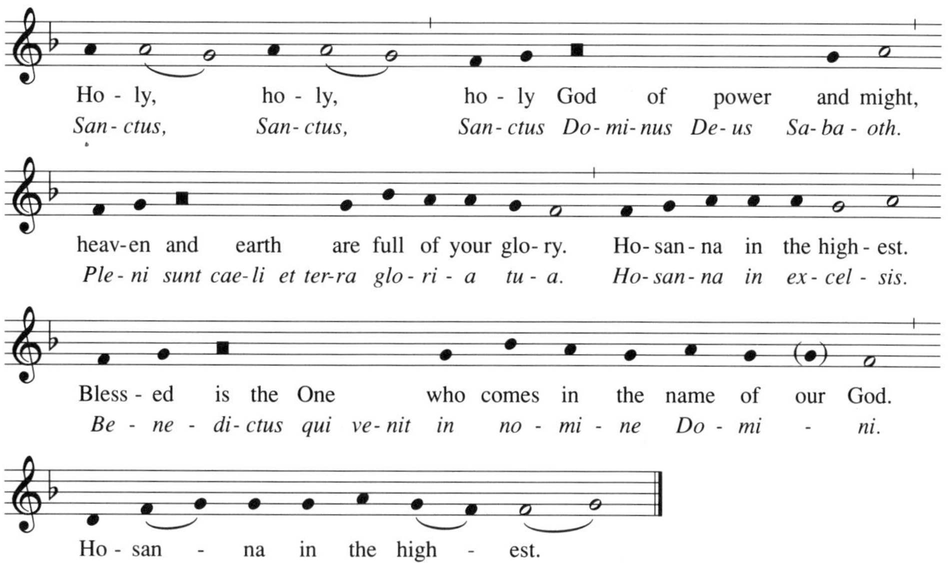
Ho - ly, ho - ly, ho - ly God of power and might,
San-ctus, San-ctus, San-ctus Do-mi-nus De-us Sa-ba - oth.
heav-en and earth are full of your glo-ry. Ho-san-na in the high - est.
Ple-ni sunt cae-li et ter-ra glo-ri - a tu - a. Ho-san-na in ex-cel - sis.
Bless - ed is the One who comes in the name of our God.
Be - ne - di-ctus qui ve-nit in no - mi - ne Do - mi - ni.
Ho - san - na in the high - est.
Ho - san - na in ex - cel - sis.

318 Holy, holy, holy

Sanctus

Music: Franz Schubert, *Deutsche Messe*, 1826; adapted by Richard Proulx, 1985

Ho - ly, ho - ly, ho - ly Lord, God of power and might,
Ho - ly, ho - ly, ho - ly Lord, God of power and might,
hea-ven and earth are full, full of your glo - ry. Ho -
san - na in the high - est. Ho - san - na in the high - est.
Bless-ed is he who comes in the name of the Lord. Ho -
san - na in the high - est. Ho - san - na in the high - est.

319 O Lamb of God

Agnus Dei

O Lamm Gottes, unschuldig

Nikolaus Decius, 1531, 1539, based on *Agnus Dei*; translated by Arthur T. Russell, 1851

Music: *O Lamm Gottes, unschuldig*, 7777777; melody adapted by Nikolaus Decius from a medieval *Agnus Dei*, c. 1539; harmony by Samuel Scheidt, 1650

1 O Lamb of God, all - ho - ly, who on the cross didst suf - fer,
2 O Lamb of God, all - ho - ly, who on the cross didst suf - fer,
3 O Lamb of God, all - ho - ly, who on the cross didst suf - fer,

and, pa - tient still and low - ly, thy - self to scorn didst of - fer:
and, pa - tient still and low - ly, thy - self to scorn didst of - fer:
and, pa - tient still and low - ly, thy - self to scorn didst of - fer:

through thee our sins are heal - ed, and God's great love re - veal-ed.
through thee our sins are heal - ed, and God's great love re - veal-ed.
through thee our sins are heal - ed, and God's great love re - veal-ed.

mer - cy on us,
Have mer - cy up - on us, Je - - su!
Have mer - cy up - on us, Je - - su!
Grant us thy peace, O Je - - su!
Have mer - cy up - on us, O Je - su!
Grant us thy peace, O Je - su!

Have mer - - - cy, Je - su!
Grant us thy peace.

320 Lamb of God

Agnus Dei

Music: Richard Felciano, 1967

Lamb of God, you take a - way the sins of the world: have mer - cy on us.
Lamb of God, you take a - way the sins of the world: have mer - cy on us.
Lamb of God, you take a - way the sins of the world: grant us peace.

321 Lamb of God

Agnus Dei

Music: Ordinarium XVIII

Lamb of God, you take a - way the sins of the world;
A - gnus De - i, qui tol - lis pec - ca - ta mun - di:
have mer - cy on us.
mi - se - re - re no - bis.

Lamb of God, you take a - way the sins of the world;
A - gnus De - i, qui tol - lis pec - ca - ta mun - di:
have mer - cy on us.
mi - se - re - re no - bis.

Lamb of God, you take a - way the sins of the world;
A - gnus De - i, qui tol - lis pec - ca - ta mun - di:
grant us peace.
do - na no - bis pa - cem.

322 Alleluia, amen

Music: Anonymous canon

1
Al - le - lu - ia, al - le - lu - ia,
A - men, a - men,
2
al - le - lu - ia, al - le - lu - ia.
a - men, a - men.

323 Alleluia

Music: Canon by Philip Hayes (1738–1797)

1 Al - le - lu - ia, al - le - lu - ia, al - le - lu - ia,

2 al - le - lu - ia, al - le - lu - ia, al - le - lu - ia,

3 al - le - lu - ia, al - le - lu - ia, al - le - lu - ia, al - le - lu - ia,

4 al - le - lu - ia, al - le - lu - ia, al - le - lu - ia, al - le - lu - ia.

324 Let us pray to the Lord

Music: Byzantine chant

Leader
For ______, let us pray to the Lord.
Response
last time:
Lord, have mer - cy.
A - men.

325 Be now, O God, exalted high

Music: no. 367

Adapted from a stanza in Tate and Brady,
New Version of the Psalms, 1696

Be now, O God, exalted high,
and as your glory fills the sky,
so let it be on earth displayed,
till you are here and now obeyed.

326 For the life that you have given

Music: no. 511

Carl P. Daw, Jr., 1987

For the life that you have given,
for the love in Christ made known,
with these fruits of time and labor,
with these gifts that are your own:
here we offer, Lord, our praises;
heart and mind and strength we bring.
Give us grace to love and serve you,
living what we pray and sing.

327 From all that dwell below the skies

Music: no. 16

Isaac Watts, 1719

1 From all that dwell below the skies
let the Creator's praise arise!
Let the Redeemer's name be sung
through every land in every tongue!

2 Eternal are your mercies, Lord,
eternal truth attends your word.
Your praise shall sound from shore to shore,
till suns shall rise and set no more.

328 God Almighty, Light-creator

Music: no. 9

Martin H. Franzmann, 1954

God Almighty, Light creator,
to thee laud and honor be;
to thee, Light of Light begotten,
praise be sung eternally;
Holy Spirit, Light-revealer,
glory, glory be to thee;
mortals, angels, now and ever
praise the Holy Trinity.

329 Praise God, from whom all blessings flow

Music: no. 1

Thomas Ken, 1674

Praise God, from whom all blessings flow;
praise him, all creatures here below;
praise him above, ye heavenly host;
praise Father, Son, and Holy Ghost.

330 Praise God, from whom all blessings flow

Music: no. 58

Brian Wren, 1989, based on Thomas Ken

Praise God, from whom all blessings flow;
praise God, all creatures high and low:
  Alleluia, alleluia!
Praise God, in Jesus fully known;
Creator, Word, and Spirit One:
  Alleluia, alleluia,
  alleluia, alleluia,
  alleluia!

331 Christ is made the sure foundation

Angularis fundamentum lapis

Sixth or seventh century; translated by John Mason Neale, 1851

Music: *Westminster Abbey*, 878787; arranged from the concluding Alleluias in Henry Purcell's "O God, thou art my God," c. 1860, by Ernest Hawkins in *The Psalmist*, 1842

1 Christ is made the sure foun-da-tion, Christ the head and cor-ner-stone,
2 All that ded-i-cat-ed ci-ty, dear-ly loved of God on high,
3 To this tem-ple, where we call you, come, O Lord of Hosts, to-day!
4 Here be-stow on all your ser-vants what they ask of you to gain;
chos-en of the Lord, and pre-cious, bind-ing all the Church in one;
in ex-ul-tant ju-bi-la-tion pours per-pe-tual mel-o-dy;
With your wont-ed lov-ing-kind-ness hear your serv-ants as they pray,
what they gain from you, for-ev-er with the bless-ed to re-tain,
Ho-ly Zi-on's help for-ev-er, and her con-fi-dence a-lone.
God the One in Three a-dor-ing in glad hymns e-ter-nal-ly.
and your full-est ben-e-dic-tion shed with-in these walls al-way.
and here-af-ter in your glo-ry ev-er-more with you to reign.

332 All things are thine

John Greenleaf Whittier, 1872

Music: *Candler*, 8888D; Scottish traditional melody

1 All things are thine; no gift have we, Lord of all gifts, to of - fer thee;
2 No lack thy per - fect full - ness knew; for hu - man needs and long - ings grew
3 All things are thine; no gift have we, Lord of all gifts, to of - fer thee;
and so with grate - ful hearts to-day thine own be-fore thy feet we lay.
this house of prayer, this home of rest, where grace is shared and truth ad-dressed.
and so with grate - ful hearts to-day thine own be-fore thy feet we lay.
Thy will in-formed the build-ers' thought; thy hand un - seen a - midst us wrought;
In weak-ness and in want we call on thee for whom the heavens are small;
Come now and deign these walls to bless; fill with thy love their emp - ti - ness;
through mor-tal mo-tive, scheme and plan thy wise e - ter - nal pur - pose ran.
thy glo - ry is thy chil-dren's good, thy joy ful-filled in ser - vant-hood.
and let their door a gate - way be to lead us from our-selves to thee.

333 God is here

"The Church of Christ," Fred Pratt Green, 1978

Music: *Abbot's Leigh*, 8787D; Cyril V. Taylor, 1941

1 God is here! As we your peo - ple meet to of - fer
2 Here are sym - bols to re - mind us of our life - long
3 Here our chil - dren find a wel - come in the Shep - herd's
4 Lord of all, of Church and king - dom, in an age of
praise and prayer, may we find in ful - ler mea - sure
need of grace; here are ta - ble, font and pul - pit;
flock and fold; here, as bread and wine are tak - en,
change and doubt keep us faith - ful to the gos - pel,
what it is in Christ we share. Here, as in the world a -
here the cross has cen - tral place. Here, in hon - es - ty of
Christ sus - tains us as of old. Here the ser - vants of the
help us work your pur - pose out. Here, in this day's ded - i -
round us, all our var - ied skills and arts wait the
preach - ing, here in si - lence, as in speech, here, in
Ser - vant seek in wor - ship to ex - plore what it
ca - tion, all we have to give, re - ceive; we, who

com - ing of the Spir - it in - to o - pen minds and hearts.
new - ness and re - new - al, God the Spir - it comes to each.
means in dai - ly liv - ing to be - lieve and to a - dore.
can - not live with - out you, we a - dore you! We be - lieve!

334 Christians, we have met to worship

George Atkins, early 19th century, and others

Music: *Holy Manna*, 8787D; melody by William Moore, 1825; harmony from *Southern Harmony*, 1835

The melody is in the tenor.

1 Chris - tians, we have met to wor - ship and a - dore the Lord our God;
2 Is there here a trem - bling jail - or, seek - ing grace and filled with fears?
3 Let us love our God su - preme - ly, let us love each oth - er, too;

pray that God the truth will teach us, as we hear the Ho - ly Word!
Is there here a weep - ing Ma - ry, pour - ing forth a flood of tears?
let us love and pray for sin - ners till our God makes all things new.

All is vain un - less the Spir - it of the Ho - ly One comes down;
Bro - thers, join your cries to help them; sis - ters, let your prayers a - bound;
When God calls us home to heav - en, at his ta - ble we'll sit down;

Chris - tians, pray, and ho - ly man - na will be show - ered all a - round.
pray, O pray that ho - ly man - na will be show - ered all a - round.
Christ will join us there and feed us with sweet man - na all a - round.

335 Christians, we have met to worship

George Atkins, early 19th century, and others

Music: *Holy Manna*, 8787D; melody by William Moore, 1825;
harmony by Margaret Mealy, 1982

1 Chris- tians, we have met to wor - ship and a - dore the Lord our God;
2 Is there here a trem-bling jail - or, seek-ing grace and filled with fears?
3 Let us love our God su - preme - ly, let us love each oth - er, too;
pray that God the truth will teach us, as we hear the Ho - ly Word!
Is there here a weep - ing Ma - ry, pour-ing forth a flood of tears?
let us love and pray for sin - ners till our God makes all things new.
All is vain un - less the Spir - it of the Ho - ly One comes down;
Bro- thers, join your cries to help them; sis- ters, let your prayers a - bound;
When God calls us home to heav - en, at his ta - ble we'll sit down;
Chris- tians, pray, and ho - ly man - na will be show-ered all a-round.
pray, O pray that ho - ly man - na will be show-ered all a-round.
Christ will join us there and feed us with sweet man - na all a-round.

336 Great God, your love has called us here

"And can it be . . . ," Brian Wren, 1973, 1989

Music: *Fillmore*, 888888; melody attributed to Jeremiah Ingalls (1764–1828); harmony by Austin C. Lovelace, 1964

1 Great God, your love has called us here, as we, by
2 We come with self - in - flict - ed pains of bro - ken
3 Great God, in Christ you call our name and then re -
4 Then take the towel, and break the bread, and hum - ble
love, for love were made. Your liv - ing like - ness still we
trust and chos - en wrong, half - free, half - bound by in - ner
ceive us as your own not through some mer - it, right or
us, and call us friends. Suf - fer and serve till all are
bear, though marred, dis - honor - ed, dis - o - beyed. We come, with
chains, by soc - ial for - ces swept a - long, by powers and
claim but by your gra - cious love a - lone. We strain to
fed and show how grand - ly love in - tends to work till
all our heart and mind your call to hear, your love to find.
sys - tems close con - fined, yet seek - ing hope for hu - man - kind.
glimpse your mer - cy seat and find you kneel - ing at our feet.
all cre - a - tion sings, to fill all worlds, to crown all things.

5 Great God, in Christ you set us free
your life to live, your joy to share.
Give us your Spirit's liberty
to turn from guilt and dull despair
and offer all that faith can do
while love is making all things new.

337 When in our music God is glorified

Fred Pratt Green, 1972

Music: *Engelberg*, 10.10.10.4; Charles Villiers Stanford, 1904

1 When in our mu - sic God is glor - i - fied, and a - dor -
2 How of - ten, mak - ing mu - sic, we have found a new di -
3 So has the Church, in lit - ur - gy and song, in faith and
4 And did not Je - sus sing a psalm that night when ut - most
5 Let ev - ery in - stru-ment be tuned for praise! Let all re -
a - tion leaves no room for pride, it is as
men - sion in the world of sound, as wor - ship
love, through cen - tur - ies of wrong, borne wit - ness
e - vil strove a - gainst the Light? Then let us
joice who have a voice to raise! And may God
though the whole cre - a - tion cried Al - le - lu - ia!
moved us to a more pro - found Al - le - lu - ia!
to the truth in ev - ery tongue, Al - le - lu - ia!
sing, for whom he won the fight, Al - le - lu - ia!
give us faith to sing al - ways
1–4

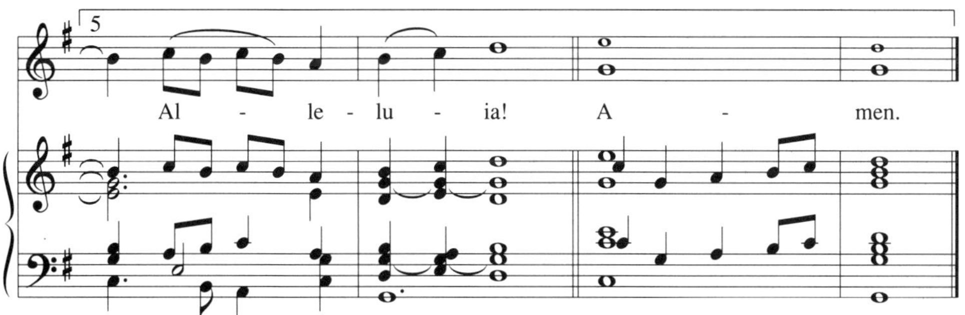
5
Al - le - lu - ia! A - men.

338 We the Lord's people

John E. Bowers, 1972

Music: *Decatur Place*, 11.11.11.5; Richard Wayne Dirksen, 1983

1 We the Lord's peo - ple, heart and voice u - nit - ing,
praise him who called us out of sin and dark - ness in - to his
own light, that he might a - noint us a roy - al priest - hood.

2 This is the Lord's house, home of all his peo - ple,
school for the faith - ful, ref - uge for the sin - ner, rest for the
pil - grim, ha - ven for the wea - ry; all find a wel - come.

3 This is the Lord's day, day of God's own mak - ing,
day of cre - a - tion, day of re - sur - rec - tion, day of the
Spi - rit, sign of hea - ven's ban - quet, day for re - joic - ing.

4 In the Lord's ser - vice bread and wine are of - fered,
that Christ may take them, bless them, break and give them to all his
peo - ple, his own life im - part - ing, food ev - er - last - ing.

339 Lord Jesus Christ, be present now

Herr Jesu Christ, dich zu uns wend

From *Cantionale Sacrum*, Gotha, 1651; in 1676 ascribed to Wilhelm II, duke of Saxe-Weimar; translation based on Catherine Winkworth, 1863

Music: *Herr Jesu Christ, dich zu uns wend*, 8888; melody in *Pensum Sacrum . . .* , Görlitz, 1648; harmony from *Cantionale Sacrum*, Gotha, 1651

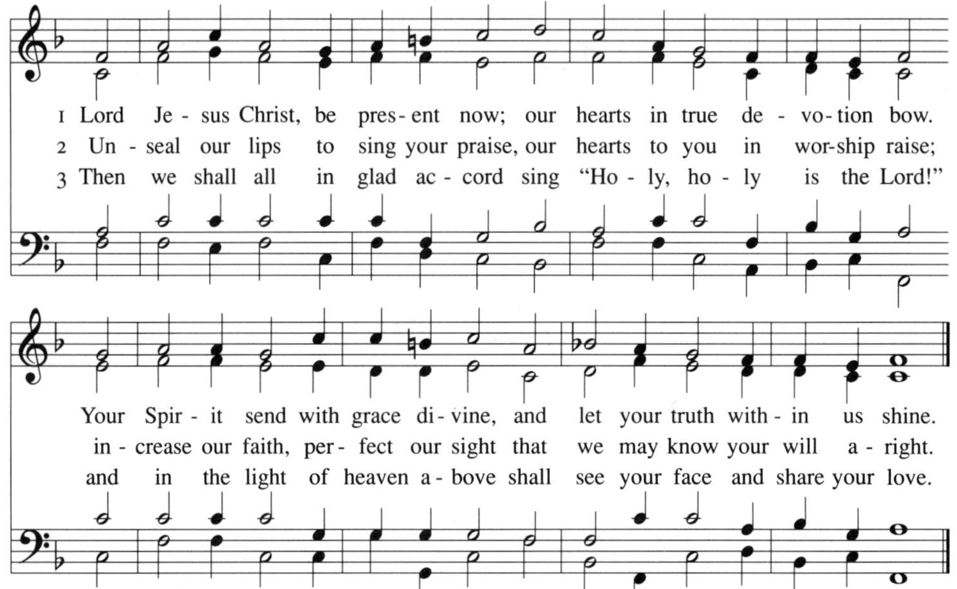
1 Lord Je - sus Christ, be pres - ent now; our hearts in true de - vo - tion bow.
2 Un - seal our lips to sing your praise, our hearts to you in wor-ship raise;
3 Then we shall all in glad ac - cord sing "Ho - ly, ho - ly is the Lord!"
Your Spir - it send with grace di - vine, and let your truth with - in us shine.
in - crease our faith, per - fect our sight that we may know your will a - right.
and in the light of heaven a - bove shall see your face and share your love.

340 What is this place

Zomaar een dak boven wat hoofden

Huub Oosterhuis (b. 1933); translated by David Smith (b. 1933)

Music: *Komt nu met zang*, 9898966; melody in Adrian Valerius's *Nederlandtsche Gedenckklanck*, 1626; harmony by Adrian Engels, 1973

1 What is this place where we are meet - ing? On - ly a house, the
2 Words from a - far, stars that are fall - ing, sparks that are sown in
3 And we ac - cept bread at God's ta - ble, brok - en and shared, a
earth its floor, walls and a roof shel - ter - ing peo - ple,
us like seed. Names for our God, dreams, signs, and won - ders
liv - ing sign. Here in this world, dy - ing and liv - ing,

win-dows for light, an o - pen door. Yet it be-comes a bod - y that lives when
sent from the past are all we need. We in this place re - mem- ber and speak a -
we are each oth-er's bread and wine. This is the place where we can re - ceive what
we are gath - ered here, and know our God is near.
gain what we have heard: God's free re - deem - ing word.
we need to in - crease: God's jus - tice and God's peace.

341 Forth in thy name

"Before work," Charles Wesley, 1749

Music: *Song 34*, 8888; melody and bass by Orlando Gibbons, 1623

These words can also be sung to *Pixham*, no. 353.

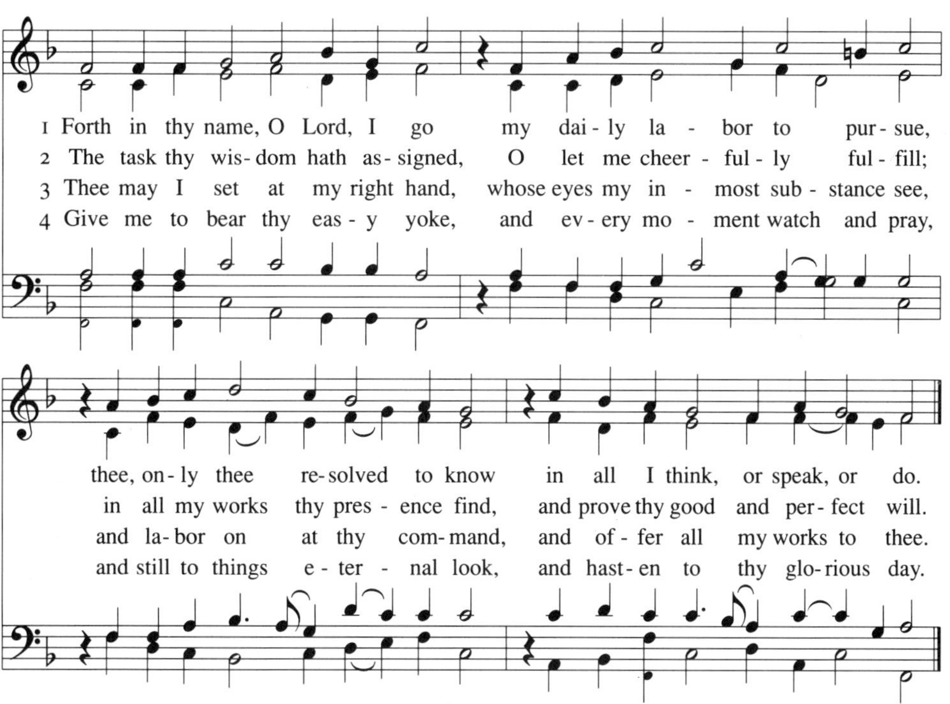
1 Forth in thy name, O Lord, I go my dai - ly la - bor to pur - sue,
2 The task thy wis - dom hath as - signed, O let me cheer - ful - ly ful - fill;
3 Thee may I set at my right hand, whose eyes my in - most sub - stance see,
4 Give me to bear thy eas - y yoke, and ev - ery mo - ment watch and pray,
thee, on - ly thee re - solved to know in all I think, or speak, or do.
in all my works thy pres - ence find, and prove thy good and per - fect will.
and la - bor on at thy com - mand, and of - fer all my works to thee.
and still to things e - ter - nal look, and hast - en to thy glo - rious day.

5 For thee delightfully employ
whate'er thy bounteous grace hath given,
and run my course with even joy,
and closely walk with thee to heaven.

342 Sent forth by God's blessing

Omer Westendorf, 1964

Music: *The Ash Grove*, 6.6.11.6.6.11.D; Welsh traditional melody; harmony by Leland Sateren, 1972

Unison
1 Sent forth by God's bless - ing, our true faith con - fess - ing,
2 With praise and thanks - giv - ing to God ev - er - liv - ing,
the peo - ple of God from this dwell - ing take leave.
the tasks of our ev - ery - day life we will face.
The ser - vice is end - ed. O now be ex - tend - ed
Our faith ev - er shar - ing, in love ev - er car - ing,
the fruits of our wor - ship in all who be - lieve.
em - brac - ing God's chil - dren of each tribe and race.
The seed of God's teach - ing, re - cep - tive souls reach - ing,
With your Word you feed us, with your light now lead us;

shall blos - som in ac - tion for God and for all.
u - nite us as one in this life that we share.

God's grace did in - vite us, and love shall u - nite us
Then may all the liv - ing with praise and thanks - giv - ing

to work for God's king - dom and an - swer the call.
give hon - or to Christ and his name that we bear.

343 Shalom

Shalom, my friends

Music: Israeli round

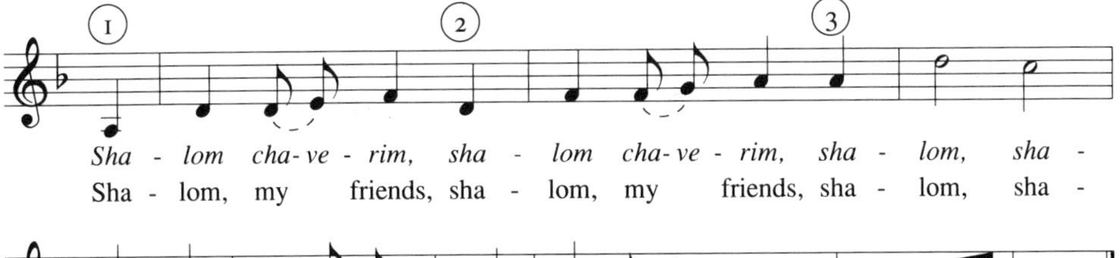
1
2
3
Sha - lom cha- ve - rim, sha - lom cha- ve - rim, sha - lom, sha -
Sha - lom, my friends, sha - lom, my friends, sha - lom, sha -

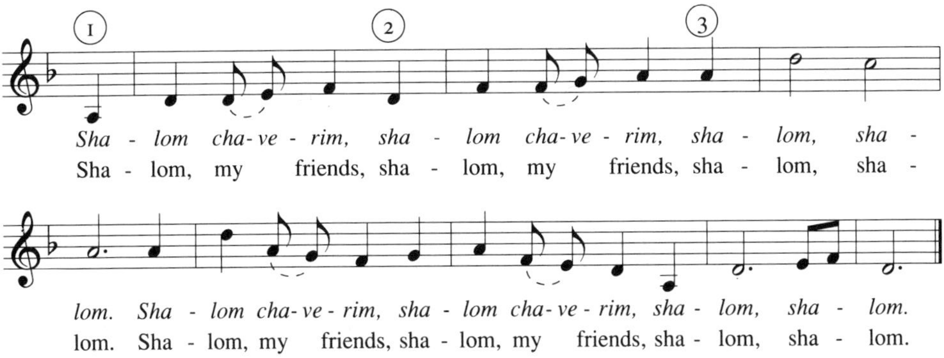

lom. Sha - lom cha- ve - rim, sha - lom cha- ve - rim, sha - lom, sha - lom.
lom. Sha - lom, my friends, sha - lom, my friends, sha - lom, sha - lom.

344 God, be with us till we meet again

Donald W. Hughes, 1964, and others, based on Jeremiah E. Rankin's hymn of c. 1880

Music: *Randolph*, 9889; Ralph Vaughan Williams, 1906

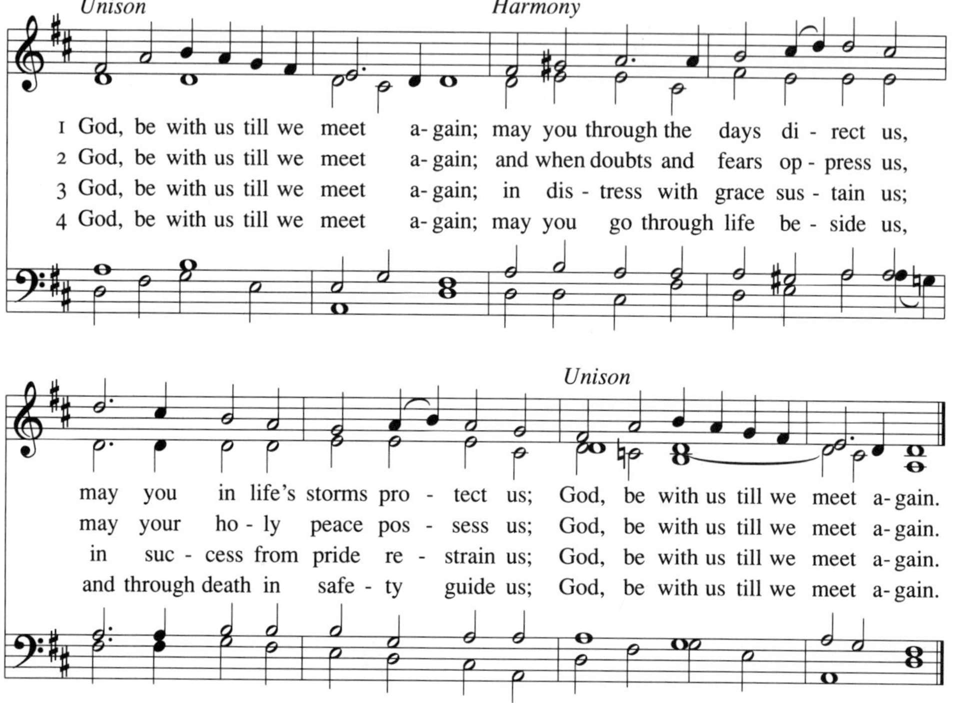
Unison
Harmony
1 God, be with us till we meet a-gain; may you through the days di - rect us,
2 God, be with us till we meet a-gain; and when doubts and fears op - press us,
3 God, be with us till we meet a-gain; in dis - tress with grace sus - tain us;
4 God, be with us till we meet a-gain; may you go through life be - side us,
Unison
may you in life's storms pro - tect us; God, be with us till we meet a-gain.
may your ho - ly peace pos - sess us; God, be with us till we meet a-gain.
in suc - cess from pride re - strain us; God, be with us till we meet a-gain.
and through death in safe - ty guide us; God, be with us till we meet a-gain.

345 Lord, dismiss us with your blessing

John Fawcett, 1773

Music: *Sicilian Mariners*, 878787; 18th-century Italian or Sicilian melody;
harmony from *The Church Hymnal*, Milwaukee, 1879

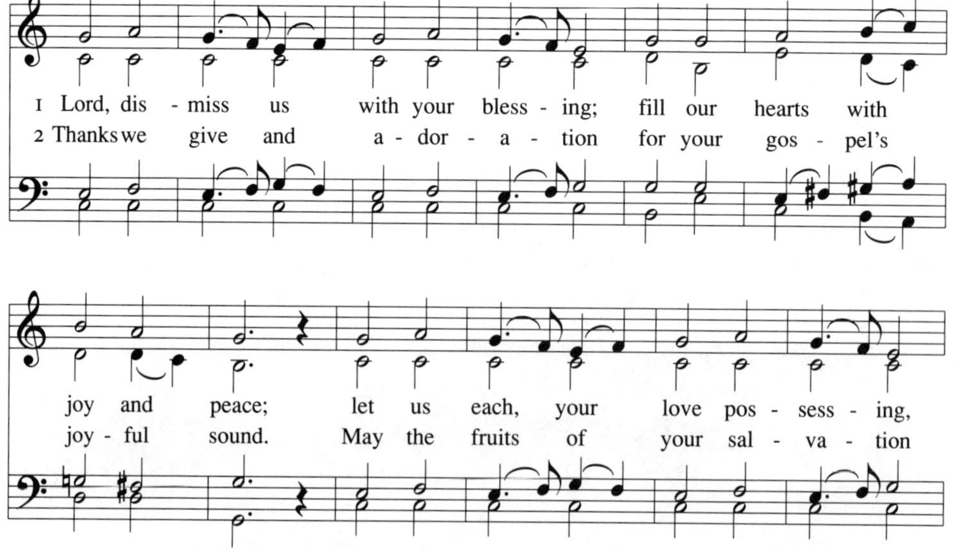
1 Lord, dis - miss us with your bless - ing; fill our hearts with
2 Thanks we give and a - dor - a - tion for your gos - pel's
joy and peace; let us each, your love pos - sess - ing,
joy - ful sound. May the fruits of your sal - va - tion

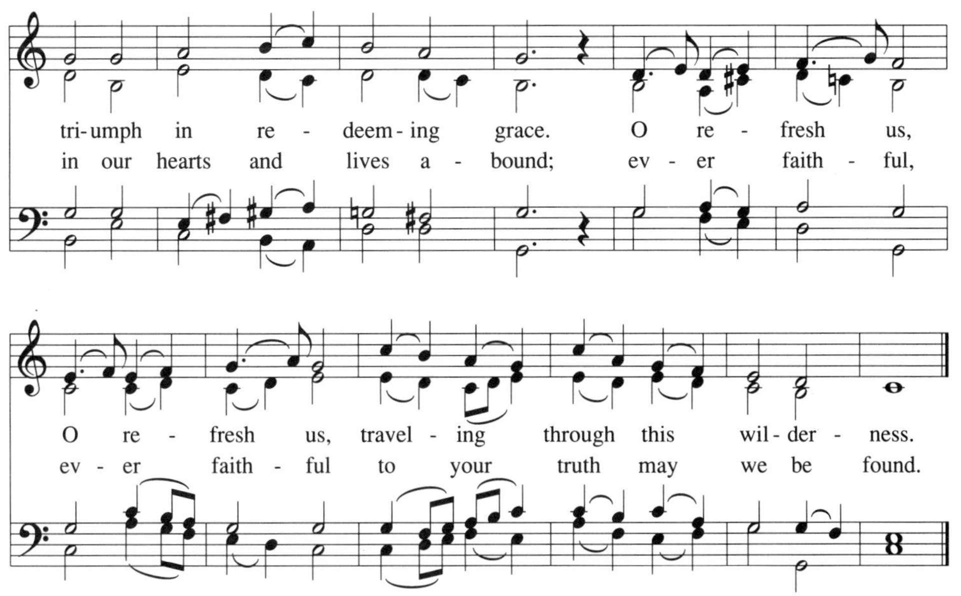
tri-umph in re - deem-ing grace. O re - fresh us,
in our hearts and lives a - bound; ev - er faith - ful,
O re - fresh us, travel - ing through this wil-der - ness.
ev - er faith - ful to your truth may we be found.

346 Lord, dismiss us with your blessing

John Fawcett, 1773

Music: *Sicilian Mariners*, 878787; 18th-century Italian or Sicilian melody; harmony by Ludwig van Beethoven in *Zwölf verschiedene Volkslieder*, 1817/18

1 Lord, dis - miss us with your bless - ing; fill our hearts with
2 Thanks we give and a - dor - a - tion for your gos - pel's
joy and peace; let us each, your love pos - sess - ing,
joy - ful sound. May the fruits of your sal - va - tion
tri-umph in re - deem-ing grace. O re - fresh us,
in our hearts and lives a - bound; ev - er faith - ful,
O re - fresh us, travel - ing through this wil-der - ness.
ev - er faith - ful to your truth may we be found.

347 Strengthen for service

Liturgy of Malabar, 4th century; paraphrase by C. W. Humphries and Percy Dearmer, 1906

Music: *Malabar*, 8787; David McK. Williams, 1941

1 Strength - en for ser - vice, Lord, the hands that ho - ly things have tak - en; let ears that now have heard your songs to clam - or nev - er wak - en.
2 Lord, may the tongues which "Ho - ly" sang keep free from all de - ceiv - ing; the eyes which saw your love be bright, your bless - ed hope per - ceiv - ing.
3 The feet that tread your hal - lowed courts from light, Lord, do not ban - ish; the bod - ies by your Bod - y fed with your new life re - plen - ish.

348 Morning has broken

Eleanor Farjeon, 1931

Music: *Bunessan*, 5554D; Gaelic traditional melody; harmony by Alec Wyton, 1982

1 Morn-ing has brok - en like the first morn - ing,
2 Sweet the rain's new fall sun - lit from heav - en,
3 Mine is the sun - light! Mine is the morn - ing
black-bird has spok - en like the first bird.
like the first dew - fall on the first grass.
born of the one light E - den saw play!
Praise for the sing - ing! Praise for the morn - ing!
Praise for the sweet - ness of the wet gar - den,
Praise with e - la - tion, praise ev - ery morn - ing,
Praise for them, spring - ing fresh from the Word!
sprung in com - plete - ness where his feet pass.
God's re - cre - a - tion of the new day!

349 Not here for high and holy things

Geoffrey A. Studdert-Kennedy, 1921

Music: *Morning Song*, 868686; melody in John Wyeth's *Repository of Sacred Music*, 1813; harmonized by Winfred Douglas, 1940

This hymn may begin with stanza 4.

1 Not here for high and ho - ly things we ren - der thanks to thee,
2 the roy - al robes of au - tumn moors, the gold - en gates of spring,
3 of faith and hope and love un - dimmed, un - dy - ing still through death,
4 A - wake, a - wake to love and work! The lark is in the sky,
but for the com - mon things of earth, the pur - ple pa - gean - try
the vel - vet of soft sum - mer nights, the sil - ver glis - ter - ing
the re - sur - rec - tion of the world, what time there comes the breath
the fields are wet with dia - mond dew, the worlds a - wake to cry
of dawn - ing and of dy - ing days, the splen - dor of the sea,
of all the mil - lion mil - lion stars, the si - lent song they sing,
of dawn that rus - tles through the trees, and that clear voice that saith:
their bless - ings on the Lord of life, as he goes meek - ly by.

5 Come, let thy voice be one with theirs,
shout with their shout of praise;
see how the giant sun soars up,
great lord of years and days!
So let the love of Jesus come
and set thy soul ablaze,

6 to give and give, and give again,
what God hath given thee:
to spend thyself nor count the cost;
to serve right gloriously
the God who gave all worlds that are,
and all that are to be.

350 O splendor of God's glory bright

Splendor paternae gloriae

Ambrose of Milan (c. 340–c. 397); translation based on *Hymns Ancient and Modern*, 1904

Music: *Puer nobis nascitur*, 8888; melody in Michael Praetorius's *Musae Sionae*, 1609; harmony by George R. Woodward, 1910

1 O splen - dor of God's glo - ry bright, who bring - est
2 come, blaz - ing Sun of truth and love, come in thy
3 Teach us to work with all our might; put Sa - tan's
4 O joy - ful be the live - long day, our thoughts as
forth the light from light; O Light, of light the
ra - diance from a - bove, and shed the Ho - ly
fierce as - saults to flight; turn all to good that
pure as morn - ing ray, our faith like noon - day's
foun - tain - spring, O Day, all days il - lu - min - ing,
Spir - it's ray on all we think or do to - day.
seems most ill; help us our call - ing to ful - fill.
glow - ing height, our souls un - dimmed by shades of night.

5 O Christ, with each returning morn
thine image to our hearts is borne;
O may we ever clearly see
our Savior and our God in thee!

351 Awake, my soul, and with the sun

Thomas Ken, 1695, 1709, from *A Manual of Prayers for Use of the Scholars of Winchester College*

Music: *Morning Hymn*, 8888; melody and most of the bass by François H. Barthélémon, c. 1789

These words can be sung to *Tallis Canon*, no. 429.

1 A - wake, my soul, and with the sun thy dai - ly stage of du - ty run;
2 A - wake, lift up thy - self, my heart, and with the an - gels bear thy part,
3 All praise to thee, who safe has kept and hast re - freshed me while I slept.
4 Lord, I my vows to thee re - new; dis - perse my sins as morn - ing dew;
shake off dull sloth, and joy - ful rise to pay thy morn - ing sac - ri - fice.
who all night long un - wear - ied sing high praise to the e - ter - nal King.
Grant, Lord, when I from death shall wake, I may of end - less light par - take.
guard my first springs of thought and will, and with thy - self my spi - rit fill.

5 Direct, control, suggest, this day,
all I design, or do, or say;
that all my powers with all their might,
in thy sole glory may unite.

352 Rise to greet the sun

Chao Tzu-ch'en (b. 1888); translated by Mildred and Bliss Wiant, 1946

Music: *Le p'ing*, 5555; Hu Te-ai (b. 1900)

1 Rise to greet the sun, redden - ing in the sky,
2 May this day be blest; trust - ing Je - sus' love,
war - rior - like and strong, come - ly as a groom;
my heart's freed from ill, fair blue sky's a - bove.

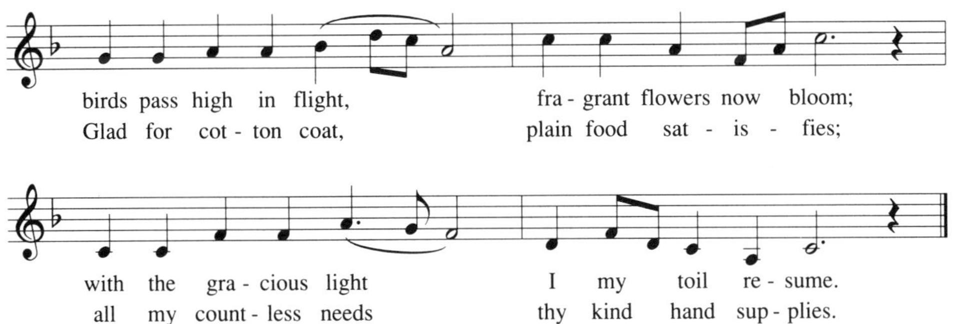
birds pass high in flight, fra - grant flowers now bloom;
Glad for cot - ton coat, plain food sat - is - fies;
with the gra - cious light I my toil re - sume.
all my count - less needs thy kind hand sup - plies.

353 Lord, as we wake we turn to you

Brian Foley, 1971, and others; based on Psalm 5

Music: *Pixham*, 8888; Horatio Parker, 1901

1 Lord, as we wake we turn to you, your - self the
2 There is no bless - ing, Lord, from you for those who
3 Your lov - ing gifts of grace to us, those fa - vors
4 Lord, make each life a life of love, keep us from

first thought of each day; our King, our God, whose
make their will their way; no praise for those who
we could nev - er earn, call for our thanks in
sin in all we do; Lord, make your law our

help is sure, your - self the help for which we pray.
will not praise, no peace for those who will not pray.
praise and prayer, call us to love you in re - turn.
on - ly law, your will our will, for love of you.

354 Christ, whose glory fills the skies

"A Morning Hymn," Charles Wesley, 1740

Music: *Ratisbon*, 777777; melody from Johann Werner's *Choralbuch*, Leipzig, 1815, based on older German sources

1 Christ, whose glo - ry fills the skies, Christ, the true, the on ly Light,
2 Dark and cheer- less is the morn un - ac - com - pan - ied by thee;
3 Vis - it then this soul of mine; pierce the gloom of sin and grief;

Sun of Righ-teous - ness, a - rise, tri- umph o'er the shades of night:
joy - less is the day's re - turn, till thy mer - cy's beams I see;
fill me, ra - dian - cy di - vine; scat - ter all my un - be - lief;

Day- spring from on high, be near; Day- star, in my heart ap - pear.
till they in - ward light im - part, glad my eyes, and warm my heart.
more and more thy - self dis - play, shin- ing to the per - fect day.

355 Lord God, we praise you

Nocte surgentes

Attributed to Gregory the Great (c. 540–604); paraphrased by Percy Dearmer, 1906, and others

Music: *Christe sanctorum*, 11.11.11.5; melody in *Paris Antiphoner*, 1681; harmony by John Wilson (b. 1905)

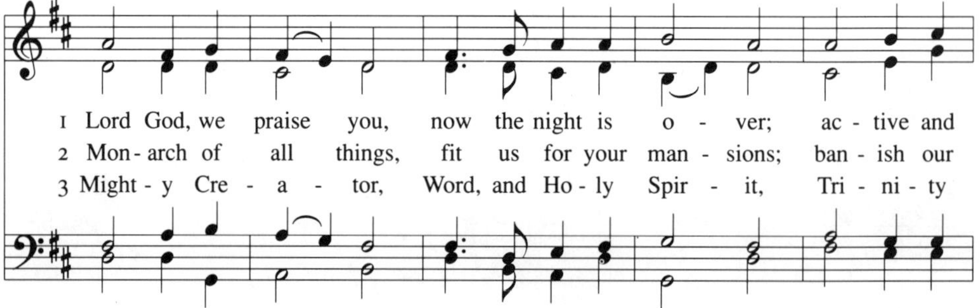
1 Lord God, we praise you, now the night is o - ver; ac - tive and
2 Mon - arch of all things, fit us for your man - sions; ban - ish our
3 Might - y Cre - a - tor, Word, and Ho - ly Spir - it, Tri - ni - ty

watch - ful, stand we all be - fore you; sing - ing we of - fer
weak - ness, health and whole - ness send - ing; bring us to heav - en,
bless - ed, send us your sal - va - tion; yours is the glo - ry,
prayer and med - i - ta - tion: thus we a - dore you.
where your saints u - nit - ed joy with - out end - ing.
gleam - ing and re - sound - ing through all cre - a - tion.

356 New every morning is the love

John Keble, 1822

Music: *Melcombe*, 8888; melody by Samuel Webbe, the elder, 1782; harmony by William H. Monk, 1875

1 New ev - ery morn - ing is the love our wak-ening and up - ris - ing prove;
2 New mer - cies, each re - turn - ing day, ho - ver a - round us while we pray;
3 If on our dai - ly course our mind be set to hal - low all we find,
4 Old friends, old scenes, will love - lier be, as more of heaven in each we see;
through sleep and dark - ness safe - ly brought, re- stored to life and power and thought.
new per - ils past, new sins for - given, new thoughts of God, new hopes of heaven.
new trea - sures still, of count - less price, God will pro - vide for sac - ri - fice.
some soft-ening gleam of love and prayer shall dawn on ev - ery cross and care.

5 The trivial round, the common task,
will furnish all we ought to ask;
room to deny ourselves—a road
to bring us daily nearer God.

6 Only, O Lord, in your dear love,
fit us for perfect rest above;
and help us, this and every day,
to live more nearly as we pray.

357 Christ, mighty Savior

Mozarabic, c. 10th century; paraphrased by Anne Lecroy, 1982,
based on Alan G. McDougall (1895–1964)

Music: *Mighty Savior*, 11.11.11.5; David Hurd, 1983

1 Christ, might - y Sa - vior, Light of all cre - a - tion, you make the
2 Now comes the day's end as the sun is set - ting: mir - ror of
3 Give heed, we pray you, to our sup - pli - ca - tion: that you may
4 Though bod - ies slum - ber, hearts shall keep their vig - il, for ev - er
day - time ra - diant with the sun - light and to the night give
day - break, pledge of re - sur - rec - tion; while in the hea - vens
grant us par - don for of - fens - es, strength for our weak hearts,
rest - ing in the peace of Je - sus, in light or dark - ness
glit - ter - ing a - dorn - ment, stars in the hea - vens.
choirs of stars ap - pear - ing hal - low the night - fall.
rest for ach - ing bo - dies, sooth - ing the wear - y.
wor - ship - ing our Sav - ior now and for ev - er.

358 God, who made the earth and heaven

Stanza 1: Reginald Heber, 1827, and others; stanza 2: William Mercer, 1864; stanza 3: Richard Whateley, 1838

Music: *Ar hyd y nos*, 84848884; Welsh traditional melody; melody in Edward Jones's *Musical Relicks of the Welsh Bards*, Dublin, 1784; harmony by L. O. Emerson, 1906

1 God, who made the earth and heav-en, dark - ness and light:
2 And when morn a - gain shall call us to run life's way,
3 Guard us wak-ing, guard us sleep-ing, and, when we die,
you the day for work have giv - en, for rest the night.
may we still, what - e'er be - fall us, your will o - bey.
may we in your might - y keep-ing all peace - ful lie.
May your an - gel guards de - fend us, slum-ber sweet your mer - cy send us,
From the power of e - vil hide us, in the nar - row path - way guide us,
When the trum-pet call shall wake us, then, O Lord, do not for - sake us,
ho - ly dreams and hopes at - tend us all through the night.
nev - er be your smile de - nied us all through the day.
but to reign in glo - ry take us with you on high.

359 God, who made the earth and heaven

Stanza 1: Reginald Heber, 1827, and others; stanza 2: William Mercer, 1864; stanza 3: Richard Whateley, 1838

Music: *Ar hyd y nos*, 84848884; Welsh traditional melody; arranged by Franz Joseph Haydn in *Scottish Songs*, 1809

1 God, who made the earth and heav-en, dark - ness and light:
2 And when morn a - gain shall call us to run life's way,
3 Guard us wak-ing, guard us sleep-ing, and, when we die,
you the day for work have giv - en, for rest the night.
may we still, what - e'er be - fall us, your will o - bey.
may we in your might - y keep-ing all peace - ful lie.

May your an - gel guards de - fend us, slum-ber sweet your mer - cy send us,
From the power of e - vil hide us, in the nar - row path-way guide us,
When the trum - pet call shall wake us, then, O Lord, do not for - sake us,
1–2
3
ho - ly dreams and hopes at - tend us all through the night.
nev - er be your smile de - nied us all through the day.
but to reign in glo - ry take us with you on high.

360 O gladsome light

Phos hilaron

Third-century Greek candlelighting hymn; translated by Robert Bridges, 1899

Music: *Nunc dimittis*, 667667; melody for the *Song of Simeon* in the *Genevan Psalter*, 1549; harmony adapted from Claude Goudimel, 1565

1 O glad-some light, O grace of our Cre - a - tor's face,
2 As fades the day's last light we see the lamps of night,
3 To you of right be - longs all praise of ho - ly songs,
the e - ter - nal splen - dor wear - ing; ce - les - tial, ho - ly, blest,
our grate - ful hymn out - pour - ing, O God of might un - known,
O Son of God, life - giv - er. You, there - fore, O Most High,
our Sa - vior Je - sus Christ, joy - ful in your ap - pear - ing!
you, the in - car - nate Son, and Spir - it blest a - dor - ing.
the world will glo - ri - fy and will ex - alt for ev - er.

361 O gracious Light

Phos hilaron

Third-century Greek candlelighting hymn; translated by F. Bland Tucker, 1982

Music: *Galilee*, 8888; Philip Armes, 1875

These words can also be sung to *Tallis Canon*, no. 429.

1 O gra - cious Light, Lord Je - sus Christ, in you the
2 Now sun - set comes, but light shines forth, the lamps are
3 Wor - thy are you of end - less praise, O Son of

Fa - ther's glo - ry shone. Im - mor - tal, ho - ly,
lit to pierce the night. Praise Fa - ther, Son, and
God, life - giv - ing Lord; where - fore you are through
blest is he, and blest are you, his ho - ly Son.
Spir - it: God who dwells in the e - ter - nal light.
all the earth and in the high - est heaven a - dored.

362 To you before the close of day

Te lucis ante terminum

Sixth century; stanzas 1 and 2 translated by the editors of *The Hymnal 1982*, stanza 3 by James Waring McCrady, 1982

Music: *Te lucis ante terminum*, 8888; plainsong; accompaniment by J. H. Arnold, 1906

1 To you be - fore the close of day, Cre - a - tor of all things, we pray
2 Save us from trou-bled, rest- less sleep, from all ill dreams your chil - dren keep;
3 A heal - thy life we ask of you, the fire of love in us re - new,
that in your con - stant cle - men - cy our guard and keep- er you would be.
so calm our minds that fears may cease and rest - ed bod- ies wake in peace.
and when the dawn new light will bring, your praise and glo - ry we shall sing.

363 O Trinity of blessed light

O lux beata Trinitas

Sixth century or earlier; translation based on John Mason Neale, 1852, and others

Music: *O lux beata Trinitas*, 8888; plainsong; accompaniment by Ernest White for *Service Book and Hymnal*, 1958

1 O Tri - ni - ty of bless - ed light,
2 To you our morn - ing song of praise,
3 To God E - ter - nal, heaven - ly Light,
O U - ni - ty of nob - lest might,
to you our even - ing prayer we raise;
to Christ re - vealed in earth - ly night,
the fier - y sun goes on its way;
O grant us, with your saints on high,
to God the Spir - it blest, we raise

shed now with - in our hearts your ray.
to praise you through e - ter - ni - ty.
our e - qual and un - ceas - ing praise.

364 The day you gave us, Lord, has ended

John Ellerton, 1870, and others

Music: *St. Clement*, 9898; Clement C. Scholefield, 1874

1 The day you gave us, Lord, has ended; the darkness
falls at your behest. To you our morning
hymns ascended; your praise shall sanctify our rest.

2 We thank you that your Church, unsleeping while earth rolls
onward into light, through all the world its
watch is keeping, and never rests by day or night.

3 Across each continent and island, as dawn leads
on another day, the voice of prayer is
never silent, nor dies the strain of praise away.

4 The sun, here having set, is waking your children
under western skies, and hour by hour, as
day is breaking, fresh hymns of thankful praise arise.

5 So be it, Lord; your throne shall never,
like earth's proud empires, pass away:
your kingdom stands, and grows forever,
till all your creatures own your sway.

365 The day you gave us, Lord, has ended

John Ellerton, 1870, and others

Music: *Cedar Springs*, 9898; Gerald Near, 1989

1 The day you gave us, Lord, has end - ed; the
2 We thank you that your Church, un - sleep - ing while
3 A cross each con - ti - nent and is - land, as
4 The sun, here hav - ing set, is wak - ing your
dark-ness falls at your be-hest. To you our morn-ing hymns as-cend -
earth rolls on-ward in - to light, through all the world its watch is keep -
dawn leads on a - no - ther day, the voice of prayer is nev - er si -
chil-dren un-der wes - tern skies, and hour by hour, as day is break -
ed; your praise shall sanc - ti - fy our rest.
ing, and nev - er rests by day or night.
lent, nor dies the strain of praise a - way.
ing, fresh hymns of thank - ful praise a - rise.

5 So be it, Lord; your throne shall never,
like earth's proud empires, pass away:
your kingdom stands, and grows forever,
till all your creatures own your sway.

366 Abide with us, O Lord

Herr, bleibe bei uns

Music: Canon by Albert Thate (b. 1903)

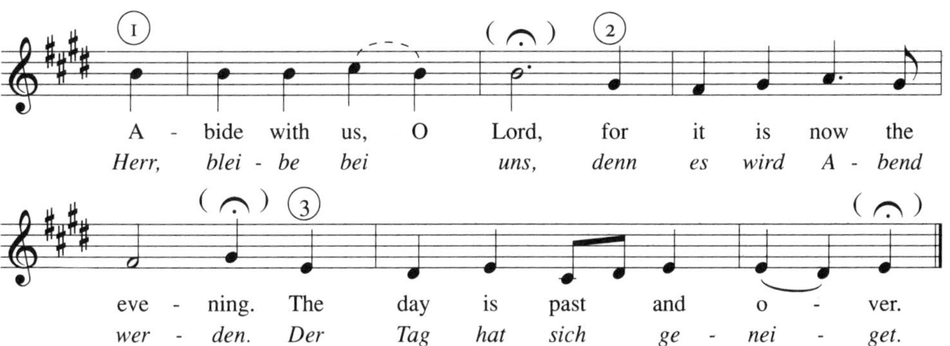
1
2
3
A - bide with us, O Lord, for it is now the
Herr, blei - be bei uns, denn es wird A - bend
eve - ning. The day is past and o - ver.
wer - den. Der Tag hat sich ge - nei - get.

367 All praise to thee, my God, this night

Thomas Ken, 1695, 1709, from *A Manual of Prayers for Use of the Scholars of Winchester College*

Music: *Tallis Canon*, 8888; melody by Thomas Tallis, 1557, shortened by Thomas Ravenscroft, 1621

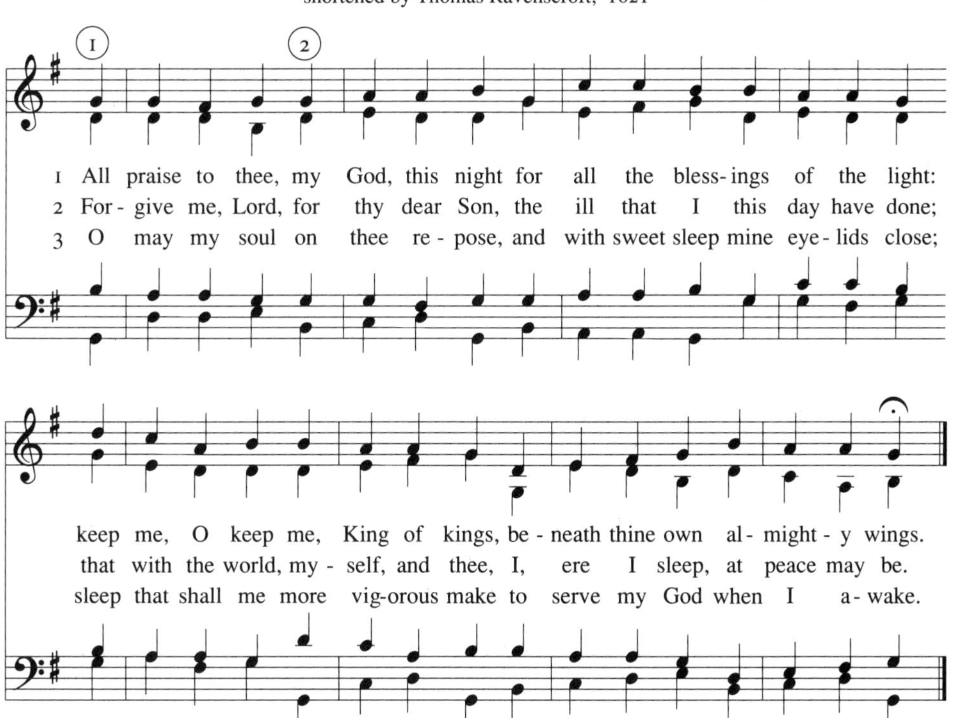
1
2
1 All praise to thee, my God, this night for all the bless-ings of the light:
2 For - give me, Lord, for thy dear Son, the ill that I this day have done;
3 O may my soul on thee re - pose, and with sweet sleep mine eye - lids close;
keep me, O keep me, King of kings, be - neath thine own al - might - y wings.
that with the world, my - self, and thee, I, ere I sleep, at peace may be.
sleep that shall me more vig-orous make to serve my God when I a - wake.

368 This is the day the Lord has made

Isaac Watts, 1719

Music: *Nun danket all*, 8686; adapted from Johann Crüger, 1653

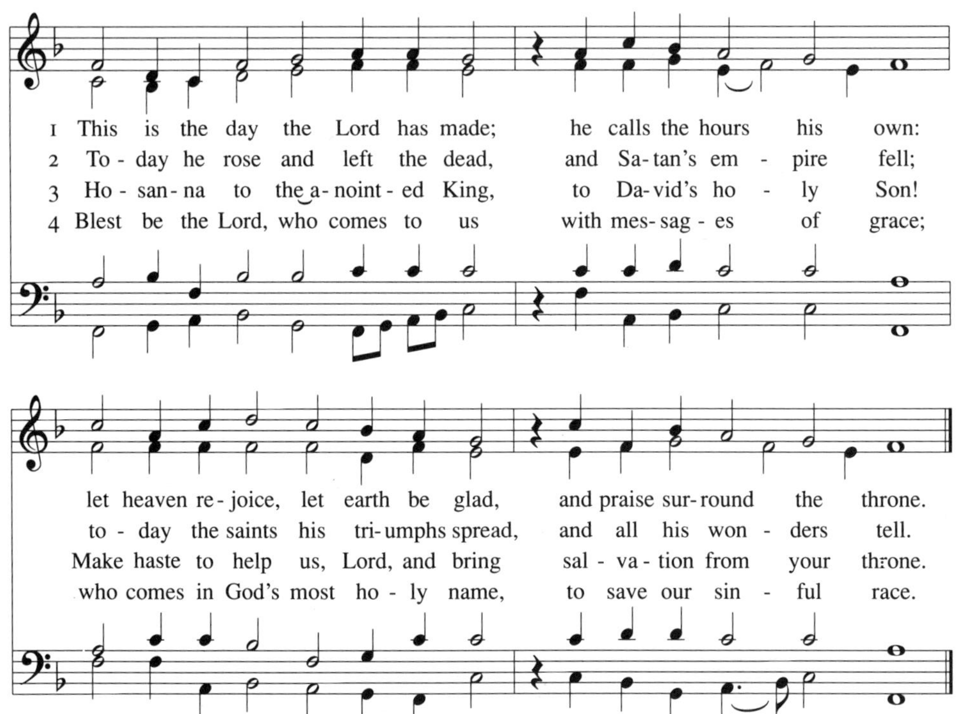
1 This is the day the Lord has made; he calls the hours his own:
2 To-day he rose and left the dead, and Sa-tan's em-pire fell;
3 Ho-san-na to the a-noint-ed King, to Da-vid's ho-ly Son!
4 Blest be the Lord, who comes to us with mes-sag-es of grace;
let heaven re-joice, let earth be glad, and praise sur-round the throne.
to-day the saints his tri-umphs spread, and all his won-ders tell.
Make haste to help us, Lord, and bring sal-va-tion from your throne.
who comes in God's most ho-ly name, to save our sin-ful race.

5 Hosanna in the highest strains
the Church on earth can raise;
the highest heavens, in which he reigns,
shall give him nobler praise.

369 Most glorious Lord of life

Edmund Spenser; Sonnet 68 in *Amoretti*, 1595

Music: *Song 1*, 10.10.10.10.(10.10); melody and bass by Orlando Gibbons, 1623

1 Most glo-rious Lord of life, that on this day
2 this joy-ous day, dear Lord, with joy be-gin,
3 and that thy love we weigh-ing wor-thi-ly,

didst make thy tri - umph o - ver death and sin,
and grant that we for whom thou did - dest die,
may like - wise love thee for the same a - gain;
and hav - ing har - rowed hell, didst bring a - way
be - ing with thy dear blood clean washed from sin,
and for thy sake, that all like dear didst buy,
cap - tiv - i - ty thence cap - tive, us to win:
may live for ev - er in fe - lic - i - ty:
with love may one a - noth - er en - ter - tain;
4 so let us love, dear Love, like as we ought;
love is the les - son which the Lord us taught.

Stanza 4 follows.

370 "God rested on the Seventh Day"

Fred Pratt Green, 1988

Music: *Dwight*, 868688; Jane Manton Marshall, 1990

Unison
1 "God rest - ed on the Sev - enth Day" re - flects a hu - man need;
2 A Day of Rest, a Day of Praise, a Day when God pro - vides
3 And yet, how soon we can de - stroy the Sab - bath God has given:
4 Be it the Sev - enth Day or First we cher - ish and ob - serve:
but what the an - cient scrip - tures say the wise will sure - ly heed:
fresh en - er - gy for work - ing days, in doubt and trou - ble guides.
to sour - ness turn our sa - cred joy, and make a hell of heaven.
as those who hun - ger still and thirst, and hum - bly seek to serve,
that God, the great Cre - a - tor, blessed
How love - ly is that dwell - ing - place
Too strict, we lose the right to choose;
God help us keep, and use with care,
this day to be a day of rest.
where we are con - scious most of grace!
too lax, our soul's di - rec - tion lose.
the pre - cious her - i - tage we share.

371 Blow ye the trumpet

Charles Wesley, 1750

Music: *Lenox*, 6666 with refrain; Lewis Edson, c. 1782

The melody is in the tenor.

1 Blow ye the trum-pet, blow! The glad-ly sol-emn sound
2 Je-sus, our great high priest, has full a-tone-ment made;
3 Ex-tol the Lamb of God, the all-a-ton-ing Lamb;
4 Prison-ers of sin and hell, your lib-er-ty re-ceive,
let all the na-tions know, to earth's re-mot-est bound:
O wear-y spir-its, rest; O mourn-ful souls, be glad:
re-demp-tion in his blood through-out the world pro-claim:
and safe in Je-sus dwell, and blest in Je-sus live:
Refrain
The year of ju-bi-lee is come! Re-turn, ye ran-somed sin-ners, home.
The year of ju-bi-lee is come! The year of ju-bi-lee is come! Re-turn, ye ran-somed sin-ners, home.
The year of ju-bi-lee is come! The year of ju-bi-lee is come! Re-turn, ye ran-somed sin-ners, home.
The year of ju-bi-lee is come! Re-turn, ye ran-somed sin-ners, home.

5 All you who sold for nought
your heritage above,
shall have it back unbought,
the gift of Jesus' love:

Refrain

6 The gospel trumpet hear,
the news of heavenly grace;
and saved from death, appear
before your Savior's face:

Refrain

372 Creator of the earth and skies

Donald W. Hughes, 1964

Music: *Uffingham*, 8888; melody and bass by Jeremiah Clark(e), 1707

These words can also be sung to *Kedron*, no. 539.

1 Cre - a - tor of the earth and skies, to whom the words of life be - long, grant us your truth to make us wise, grant us your power to make us strong.
2 We have not known you: to the skies our mon - u - ments of fol - ly soar, and all our self - wrought mis - er - ies have made us trust our - selves the more.
3 We have not loved you: far and wide the wreck - age of our ha - tred spreads, and e - vils wrought by hu - man pride re - coil on un - re - pent - ant heads.
4 For this, our fool - ish con - fi - dence, our pride of know - ledge and our sin, we come to you in pen - i - tence; in us the work of grace be - gin.

5 Teach us to know and love you, Lord,
and humbly follow in your way.
Speak to our souls the quickening word,
and turn our darkness into day.

373 Dear Lord, embracing humankind

John Greenleaf Whittier, 1872, and others

Music: *Repton*, 868866; arranged in George Gilbert's *Repton School: Hymns for Use in Chapel*, 1924, from a song in C. Hubert H. Parry's *Judith*, 1888

1 Dear Lord, em- brac- ing hu - man- kind, for - give our fool- ish ways!
2 In sim - ple trust like theirs who heard, be - side the Syr- ian sea,
3 O Sab- bath rest by Gal - i - lee! O calm of hills a - bove,
4 Drop thy still dews of qui - et - ness, till all our striv-ings cease:
Re - clothe us in our right - ful mind, in pur - er lives thy ser- vice find,
the gra- cious call - ing of the Lord, let us, like them, with- out a word,
where Je - sus knelt to share with thee the si - lence of e - ter - ni - ty,
take from our souls the strain and stress, and let our or- dered lives con-fess
in deep - er rev - erence, praise, in deep- er rev - erence, praise.
rise up and fol - low thee, rise up and fol - low thee.
in - ter - pret - ed by love, in - ter- pret - ed by love!
the beau - ty of thy peace, the beau - ty of thy peace.

374 O God of truth

Thomas Hughes, 1859

Music: *Martyrs*, 8686; melody in *Scottish Psalter*, 1635

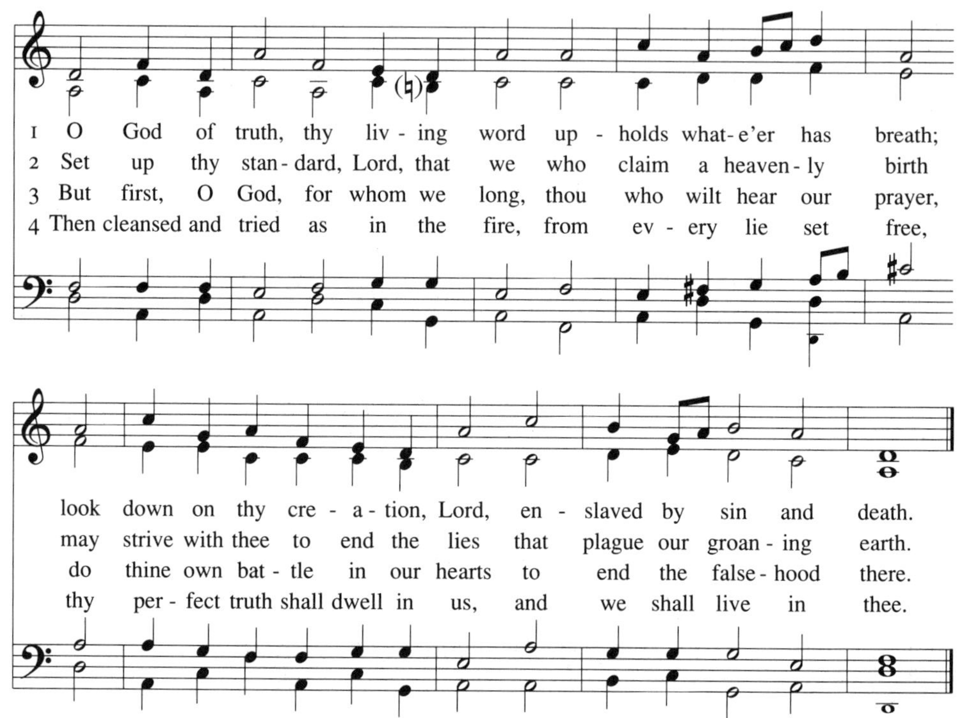
1 O God of truth, thy liv - ing word up - holds what-e'er has breath;
2 Set up thy stan - dard, Lord, that we who claim a heaven - ly birth
3 But first, O God, for whom we long, thou who wilt hear our prayer,
4 Then cleansed and tried as in the fire, from ev - ery lie set free,
look down on thy cre - a - tion, Lord, en - slaved by sin and death.
may strive with thee to end the lies that plague our groan - ing earth.
do thine own bat - tle in our hearts to end the false - hood there.
thy per - fect truth shall dwell in us, and we shall live in thee.

375 Another harmonization (from *Songs of Praise*, 1931):

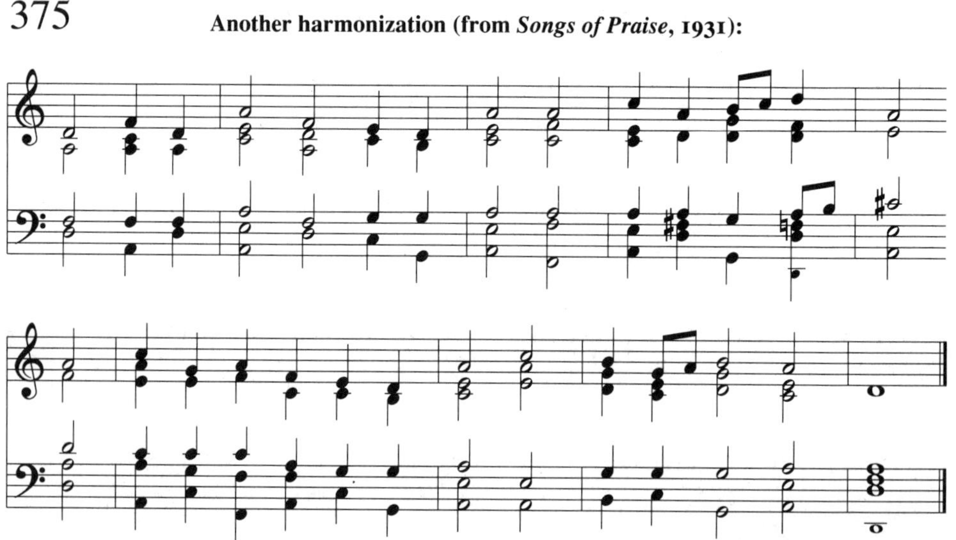

376 Out of the depths I cry to you

Aus tiefer Not schrei ich zu dir

Martin Luther, 1524; based on Psalm 130; translated by Gracia Grindal

Music: *Aus tiefer Not*, 8787887; attributed to Martin Luther, 1524; harmony mostly by Johann Hermann Schein, 1627

1 Out of the depths I cry to you; O Lord, now hear me call - ing.
2 All things you send are full of grace; you crown our lives with fa - vor.
3 It is in God that we shall hope, and not in our own mer - it;
4 My soul is wait-ing for the Lord as one who longs for morn - ing;
In - cline your ear to my dis - tress in spite of my re - bell - ing.
All our good works are done in vain with-out our Lord and Sa - vior.
we rest our fears in God's good Word and trust the Ho - ly Spir - it,
no watch - er waits with great - er hope than I for Christ's re - turn - ing.
Do not re - gard my sin - ful deeds. Send me the grace my spir - it needs;
We praise the God who gives us faith and saves us from the grip of death;
whose pro - mise keeps us strong and sure; we trust the ho - ly sig - na - ture
I hope as Is - rael in the Lord, who sends re - demp - tion through the Word.
with - out it I am noth - ing.
our lives are in God's keep - ing.
in - scribed up - on our tem - ples.
Praise God for end - less mer - cy.

377 Wilt thou forgive that sin

John Donne, 1633

Music: *Donne*, 10.10.10.10.8.4; melody and bass by John Hilton (c. 1621); inner voices by Roy F. Kehl, 1984

1 Wilt thou for-give that sin, where I be - gun, which is my sin, though
2 Wilt thou for-give that sin, by which I've won oth - ers to sin, and
3 I have a sin of fear that when I've spun my last thread, I shall
it were done be - fore? Wilt thou for-give those
made my sin their door? Wilt thou for-give that
per - ish on that shore; swear by thy-self, that
sins through which I run, and do run still, though
sin which I did shun a year or two, but
at my death thy Son shall shine as he shines
still I do de - plore? When thou hast done,
wal - lowed in a score? When thou hast done,
now, and here - to - fore. And hav - ing done
(♮)
(♮)
(♮)
(♮)

1–2
3
thou hast not done, for I have more.
thou hast not done, for I have more.
that, thou hast done, I fear no more.

378 "Forgive our sins as we forgive"

Rosamond J. Herklots, 1969

Music: *Detroit*, 8686; melody from *Supplement to Kentucky Harmony*, 1820; harmony by Margaret W. Mealy, 1985

1 "For - give our sins as we for - give," you taught us, Lord, to pray,
but you a - lone can grant us grace to live the words we say.

2 How can your par - don reach and bless the un - for - giv - ing heart
that broods on wrongs and will not let old bit - ter - ness de - part?

3 In blaz - ing light your cross re - veals the truth we dim - ly knew:
what triv - ial debts are owed to us, how great our debt to you.

4 Lord, cleanse the depths with - in our souls and bid re - sent - ment cease.
Then, bound to all in bonds of love, our lives will spread your peace.

379 Deep in the shadows of the past

"The quest," Brian Wren, 1973

Music: *Kingsfold*, 8686D; English traditional melody;
arranged by Ralph Vaughan Williams, 1906

1 Deep in the sha-dows of the past, far out from set - tled lands,
2 While oth-ers bowed to change-less gods, they met a mys - ter - y:
3 From A - bra - ham to Naz - a - reth the pro-mise changed and grew,
4 For all the writ-ings that sur-vived, for lead-ers, long a - go,
some no - mads trav - elled with their God a - cross the des - ert sands.
God with an un - com - plet - ed name, "I am what I will be";
while some, re - mem - ber - ing the past, re - cord - ed what they knew,
who sift - ed, chose, and then pre-served the Bi - ble that we know,
The dawn of hope for hu - man - kind was glimpsed by them a - lone —
and by their tents, a - round their fires, in sto - ry, song, and law,
and some, in let - ters or la - ments, in pro - phe - cy and praise,
give thanks, and find its pro - mise yet our com - fort, strength, and call,
a pro - mise call - ing them a - head, a fu - ture yet un - known.
they praised, re - mem - bered, hand - ed on a past that pro - mised more.
re - cov - ered, held, and re - ex - pressed new hope for chang - ing days.
the work - ing mod - el for our faith, a - live with hope for all.

380 O Word of God incarnate

William Walsham How, 1867

Music: *Munich*, 7676D; melody in *Neuvermehrtes Meiningisches Gesangbuch*, 1693; harmony adapted from a quartet in Mendelssohn's *Elijah*, 1847

1 O Word of God in - car - nate, O Wis - dom from on high,
2 The Church from you, dear Mas - ter, re - ceived the gift di - vine;
3 O make your Church, dear Sa - vior, a lamp of bur - nished gold
O Truth un-changed, un - chang - ing, O Light of our dark sky:
and still that light is lift - ed o'er all the earth to shine.
to bear be - fore the na - tions your true light, as of old;
we praise you for the ra - diance that from the hal-lowed page,
It is the chart and com - pass that, all life's voy - age through,
O teach your wan-dering pil - grims by this their path to trace,
a lan - tern to our foot - steps, shines on from age to age.
mid mists and rocks and quick - sands still guides, O Christ, to you.
till, clouds and dark-ness end - ed, they see you face to face.

381 Thanks to God whose Word was spoken

R. T. Brooks, 1954

Music: *Wylde Green*, 8787 with refrain; Peter Cutts, 1955, 1956

1 Thanks to God whose Word was spok - en in the deed that made the earth.
2 Thanks to God whose Word in - car - nate our new life on earth be - gan.
3 Thanks to God whose word was writ - ten in the Bi - ble's sa - cred page,
4 Thanks to God whose word is pub-lished in the tongues of ev - ery race.
His the voice that called a na - tion; his the fires that tried its worth.
Deeds and words and death and ris - ing tell the grace in heav-en's plan.
re - cord of the re - ve - la - tion show - ing God to ev - ery age.
See its glo - ry un - di - min - ished by the change of time or place.
God has spok - en: praise God for his o - pen word.
God has spok - en: praise God for his o - pen word.
God has spok - en: praise God for his o - pen word.
God has spok - en: praise God for his o - pen word.

5 Thanks to God whose Word is answered
by the Spirit's voice within.
Here we drink of joy unmeasured,
life redeemed from death and sin.
God is speaking:
praise God for his open word.

382 We limit not the truth of God

George Rawson, 1853; based on John Robinson's letter to the departing Pilgrims, 1620
(see also hymn no. 490)

Music: *Halifax*, 8686D; adapted in Butts's *Harmonia Sacra*, 1753, from an aria in G. F. Handel's *Susanna*, 1748; harmony based on Handel by David Hurd, 1984

1 We lim - it not the truth of God to our poor reach of mind,
2 Who dares to bind to our dull sense the or - a - cles of heaven,
3 O Tri - ni - ty most ho - ly, send us in-crease from a - bove;
to no-tions of our time and place, crude, par-tial, and con- fined;
for all the na-tions, tongues, and climes and all the a - ges given?
en-large, ex-pand all liv - ing souls to com-pre-hend your love;
no, let a new and bet - ter hope with - in our hearts be stirred;
The u - ni-verse, how much un-known! The o-cean un - ex - plored!
and make us all go on to know, with nob-ler powers con - ferred:
Refrain
the Lord has yet more light and truth to break forth from his word.

383 Yi-yi-yi-yisrael v'oraita

Open your ears, O faithful people

From the *Talmud*: "Israel and the Torah are one";
English words by Willard F. Jabusch, b. 1930

Music: *Yisrael v'oraita*, 10.6.10.6 with refrain; Hasidic melody;
harmony by Richard Proulx, 1984

1 Yi - yi - yi - yis - ra - el, yi - yis - ra - el v' - o - rai - ta had hu Yi - yi - yi - yis - ra - el, yi - yis - ra - el v' - o - rai - ta had hu
1 O - pen your ears, O faith - ful peo - ple, o - pen your ears and hear God's word. O - pen your hearts, O faith - ful peo - ple, God now speaks to you.
2 They who have ears to hear the mes - sage, they who have ears, now let them hear. They who would learn the way of wis - dom, let them hear God's word.

Refrain
Tor - ah or - a, Tor - ah or - a, Hal - le - lu - yah,
God has spok - en to the peo - ple, Hal - le - lu - yah!
Tor - ah or - a, Tor - ah or - a, Hal - le - lu - yah. Hal - le - lu - yah.
and his words are words of wis - dom, Hal - le - lu - yah! Hal - le - lu - yah!
Tor - ah or - a, Tor - ah or - a, Hal - le - lu - yah,
Tor - ah or - a, Tor - ah or - a, Hal - le - lu - yah!
Tor - ah or - a, Tor - ah or - a, Hal - le - lu - yah.
Tor - ah or - a, Tor - ah or - a, Hal - le - lu - yah!
3
3

384 When seed falls on good soil

Norman P. Olsen, 1976

Music: *Walhof*, 668866; Frederick F. Jackish, 1976

Unison

1 When seed falls on good soil, it's born through qu - iet toil;
2 God's Word in Christ is seed; good soil its ur - gent need;
3 Plow up the trod - den way, and clear the stone a - way;

where soil re - ceives, the earth con - ceives the blade, the stem, the fruit, the leaves.
for it must find in hu - man - kind the fer - tile soil in heart and mind.
tear out the weed, and sow the seed. Pre - pare our hearts your Word to heed,

Good soil, O mo - ther earth, the womb, where seed takes birth.
Good soil! A hu - man field! A hun - dred - fold to yield.
that we good soil may be. Be - gin, O Lord, with me!

385 We know that Christ is raised

John B. Geyer, 1967

Music: *Engelberg*, 10.10.10.4; Charles Villiers Stanford, 1904

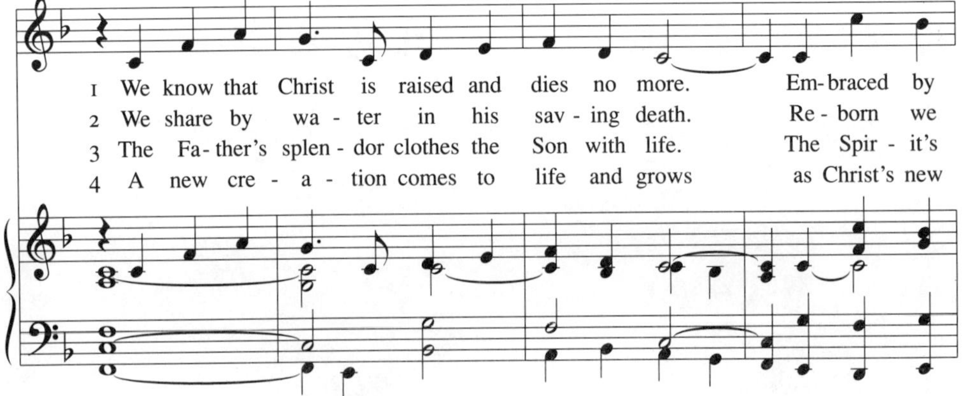
1 We know that Christ is raised and dies no more. Em - braced by
2 We share by wa - ter in his sav - ing death. Re - born we
3 The Fa - ther's splen - dor clothes the Son with life. The Spir - it's
4 A new cre - a - tion comes to life and grows as Christ's new

death he broke its fear - ful hold; and our de -
share with him an Eas - ter life as liv - ing
pow - er shakes the Church of God. Bap - tized we
Bod - y takes on flesh and blood. The u - ni -
1–3
spair he turned to blaz - ing joy. Al - le - lu - ia!
mem - bers of a liv - ing Christ. Al - le - lu - ia!
live with God the Three in One. Al - le - lu - ia!
verse re - stored and whole will sing:
4
Al - le - lu - ia! A - men.

386 I bind unto myself today

Attributed to St. Patrick (c. 386–c. 460); paraphrased by Cecil Frances Alexander, 1889

Music: *St. Patrick's Breastplate*, 8888D; Irish traditional melody arranged by Charles Villiers Stanford, 1902, 1906

Unison
1 I bind un - to my - self to - day the strong name
2 I bind this day to me for ev - er, by power of
3 I bind un - to my - self the power of the great
4 I bind un - to my - self to - day the vir - tues
5 I bind un - to my - self to - day the power of
of the Trin - i - ty, by in - vo - ca - tion
faith, Christ's in - car - na - tion; his bap - tism in the
love of cher - u - bim; the sweet "Well done" in
of the star - lit heaven — the glo - rious sun's life -
God to hold and lead, God's eye to watch, and
Stanza 1 ends here.
of the same, the Three in One, and One in Three.
Jor - dan riv - er; his death on cross for my sal - va - tion;
judg - ment hour; the ser - vice of the ser - a - phim;
giv - ing ray, the white - ness of the moon at even,
might to stay, and ear to heark - en to my need;
2 his burst - ing from the spic - ed tomb; his rid - ing
3 con - fess - ors' faith, a - pos - tles' word, the pa - triarchs'
4 the flash - ing of the light - ning free, the whirl - ing
5 the wis - dom of my God to teach, with hand to

up the heaven - ly way; his com - ing at the
prayers, the pro - phets' scrolls; all good deeds done un -
wind's tem - pes - tuous shocks, the sta - ble earth, the
guide, and shield to ward; the word of God to
day of doom: I bind un - to my - self to - day.
to the Lord, and pu - ri - ty of faith - ful souls.
deep salt sea, a - round the old e - ter - nal rocks.
give me speech, the heaven - ly host to be my guard.

5 I bind unto myself today
the power of God to hold and lead,
God's eye to watch, and might to stay,
and ear to hearken to my need;
the wisdom of my God to teach,
with hand to guide, and shield to ward;
the word of God to give me speech,
the heavenly host to be my guard.

For stanza 6, continue with hymn 387, "Christ be with me"; then return for stanza 7.

7 I bind unto myself the name,
the strong name of the Trinity,
by invocation of the same,
the Three in One, and One in Three.
Of whom all nature hath creation,
eternal Father, Spirit, Word:
praise to the Lord of my salvation,
salvation is of Christ the Lord.

387 Christ be with me

Attributed to St. Patrick (c. 386–c. 460); paraphrased by Cecil Frances Alexander, 1889

Music: *Deirdre*, 8888; Irish traditional melody, adapted by Charles Villiers Stanford, 1904

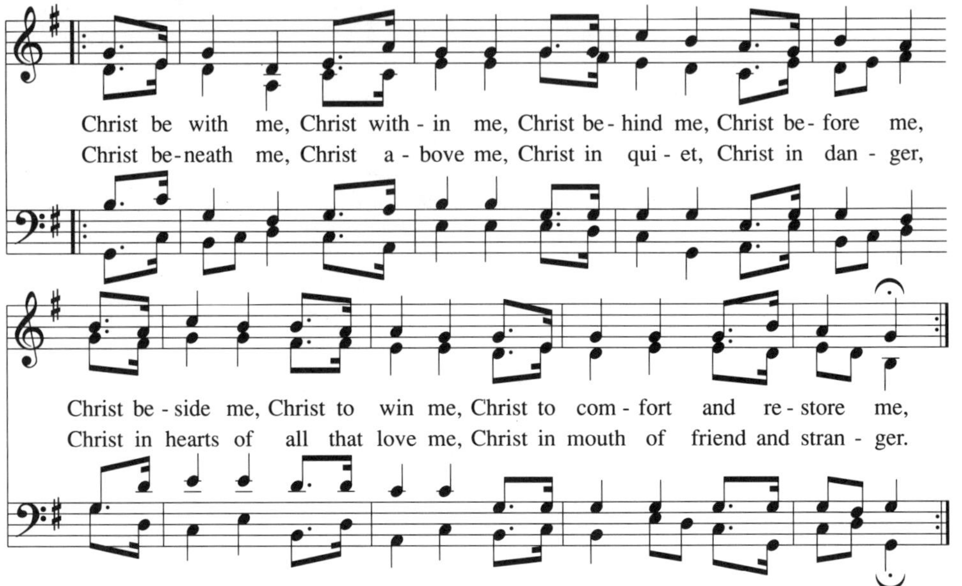
Christ be with me, Christ with - in me, Christ be - hind me, Christ be - fore me,
Christ be - neath me, Christ a - bove me, Christ in qui - et, Christ in dan - ger,
Christ be - side me, Christ to win me, Christ to com - fort and re - store me,
Christ in hearts of all that love me, Christ in mouth of friend and stran - ger.

388 This is the Spirit's entry now

Thomas E. Herbranson, 1965

Music: *Perry*, 8686; Leo Sowerby, 1962

1 This is the Spir - it's en - try now: the wa - ter and the Word,
2 This mir - a - cle of life re - born comes from the Lord of breath;
3 Let wa - ter be the sa - cred sign that we must die each day
4 Re - new - ing Spir - it, hear our praise for your bap - tis - mal power
the cross of Je - sus on your brow, the seal both felt and heard.
the per - fect One from life was torn; our life comes through Christ's death.
to rise a - gain by his de - sign as fol - lowers of his way.
that wash - es us through all our days. Lord, cleanse a - gain this hour.

389 Lord, we have come at your own invitation

"Confirmation and Commitment," Fred Pratt Green, 1977

Music: *O quanta qualia*, 11.10.11.10; melody in *Paris Antiphoner*, 1681; harmony by John Bacchus Dykes, 1868

1 Lord, we have come at your own in - vi - ta - tion,
2 Here, at your ta - ble, con - firm our in - ten - tion
3 When, at your ta - ble, each time of re - turn - ing,
4 So, in the world where each du - ty as - signed us
chos - en by you to be count - ed as friends:
ev - er to cher - ish the gifts you pro - vide;
vows are re - newed, and our cour - age re - stored:
gives us the chance to cre - ate or de - stroy,
yours is the strength that sus - tains our vo - ca - tion,
teach us to serve with - out pride or pre - ten - sion,
may we in - creas - ing - ly glo - ry in learn - ing
help us to make those de - ci - sions that bind us,
ours a com - mit - ment we know nev - er ends.
led by your Spir - it, de - fend - er and guide.
all that it means to ac - cept you as Lord.
Lord, to your - self, in o - bed - ience and joy.

390 Spirit of God, unleashed on earth

John W. Arthur, 1972

Music: *Lledrod*, 8888; melody in *Caniadaeth y Cysegr*, 1839

1 Spir - it of God, un - leashed on earth with rush of
2 You came in power; the Church was born; O Ho - ly
3 With burn - ing words of vic - tory won in - spire our

wind and roar of flame! With tongues of fire saints
Spir - it, come a - gain! From liv - ing wa - ters
hearts grown cold with fear, re - vive in us bap -

spread good news; earth, kin - dling, blazed its loud ac - claim.
raise new saints; let new tongues hail the ris - en Lord.
tis - mal grace, and fan our smol - dering lives to flame.

391 This is the hour of banquet

Horatius Bonar, 1855

Music: *Nyack*, 10.10.10.10; Warren Swenson, 1985

These words can also be sung to *Sursum corda*, no. 392.

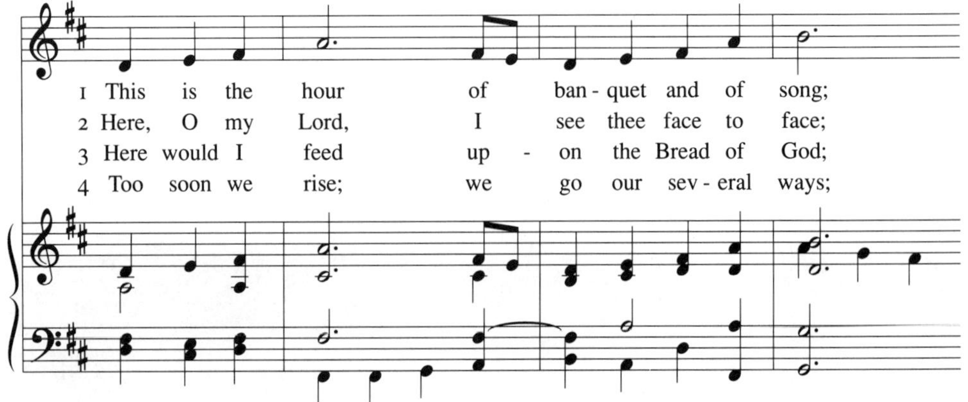
1 This is the hour of ban - quet and of song;
2 Here, O my Lord, I see thee face to face;
3 Here would I feed up - on the Bread of God;
4 Too soon we rise; we go our sev - eral ways;

this is the heaven - ly ta - ble spread for me;
here would I touch and han - dle things un - seen;
here drink with thee the roy - al Wine of heaven;
the feast, though not the love, is past and gone,
here let me feast, and, feast - ing, still pro - long
here grasp with firm - er hand e - ter - nal grace,
here would I lay a - side each earth - ly load,
the Bread and Wine con - sumed: yet all our days
the brief, bright hour of fel - low - ship with thee.
and all my wea - ri - ness up - on thee lean.
here taste a - fresh the calm of sin for - given.
thou still art here with us — our Shield and Sun.

392 Come, risen Lord

George W. Briggs, 1931

Music: *Sursum corda*, 10.10.10.10; Alfred M. Smith, 1941

1 Come, ris - en Lord, and deign to be our guest; nay, let us be thy
2 We meet, as in that up - per room they met; thou at the ta - ble,
3 One bo - dy we, who now one Bo - dy take, one Church u - nit - ed
4 One with each o - ther, Lord, for one in thee, who art one Sa - vior
guests; the feast is thine; thy - self at thine own board make man - i -
bless - ing, yet dost stand: "This is my Bo - dy": so thou giv - est
in com - mun - ion blest; one name we bear, one Bread of life we
and one liv - ing Head; then o - pen thou our eyes, that we may
fest in thine own sac - ra - ment of bread and wine.
yet; faith still re - ceives the cup as from thy hand.
break, with all thy saints on earth and saints at rest.
see; be known to us in break - ing of the Bread.

393 Let us break bread together

African American spiritual, probably 18th century, stanzas 1 and 2 are probably 19th-century additions

Music: *Let us break bread together*, 10.10 with refrain; African American spiritual; harmony by David Hurd, 1983

1 Let us break bread to - geth- er on our knees;
2 Let us drink wine to - geth- er on our knees;
3 Let us praise God to - geth- er on our knees;
let us break bread to - geth-er on our knees;
let us drink wine to - geth-er on our knees;
let us praise God to - geth-er on our knees;
Refrain
when I fall on my knees, with my face to the ris - ing sun,
O Lord, have mer- cy on me.
1–2
3

394 An upper room did our Lord prepare

Fred Pratt Green, 1973

Music: *O Waly Waly*, 9898; English traditional melody; harmony by John Wilson, 1974

1 An up - per room did our Lord pre - pare for those he
2 A last - ing gift Je - sus gave his own: to share his
3 And af - ter sup - per he washed their feet, for ser - vice,
4 No end there is! We de - part in peace. He loves be -
loved un - til the end, and his dis - ci - ples still ga - ther
bread, his lov - ing cup. What - ev - er bur - dens may bow us
too, is sac - ra - ment. In him our joy shall be made com -
yond our ut - ter - most: in ev - ery room in our Fa - ther's
there, to cel - e - brate their ris - en friend.
down, he by his cross shall lift us up.
plete, sent out to serve, as he was sent.
house, he will be there, as Lord and host.

395 At the Lamb's high feast we sing

Ad regias Agni dapes

From the *Roman Breviary* of 1631; based on the medieval *Ad coenam Agni providi*; translated by Robert Campbell, 1849

Music: *Salzburg*, 7777D; melody by Jakob Hintze, 1678; harmony adapted from J. S. Bach (1685–1750)

1 At the Lamb's high feast we sing praise to our vic - to - rious King,
2 Where the Pas - chal blood is poured, death's dark an - gel sheathes his sword:
3 Might - y vic - tim from on high, hell's fierce powers be - neath you lie;
4 Eas - ter tri - umph, Eas - ter joy, you a - lone can sin de - stroy.
who has washed us in the tide flow - ing from his pierc - ed side;
Is - rael's hosts tri - umph - ant go through the wave that drowns the foe.
you have con - quered in the fight, you have brought us life and light:
From sin's power now set us free, new - born souls, O Lord, to be.
praise we him, whose love di - vine gives his sa - cred blood for wine,
Praise we Christ, whose blood was shed, Pas - chal vic - tim, Pas - chal bread;
now no more can death ap - pall, now no more the grave en - thrall;
Hymns of glo - ry, songs of praise, gra - cious God, to you we raise;
gives his bod - y for the feast, Christ the vic - tim, Christ the priest.
with sin - cer - i - ty and love eat we man - na from a - bove.
you have o - pened par - a - dise, and in you your saints shall rise.
ris - en Lord and Spir - it blest, prais - es be to you ad - dressed.

396 Draw us in the Spirit's tether

Percy Dearmer, 1931

Music: *Union Seminary*, 8787447; Harold Friedell, 1957

1 Draw us in the Spir-it's teth - er, for when hum - bly in thy name two or three are met to - geth - er, thou art in the midst of them; Al - le - lu - ia! Al - le - lu - ia! Touch we now thy gar - ment's hem.
2 As dis - ci - ples used to gath - er in the name of Christ to sup, then with thanks to God the Giv - er break the bread and bless the cup, Al - le - lu - ia! Al - le - lu - ia! so now bind our friend - ship up.
3 All our meals and all our liv - ing make as sac - ra - ments of thee, that by car - ing, help-ing, giv - ing, we may true dis - ci - ples be. Al - le - lu - ia! Al - le - lu - ia! We will serve thee faith - ful - ly.

397 Father, we thank you that you planted

F. Bland Tucker, 1939, and others; based on prayers in the *Didache*, 2d century

Music: *Rendez à Dieu*, 9898D; melody in *La Forme des prières et chants ecclésiastiques*, Strasbourg, 1545; harmony adapted from Claude Goudimel, 1565

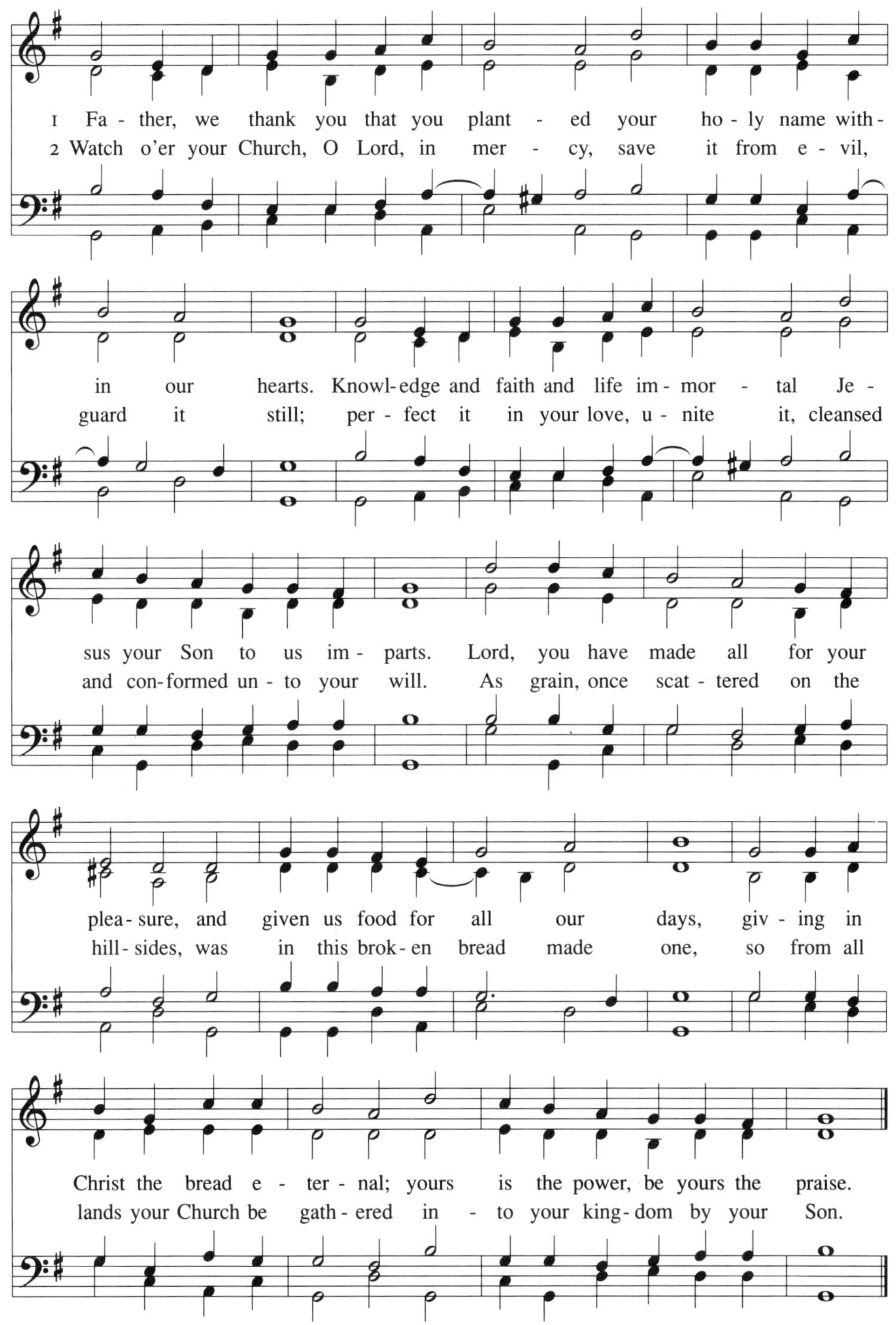
1 Fa - ther, we thank you that you plant - ed your ho - ly name with - in our hearts. Knowl - edge and faith and life im - mor - tal Je - sus your Son to us im - parts. Lord, you have made all for your plea - sure, and given us food for all our days, giv - ing in Christ the bread e - ter - nal; yours is the power, be yours the praise.
2 Watch o'er your Church, O Lord, in mer - cy, save it from e - vil, guard it still; per - fect it in your love, u - nite it, cleansed and con - formed un - to your will. As grain, once scat - tered on the hill - sides, was in this brok - en bread made one, so from all lands your Church be gath - ered in - to your king - dom by your Son.

398 Father, we thank you that you planted

F. Bland Tucker, 1939, and others; based on prayers in the *Didache*, 2d century

Music: *Albright*, 9898D; William Albright, 1973

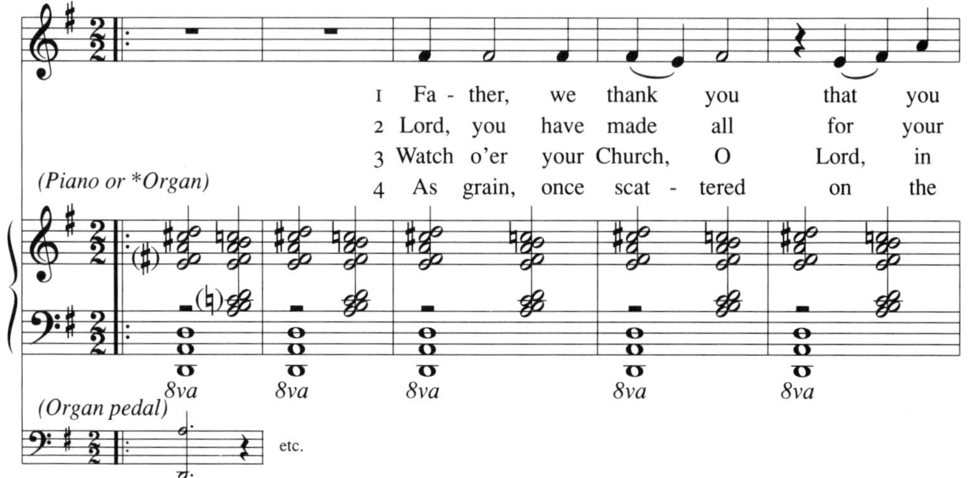

1 Fa - ther, we thank you that you
2 Lord, you have made all for your
3 Watch o'er your Church, O Lord, in
4 As grain, once scat - tered on the
(Piano or *Organ)
8va
(Organ pedal)
etc.

**Tie all repeated notes in hands.*

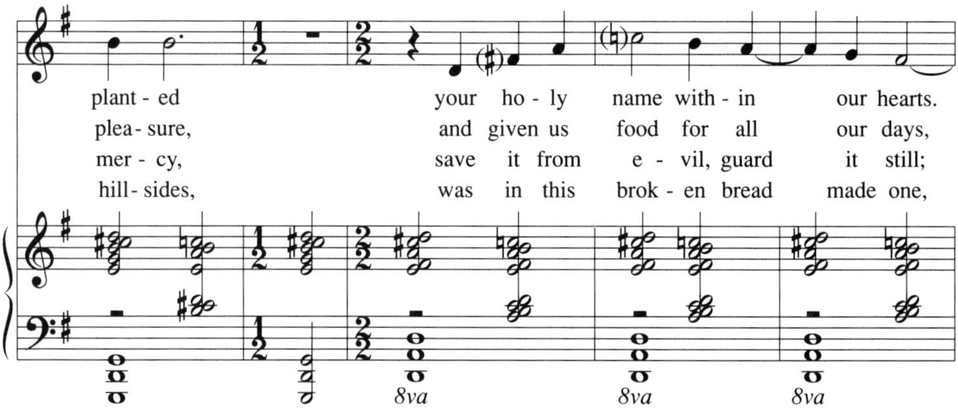

plant - ed your ho - ly name with - in our hearts.
plea - sure, and given us food for all our days,
mer - cy, save it from e - vil, guard it still;
hill - sides, was in this brok - en bread made one,

8va

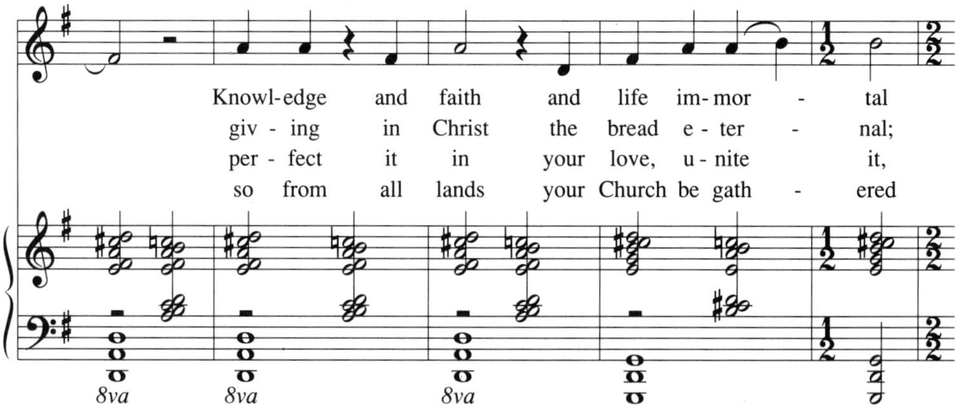

Knowl - edge and faith and life im - mor - tal
giv - ing in Christ the bread e - ter - nal;
per - fect it in your love, u - nite it,
so from all lands your Church be gath - ered

8va

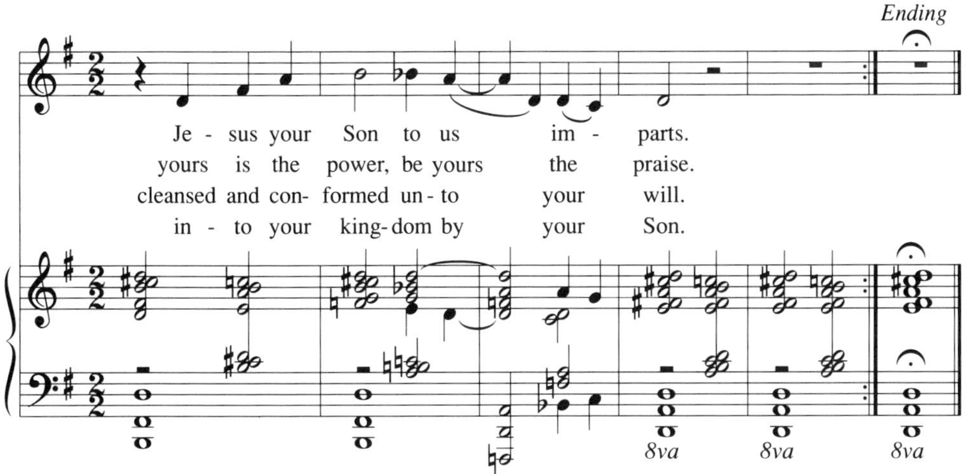
Ending
Je - sus your Son to us im - parts.
yours is the power, be yours the praise.
cleansed and con- formed un- to your will.
in - to your king- dom by your Son.
8va
8va
8va

399 Bread of the world in mercy broken

Reginald Heber, 1827 (posth.)

Music: *Les Commandemens de Dieu*, 9898; melody in *La Forme des prières et chants ecclésiastiques*, Strasbourg, 1545; harmony adapted from Claude Goudimel, 1565

These words can also be sung to *Rendez à Dieu*, no. 397.

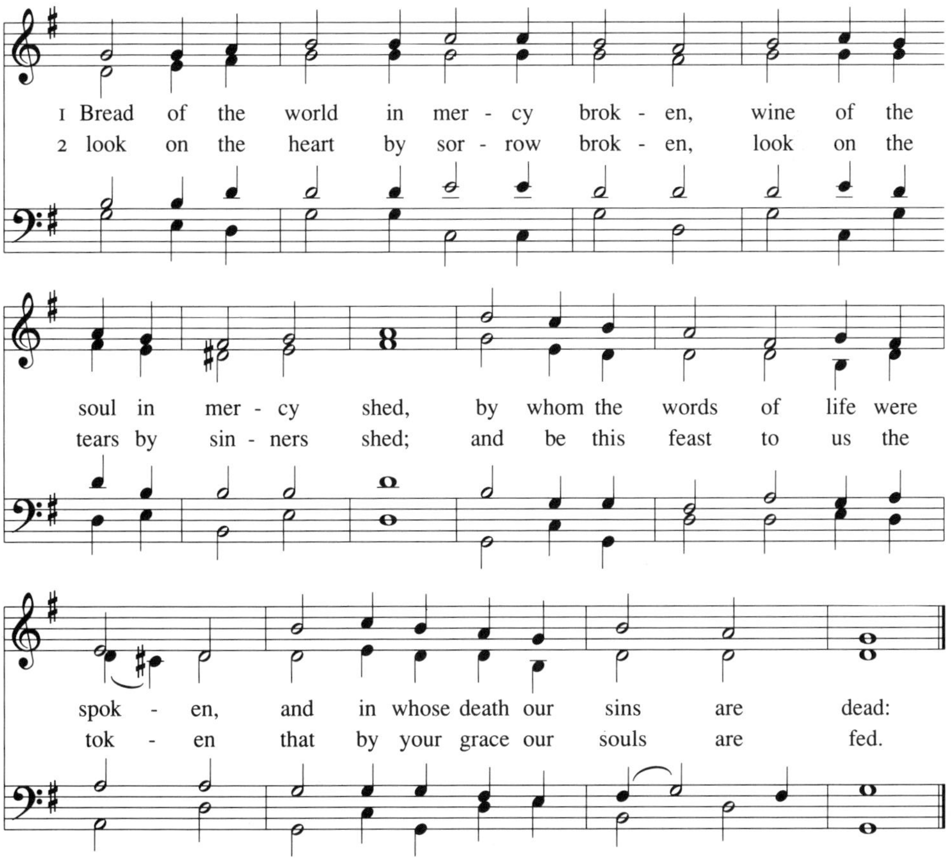

1 Bread of the world in mer - cy brok - en, wine of the
2 look on the heart by sor - row brok - en, look on the

soul in mer - cy shed, by whom the words of life were
tears by sin - ners shed; and be this feast to us the

spok - en, and in whose death our sins are dead:
tok - en that by your grace our souls are fed.

400 The King of love my shepherd is

Henry W. Baker, 1868, based on Psalm 23

Music: *St. Columba*, 8787; Irish traditional melody

3
1 The King of love my shep - herd is, whose good - ness
2 Where streams of liv - ing wa - ter flow, my ran - somed
3 Per - verse and fool - ish oft I strayed, but yet in
4 In death's dark vale I fear no ill with thee, dear
fail - eth nev - er; I noth - ing lack if
soul he lead - eth; and where the ver - dant
love he sought me, and on his shoul - der
Lord, be - side me; thy rod and staff my
I am his, and he is mine for ev - er.
pas - tures grow, with food ce - les - tial feed - eth.
gent - ly laid, and home, re - joic - ing, brought me.
com - fort still, thy cross be - fore to guide me.

5 Thou spread'st a table in my sight;
thy unction grace bestoweth;
and O what transport of delight
from thy pure chalice floweth!

6 And so through all the length of days
thy goodness faileth never:
Good Shepherd, may I sing thy praise
within thy house forever.

401 You satisfy the hungry heart

Omer Westendorf, 1976

Music: *Bicentennial*, 8686 with refrain; Robert E. Kreutz, 1976

Refrain
You sat-is-fy the hun-gry heart with gift of fin-est wheat;
come give to us, O sav-ing Lord, the bread of life to eat.
Fine
As when a shep-herd calls the sheep, they know and heed that voice,
With joy-ful lips we sing to you our praise and grat-i-tude,
Is not the cup we bless and share the blood of Christ out-poured?
The mys-tery of your pres-ence, Lord, no mor-tal tongue can tell:
so when you call your fam-ily, Lord, we fol-low and re-joice.
that you should count us wor-thy, Lord, to share this heaven-ly food.
Do not one cup, one loaf, de-clare our one-ness in the Lord?
whom all the world can-not con-tain comes in our hearts to dwell.
D.C.

6 You give yourself to us, O Lord;
then selfless let us be,
to serve each other in your name
in truth and charity.

Refrain

402 Deck thyself, my soul, with gladness

Schmücke dich, o liebe Seele

Johann Franck, 1649; translated by Catherine Winkworth, 1858

Music: *Schmücke dich*, 8888D; melody by Johann Crüger, 1649; harmony from *The English Hymnal*, 1906

1 Deck thy - self, my soul, with glad - ness, leave the gloom - y haunts of sad - ness, come in - to the day-light's splen - dor, there with joy thy prais-es ren - der un - to Christ whose grace un - bound - ed hath this won - drous ban - quet found - ed; high o'er
2 Sun, who all my life dost bright - en; Light, who dost my soul en - light - en; Joy, the best that an - y know - eth; Fount, whence all my be - ing flow - eth: at thy feet I cry, "My Mak - er, let me be a fit par - tak - er of this
3 Je - sus, bread of life, I pray thee, let me glad - ly here o - bey thee; nev - er to my hurt in - vit - ed, be thy love with love re - quit - ed; from this ban - quet let me mea - sure, Lord, how vast and deep its trea - sure; through the

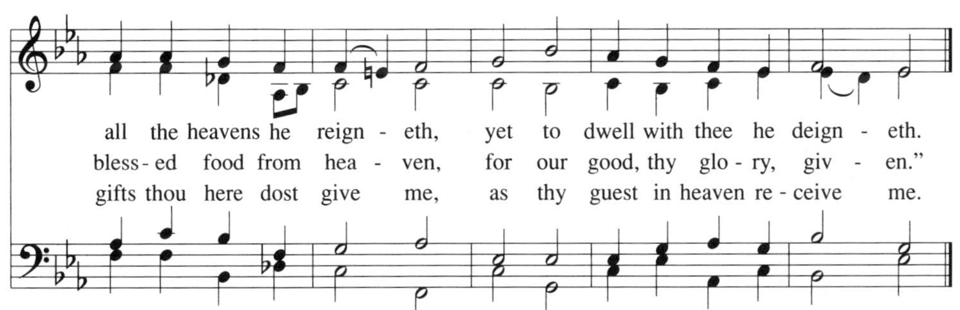
all the heavens he reign - eth, yet to dwell with thee he deign - eth.
bless - ed food from hea - ven, for our good, thy glo - ry, giv - en."
gifts thou here dost give me, as thy guest in heaven re - ceive me.

403 I come with joy to meet my Lord

"Christ making friends," Brian Wren, 1968, 1977

Music: *Land of Rest*, 8686; American folk melody;
adapted and harmonized by Annabel Morris Buchanan, 1938

1 I come with joy to meet my Lord, for - giv - en, loved, and free, in awe and won - der to re - call his life laid down for me.

2 I come with Chris - tians far and near to find, as all are fed, the new com - mu - ni - ty of love in Christ's com - mun - ion bread.

3 As Christ breaks bread and bids us share, each proud di - vi - sion ends; the love that made us, makes us one, and stran - gers now are friends.

4 And thus with joy we meet our Lord; his pres - ence, al - ways near, is in such friend - ship bet - ter known: we see and praise him here.

5 Together met, together bound,
we'll go our different ways,
and as his people in the world
we'll live and speak his praise.

404 Now, my tongue, the mystery telling

Pange lingua gloriosi

Attributed to Thomas Aquinas, 1263; based on Fortunatus's hymn *Pange lingua gloriosi* (see no. 261); translation adapted from *The Hymnal 1940*

Music: *Pange lingua*, 878787; plainsong; harmony by Ivan Florjanc in *Slavimo Gospoda*, Celje, 1988

1 Now, my tongue, the mys-tery tell - ing, of the glo - rious bo - dy sing,
2 Given for us, and con - de - scend - ing to be born for us be - low,
3 That last night at sup - per ly - ing mid the twelve, his cho - sen band,
4 Word made flesh, the bread he tak - eth, by his word his flesh to be;
and the blood, all price ex - cell - ing, which the Gen - tiles' Lord and King,
with his own in con - verse blend - ing he the seed of truth did sow,
Je - sus, with the Law com - ply - ing, keeps the feast its rites de - mand;
wine his sa - cred blood he mak - eth, though the sens - es fail to see;
once on earth a - mong us dwell - ing, shed for this world's ran - som - ing.
till he closed with won - drous end - ing his most pa - tient life of woe.
then, more pre - cious food sup - ply - ing, gives him - self with his own hand.
faith a - lone the true heart wak - eth to be - hold the mys - ter - y.

405 Now, my tongue, the mystery telling

Pange lingua gloriosi

Attributed to Thomas Aquinas, 1263; based on Fortunatus's hymn *Pange lingua gloriosi* (see no. 261); translation adapted from *The Hymnal 1940*

Music: *Grafton*, 878787; melody in *Le Recueil noté*, Lyon, 1871; harmony from *Songs of Praise*, 1925

1 Now, my tongue, the mys-tery tell-ing, of the glo-rious bo-dy sing,
2 Given for us, and con-de-scend-ing to be born for us be-low,
3 That last night at sup-per ly-ing mid the twelve, his cho-sen band,
4 Word made flesh, the bread he tak-eth, by his word his flesh to be;
and the blood, all price ex-cell-ing, which the Gen-tiles' Lord and King,
with his own in con-verse blend-ing he the seed of truth did sow,
Je-sus, with the Law com-ply-ing, keeps the feast its rites de-mand;
wine his sa-cred blood he mak-eth, though the sens-es fail to see;
once on earth a-mong us dwell-ing, shed for this world's ran-som-ing.
till he closed with won-drous end-ing his most pa-tient life of woe.
then, more pre-cious food sup-ply-ing, gives him-self with his own hand.
faith a-lone the true heart wak-eth to be-hold the mys-ter-y.

406 Una espiga

Sheaves of summer

Cesareo Gabaraín, 1973; translated by George Lockwood

Music: *Una espiga*, 10.10.13.10; Cesareo Gabaraín, 1973; harmony by Skinner Chavez-Melo, 1973

1 U - na es - pi - ga do - ra - da por el sol,
2 Com - par - ti - mos la mis - ma co - mu - nión,
1 Sheaves of sum - mer turned gold - en by the sun,
2 We are shar - ing the same com - mun - ion meal,
el ra - ci - mo que cor - ta el vi - ña - dor,
so - mos tri - go del mis - mo sem - bra - dor,
grapes in bunch - es, cut down when ripe and red,
we are wheat by the same great Sow - er sown;
se con - vier - ten a - ho - ra en pan y vi - no de a - mor,
un mo - li - no a la vi - da nos tri - tu - ra con do - lor,
are con - vert - ed in - to the bread and wine of God's love
like a mill - stone life grinds us down with sor - row and pain,
en el cuer - po y la san - gre del Se - ñor.
Dios nos ha - ce pue - blo nue - vo en el a - mor.
in the bod - y and blood of our dear Lord.
but God makes us new peo - ple bound by love.

3 *Como granos que han hecho el mismo pan,*
como notas que tejen un cantar,
como gotas de agua que se funden en el mar,
los cristianos un cuerpo formarán.

4 *En la mesa de Dios se sentarán,*
como hijos su pan compartirán,
una misma esperanza caminando cantarán,
en la vida como hermanos se amarán.

3 Like the grains which become one same whole loaf,
like the notes that are woven into song,
like the droplets of water that are blended in the sea,
we, as Christians, one body shall become.

4 At God's table together we will sit.
As God's children, Christ's body we will share.
One same hope we will sing together as we walk along.
Brothers, sisters, in life, in love, we'll be.

407 Now the silence

Jaroslav J. Vajda, 1968

Music: *Now*, irregular meter; Carl Schalk, 1969

Now the si - lence Now the peace Now the emp - ty hands up- lift - ed
Now the kneel- ing Now the plea Now the Fa- ther's arms in wel- come
Now the hear- ing Now the power Now the ves - sel brimmed for pour - ing

Now the bod - y Now the blood Now the joy - ful cel - e - bra - tion
Now the wed- ding Now the songs Now the heart for- giv - en leap - ing
Now the Spir - it's vis - i - ta - tion Now the Son's e - pi - pha - ny
Now the Fa - ther's bless - ing Now Now Now

408 Let all mortal flesh keep silence

From the *Liturgy of St. James*, 4th century; translated by Gerard Moultrie, 1864

Music: *Picardy*, 878787; French folk melody

Unison
1 Let all mor - tal flesh keep si - lence, and with fear and
2 King of kings, yet born of Ma - ry, as of old on
3 Rank on rank the host of heav - en spreads its van - guard
4 At his feet the six - winged ser - aph; cher - u - bim with
trem - bling stand; pon - der noth - ing earth - ly mind - ed,
earth he stood, Lord of lords, in hu - man ves - ture —
on the way, as the Light of light de - scend - eth
sleep - less eye veil their fac - es to the Pres - ence,
for with bless - ing in his hand Christ our God to earth de -
in the Bo - dy and the Blood — he will give to all the
from the realms of end - less day, that the powers of hell may
as with cease - less voice they cry, "Al - le - lu - ia! Al - le -
scend - eth, our full hom - age to de - mand.
faith - ful his own self for heaven - ly food.
va - nish as the dark - ness clears a - way.
lu - ia! Al - le - lu - ia! Lord most high."

409 Humbly I adore thee

Adoro te devote

Attributed to Thomas Aquinas (1227–1274); translation from *The Hymnal 1982*

Music: *Adoro te devote*, 11.11.11.11; melody in *Processionale*, Paris, 1697; harmony by Frederick F. Jackisch, 1978

1 Hum - bly I a - dore thee, Ver - i - ty un - seen,
2 Taste and touch and vi - sion to dis - cern thee fail;
3 O me - mo - rial won - drous of the Lord's own death;
4 Je - sus, whom now hid - den I by faith be - hold,
who thy glo - ry hid - est 'neath these sha - dows mean;
faith, that comes by hear - ing, pierc - es through the veil.
liv - ing Bread that giv - est all thy crea - tures breath,
what my soul doth long for, that thy word fore - told:
lo, to thee sur - ren - dered, my whole heart is bowed,
I be - lieve what - e'er the Son of God hath told;
grant my spir - it ev - er by thy life may live,
face to face thy splen - dor I at last shall see,

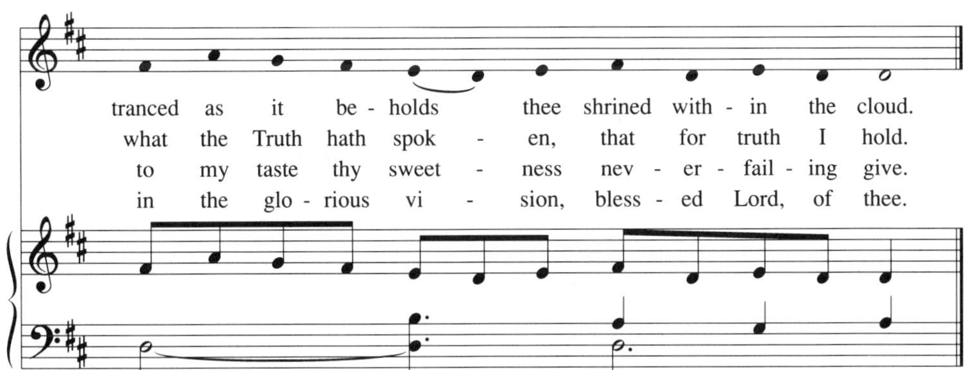
tranced as it be - holds thee shrined with - in the cloud.
what the Truth hath spok - en, that for truth I hold.
to my taste thy sweet - ness nev - er - fail - ing give.
in the glo - rious vi - sion, bless - ed Lord, of thee.

410 Lord, enthroned in heavenly splendor

George Hugh Bourne, 1874

Music: *St. Helen*, 8787447; George Martin, 1881

Unison

1 Lord, en - throned in heaven - ly splen - dor, first be - got - ten from the dead,
2 Here our hum - blest hom - age pay we; here in lov - ing rev - erence bow;
3 Though the low - liest form now veils you as of old in Beth - le - hem,
4 Pas - chal Lamb, your offer - ing, fin - ished once for all when you were slain,

Harmony

you a - lone, our strong de - fend - er, now lift up your peo - ple's head.
here for faith's dis - cern - ment pray we, lest we fail to know you now.
here as there your an - gels hail you, branch and flower of Jes - se's stem.
in its full - ness un - di - min - ished shall for ev - er - more re - main.

Al - le - lu - ia! Al - le - lu - ia! Je - sus, true and liv - ing Bread!
Al - le - lu - ia! Al - le - lu - ia! You are here, we ask not how.
Al - le - lu - ia! Al - le - lu - ia! We in wor - ship join with them.
Al - le - lu - ia! Al - le - lu - ia! Cleans - ing souls from ev - ery stain.

5 Life-imparting heavenly manna,
stricken rock with streaming side,
heaven and earth with loud hosanna
worship you, the Lamb who died.
Alleluia! Alleluia!
Risen, ascended, glorified!

411 Thine the amen thine the praise

Herbert Brokering, 1983

Music: *Thine the amen*, 7.7.7.7.8.7.14; Carl Schalk, 1983

1 Thine the a - men thine the praise al - le - lu - ias an - gels raise
2 life e - ter - nal - ly thine the prom - ise let there be
3 tru - ly thine the yes thine the ta - ble we the guest
4 king-dom thine the prize thine the won - der full sur - prise
thine the ev - er - last - ing head thine the break - ing of the bread
thine the vi - sion thine the tree all the earth on bend - ed knee
thine the mer - cy all from thee thine the glo - ry yet to be
thine the ban - quet then the praise then the jus - tice of thy ways
thine the glo - ry thine the sto - ry thine the har - vest then the cup
gone the nail - ing gone the rail - ing gone the plead - ing gone the cry
then the ring - ing and the sing - ing then the end of all the war
thine the glo - ry thine the sto - ry then the wel - come to the least

thine the vine - yard then the cup is lift - ed
gone the sigh - ing gone the dy - ing what was
thine the liv - ing thine the lov - ing ev - er -
then the won - der all in - creas - ing at thy
1–4
5
up lift - ed up.
loss lift - ed high.
more ev - er - more.
feast at thy feast.
(2) Thine the
(3) Thine the
(4) Thine the
(5) Thine the
(5) thee.

5 Thine the glory in the night
no more dying only light
thine the river thine the tree
then the Lamb eternally
then the holy holy holy
celebration jubilee
thine the spendor thine the brightness
only thee only thee.

412 The bread of life

Jiu shi zhi shen

Timothy Tingfang Lew, 1935; translated by Walter Reginald Oxenham Taylor, 1943

Music: *Sheng en*, 9898; melody by Su Yin-Lan, 1934; harmony by I-to Loh, 1984

1 *Jiu shi zhi shen, wei zhong-sheng bo - kai,*
1 The bread of life for all is brok - en!
2 With god - ly fear we seek your pres - ence,
3 O Lord, we pray, come now a - mong us,
Zai Gu - lou di, tong in ku - bei;
Christ drank the cup of Gol - go - tha.
our hearts dis - tressed by peo - ple's grief.
light - en our eyes, bright - ly ap - pear!
Meng en xin - zhong, feng ming chang ji - nian,
God's grace we trust, and spread with rev - erence
Your ho - ly face is stained with bit - ter tears;
Em - man - u - el, heaven's joy un - end - ing,
Jing she sheng - yan, zhu - i dang nian.
this ho - ly feast, and thus re - mem - ber.
our hu - man pain you share each day with us.
our life with yours for - ev - er blend - ing.

413 O Christ, the healer

"A Prayer for Wholeness," Fred Pratt Green, 1967

Music: *Distress*, 8888; melody in William Walker's *Southern Harmony*, 1835;
harmony by Russell Schulz-Widmar, 1990

1 O Christ, the heal - er, we have come to
2 From ev - ery ail - ment flesh en - dures our
3 How strong, O Lord, are our de - sires, how
4 In con - flicts that de - stroy our health we
pray for health, to plead for friends. How can we fail to
bod - ies clam - or to be freed; yet in our hearts we
weak our knowl - edge of our - selves! Re - lease in us those
rec - og - nize the world's dis - ease; our com - mon life de -
be re - stored when reached by love that nev - er ends?
would con - fess that whole - ness is our deep - est need.
heal - ing truths un - con - scious pride re - sists or shelves.
clares our ills. Is there no cure, O Christ, for these?

5 Grant that we all, made one in faith,
in your community may find
the wholeness that, enriching us,
shall reach the whole of humankind.

414 "Silence! Frenzied, unclean spirit"

Thomas H. Troeger, 1984

Music: *Authority*, 8787D; Carol Doran, 1984

These words can also be sung to *Geneva*, no. 423.

(f, f, mf)
1 "Si-lence! Fren-zied, un-clean spir-it," cried God's heal-ing Ho-ly One.
2 Lord, the de-mons still are thriv-ing in the gray cells of the mind:
3 Si-lence, Lord, the un-clean spir-it, in our mind and in our heart.
(f, f, mf)
"Cease your rant-ing! Flesh can't bear it. Flee as night be-
ty-rant voic-es, shrill and driv-ing, twist-ed thoughts that
Speak your word that when we hear it, all our de-mons
fore the sun." At Christ's voice the de-mon trem-bled,
grip and bind, doubts that stir the heart to pan-ic,
shall de-part. Clear our thought and calm our feel-ing,
from its vic-tim mad-ly rushed, while the crowd that
fears dis-tort-ing rea-son's sight, guilt that makes our
still the frac-tured, war-ring soul. By the pow-er

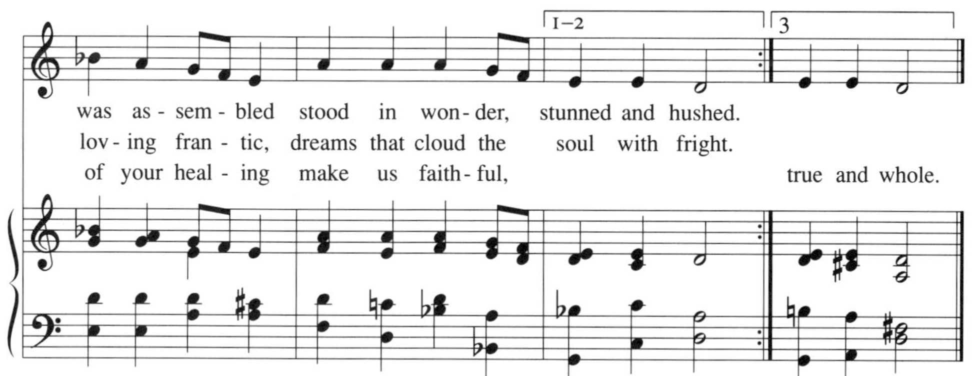
1–2
3
was as - sem - bled stood in won - der, stunned and hushed.
lov - ing fran - tic, dreams that cloud the soul with fright.
of your heal - ing make us faith - ful, true and whole.

415 In the hour of my distress

"Litany to the Holy Spirit," Robert Herrick, *Hesperides*, 1648

Music: *St. Bees*, 7776; John Bacchus Dykes, 1862

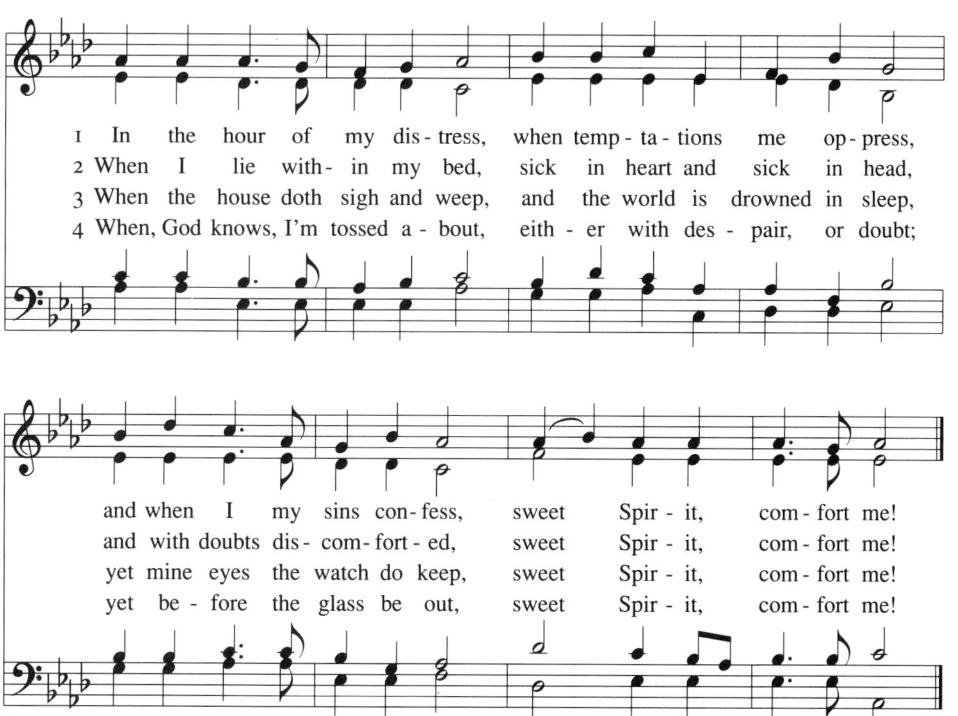
1 In the hour of my dis - tress, when temp - ta - tions me op - press,
2 When I lie with - in my bed, sick in heart and sick in head,
3 When the house doth sigh and weep, and the world is drowned in sleep,
4 When, God knows, I'm tossed a - bout, eith - er with des - pair, or doubt;
and when I my sins con - fess, sweet Spir - it, com - fort me!
and with doubts dis - com - fort - ed, sweet Spir - it, com - fort me!
yet mine eyes the watch do keep, sweet Spir - it, com - fort me!
yet be - fore the glass be out, sweet Spir - it, com - fort me!

416 Your hands, O Lord, in days of old

Edward H. Plumptre, 1864, and others

Music: *St. Matthew*, 8686D; melody in *A Supplement to the New Version*, 1708; probably by William Croft

1 Your hands, O Lord, in days of old were strong to heal and save; they tri - umphed o'er dis - ease and death, o'er dark - ness and the grave. To you they went, the blind, the deaf, the pal - sied, and the lame, the lep - er
2 And then your touch brought life and health, gave hear - ing, strength, and sight; and youth re - newed and health re - stored praised you, the Lord of light: and so, O Lord, be near to bless, with all your heal - ing power, in troub - led
3 O be our gra - cious lead - er still, great Lord of life and death; re - store and strength - en, soothe and bless with your al - might - y breath: on hands that work and eyes that see, your heal - ing wis - dom pour, that whole and

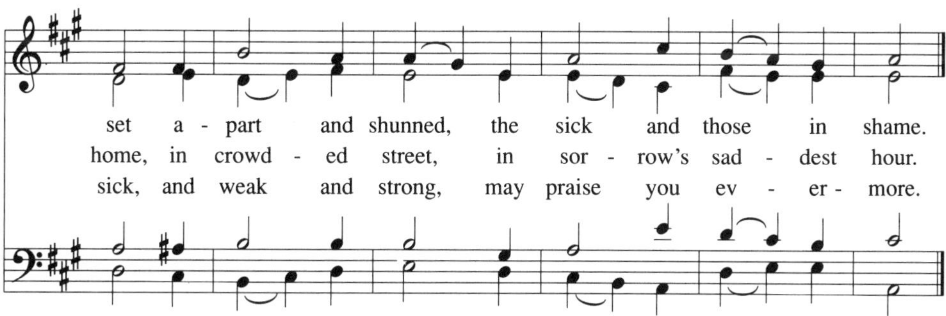
set a - part and shunned, the sick and those in shame.
home, in crowd - ed street, in sor - row's sad - dest hour.
sick, and weak and strong, may praise you ev - er - more.

417 Your love, O God, has called us here

Russell Schulz-Widmar, 1982

Music: *Gardiner*, 8888; melody "from Beethoven" in William Gardiner's *Sacred Melodies*, 1815

1 Your love, O God, has called us here, for all love
2 O gra - cious God, you con - se - crate all that is
3 O God of love, in - spire our life, re - veal your

finds its source in you, the per - fect love that
love - ly, good, and true. Bless those who in your
will in all we do; join ev - ery hus - band,

casts out fear, the love that Christ makes ev - er new.
pres - ence wait and ev - ery day their love re - new.
ev - ery wife in mu - tual love and love for you.

418 When love is found

"Love song," Brian Wren, 1978

Music: *O Waly Waly*, 8888; English traditional melody; harmony by Martin West, 1983

1 When love is found and hope comes home, sing and be
2 When love has flowered in trust and care, build both each
3 When love is tried as loved ones change, hold still to
4 When love is torn and trust be - trayed, pray strength to
glad that two are one. When love ex - plodes and fills the
day, that love may dare to reach be - yond home's warmth and
hope though all seems strange, till ease re - turns, and love grows
love till tor- ments fade, till lov - ers keep no score of
sky, praise God and share our Mak - er's joy.
light, to serve and strive for truth and right.
wise through listen - ing ears and o - pened eyes.
wrong, but hear through pain love's East - er song.

5 Praise God for love,
praise God for life,
in age or youth,
in husband, wife.
Lift up your hearts,
let love be fed
through death and life
in wine and bread.

419 O Father, all-creating

John Ellerton, 1876

Music: *Aurelia*, 7676D; Samuel Sebastian Wesley, 1864

1 O Fa - ther, all - cre - a - ting, whose wis - dom, love, and power
2 O Sa - vior, guest most gen - erous of old in Ga - li - lee,
3 O Spir - it, ev - er mov - ing, breathe on them from a - bove,
4 Ex - cept thou build it, Fa - ther, the house is built in vain;
first bound two lives to - geth - er in E - den's pri - mal hour,
re - veal to - day thy pres - ence with these who call on thee;
so might - y in thy pure - ness, so ten - der in thy love;
ex - cept thou, Sa - vior, bless it, the joy will turn to pain;
to - day to these thy chil - dren thine ear - liest gifts re - new —
their store of earth - ly glad - ness trans - form to heaven - ly wine,
that, guard - ed by thy pres - ence, from sin and strife kept free,
but nought can break the un - ion of hearts in thee made one,
a home by thee made hap - py, a love by thee kept true.
and teach them, in the tast - ing, to know the gift is thine.
their lives may own thy guid - ance, their hearts be ruled by thee.
and love thy Spir - it hal - lows is end - less love be - gun.

420 Crown with love, Lord, this glad day

Ian M. Fraser, 1966

Music: *Harts*, 777777; melody and most of the harmony by Benjamin Milgrove, 1768

1 Crown with love, Lord, this glad day, love to hum - ble and de - light,
2 Crown with joy, Lord, this glad day, joy to face life's hurt and ill,
3 Crown with peace, Lord, this glad day, peace the world may not in - vent,

love which un - til death will stay, test - ing all life's depth and height;
all that tests the wed - ded way, forg - ing un - ion deep - er still;
nor mis - for - tune strip a - way from two hearts in you con - tent,

such a love as took our part, spend - thrift in its gen - erous art.
joy like his who, for our gain, light - ly weighed the cross and pain.
know - ing love will nev - er cease from that source who is our peace.

421 O God, whom neither time nor space can limit

Horace Smith (1836–1922) and others

Music: *London New*, 8686; melody in *Scottish Psalter*, 1635;
harmony from *Hymns for Church and School*, 1964

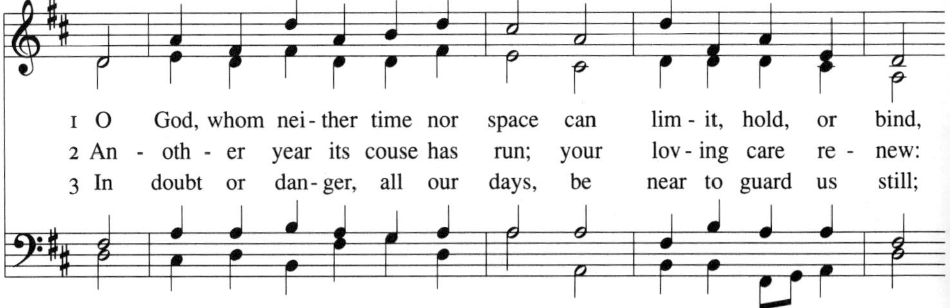
1 O God, whom nei - ther time nor space can lim - it, hold, or bind,
2 An - oth - er year its couse has run; your lov - ing care re - new:
3 In doubt or dan - ger, all our days, be near to guard us still;

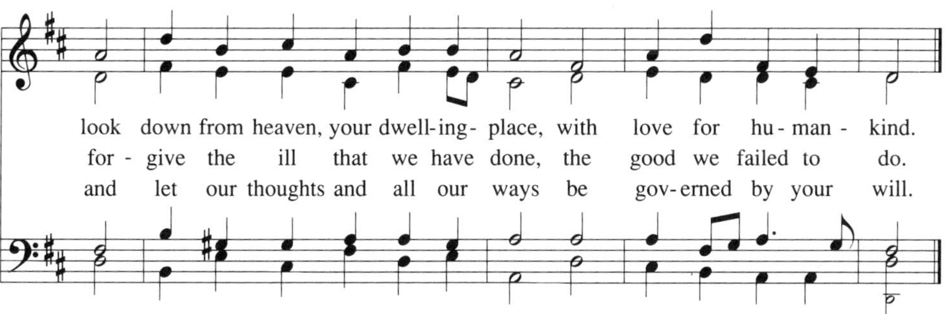
look down from heaven, your dwell-ing- place, with love for hu - man - kind.
for - give the ill that we have done, the good we failed to do.
and let our thoughts and all our ways be gov-erned by your will.

422 Great God, we sing that mighty hand

Philip Doddridge, 1755 (posth.)

Music: *Wareham*, 8888; melody by William Knapp, 1738

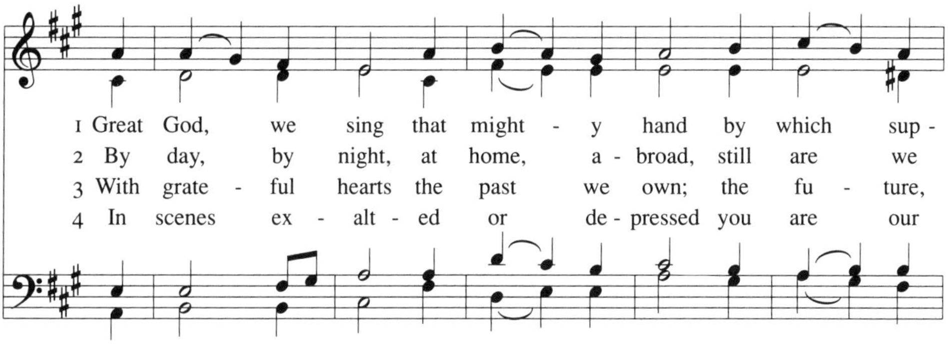

1 Great God, we sing that might - y hand by which sup -
2 By day, by night, at home, a - broad, still are we
3 With grate - ful hearts the past we own; the fu - ture,
4 In scenes ex - alt - ed or de - pressed you are our

port - ed still we stand; the o - pening year your
guard - ed by our God; with an in - ces - sant
all to us un - known, we to your guard - ian
joy, and you our rest; your good - ness all our

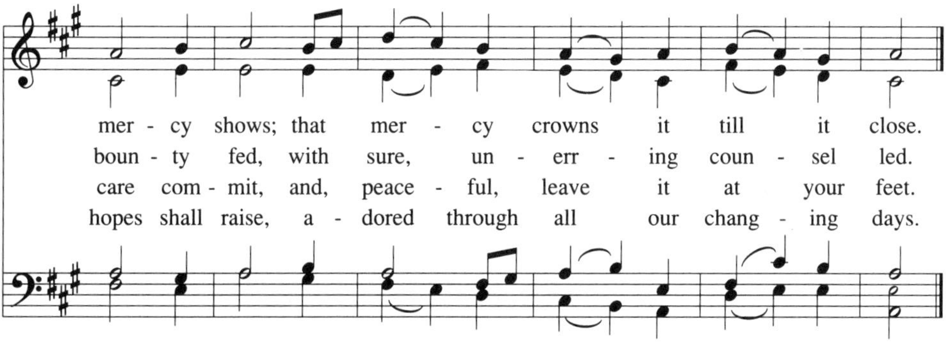

mer - cy shows; that mer - cy crowns it till it close.
boun - ty fed, with sure, un - err - ing coun - sel led.
care com - mit, and, peace - ful, leave it at your feet.
hopes shall raise, a - dored through all our chang - ing days.

423 Praise the Source of faith and learning

Thomas H. Troeger, 1987, 1989

Music: *Geneva*, 8787D; George Henry Day, 1940

1 Praise the Source of faith and learn - ing who has sparked and stoked the mind
2 God of wis - dom, we ac - knowl-edge that our sci - ence and our art
3 May our faith re - deem the blun - der of be - liev - ing that our thought
4 As two cur - rents in a riv - er fight each oth - er's un - der - tow
with a pas - sion for dis - cern - ing how the world has been de - signed.
and the breadth of hu - man knowl-edge on - ly par - tial truth im - part.
has dis - placed the grounds for won - der which the an - cient proph - ets taught.
till con - verg - ing they de - liv - er one co - her - ent stead - y flow,
Let the sense of won - der flow - ing from the won - ders we sur - vey
Far be - yond our cal - cu - la - tion lies a depth we can - not sound
May our learn - ing curb the er - ror which un - think - ing faith can breed
blend, O God, our faith and learn - ing till they carve a sin - gle course,
keep our faith for - ev - er grow - ing and re - new our need to pray:
where your pur - pose for cre - a - tion and the pulse of life are found.
lest we jus - ti - fy some ter - ror with an an - ti - quat - ed creed.
till they join as one, re - turn - ing praise and thanks to you, their Source.

424 Lord, you have brought us to our journey's end

Cyril A. Alington, 1936, and others

Music: *Sheldonian*, 10.10.10.10; Cyril V. Taylor, 1943

1 Lord, you have brought us to our jour - ney's end:
2 If we have learned to feel our neigh - bor's need,
3 If from your paths, by judg - ment un - dis - mayed,
4 For all the joys which you have deigned to share,
once more to you our grate - ful prayers as - cend;
to fight for truth in thought and word and deed;
and for your gifts un - grate - ful, we have strayed,
for all the pains which you have helped to bear,
once more we stand to praise you for the past;
if these are les - sons which the years have taught,
if day by day our prayers were faint and few,
for all our friends, in life and death the same,
grant prayer and praise be hon - est to the last.
con - firm then, Lord, what you in us have wrought.
for - give, O Lord, and build our hearts a - new.
we thank you, Lord, and praise your glo - rious name.

425 For the splendor of creation

Carl P. Daw, Jr., 1989

Music: *Thaxted*, 8686x3; adapted by Gustav Holst from his 1916 orchestral suite *The Planets*; harmonization, adapted from Holst, from *Hymns for Church and School*, 1964

Unison
1 For the splen - dor of cre - a - tion that draws us to in - quire,
2 For the schol - ars past and pres - ent whose boun - ty we di - gest,
for the mys - ter - ies of knowl - edge to which our hearts as - pire,
for the teach - ers who in - spire us to sum - mon forth our best,
for the deep and sub - tle beau - ties which de - light the eye and ear,
for our ri - vals and com - pan - ions, some - times fool - ish, some - times wise,
for the dis - ci - pline of log - ic, the strug - gle to be clear,
for the hu - man web up - hold - ing this no - ble en - ter - prise,
for the un - ex - plained re - main - der, the puz - zling and the odd:
for the com - mon life that binds us through days that soar or plod:

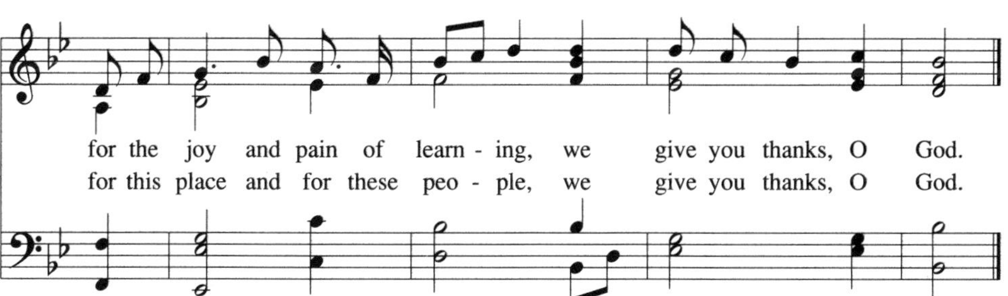
for the joy and pain of learn - ing, we give you thanks, O God.
for this place and for these peo - ple, we give you thanks, O God.

426 Come, let us anew

Charles Wesley, 1749

Music: *Sutton Courtenay*, 5.5.5.11; Erik Routley, 1943

Unison
1 Come, let us a - new our jour- ney pur - sue, roll round with the year, and nev - er stand still till the Mas - ter ap - pear.
2 His a - dor - a - ble will let us glad - ly ful - fill, and our tal - ents im - prove, by the pa- tience of hope and the la - bor of love.
3 Our life is a dream, our time as a stream glides swift - ly a - way, and the fug - i - tive mo - ment re - fus - es to stay.
4 The ar- row is flown, the mo- ment is gone; the mil - len - ni - al year rush- es on to our view, and e - ter - ni - ty's here.

5 O that each in the day
of his coming may say:
"I have fought my way through,
I have finished the work that you gave me to do!"

6 O that each from the Lord
may receive the glad word:
"Well and faithfully done;
enter into my joy, and sit down on my throne!"

427 We come unto our Savior God

Thomas Hornblower Gill, 1868, and others

Music: *Nun freut euch*, 8787887; melody in Josef Klug's *Geistliche Lieder*, Wittenberg,

1 We come un - to our Sa - vior God with each past gen - er - a - tion;
2 Their joy un - to their Lord we bring; their song to us de - scend - eth;
3 Ye saints to come, take up the strain, the same sweet theme en - deav - or;
the e - ter - nal arms, their dear a - bode, we make our hab - i - ta - tion.
the Spir - it who in them did sing to us fresh mu - sic lend - eth;
un - brok - en be the gold - en chain! Keep on the song for ev - er!
We bring thee, Lord, the praise they brought; we seek thee as thy
the song in them, in us, is one; we raise it high, we
Safe in the same dear dwell - ing place, rich with the same e -
saints have sought, in hope of our sal - va - tion.
send it on — the song that nev - er end - eth.
ter - nal grace, bless the same bound - less Giv - er!

428 O gracious God, your servants first built

George Wallace Briggs, 1920, and others

Music: *King's Lynn*, 7676D; English traditional melody, arranged by Ralph Vaughan Williams, 1906

Unison
1 O gra - cious God, your ser - vants first built this school of old;
2 The change - ful years un - rest - ing their si - lent course have sped,
3 They reap not where they la - bored; we reap what they have sown:
your hand has crowned their chil - dren with bless - ings man - i - fold.
new stu - dents ev - er bring - ing in stu - dents' steps to tread:
our har - vest will be gath - ered by a - ges yet un - known.
For your un - fail - ing mer - cies, far strewn a - long our way,
and some are long for - got - ten, long spent their hopes and fears;
The days of old have showered us with gifts be - yond all praise;
with all who passed be - fore us, we praise your name to - day.
safe rest they in your keep - ing, un - chang - ing with the years.
O make us ev - er faith - ful to serve the com - ing days.

429 O gracious Power

Oliver Wendell Holmes, 1869, for the 40-year reunion of the Harvard class of 1829

Music: *Tallis Canon*, 8888; Thomas Tallis, 1557, shortened by Thomas Ravenscroft, 1621

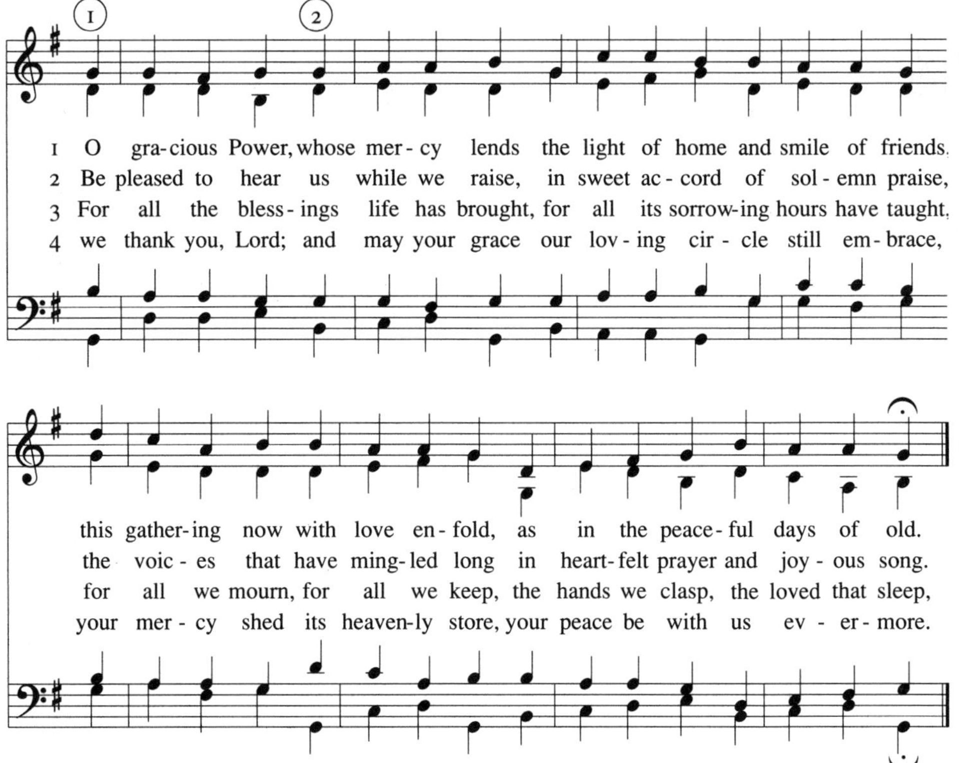

1
2
1 O gra-cious Power, whose mer - cy lends the light of home and smile of friends,
2 Be pleased to hear us while we raise, in sweet ac - cord of sol - emn praise,
3 For all the bless - ings life has brought, for all its sorrow-ing hours have taught,
4 we thank you, Lord; and may your grace our lov - ing cir - cle still em - brace,
this gather-ing now with love en - fold, as in the peace - ful days of old.
the voic - es that have ming-led long in heart-felt prayer and joy - ous song.
for all we mourn, for all we keep, the hands we clasp, the loved that sleep,
your mer - cy shed its heaven-ly store, your peace be with us ev - er - more.

430 God is Love

Timothy Rees, 1922

Music: *Abbot's Leigh*, 8787D; Cyril V. Taylor, 1941

These words can also be sung to *Hyfrydol*, no. 560.

1 God is Love, let heaven a - dore him; God is Love, let
2 God is Love; and love en - folds us, all the world in
3 God is Love; and though with blind-ness sin af - flicts all

earth re - joice; let cre - a - tion sing be - fore him
one em - brace: with un - fail - ing grasp God holds us,
hu - man life, God's e - ter - nal lov - ing - kind-ness
and ex - alt him with one voice. God who laid the earth's foun-
ev - ery child of ev - ery race. And when hu - man hearts are
guides us through our earth - ly strife. Sin and death and hell shall
da - tion, God who spread the heavens a - bove, God who
break - ing un - der sor - row's i - ron rod, then we
nev - er o'er us fi - nal tri - umph gain; God is
breathes through all cre - a - tion: God is Love, e - ter - nal Love.
find that self - same ach - ing deep with - in the heart of God.
Love, so Love for ev - er o'er the u - ni - verse must reign.

431 God of the nations

"At a war memorial," Fred Pratt Green, 1987

Music: *Toulon*, 10.10.10.10; abridged form of a melody in the *Genevan Psalter*, 1551; harmony adapted from Claude Goudimel, 1565

1 God of the na - tions, God of all who live,
2 Some died sus - tained by prom - ise of suc - cess;
3 "When you re - mem - ber us," we hear them cry,
4 We lay our wreathes, per - form the sim - ple rite,
how man - y gave us all they had to give!
some in de - feat's de - spair and bit - ter - ness;
"take great - er care how you let oth - ers die;
anx - ious that we may see in clear - er light,
Now, in re - mem - brance of our na - tion's dead,
some died the vic - tims of in - com - pe - tence:
what - ev - er God you wor - ship, or if none,
as those for whom a na - tion's blood was shed,
in pride and hon - est - y let prayers be said.
through years of per - il they were our de - fense.
pray that the na - tions learn to live as one."
how best to serve the liv - ing and the dead.

5 God of the nations, God of friend and foe,
under whose judgment all must come and go,
in your compassion show us how to end
fear of our foes and make of each a friend.

432 Rest in peace

"The Future Life," Fred Pratt Green, 1982

Music: *Moehr*, 88778338; Russell Schulz-Widmar, 1987

1 Rest in peace, earth's jour-ney end-ed, you whom Christ re-deemed, de-fend-ed:
2 Hap-py soul, to Christ u-nit-ed, calm-er now and clear-er sight-ed:
3 May we meet, dear Lord, in heav-en, each for-giv-ing and for-giv-en;
to the place where saints are one safe-ly brought by him a-lone.
your new jour-ney now be-gins, freed from earth's be-set-ting sins.
each more gift-ed to pur-sue all you have for us to do.
May he grant us like pro-tect-ion, rest in peace, rest in peace,
Press-ing on to-wards per-fect-ion, hap-py soul, hap-py soul,
By your Spir-it's sure di-rect-ion may we meet, may we meet,
rest in peace, earth's jour-ney end-ed.
hap-py soul, to Christ u-nit-ed.
may we meet, dear Lord in heav-en.

433 Christ the Victorious

Carl P. Daw, Jr., 1982

Music: *Russian Anthem*, 11.10.11.9; Alexis Lvov, 1833, for the national hymn of Russia

1 Christ the Vic - to - ri - ous, give to your ser - vants
2 On - ly Im - mor - tal One, Might - y Cre - a - tor!
3 God - spok - en pro - phe - cy, word at cre - a - tion:
4 Christ the Vic - to - ri - ous, give to your ser - vants
rest with your saints in the re - gions of light.
We are your crea - tures and chil - dren of earth.
"You came from dust and to dust shall re - turn."
rest with your saints in the re - gions of light.
Grief and pain end - ed, and sigh - ing no long - er,
From earth you formed us, both glo - rious and mor - tal,
Yet at the grave shall we raise up our glad song:
Grief and pain end - ed, and sigh - ing no long - er,
there may they find ev - er - last - ing life.
and to the earth shall we all re - turn.
"Al - le - lu - ia, al - le - lu - ia!"
there may they find ev - er - last - ing life.

434 King of glory, King of peace

George Herbert, 1633 (posth.)

Music: *General Seminary*, 7474D; David C. Walker, 1976

1 King of glo - ry, King of peace, I will love thee;
2 Where-fore with my ut-most art I will sing thee,
3 Seven whole days, not one in seven, I will praise thee;
and that love may nev-er cease, I will move thee.
and the cream of all my heart I will bring thee.
in my heart, though not in heaven, I can raise thee.
Thou hast grant-ed my re - quest, thou hast heard me;
Though my sins a - gainst me cried, thou didst clear me;
Small it is in this poor sort to en - roll thee;
thou didst note my work-ing breast, thou hast spared me.
and a - lone, when they re - plied, thou didst hear me.
e'en e - ter - ni - ty's too short to ex - tol thee.

435 Come down, O Love divine

Discendi, amor santo

Bianca da Siena (d. 1434); translated by Richard F. Littledale, 1867

Music: *Down Ampney*, 6.6.11.6.6.11; Ralph Vaughan Williams, 1906

1 Come down, O Love di - vine, seek thou this soul of mine,
2 O let it free - ly burn, till earth - ly pas - sions turn
3 And so the yearn - ing strong, with which the soul will long,
and vis - it it with thine own ar - dor glow - ing;
to dust and ash - es in its heat con - sum - ing;
shall far out - pass the power of hu - man tell - ing;
O Com - fort - er, draw near, with - in my heart ap - pear,
and let thy glo - rious light shine ev - er on my sight,
for none can guess its grace, till they be - come the place
and kin - dle it, thy ho - ly flame be - stow - ing.
and clothe me round, the while my path il - lum - ing.
where - in the Ho - ly Spir - it makes a dwell - ing.

436 Blessed assurance

Fanny Crosby (Frances Jane van Alstyne), 1873

Music: *Assurance*, 9.10.9.9 with refrain; Phoebe P. Knapp, 1873

1 Bless-ed as-sur-ance, Je-sus is mine! O what a fore-taste of glo-ry di-vine!
2 Per-fect sub-mis-sion, per-fect de-light, vi-sions of rap-ture now burst on my sight;
3 Per-fect sub-mis-sion, all is at rest; I in my Sa-vior am hap-py and blest,
Heir of sal-va-tion, pur-chase of God, born of his Spir-it, washed in his blood.
an-gels de-scend-ing bring from a-bove e-choes of mer-cy, whis-pers of love.
watch-ing and wait-ing, look-ing a-bove, filled with his good-ness, lost in his love.
Refrain
This is my sto-ry, this is my song, prais-ing my Sa-vior all the day long;
this is my sto-ry, this is my song, prais-ing my Sa-vior all the day long.

437 Come, thou fount of every blessing

Robert Robinson, 1758

Music: *Nettleton*, 8787D; melody in John Wyeth's *Repository of Sacred Music, Part Second*, Harrisburg, Pennsylvania, 1813; harmony by Gerre Hancock, 1971

1 Come, thou fount of ev - ery bless - ing, tune my heart to sing thy grace;
2 Here I find my great-est trea - sure; hith - er by thy help I've come;
3 O to grace how great a debt - or dai - ly I'm con - strained to be!
streams of mer - cy, nev - er ceas - ing, call for songs of loud - est praise.
and I hope, by thy good plea - sure, safe - ly to ar - rive at home.
Let thy good - ness, like a fet - ter, bind my wan-dering heart to thee.
Teach me some me - lo - dious son - net, sung by flam - ing tongues a - bove.
Je - sus sought me when a stran - ger wan-dering from the fold of God;
Prone to wan - der, Lord, I feel it, prone to leave the God I love;
Praise the mount! I'm fixed up - on it, mount of thy re - deem - ing love.
he, to res - cue me from dan - ger, in - ter - posed his pre - cious blood.
here's my heart, O take and seal it, seal it for thy courts a - bove.

438 An'im z'mirot

Sweet hymns and songs

Jewish traditional

Music: *An'im z'mirot*, 8888; Jewish traditional melody; arranged by Charles Davidson, 1987

1 An' - im z' - mi - rot v' - shi - rim e - e - rog,
2 Mi - dei da - b' - ri bich - vo - de - cha, ho -
1 Sweet hymns and songs will I re - cite to
2 My med - i - ta - tion day and night, may
ki ei - le - cha naf - shi ta - a - rog. Naf - shi cham - dah b' -
meh li - bi el do - de - cha. Ye - e - rav - na si -
sing of you by day and night, of you, who are my
it be pleas - ant in your sight, for you are all my
tzeil ya - de - cha la - da - at kol raz so - de - cha.
chi a - le - cha, ki naf - shi ta - a - rog ei - le - cha.
soul's de - light, of you, who are my soul's de - light.
soul's de - light, for you are all my soul's de - light.

439 I love thee, Lord

No me mueue, mi Dios

Spanish, 17th century; translated by Edward Caswall, 1849, and others

Music: *St. Fulbert*, 8686; Henry J. Gauntlett, 1852

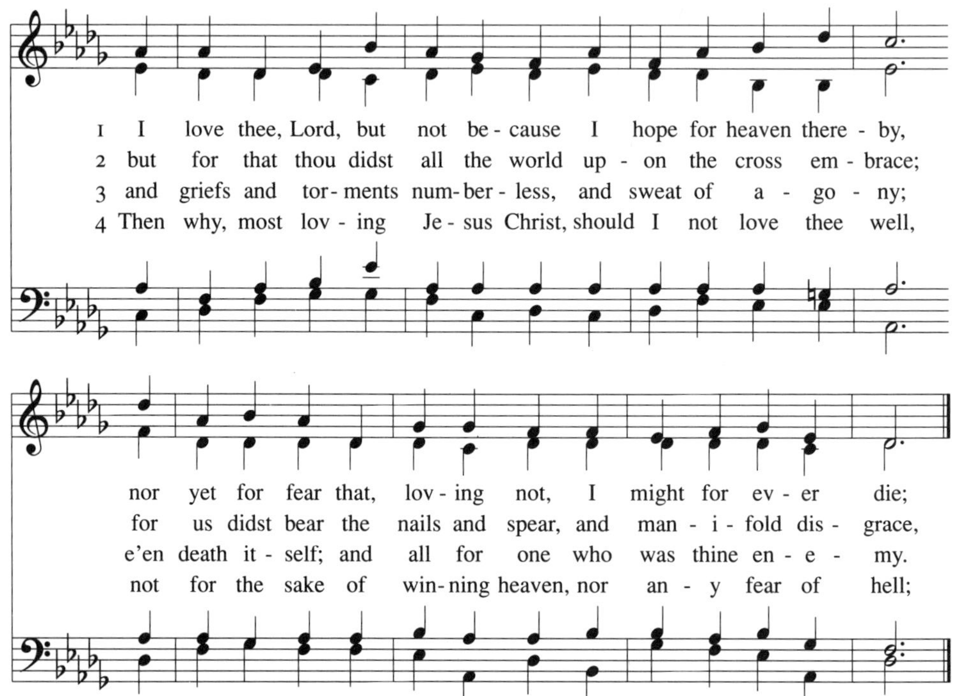
1 I love thee, Lord, but not be - cause I hope for heaven there - by,
2 but for that thou didst all the world up - on the cross em - brace;
3 and griefs and tor - ments num - ber - less, and sweat of a - go - ny;
4 Then why, most lov - ing Je - sus Christ, should I not love thee well,
nor yet for fear that, lov - ing not, I might for ev - er die;
for us didst bear the nails and spear, and man - i - fold dis - grace,
e'en death it - self; and all for one who was thine en - e - my.
not for the sake of win - ning heaven, nor an - y fear of hell;

5 not with the hope of gaining aught,
not seeking a reward;
but with thy costly love for me,
O ever loving Lord!

6 E'en so I love thee, and will love,
and in thy praise will sing,
solely because thou art my God
and my eternal King.

440 To Mercy, Pity, Peace and Love

William Blake, *Songs of Innocence*, 1789

Music: *Poldhu*, 8686; Peter Cutts, 1985

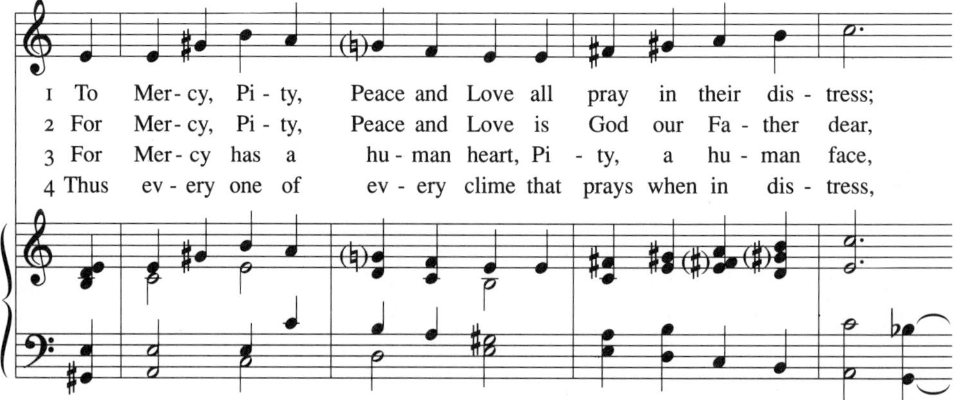
1 To Mer - cy, Pi - ty, Peace and Love all pray in their dis - tress;
2 For Mer - cy, Pi - ty, Peace and Love is God our Fa - ther dear,
3 For Mer - cy has a hu - man heart, Pi - ty, a hu - man face,
4 Thus ev - ery one of ev - ery clime that prays when in dis - tress,

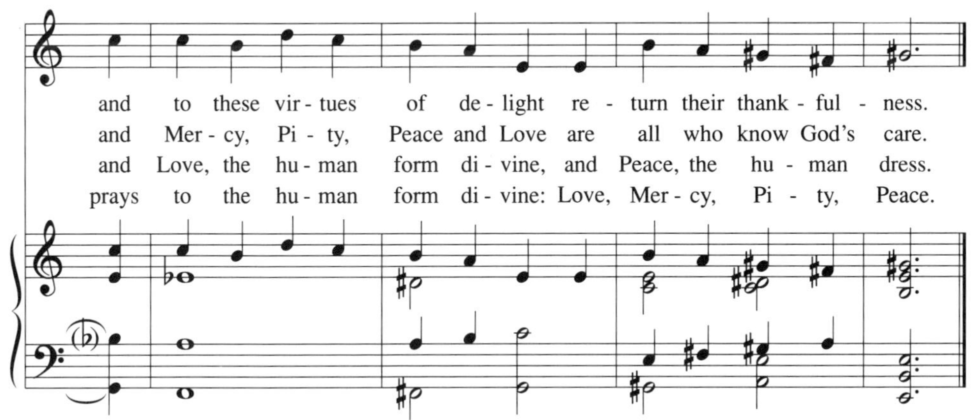
and to these vir- tues of de- light re - turn their thank - ful - ness.
and Mer - cy, Pi - ty, Peace and Love are all who know God's care.
and Love, the hu - man form di - vine, and Peace, the hu - man dress.
prays to the hu - man form di - vine: Love, Mer - cy, Pi - ty, Peace.

5 And all must love the human form
   of every race and hue;
where Mercy, Love and Pity dwell,
   there God is dwelling too.

441 Immortal love for ever full

John Greenleaf Whittier, 1867; selected stanzas from "Our Master"

Music: *Detroit*, 8686; melody in *Supplement to Kentucky Harmony*, 1820; harmony by Russell Schulz-Widmar, 1990

1 Im - mor - tal love for ev - er full, for ev - er flow - ing free,
2 Our out - ward lips con- fess the name all oth - er names a - bove;
3 We may not climb the heaven - ly steeps to bring the Lord Christ down;
4 but warm, sweet, ten - der, ev - en yet a pres - ent help is he;
for ev - er shared, for ev - er whole, a nev - er - ebb - ing sea!
love on - ly know - eth whence it came and com - pre - hend - eth love.
in vain we search the low - est deeps, for him no depths can drown;
and faith has still its O - liv - et, and love its Ga - li - lee.

5 The healing of his seamless dress
   is by our beds of pain;
we touch him in life's throng and press,
   and we are whole again.

6 Alone, O love ineffable,
   thy saving name is given;
to turn aside from thee is hell,
   to walk with thee is heaven.

442 Eternal Spirit of the living Christ

Frank von Christierson, 1974, 1979

Music: *Sursum corda*, 10.10.10.10; Alfred M. Smith, 1941

Unison
1 E - ter - nal Spir - it of the liv - ing Christ,
2 Come, pray in me the prayer I need this day;
3 Come with the vi - sion and the strength I need
I know not how to ask or what to say;
help me to see your pur - pose and your will,
to serve my God, and all hu - man - i - ty;
I on - ly know my need, as deep as life,
where I have failed, what I have done a - miss;
ful - fill - ment of my life in love out - poured —
and on - ly you can teach me how to pray.
held in for - giv - ing love, let me be still.
my life in you, O Christ, your love in me.

443 Jesus, priceless treasure

Jesu, meine Freude

Johann Franck, 1653, patterned after Alberti's love song "Flora, meine Freude"; translation adapted from various sources

Music: *Jesu, meine Freude*, 665665786; melody by Johann Crüger, 1653, based on a German traditional melody; harmony by Georg Philipp Telemann, 1719

1 Je - sus, price - less trea - sure, source of pur - est plea - sure,
2 Ban - ish thoughts of sad - ness, for our fount of glad - ness,
friend for - ev - er dear: though the earth is shak - ing,
Je - sus, en - ters in; though the clouds may gath - er,
and the na - tions quak - ing, you will calm our fear.
those who love the Sa - vior still have peace with - in.
Sa - tan's force must run its course and life's bit - ter storms as - sail
Though we bear much sor - row here, still in you lies pur - est plea -
us, yet you will not fail us.
sure, Je - sus, price - less trea - sure!

444 Send me, Lord

South African traditional

Music: *Thuma mina*, 387; South African traditional

Leader

Send me, Lord.

All

1 Send me, Jesus, send me, Jesus, send me, Jesus, send me, Lord. 2 Lead me,
Jesus, lead me, Jesus, lead me, Jesus, lead me, Lord. 3 Fill me,
Jesus, fill me, Jesus, fill me, Jesus, fill me, Lord.

1–2 | 3

2 Lead me, Lord.
3 Fill me, Lord.

Additional stanzas may be improvised.

445 There was a maid in Nazareth

Herbert O'Driscoll, 1980

Music: *There was a Maid*, 8684; Alice Parker, 1989

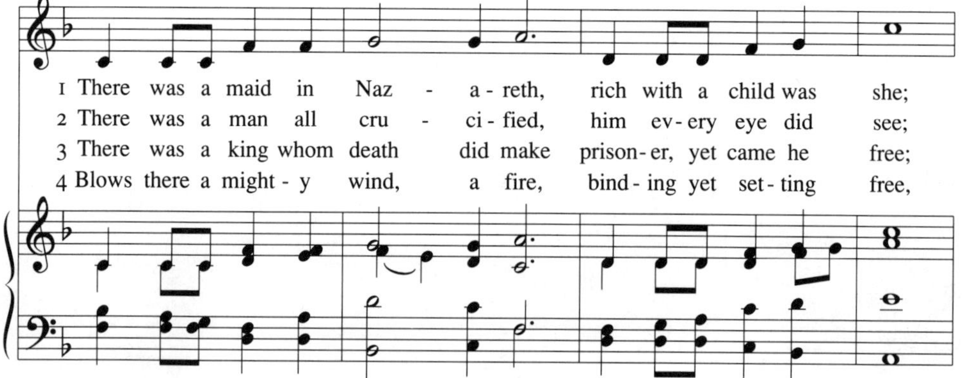
1 There was a maid in Naz - a - reth, rich with a child was she;
2 There was a man all cru - ci - fied, him ev - ery eye did see;
3 There was a king whom death did make prison - er, yet came he free;
4 Blows there a might - y wind, a fire, bind - ing yet set - ting free,

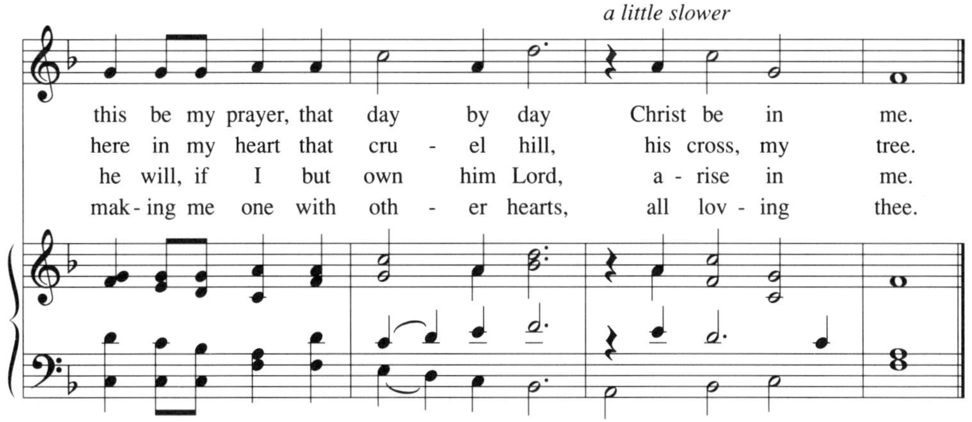
a little slower
this be my prayer, that day by day Christ be in me.
here in my heart that cru - el hill, his cross, my tree.
he will, if I but own him Lord, a - rise in me.
mak - ing me one with oth - er hearts, all lov - ing thee.

446 Come, my way, my truth, my life

"The Call," George Herbert, 1633 (posth.)

Music: *The Call*, 7777; Ralph Vaughan Williams, 1911; adapted by E. Harold Geer in *Hymnal for Colleges and Schools*, 1956

Unison

1 Come, my way, my truth, my life: such a way as gives us
2 Come, my light, my feast, my strength: such a light as shows a
3 Come, my joy, my love, my heart: such a joy as none can

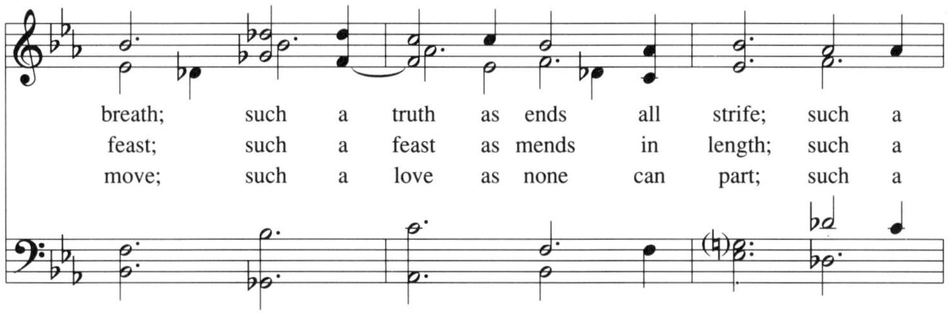

breath; such a truth as ends all strife; such a
feast; such a feast as mends in length; such a
move; such a love as none can part; such a

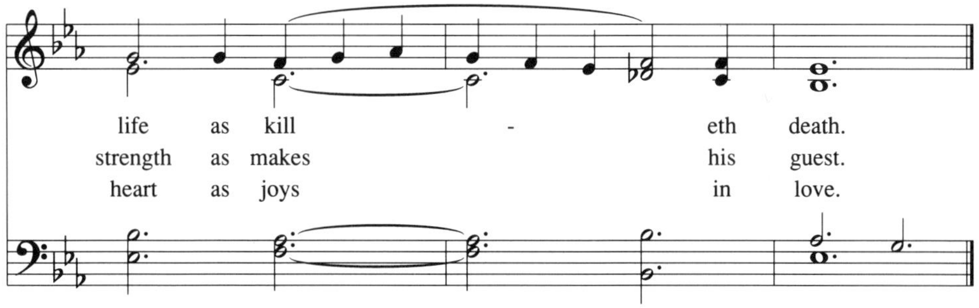

life as kill - eth death.
strength as makes his guest.
heart as joys in love.

447 O thou whose power o'er moving worlds presides

O qui perpetua mundum ratione gubernans

Anicius Manlius Severinus Boethius, c. 475–525; translated by Samuel Johnson, 1750

Music: *Song 4*, 10.10.10.10; melody and bass by Orlando Gibbons, 1623

1 O thou whose power o'er mov - ing worlds pre - sides,
2 'Tis thine a - lone to calm the trou - bled breast
whose voice cre - a - ted, and whose wis - dom guides,
with si - lent con - fi - dence and ho - ly rest:
on dark - ened souls in pure ef - ful - gence shine,
from thee, great God, we spring, to thee we tend —
and cheer the cloud - ed mind with light di - vine.
path, mo - tive, guide, o - rig - i - nal, and end.

448 What wondrous love is this

American folk hymn, early 19th century

Music: *Wondrous Love*, 12.9.12.12.9; William Walker's *Southern Harmony*, 1835

The melody is in the tenor.
1 What won - drous love is this, O my soul, O my soul,
2 When I was sink - ing down, sink - ing down, sink - ing down,
3 To God and to the Lamb I will sing, I will sing,
4 And when from death I'm free, I'll sing on, I'll sing on,
what won - drous love is this, O my soul!
when I was sink - ing down, sink - ing down,
to God and to the Lamb I will sing;
and when from death I'm free, I'll sing on;
What won - drous love is this that caused the Lord of bliss
when I was sink - ing down be - neath God's righ - teous frown,
to God and to the Lamb who is the great I AM,
and when from death I'm free, I'll sing and joy - ful be,
to bear the dread - ful curse for my soul, for my soul,
Christ laid a - side his crown for my soul, for my soul,
while mi - lions join the theme I will sing, I will sing,
and through e - ter - ni - ty I'll sing on, I'll sing on,
to bear the dread - ful curse for my soul.
Christ laid a - side his crown for my soul.
while mi - lions join the theme I will sing.
and through e - ter - ni - ty I'll sing on.

449 What wondrous love is this

American folk hymn, early 19th century

Music: *Wondrous Love*, 12.9.12.12.9; melody in William Walker's *Southern Harmony*, 1835; harmony by Paul J. Christiansen, 1955

1 What won-drous love is this, O my soul, O my soul,
2 When I was sink-ing down, sink-ing down, sink-ing down,
3 To God and to the Lamb I will sing, I will sing,
4 And when from death I'm free, I'll sing on, I'll sing on,
what won-drous love is this, O my soul!
when I was sink-ing down, sink-ing down,
to God and to the Lamb I will sing;
and when from death I'm free, I'll sing on;
What won-drous love is this that caused the Lord of bliss
when I was sink-ing down be-neath God's righ-teous frown,
to God and to the Lamb who is the great I AM,
and when from death I'm free, I'll sing and joy-ful be,
to bear the dread-ful curse for my soul, for my soul,
Christ laid a-side his crown for my soul, for my soul,
while mi-lions join the theme I will sing, I will sing,
and through e-ter-ni-ty I'll sing on, I'll sing on,

to bear the dread - ful curse for my soul.
Christ laid a - side his crown for my soul.
while mi - lions join the theme I will sing.
and through e - ter - ni - ty I'll sing on.

450 Fairest Lord Jesus

Schönster Herr Jesu

Stanzas 1 and 3 from *Münster Gesangbuch*, 1677; stanza 2 from *Schlesische Volkslieder*, Leipzig, 1842; translation from Richard Storrs Willis's *Church Chorals and Choir Studies*, New York, 1850

Music: *Schönster Herr Jesu*, 568558; melody in A. H. Hoffman von Fallersleben's *Schlesische Volkslieder*, Leipzig, 1842; harmony by Richard S. Willis, 1850

1 Fair - est Lord Je - sus, Rul - er of all na - ture,
2 Fair are the mea - dows, fair - er still the wood - lands,
3 Fair is the sun - shine, fair - er still the moon - light,

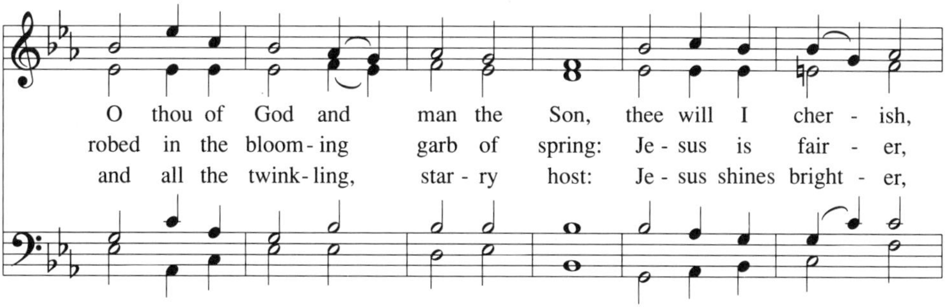

O thou of God and man the Son, thee will I cher - ish,
robed in the bloom - ing garb of spring: Je - sus is fair - er,
and all the twink - ling, star - ry host: Je - sus shines bright - er,

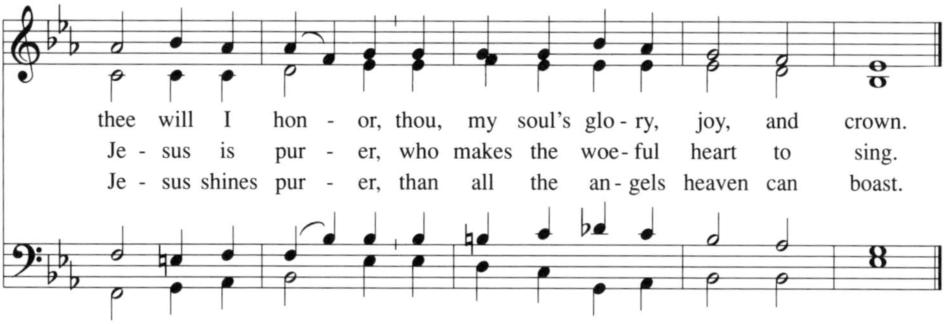

thee will I hon - or, thou, my soul's glo - ry, joy, and crown.
Je - sus is pur - er, who makes the woe - ful heart to sing.
Je - sus shines pur - er, than all the an - gels heaven can boast.

451 Fairest Lord Jesus

Schönster Herr Jesu

Stanzas 1 and 3 from *Münster Gesangbuch*, 1677; stanza 2 from *Schlesische Volkslieder*, Leipzig, 1842; translation from Richard Storrs Willis's *Church Chorals and Choir Studies*, New York, 1850

Music: *Schönster Herr Jesu*, 568558; melody in A. H. Hoffman von Fallersleben's *Schlesische Volkslieder*, Leipzig, 1842; harmony by Russell Schulz-Widmar, 1990

1 Fair - est Lord Je - sus, Rul - er of all na - ture,
2 Fair are the mea - dows, fair - er still the wood - lands,
3 Fair is the sun - shine, fair - er still the moon - light,
O thou of God and man the Son, thee will I cher - ish,
robed in the bloom - ing garb of spring: Je - sus is fair - er,
and all the twink - ling, star - ry host: Je - sus shines bright - er,
thee will I hon - or, thou, my soul's glo - ry, joy, and crown.
Je - sus is pur - er, who makes the woe - ful heart to sing.
Je - sus shines pur - er, than all the an - gels heaven can boast.

452 I've got peace like a river

African American spiritual

Music: *Peace Like a River*, 7.7.10; African American spiritual

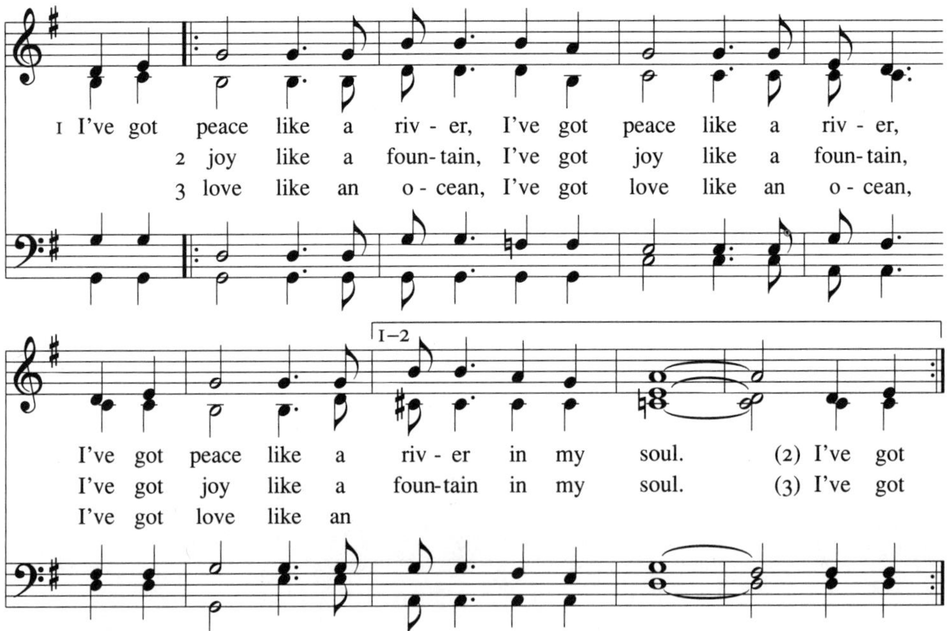
1 I've got peace like a riv - er, I've got peace like a riv - er,
2 joy like a foun - tain, I've got joy like a foun - tain,
3 love like an o - cean, I've got love like an o - cean,
1–2
I've got peace like a riv - er in my soul. (2) I've got
I've got joy like a foun - tain in my soul. (3) I've got
I've got love like an

3
o - cean in my soul.

453 Lord, as a pilgrim through life I go

Oi Herra, jos mä matkamies maan

Wilhelmi Malmivaara, 1903; translated by Gilbert E. Doan, 1978

Music: *Oi Herra, jos mä matkamies maan*, 99554; melody by Berndt Mikael Nyberg, 1920; harmony by Walter Pelz, 1978

Unison

1 Lord, as a pilgrim through life I go;
each day your loving presence I know.
Travel beside me, strengthen and guide me,
Shepherd divine!

2 Friends have forsaken, you have stood fast;
you have been faithful, true to the last;
much I offended, yet you extended
friendship divine!

3 You are my refuge; grant me, I pray,
strength for each burden, light for each day,
comfort in sorrow, grace for tomorrow,
Savior divine!

4 Lord, let your presence brighten the night
till the last sunrise; then, in your might,
pardon and spare me, summon and bear me
homeward at last.

454 When I survey the wondrous cross

Isaac Watts, 1707

Music: *Hamburg*, 8888; Lowell Mason, 1824, based on Gregorian psalm tone I

1 When I sur - vey the won - drous cross on which the
2 For - bid it, Lord, that I should boast, save in the
3 See, from his head, his hands, his feet, sor - row and
4 Were the whole realm of na - ture mine, that were an

Prince of Glo - ry died, my rich - est gain I
death of Christ, my God: all the vain things that
love flow min - gled down! Did e'er such love and
offer - ing far too small; love so a - maz - ing,

count but loss, and pour con- tempt on all my pride.
charm me most, I sac - ri - fice them to his blood.
sor - row meet, or thorns com- pose so rich a crown?
so di - vine, de - mands my soul, my life, my all.

455 When I survey the wondrous cross

Isaac Watts, 1707

Music: *Rockingham*, 8888; melody adapted by Edward Miller in 1790 from a melody in Aaron Williams's *A Second Supplement*, c. 1780

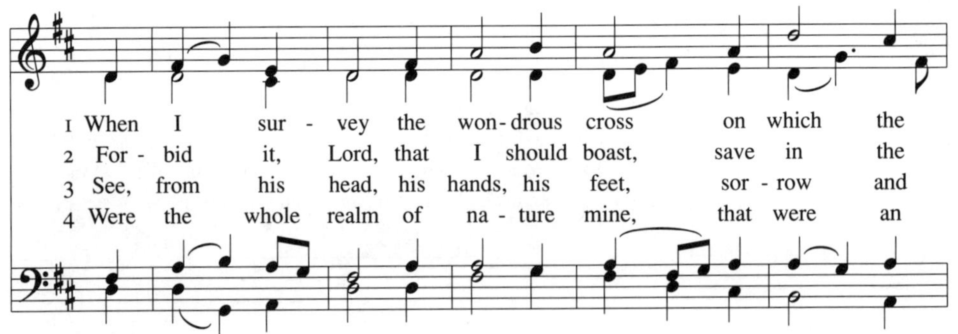
1 When I sur - vey the won- drous cross on which the
2 For - bid it, Lord, that I should boast, save in the
3 See, from his head, his hands, his feet, sor - row and
4 Were the whole realm of na - ture mine, that were an

Prince of Glo - ry died, my rich - est gain I
death of Christ, my God: all the vain things that
love flow min - gled down! Did e'er such love and
offer - ing far too small; love so a - maz - ing,
count but loss, and pour con - tempt on all my pride.
charm me most, I sac - ri - fice them to his blood.
sor - row meet, or thorns com - pose so rich a crown?
so di - vine, de - mands my soul, my life, my all.

456 Thou art the Way

George Washington Doane, 1824

Music: *St. James*, 8686; melody in *Select Psalms and Hymns*, London, 1697; probably by Raphael Courteville

1 Thou art the Way; to thee a - lone from sin and death we flee;
2 Thou art the Truth; thy word a - lone true wis - dom can im - part;
3 Thou art the Life; the rend - ing tomb pro - claims thy con - quering arm;
4 Thou art the Way, the Truth, the Life; grant us that way to know,
and all who would the Fa - ther seek, must seek him, Lord, by thee.
no oth - er can in - form the mind and pur - i - fy the heart.
and those who put their trust in thee nor death nor hell can harm.
that truth to keep, that life to win, whose joys e - ter - nal flow.

457 Jesus, the very thought of you

Jesu, dulcis memoria

Twelfth century; translated by Edward Caswall, 1849

Music: *Windsor*, 8686; melody in William Damon's *Booke of Musicke*, 1591

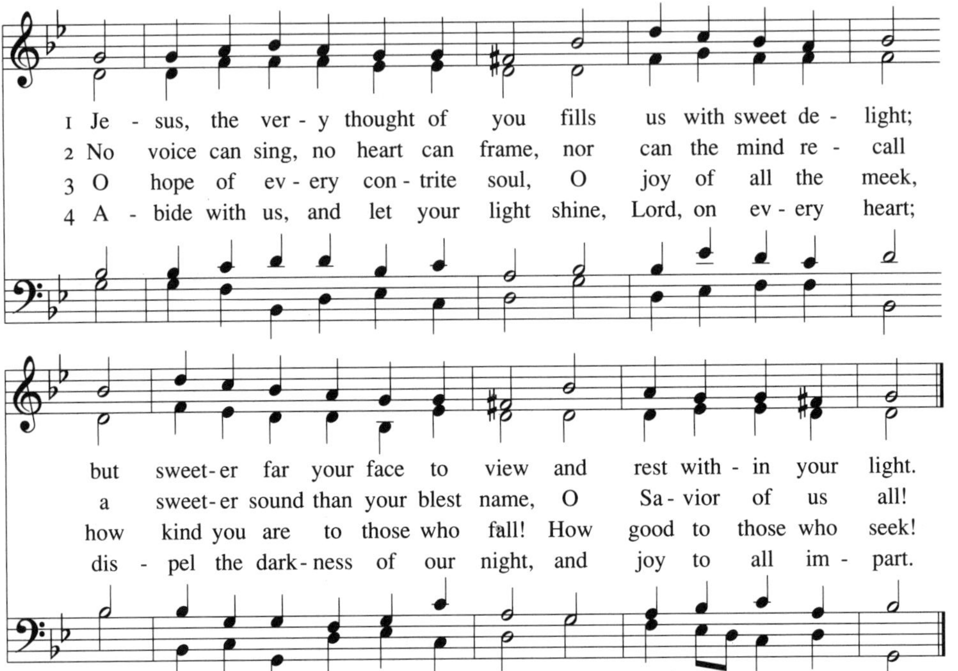
1 Je - sus, the ver - y thought of you fills us with sweet de - light;
2 No voice can sing, no heart can frame, nor can the mind re - call
3 O hope of ev - ery con - trite soul, O joy of all the meek,
4 A - bide with us, and let your light shine, Lord, on ev - ery heart;
but sweet- er far your face to view and rest with - in your light.
a sweet- er sound than your blest name, O Sa - vior of us all!
how kind you are to those who fall! How good to those who seek!
dis - pel the dark- ness of our night, and joy to all im - part.

458 Amazing grace

John Newton, 1779

Music: *New Britain*, 8686; 19th-century American melody; harmony by Edwin O. Excell, 1900

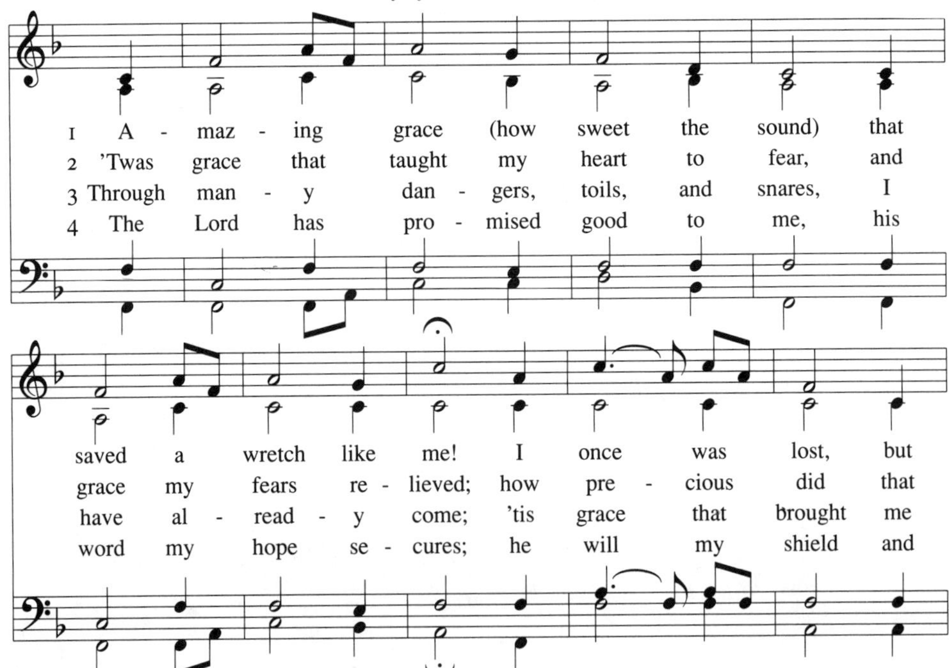
1 A - maz - ing grace (how sweet the sound) that
2 'Twas grace that taught my heart to fear, and
3 Through man - y dan - gers, toils, and snares, I
4 The Lord has pro - mised good to me, his
saved a wretch like me! I once was lost, but
grace my fears re - lieved; how pre - cious did that
have al - read - y come; 'tis grace that brought me
word my hope se - cures; he will my shield and

now am found, was blind, but now I see.
grace ap - pear the hour I first be - lieved.
safe thus far, and grace will lead me home.
por - tion be as long as life en - dures.

5 And, when this flesh and heart shall fail,
and mortal life shall cease,
I shall possess, within the veil,
a life of joy and peace.

459 He comes to us as one unknown

Timothy Dudley-Smith, 1982; first line from Albert Schweitzer's *The Quest of the Historical Jesus*, 1910

Music: *Lobt Gott, ihr Christen*, 86886; Nikolaus Hermann, 1554; adapted and harmonized by J. S. Bach, in Cantata no. 151, 1725

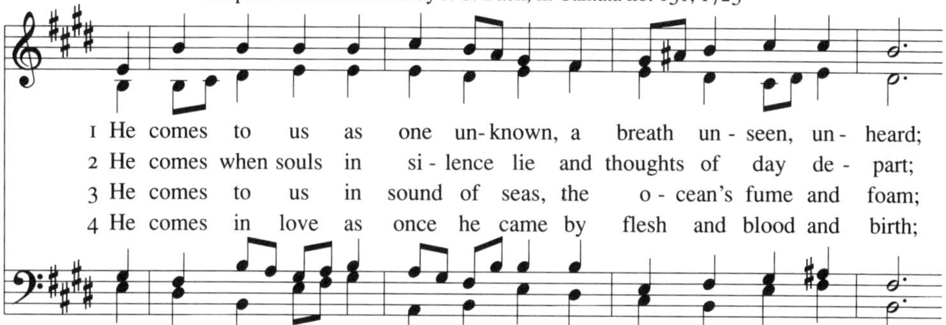

1 He comes to us as one un-known, a breath un - seen, un - heard;
2 He comes when souls in si - lence lie and thoughts of day de - part;
3 He comes to us in sound of seas, the o - cean's fume and foam;
4 He comes in love as once he came by flesh and blood and birth;

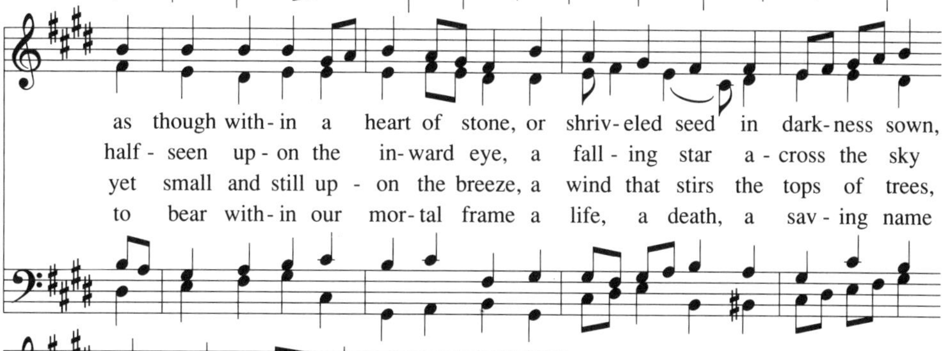

as though with - in a heart of stone, or shriv - eled seed in dark - ness sown,
half - seen up - on the in - ward eye, a fall - ing star a - cross the sky
yet small and still up - on the breeze, a wind that stirs the tops of trees,
to bear with - in our mor - tal frame a life, a death, a sav - ing name

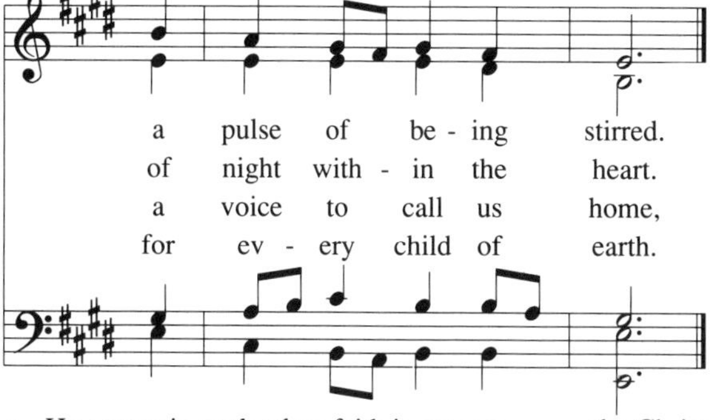

a pulse of be - ing stirred.
of night with - in the heart.
a voice to call us home,
for ev - ery child of earth.

5 He comes in truth when faith is grown;
believed, obeyed, adored:
the Christ in all the scriptures shown,
as yet unseen, but not unknown,
our Savior and our Lord.

460 A mighty fortress is our God

Ein' feste Burg ist unser Gott

Martin Luther, 1529; based on Psalm 46; translated by Frederick H. Hedge, 1853

Music: *Ein' feste Burg*, 878766667; melody by Martin Luther, 1529; harmony from *The New Hymnal for American Youth*, 1930

1 A might - y for - tress is our God, a bul - wark nev - er fail - ing;
2 Did we in our own strength con - fide, our striv - ing would be los - ing,
3 And though this world, with de - vils filled, should threat - en to un - do us,
4 That word a - bove all earth - ly powers, no thanks to them, a - bid - eth;
our help - er sure a - mid the flood of mor - tal ills pre - vail - ing:
were not the right man on our side, the man of God's own choos - ing:
we will not fear, for God hath willed the truth to tri - umph through us:
the Spir - it and the gifts are ours through Christ who with us sid - eth:
for still our an - cient foe doth seek to work us woe;
dost ask who that may be? Christ Je - sus, it is he;
the prince of dark - ness grim, we trem - ble not for him;
let goods and kin - dred go, this mor - tal life al - so;
with power and ma - lice great, and armed with cru - el hate,
Lord Sab - a - oth his name, from age to age the same,
his rage we can en - dure, for lo! his doom is sure,
the bo - dy they may kill: God's truth a - bid - eth still,

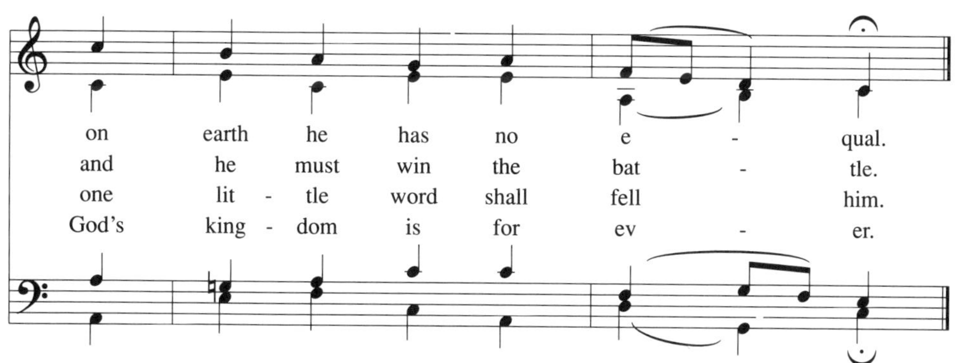
on earth he has no e - qual.
and he must win the bat - tle.
one lit - tle word shall fell him.
God's king - dom is for ev - er.

461 The tree of life my soul hath seen

From Joshua Smith's *Divine Hymns or Spiritual Songs*, New Hampshire, 1784

Music: *Jesus Christ the Apple Tree*, 888888; Elizabeth Poston, 1967

1 The tree of life my soul hath seen, lad - en with fruit, and al - ways green,
2 Such beau - ty doth all things ex - cel: by faith I know, but ne'er can tell,
3 For hap - pi - ness I long have sought, and plea - sure dear - ly I have bought,
4 I'm wear - y with my for - mer toil, here I will sit and rest a - while,

the tree of life my soul hath seen, lad - en with fruit, and al - ways green:
such beau - ty doth all things ex - cel: by faith I know, but ne'er can tell
for hap - pi - ness I long have sought, and plea - sure dear - ly I have bought:
I'm wear - y with my for - mer toil, here I will sit and rest a - while:

the trees of na - ture fruit - less be com - pared with Christ the ap - ple tree.
the glo - ry which I now can see in Je - sus Christ the ap - ple tree.
I missed in all; but now I see 'tis found in Christ the ap - ple tree.
un - der the sha - dow I will be of Je - sus Christ the ap - ple tree.

5 This fruit doth make my soul to thrive,
it keeps my dying faith alive;
this fruit doth make my soul to thrive,
it keeps my dying faith alive;
which makes my soul in haste to be
with Jesus Christ the apple tree.

462 The tree of life my soul hath seen

From Joshua Smith's *Divine Hymns or Spiritual Songs*, New Hampshire, 1784

Music: *Pinkham*, 8888; Daniel Pinkham, 1989

1 The tree of life my soul hath seen, lad - en with fruit, and
2 Such beau - ty doth all things ex - cel: by faith I know, but
3 For hap - pi - ness I long have sought, and plea - sure dear - ly
4 I'm wear - y with my for - mer toil, here I will sit and
al - ways green: the trees of na - ture fruit - less be com - pared with
ne'er can tell the glo - ry which I now can see in Je - sus
I have bought: I missed in all; but now I see 'tis found in
rest a - while: un - der the sha - dow I will be of Je - sus
1–4
Christ the ap - ple tree.
Christ the ap - ple tree.
Christ the ap - ple tree.
Christ the ap - ple tree.
5
5 Christ the ap - ple tree.

5 This fruit doth make my soul to thrive,
it keeps my dying faith alive;
which makes my soul in haste to be
with Jesus Christ the apple tree.

463 Father, with all your Gospel's power

Erhalt uns, Herr

Martin Luther, 1524; paraphrased by Erik Routley, 1974

Music: *Erhalt uns, Herr*, 8888; melody in Klug's *Geistliche Lieder*, 1543; harmony by Michael Praetorius, 1609

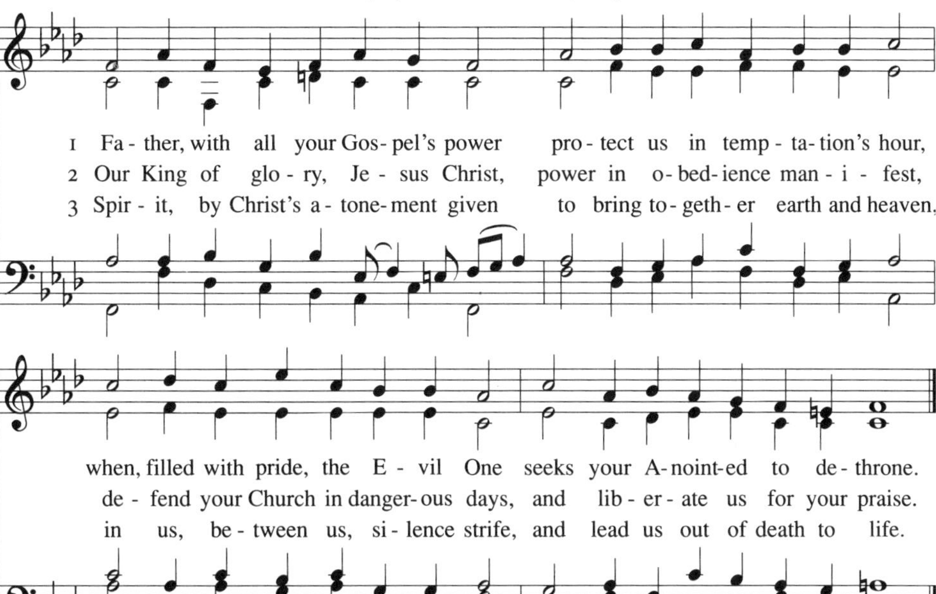

1 Fa - ther, with all your Gos - pel's power pro - tect us in temp - ta - tion's hour,
2 Our King of glo - ry, Je - sus Christ, power in o - bed - ience man - i - fest,
3 Spir - it, by Christ's a - tone - ment given to bring to - geth - er earth and heaven,
when, filled with pride, the E - vil One seeks your A - noint - ed to de - throne.
de - fend your Church in danger - ous days, and lib - er - ate us for your praise.
in us, be - tween us, si - lence strife, and lead us out of death to life.

464 A God and yet a man?

English, 15th century

Music: *Divine Paradox*, 6767; adapted from a song by John Dowland (c. 1563–1626) by the editors of *New Catholic Hymnal*, 1971

1 A God and yet a man? A maid and yet a mo - ther?
2 A God and can he die? A dead man, can he live?
3 God, truth it - self does teach; our thoughts sink too far un - der
Thought won - ders how thought can con - ceive one or the o - ther.
What can thought well re - ply? What rea - son rea - son give?
for rea - son's power to reach. Be - lieve and leave to wond - er!

465 All my hope on God is founded

Meine Hoffnung stehet feste

Joachim Neander, 1680; paraphrased by Robert Bridges, 1899

Music: *Michael*, 8787337; Herbert Howells, 1930, 1977

1 All my hope on God is found - ed who doth still my trust re - new, who through change and chance will guide me, on - ly good and on - ly true. God un - known, who a -
2 Pride of life and earth - ly glo - ry, sword and crown be - tray our trust; what with care and toil we fash - ion, tower and tem - ple, fall to dust. But God's power, hour by
3 God's great good-ness ay en - dur - eth; deep God's wis - dom, pass - ing thought; splen - dor, light and life a - bound there, beau - ty spring - eth out of nought. Ev - er - more from God's
4 Dai - ly doth the al - mighty Giv - er boun - teous gifts on us be - stow; God's de - sire our soul de - light - eth, pleas - ure leads us where we go. Love doth stand at God's

lone calls my heart to be God's own.
hour, is my tem - ple and my tower.
store new - born worlds rise and a - dore.
hand; joy doth wait at God's com - mand.

5 Still from earth to God eternal
sacrifice of praise be done,
high above all praises praising
for the gift of God's own Son.
Christ doth call one and all:
ye who follow shall not fall.

466 God moves in a mysterious way

William Cowper, 1774

Music: *London New*, 8686; melody in *Scottish Psalter*, 1635; harmony from *Hymns for Church and School*, 1964

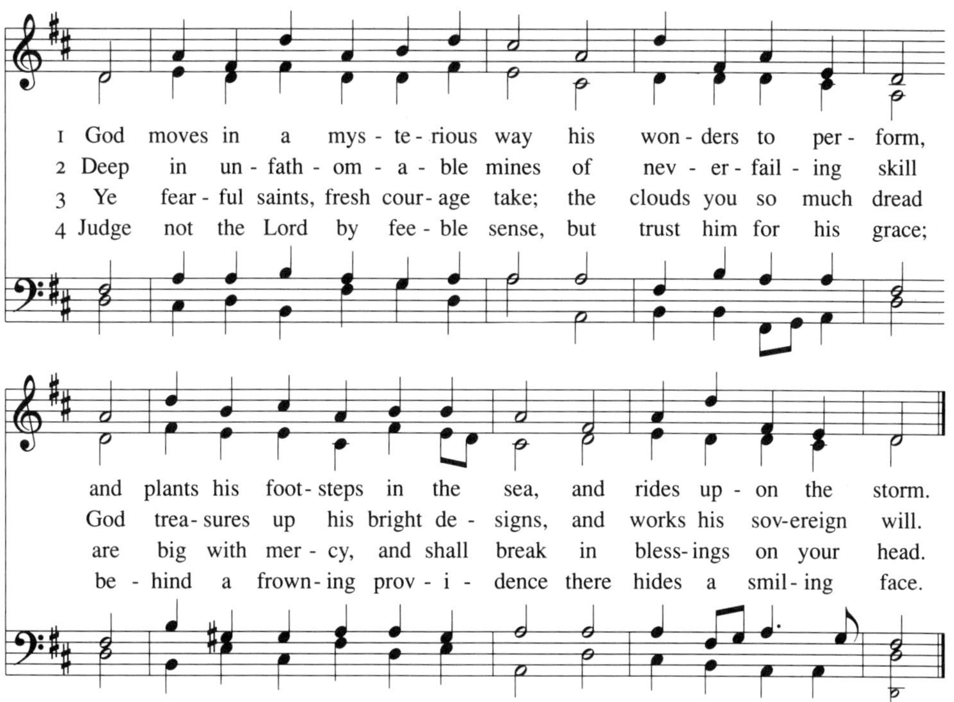
1 God moves in a mys - te - rious way his won - ders to per - form,
2 Deep in un - fath - om - a - ble mines of nev - er - fail - ing skill
3 Ye fear - ful saints, fresh cour - age take; the clouds you so much dread
4 Judge not the Lord by fee - ble sense, but trust him for his grace;
and plants his foot - steps in the sea, and rides up - on the storm.
God trea - sures up his bright de - signs, and works his sov-ereign will.
are big with mer - cy, and shall break in bless - ings on your head.
be - hind a frown - ing prov - i - dence there hides a smil - ing face.

5 God's purposes will ripen fast,
unfolding every hour:
the bud may have a bitter taste,
but sweet will be the flower.

6 Blind unbelief is sure to err,
and scan his work in vain;
God is his own interpreter,
and God will make it plain.

467 By gracious powers

Von guten Mächten

Dietrich Bonhoeffer, 1944; a New Year's Eve poem from prison; translated by Fred Pratt Green, 1972

Music: *Intercessor*, 11.10.11.10; C. Hubert H. Parry, 1904

1 By gra - cious powers so won - der - ful - ly shel - tered,
2 Yet is this heart by its old foe tor - ment - ed,
3 And when this cup you give is filled to brim - ming
4 Yet when a - gain in this same world you give us
and con - fi - dent - ly wait - ing come what may,
still e - vil days bring bur - dens hard to bear;
with bit - ter suffer - ing, hard to un - der - stand,
the joy we had, the bright - ness of your Sun,
we know that God is with us night and morn - ing,
O give our fright - ened souls the sure sal - va - tion,
we take it thank - ful - ly and with - out trem - bling,
we shall re - mem - ber all the days we lived through,
and nev - er fails to greet us each new day.
for which, O Lord, you taught us to pre - pare.
out of so good and so be - loved a hand.
and our whole life shall then be yours a - lone.

468 Guide me ever, great Redeemer

Arglwydd, arwain trwy'r anialwch

William Williams, 1745; translated by Peter Williams, 1771,
William or John Williams, 1772, and others

Music: *Cwm Rhondda*, 8787877; John Hughes, 1905

1 Guide me ev - er, great Re - deem - er, pil - grim through this bar - ren land;
2 O - pen now the crys - tal foun - tain where the heal - ing wa - ters flow;
3 When I tread the verge of Jor - dan, bid my anx - ious fears sub - side;
I am weak, but you are might - y; hold me with your power - ful hand:
let the fire and cloud - y pil - lar guide me all my jour - ney through:
death of death, and hell's de - struc - tion, land mc safe on Ca - naan's side:
Bread of heav - en, Bread of heav - en, feed me till I want no
strong De - liv - erer, strong De - liv - erer, be for me my strength and
songs of prais - es, songs of prais - es I will ev - er give to
more, feed me till I want no more.
shield, be for me my strength and shield.
you, I will ev - er give to you.

469 No hay que temer

St. Teresa de Jesús (Teresa of Avila, 1515–1582): "There is nothing to fear. Sleep not, for there is no peace on earth. Let us venture forth into life."

Music: Canon by Jacques Berthier and the Community of Taizé, 1986

1
No hay que te-mer, no hay que te-mer.
2
No dur-máis, no dur-máis,
3
pues que no hay paz en la tie - rra.
4
A-ven-tu-re-mos la vi - da.

470 Come, O thou Traveler unknown

"Wrestling Jacob," Charles Wesley, 1739

Music: *Woodbury*, 888888; Erik Routley, 1969

1 Come, O thou Trav - el - er un - known, whom still I hold, but can - not see! My com - pa -
2 I need not tell thee who I am, my mis - er - y and sin de - clare; thy - self hast
3 Yield to me now, for I am weak but con - fi - dent in self - de - spair! Speak to my
4 'Tis Love! 'tis Love! thou diedst for me! I hear thy whis - per in my heart; the morn - ing

ny be- fore is gone, and I am left a - lone with
called me by my name, look on thy hands and read it
heart, in bless- ing speak, be con- quered by my in - stant
breaks, the shad- ows flee, pure U - ni - ver - sal Love thou
thee; with thee all night I mean to stay and wres- tle till the
there. But who, I ask thee, who art thou? Tell me thy name, and
prayer; speak, or thou nev - er hence shalt move, and tell me if thy
art; to me, to all, thy mer- cies move: thy na- ture and thy
break of day.
tell me now.
name is Love.
name is Love.
1–4
5
Love.

5 Lame as I am, I'll run my race,
hell, death, and sin by faith o'ercome;
I'll leap for joy, increase my pace,
and as a bounding hart fly home,
through all eternity to prove
thy nature and thy name is Love.

471 I Come, O thou Traveler unknown

"Wrestling Jacob," Charles Wesley, 1739

Music: *Carey*, 888888; melody by Henry Carey in Church's *Introduction to Psalmody*, c. 1723; harmony mostly from *Hymns for Church and School*, 1964

1 Come, O thou Trav - el - er un - known, whom still I hold, but can - not see! My com - pa - ny be - fore is gone, and I am left a - lone with thee; with thee all night I mean to
2 I need not tell thee who I am, my mis - er - y and sin de - clare; thy - self hast called me by my name, look on thy hands and read it there. But who, I ask thee, who art
3 Yield to me now, for I am weak but con - fi - dent in self - de - spair! Speak to my heart, in bless - ing speak, be con - quered by my in - stant prayer; speak, or thou nev - er hence shalt
4 'Tis Love! 'tis Love! thou diedst for me! I hear thy whis - per in my heart; the morn - ing breaks, the shad - ows flee, pure U - ni - ver - sal Love thou art; to me, to all, thy mer - cies

stay and wres - tle till the break of day.
thou? Tell me thy name, and tell me now.
move, and tell me if thy name is Love.
move: thy na - ture and thy name is Love.

5 Lame as I am, I'll run my race,
hell, death, and sin by faith o'ercome;
I'll leap for joy, increase my pace,
and as a bounding hart fly home,
through all eternity to prove
thy nature and thy name is Love.

472 There's a wideness in God's mercy

Frederick W. Faber, 1854

Music: *Beng-li*, 8787; I-to Loh, 1970

These words can also be sung to *In Babilone*, no. 511.

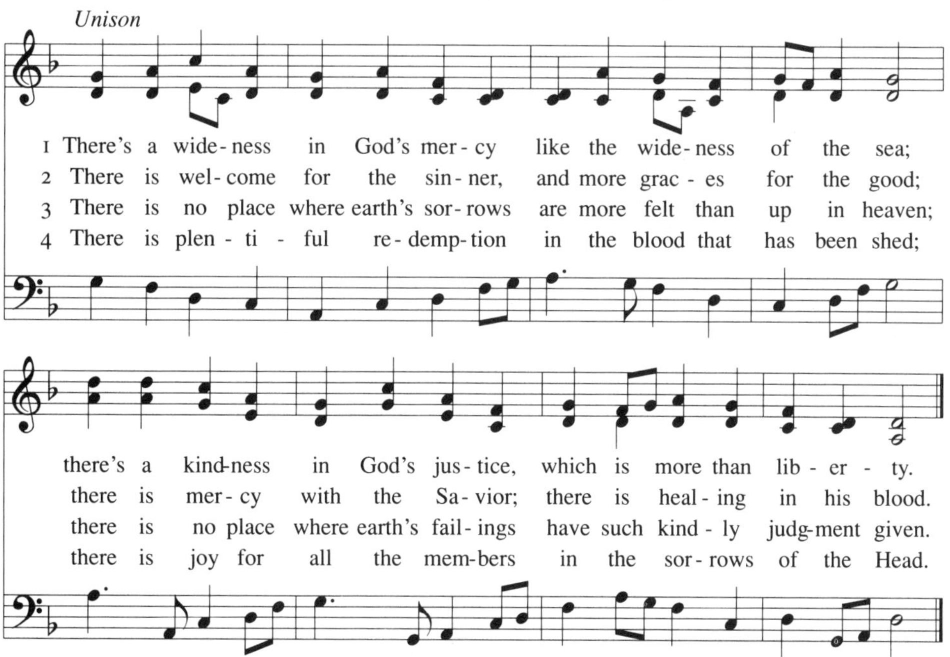
Unison
1 There's a wide-ness in God's mer-cy like the wide-ness of the sea;
2 There is wel-come for the sin-ner, and more grac-es for the good;
3 There is no place where earth's sor-rows are more felt than up in heaven;
4 There is plen-ti-ful re-demp-tion in the blood that has been shed;
there's a kind-ness in God's jus-tice, which is more than lib-er-ty.
there is mer-cy with the Sa-vior; there is heal-ing in his blood.
there is no place where earth's fail-ings have such kind-ly judg-ment given.
there is joy for all the mem-bers in the sor-rows of the Head.

5 For the love of God is broader
than the measure of the mind;
and the heart of the Eternal
is most wonderfully kind.

6 If our love were but more faithful,
we should take him at his word;
and our life would be thanksgiving
for the goodness of the Lord.

473 There's a wideness in God's mercy

Frederick W. Faber, 1854

Music: *St. Helena*, 8787D; Calvin Hampton, 1978

These words can also be sung to *In Babilone*, no. 511.

Introduction
Descant for flute or violin (last time only)
1 There's a wide - ness in God's mer - cy like the wide - ness
2 There is no place where earth's sor - rows are more felt than
3 For the love of God is broad - er than the mea - sure
of the sea; there's a kind - ness in God's jus -
up in heaven; there is no place where earth's fail -
of the mind; and the heart of the E - ter -

tice, which is more than lib - er - ty. There is wel - come
ings have such kind - ly judg - ment given. There is plen - ti -
nal is most won - der - ful - ly kind. If our love were
for the sin - ner, and more grac - es for the good; there is mer - cy
ful re - demp - tion in the blood that has been shed; there is joy for
but more faith - ful, we should take him at his word; and our life would
with the Sa - vior; there is heal - ing in his blood.
all the mem - bers in the sor - rows of the Head.
be thanks - giv - ing for the good - ness of the Lord.

474 How can we name a love

"The Beyond in the midst of life," Brian Wren, 1973

Music: *Mercer Street*, 6686D; Malcolm Williamson, 1973

1 How can we name a love deep - er than heart and mind,
2 If we a - woke to life built on a rock of care
3 If in an - oth - er's arms close-ness and joy as- tound,
4 When in a job or task oth - ers with us u - nite,
ba - sic to all we know or think or do or seek or find?
that asked no great re- ward, but firm, as-sured, was sim - ply there,
and as we take and give we die and live, are lost and found,
work - ing at some-thing new to make or do with shared de - light,
"Look at your life, your world: in each fa - mil - iar face
we can, with par - ents' names, pic - ture and then a - dore
or if by oth - ers' trust shy-ness and pride un - bend,
think how our Part - ner's aims cry to be un - der - stood:
where joy is found love's ech - oes sound, hid in the com - mon - place."
love's cos - mic mind, our Fa - ther kind, our Mo - ther strong and sure.
we glimpse God's ways and hush to praise our Lov - er and our Friend.
that small and great con - ceive, cre - ate, and know that life is good.

5 So, in a hundred names
daily we all can meet
signals of love unknown at work,
at home or in the street.

Yet on these terms alone
faith would be weak and dim:
in Christ we see love's guarantee
and fix our hopes on him.

475 O day full of grace

Den signede Dag

Nikolai F. S. Grundtvig, 1826, based on older versions; translated by Gerald Thorson, 1978

Music: *Den signede dag*, 989898; medieval Nordic melody; harmony from *Den Svenska Psalm Boken*, 1939

1 O day full of grace that now we see ap - pear - ing on
2 O day full of grace, O bless - ed time, our Lord on the
3 For Christ bore our sins, and not his own, when he on the
4 When we on that fi - nal jour - ney go that Christ is for
earth's hor - i - zon, bring light from our God that we may
earth ar - riv - ing; then came to the world that light sub -
cross was hang - ing; and then he a - rose and moved the
us pre - par - ing, we'll gath - er in song, our hearts a -
be a - bound - ing in joy this sea - son. God, shine for us
lime, great joy for us all re - triev - ing; for Je - sus all
stone, that we, un - to him be - long - ing, might join with an -
glow, all joy of the heav - ens shar - ing, and walk in the
now in this dark place; your name on our hearts em - blaz - on.
mor - tals did em - brace, all dark - ness and shame re - mov - ing.
gel - ic hosts to raise our voic - es in end - less sing - ing.
light of God's own place, with an - gels his name a - dor - ing.

476 Earth's scattered isles and contoured hills

Jeffery Rowthorn, 1974, based on Psalm 97

Music: *Meadville*, 888888; adapted by W. Thomas Jones, 1980, from an anthem by Walter L. Pelz, 1977

1 Earth's scat - tered isles and con-toured hills which part the
2 God's judg - ment passed on so - cial ills that thwart a -
3 The con - stant care which Is - rael knew a - like in
4 The light which shines through no - ble acts, the quest for
seas and mold the land, and vis - tas new - ly
while God's firm in - tent, the flag - ging dreams of
faith and faith - less - ness, the sub - tle prov - i -
truth dis - pel - ling lies, the grace of Christ re -
seen from space that show a world awe - some and
wea - ry folk whose brave new world lies torn and
dence which guides a pil - grim Church through change and
newed in us so love lives on and dis - cord

grand, all won-drous-ly u-nite to sing: take
rent, in pain-ful form their mes-sage bring: take
stress, in-spire us grate-ful-ly to sing: take
dies, all blend their song, good news to bring: take

heart, take hope, the Lord is King!
heart, take hope, the Lord is King!
heart, take hope, the Lord is King!
heart, take hope, the Lord is King!

477 Can I see another's woe

William Blake, 1789

Music: *Song 13*, 7777; adapted from Orlando Gibbons, 1623

1 Can I see an-oth-er's woe, and not be in sor-row too?
2 Can I see a fall-ing tear, and not feel my sor-row's share?
3 Think not thou canst sigh a sigh, and thy Mak-er is not by;
4 O! God give to us his joy that our grief he may de-stroy:
Can I see an-oth-er's grief, and not seek for kind re-lief?
Can a par-ent see a child weep, nor be with sor-row filled?
think not thou canst weep a tear, and thy Mak-er is not near.
till our pain and sor-row leave, God doth sit by us and grieve.

478 How firm a foundation

"K" in John Rippon's *Selection of Hymns*, 1787

Music: *Foundation*, 11.11.11.11; melody in Joseph Funk's *A Compilation of Genuine Church Music*, Winchester, Virginia, 1832; harmony by Calvin Hampton, 1982

1 How firm a foun - da - tion, you saints of the Lord,
2 "Fear not, I am with you, O be not dis - mayed,
3 "When through the deep wa - ters I call you to go,
4 "When through fier - y tri - als your path - way shall lie,
is laid for your faith in his ex - cel - lent word!
for I am your God and will still give you aid:
the riv - ers of sor - row shall not ov - er - flow;
my grace, all - suf - fi - cient, shall be your sup - ply;
What more can God say than to you he has said,
I'll strength - en you, help you, and cause you to stand,
for I will be with you, your trou - bles to bless,
the flame shall not hurt you; I on - ly de - sign

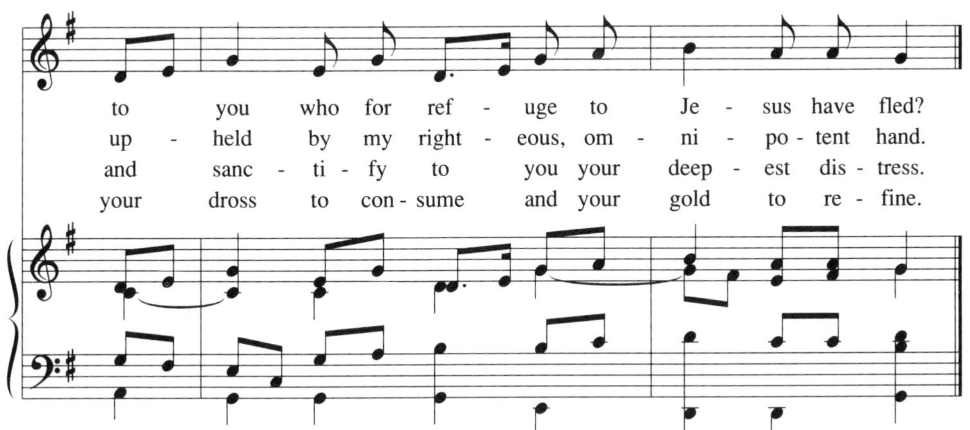
to you who for ref - uge to Je - sus have fled?
up - held by my right - eous, om - ni - po - tent hand.
and sanc - ti - fy to you your deep - est dis - tress.
your dross to con - sume and your gold to re - fine.

5 "The soul that on Jesus has leaned for repose,
I will not, I will not desert to its foes;
that soul, though all hell shall endeavor to shake,
I'll never, no, never, no, never forsake."

479 Christ be my leader

Timothy Dudley-Smith, 1961

Music: *Slane*, 10.10.10.10; Irish folk melody; harmony by Martin Shaw, 1925

1 Christ be my lead - er by night as by day; safe through the
2 Christ be my teach - er in age as in youth, drift - ing or
3 Christ be my Sa - vior in calm as in strife; death can - not

dark - ness, for he is the way. Glad - ly I fol - low, my
doubt - ing, for he is the truth. Grant me to trust him; though
hold me, for he is the life. Nor dark - ness, nor doubt - ing, nor

fu - ture his care; dark - ness is day - light when Je - sus is there.
shift - ing as sand, doubt can - not daunt me; in Je - sus I stand.
sin and its stain can touch my sal - va - tion: with Je - sus I reign.

480 Here hangs a man discarded

"Hope against hope," Brian Wren, 1973

Music: *Shrub End*, 7676; Peter Cutts, 1975

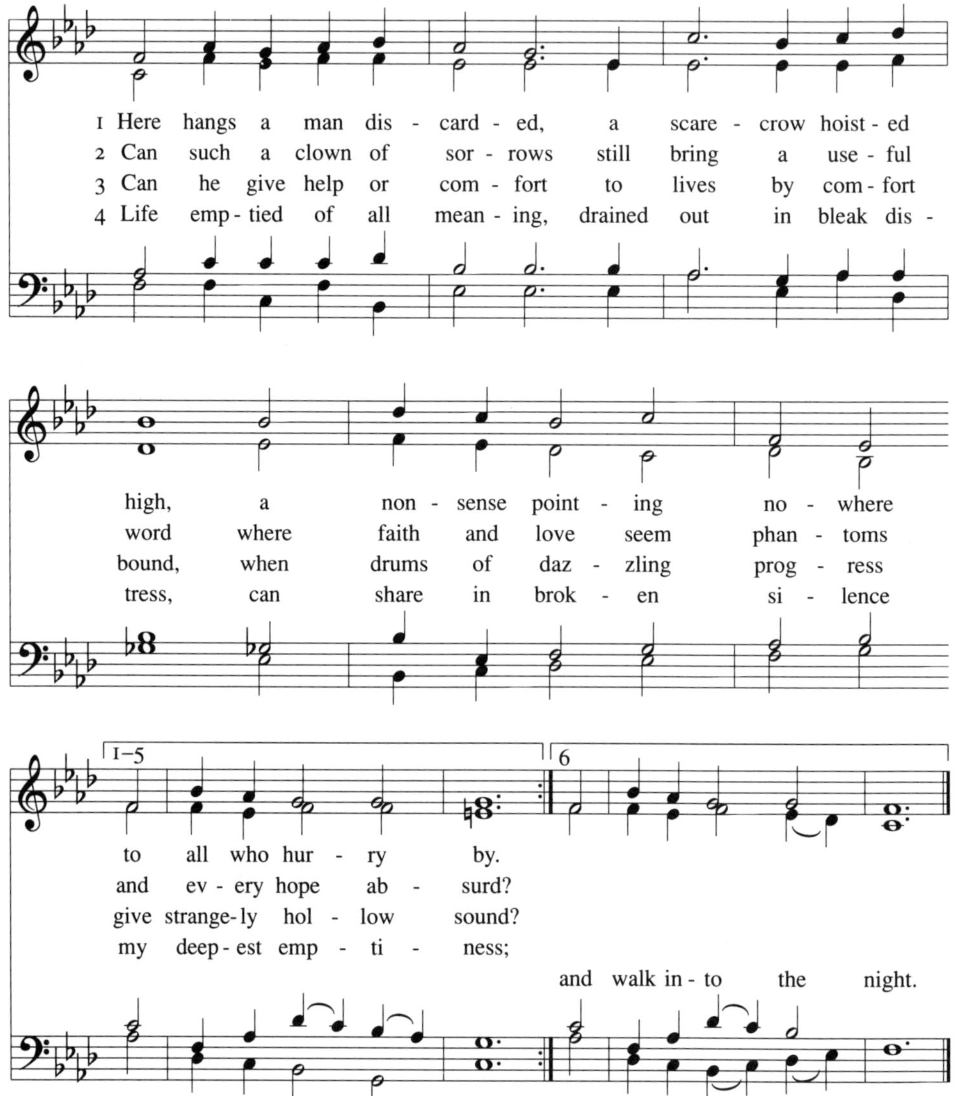
1 Here hangs a man dis - card - ed, a scare - crow hoist - ed
2 Can such a clown of sor - rows still bring a use - ful
3 Can he give help or com - fort to lives by com - fort
4 Life emp - tied of all mean - ing, drained out in bleak dis -
high, a non - sense point - ing no - where
word where faith and love seem phan - toms
bound, when drums of daz - zling prog - ress
tress, can share in brok - en si - lence
1–5
6
to all who hur - ry by.
and ev - ery hope ab - surd?
give strange - ly hol - low sound?
my deep - est emp - ti - ness;
and walk in - to the night.

5 and love that freely entered
the pit of life's despair
can name our hidden darkness
and suffer with us there.

6 Lord, if you now are risen,
help all who long for light
to hold the hand of promise
and walk into the night.

481 If thou but suffer God to guide thee

Wer nur den lieben Gott lässt walten

Georg Neumark, 1657; translated by Catherine Winkworth, 1863

Music: *Wer nur den lieben Gott*, 989888; melody by Georg Neumark, 1657

1 If thou but suf - fer God to guide thee, and hope in God through
2 On - ly be still, and wait God's lei - sure in cheer- ful hope, with
3 Sing, pray, and keep God's ways un - swerv- ing; so do thine own part
all thy ways, God will give strength, what - e'er be - tide thee,
heart con - tent to take what - e'er thy Mak - er's plea - sure
faith - ful - ly, and trust God's word; though un - de - serv - ing,
and bear thee through the e - vil days. Who trusts in God's un -
and all - dis - cern - ing love hath sent; doubt not thy in - most
thou yet shalt find it true for thee. God nev - er yet for -
chang - ing love builds on the rock that naught can move.
wants are known, for thou art called to be God's own.
sook at need the soul that trust - ed God in - deed.

482 Two roads diverged in a yellow wood

"The Road Not Taken," Robert Frost, 1916

Music: *The Road Not Taken*, irregular meter; Randall Thompson, from *Frostiana*, 1959

1 Two
2 then
3 and
4 I
p legato
roads di - verged in a yel - low wood and sor - ry I could not
took the oth - er, as just as fair, and hav - ing per - haps the
both that morn - ing e - qual - ly lay in leaves no step had
shall be tell - ing this with a sigh some - where ag - es and
trav - el both and be one trav - eler, long I stood and
bet - ter claim, be - cause it was grass - y and want - ed wear; though
trod - den black. Oh, I kept the first for an - oth - er day! Yet
ag - es hence: two roads di - verged in a wood, and I — I

looked down one as far as I could to where it bent in the
as for that the pass - ing there had worn them real - ly a -
know-ing how way leads on to way, I doubt-ed if I should
took the one less trav - eled by, and that has made
1–3
4
un - der - growth;
bout the same,
ev - er come back.
all the dif - fer - - - ence.
rall.
pp
ppp

483 I heard the voice of Jesus say

"The Voice from Galilee," Horatius Bonar, 1846

Music: *The Third Tune*, 8686D; Thomas Tallis, c. 1557

1 I heard the voice of Je - sus say, "Come un - to me and rest;
2 I heard the voice of Je - sus say, "Be - hold, I free - ly give
3 I heard the voice of Je - sus say, "I am this dark world's light;
lay down, O wea - ry one, lay down your head up - on my breast."
the liv - ing wa - ter; thirst - y one, stoop down, and drink, and live."
look un - to me, your morn shall rise, and all your day be bright."
I came to Je - sus as I was, wea - ry, and worn, and sad;
I came to Je - sus, and I drank of that life - giv - ing stream;
I looked to Je - sus, and I found in him my Star, my Sun;
I found in him a rest - ing place, and he has made me glad.
my thirst was quenched, my soul re - vived, and now I live in him.
and in that Light of life I'll walk till travel-ing days are done.

484 My hope is built

Edward Mote, c. 1832

Music: *Solid Rock*, 8888 with refrain; William Bradbury, 1863

These words can also be sung to *Melita*, no. 508.

1 My hope is built on no-thing less than Je-sus' blood and right-eous-ness;
2 When dark-ness veils his love-ly face, I rest on his un-chang-ing grace;
3 His oath, his cov-e-nant, his blood sus-tain me in the rag-ing flood;
4 When he shall come with trum-pet sound, O may I then in him be found,
no mer-it of my own I claim, but whol-ly lean on Je-sus' name.
in ev-ery high and storm-y gale my an-chor holds with-in the veil.
when all sup-ports are washed a-way, he then is all my hope and stay.
clothed in his right-eous-ness a-lone, fault-less to stand be-fore the throne!
Refrain
On Christ, the sol-id rock, I stand; all oth-er ground is
sink-ing sand, all oth-er ground is sink-ing sand.

485 Lord of all hopefulness

"All-Day Hymn," Jan Struther, 1931

Music: *Slane*, 10.11.11.12; Irish folk melody;
harmony by the editors of *The Hymnal 1982*

1 Lord of all hope-ful-ness, Lord of all joy, whose trust, ev - er
2 Lord of all ea - ger-ness, Lord of all faith, whose strong hands were
3 Lord of all kind-li-ness, Lord of all grace, your hands swift to
4 Lord of all gen-tle-ness, Lord of all calm, whose voice is con -
child-like, no cares could de - stroy, be there at our wak - ing, and
skilled at the plane and the lathe, be there at our la - bors, and
wel-come, your arms to em - brace, be there at our hom - ing, and
tent-ment, whose pres-ence is balm, be there at our sleep - ing, and
give us, we pray, your bliss in our hearts, Lord, at the break of the day.
give us, we pray, your strength in our hearts, Lord, at the noon of the day.
give us, we pray, your love in our hearts, Lord, at the eve of the day.
give us, we pray, your peace in our hearts, Lord, at the end of the day.

486 God, my Lord, my strength

Pán Bůh jest má sila

From *Tranoscious*, Levoca, 1636; translated by Jaroslav J. Vajda, 1967

Music: *Pán Bůh*, 10.4.7.5.6.5; melody in *Gradual*, Prague, 1567; harmony by Theodore Beck, 1969

1 God, my Lord, my strength, my place of hid-ing and con - fid - ing
2 Christ in me, and I am freed for liv-ing and for - giv - ing,
3 Up, weak knees and spir - it bowed in sor-row! No to - mor - row
in all needs by night and day; though foes sur - round me,
heart of flesh for life - less stone; now bold to serve him,
shall a - rise to beat you down; God goes be - fore you
and Sa - tan mark his prey, God shall have his way.
now cheered his love to own, nev - er - more a - lone.
and an - gels all a - round; on your head a crown!

487 These things did Thomas count as real

Thomas H. Troeger, 1984 (adapted)

Music: *Merle Marie*, 8888; Carol Doran, 1984

1 These things did Thom - as count as real: the warmth of blood, the chill of steel, the grain of wood, the heft of stone, the last frail twitch of flesh and bone.
2 The vi - sion of his skep - tic mind was keen e - nough to make him blind to an - y un - ex - pect - ed act too large for his small world of fact.
3 His rea - soned cer - tain - ties de - nied that one could live when one had died, un - til his fin - gers read like Braille the mark - ings of the spear and nail.
4 May we, O God, by grace be - lieve and thus the ris - en Christ re - ceive, whose raw, im - print - ed hands reach out to beck - on us be - yond our doubt.

488 There is no moment of my life

Brian Foley, 1971, based on Psalm 139:1–18

Music: *St. Botolph*, 8686; Gordon Slater, 1929, 1931

1 There is no mo - ment of my life, no
2 Be - fore I speak, my words are known, and
3 If I should close my eyes to him, God
4 God knew my days be - fore all days, be -
place where I may go, no ac - tion which God
all that I de - cide, to come or go: God
comes to give me sight; if I should go where
fore I came to be; God keeps me, loves me,
does not see, no thought God does not know.
knows my choice, and makes him - self my guide.
all is dark, God makes my dark - ness light.
in my ways: no lov - er such as he.

489 Light of the minds that know him

Timothy Dudley-Smith, 1976, based on a prayer of Augustine of Hippo

Music: *Moville*, 7676D; Irish traditional melody; harmony by Charles H. Kitson, 1927

1 Light of the minds that know him, may Christ be light to mine;
2 Life of the souls that love him, may Christ be ours in-deed;
3 Strength of the wills that serve him, may Christ be strength to me,
4 May it be ours to know him that we may tru - ly love,
my sun in ris - en splen - dor, my light of truth di - vine;
the liv - ing bread from heav - en on whom our spir - its feed;
who stilled the storm and tem - pest, who calmed the toss - ing sea;
and, lov - ing, ful - ly serve him as serve the saints a - bove;
my guide in doubt and dark - ness, my true and liv - ing way,
who died for love of sin - ners to bear our guilt - y load,
his Spir - it's power to move me, his will to mas - ter mine,
till in that home of glo - ry, with fade - less splen-dor bright,

my clear light ev - er shin - ing, my dawn of heav - en's day.
and make of life's brief jour - ney a new Em - ma - us road.
his cross to car - ry dai - ly and con - quer in his sign.
we serve in per - fect free - dom our Strength, our Life, our Light.

490 Not far beyond the sea

George B. Caird, c. 1945; based in part on John Robinson's letter to the departing Pilgrims, 1620 (see also hymn no. 382)

Music: *Cornwall*, 886886; Samuel Sebastian Wesley, 1872

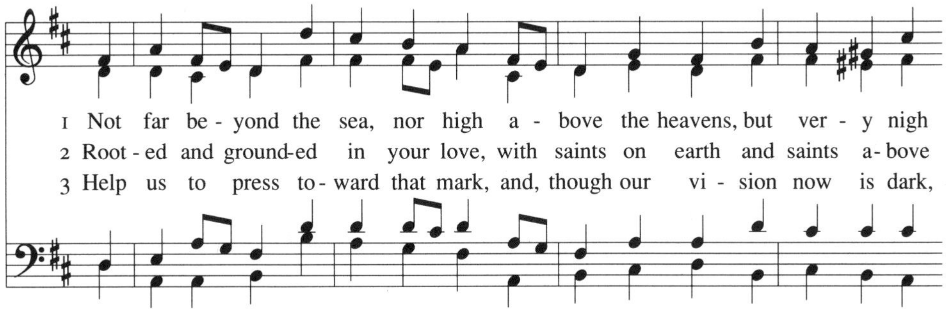

1 Not far be - yond the sea, nor high a - bove the heavens, but ver - y nigh
2 Root - ed and ground-ed in your love, with saints on earth and saints a - bove
3 Help us to press to - ward that mark, and, though our vi - sion now is dark,

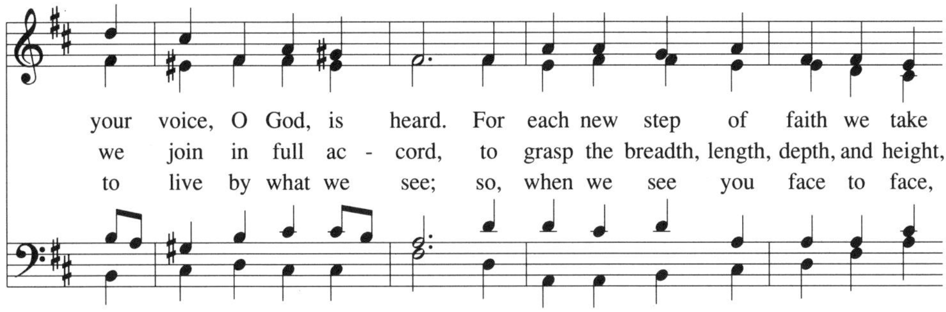

your voice, O God, is heard. For each new step of faith we take
we join in full ac - cord, to grasp the breadth, length, depth, and height,
to live by what we see; so, when we see you face to face,

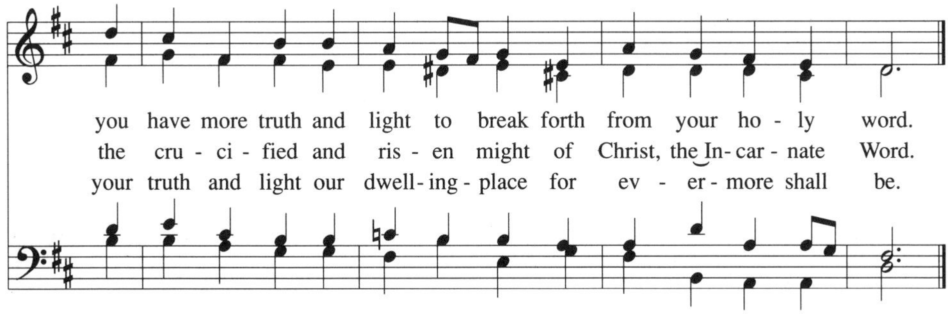

you have more truth and light to break forth from your ho - ly word.
the cru - ci - fied and ris - en might of Christ, the In - car - nate Word.
your truth and light our dwell - ing - place for ev - er - more shall be.

491 There is a balm in Gilead

African American spiritual

Music: *Balm in Gilead*, 7676 with refrain; African American spiritual; harmony by David Hurd, 1983

Refrain
There is a balm in Gil-e-ad to make the wound-ed whole.
There is a balm in Gil-e-ad to heal the sin-sick soul.
1 Some-times I feel dis-cour-aged, and think my work's in vain, but
2 If you can-not preach like Pe-ter, if you can-not pray like Paul, you can
then the Ho-ly Spir-it re-vives my soul a-gain.
tell the love of Je-sus and say, "He died for all!"
D.C.

492 Who would true valor see

Adapted from Mr. Valiant-for-Truth's song in John Bunyan's *The Pilgrim's Progress*, part 2, 1684

Music: *St. Dunstan's*, 65656665; Winfred Douglas, 1917

1 Who would true val - or see 'gainst all di - sas - ter,
2 Who so be - set you round with dis - mal sto - ries
3 Hob - gob - lin nor foul fiend can daunt your spir - it;
come forth, and con - stant be; fol - low the Mas - ter.
do but them - selves con - found; your strength the more is.
you know you at the end shall life in - her - it.
There's no dis - cour - age - ment shall make you once re - lent
No li - on can you fright, you'll with a gi - ant fight,
Then fan - cies fly a - way! Fear not what oth - ers say,
your first a - vowed in - tent to be a pil - grim.
but you will have the right to be a pil - grim.
but la - bor night and day to be a pil - grim.

493 Author of faith, eternal Word

Charles Wesley, 1740

Music: *Song 34*, 8888; melody and bass by Orlando Gibbons, 1623

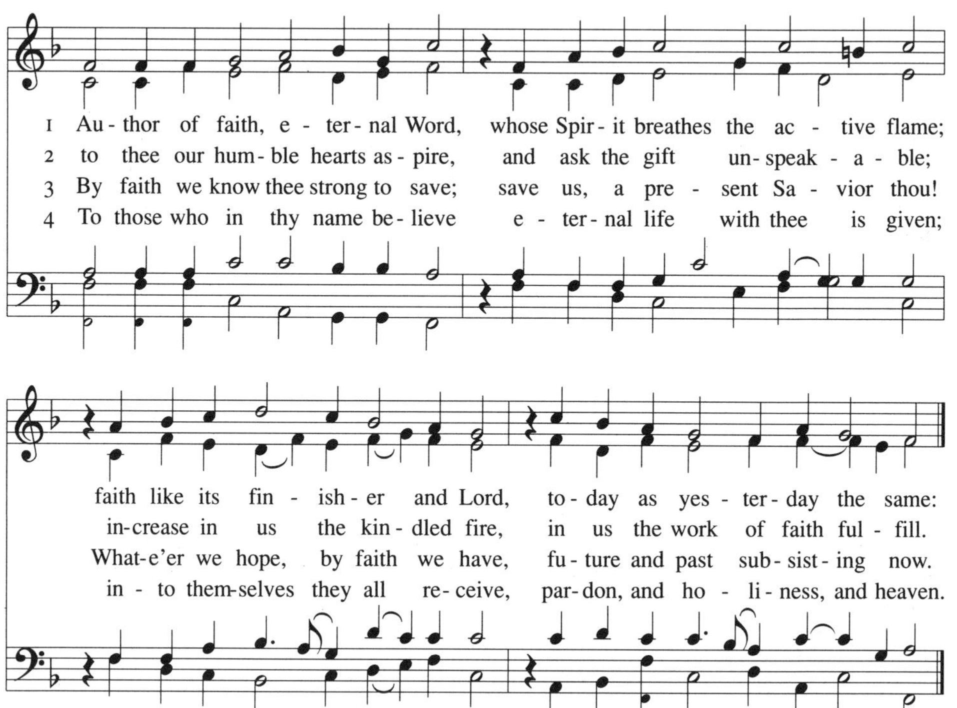
1 Au - thor of faith, e - ter - nal Word, whose Spir - it breathes the ac - tive flame;
2 to thee our hum - ble hearts as - pire, and ask the gift un - speak - a - ble;
3 By faith we know thee strong to save; save us, a pre - sent Sa - vior thou!
4 To those who in thy name be - lieve e - ter - nal life with thee is given;
faith like its fin - ish - er and Lord, to - day as yes - ter - day the same:
in-crease in us the kin - dled fire, in us the work of faith ful - fill.
What-e'er we hope, by faith we have, fu - ture and past sub - sist - ing now.
in - to them-selves they all re - ceive, par - don, and ho - li - ness, and heaven.

5 The things unknown to feeble sense,
unseen by reason's glimmering ray,
with strong commanding evidence
their heavenly origin display.

6 Faith lends its realizing light,
the clouds disperse, the shadows fly;
the invisible appears in sight,
and God is seen by mortal eye.

494 Our journey had advanced

Emily Dickinson, 1830–1886

Music: *London*, 6686; *Ravenscroft's Psalter*, 1621

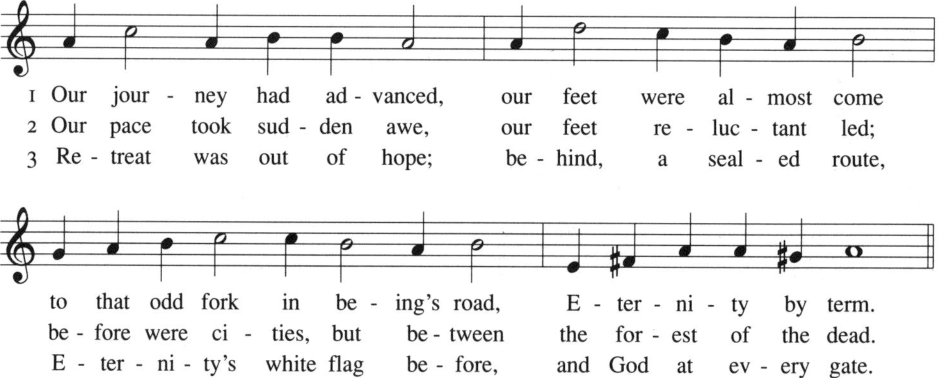
1 Our jour - ney had ad - vanced, our feet were al - most come
2 Our pace took sud - den awe, our feet re - luc - tant led;
3 Re - treat was out of hope; be - hind, a seal - ed route,
to that odd fork in be - ing's road, E - ter - ni - ty by term.
be - fore were ci - ties, but be - tween the for - est of the dead.
E - ter - ni - ty's white flag be - fore, and God at ev - ery gate.

Harmony version, with melody in the tenor:

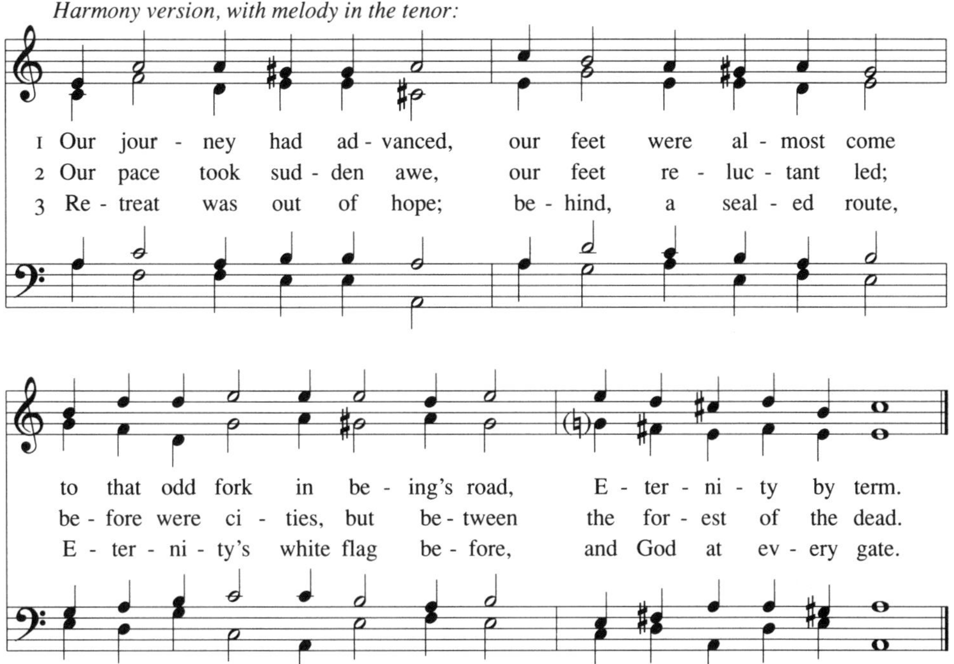
1 Our jour - ney had ad - vanced, our feet were al - most come
2 Our pace took sud - den awe, our feet re - luc - tant led;
3 Re - treat was out of hope; be - hind, a seal - ed route,
to that odd fork in be - ing's road, E - ter - ni - ty by term.
be - fore were ci - ties, but be - tween the for - est of the dead.
E - ter - ni - ty's white flag be - fore, and God at ev - ery gate.

495 Lord, it is in thy tender care

"The Covenant and Confidence of Faith," Richard Baxter, 1681, and others

Music: *Wigtown*, 8686; melody and most of the harmony from *Scottish Psalter*, 1635

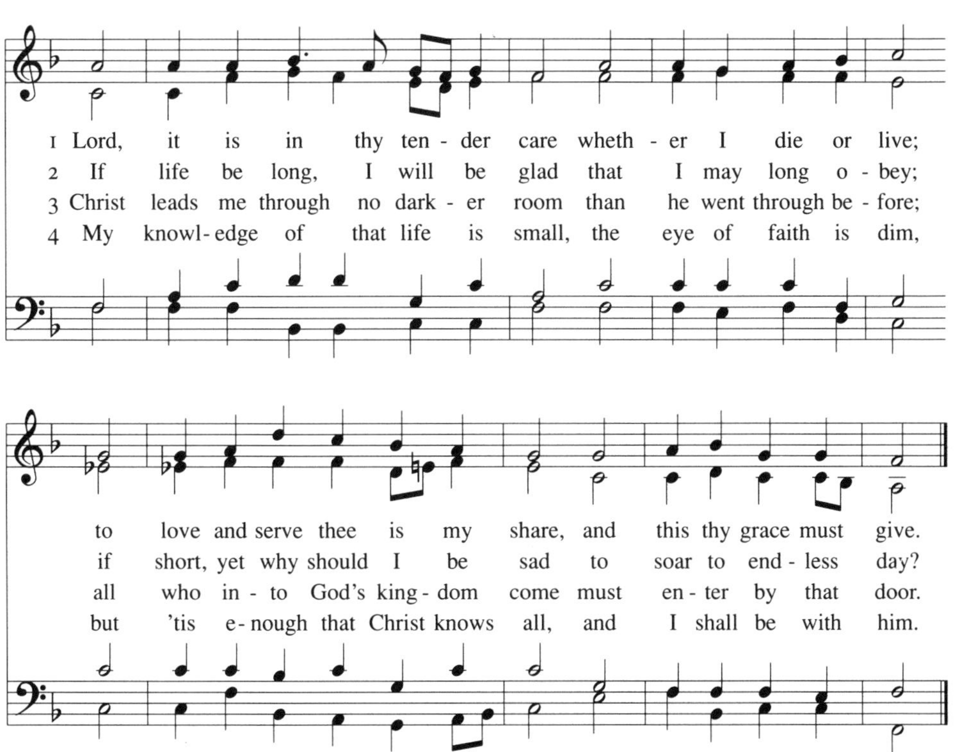
1 Lord, it is in thy ten - der care wheth - er I die or live;
2 If life be long, I will be glad that I may long o - bey;
3 Christ leads me through no dark - er room than he went through be - fore;
4 My knowl - edge of that life is small, the eye of faith is dim,
to love and serve thee is my share, and this thy grace must give.
if short, yet why should I be sad to soar to end - less day?
all who in - to God's king - dom come must en - ter by that door.
but 'tis e - nough that Christ knows all, and I shall be with him.

496 God made from one blood

Thomas H. Troeger, 1988 (adapted)

Music: *Normandy*, 11.11.11.11; Basque carol collected and extended by C. Edgar Pettman (1865–1943); harmonized by the music editors of *The BBC Hymn Book*, 1951

1 God made from one blood all the fam - ilies of earth, the cir - cles of nur - ture that raise us from birth, com - pan - ions who join us to walk through each stage of child - hood and youth and a - dult - hood and age.
2 We turn to you, God, with our thanks and our tears for all of the fam - ilies we've known through the years, the in - ti - mate net - works on whom we de - pend of par - ents and spous - es and chil - dren and friends.
3 Through fam - ilies we've tast - ed the val - ue of trust and felt what it means to be lov - ing and just, yet fam - ilies have al - so be - trayed their best goals, mis - treat - ing their mem - bers and bruis - ing their souls.
4 Help fam - ilies in all of their var - i - ous forms to face with in - teg - ri - ty strug - gles and storms; grant peace to our homes that will nur - ture the bud of peace for the fam - ilies you made from one blood.

497 Lord of all being

Oliver Wendell Holmes, 1859

Music: *Mendon*, 8888; melody from *Methodist Harmonist*, 1821; adapted and harmonized by Lowell Mason, 1859

These words can also be sung to *Duke Street*, no. 16.

1 Lord of all be - ing, throned a - far, thy glo - ry flames from sun and star; cen - ter and soul of ev - ery sphere, yet to each lov - ing heart how near!
2 Sun of our life, thy quick - ening ray sheds on our path the glow of day; star of our hope, thy soft - ened light cheers the long watch - es of the night.
3 Our mid-night is thy smile with - drawn; our noon - tide is thy gra - cious dawn; our rain - bow arch, thy mer - cy's sign; all, save the clouds of sin, are thine.
4 Lord of all life, be - low, a - bove, whose light is truth, whose warmth is love, be - fore thy ev - er - blaz - ing throne we ask no lus - ter of our own.

5 Grant us thy truth to make us free,
and kindling hearts that burn for thee,
till all thy living altars claim
one holy light, one heavenly flame.

498 Eternal Ruler of the ceaseless round

John White Chadwick, 1864, for his graduation from Harvard Divinity School

Music: *Song 1*, 10.10.10.10.10.10; melody and bass by Orlando Gibbons, 1623

1 E - ter - nal Ru - ler of the cease - less round
2 We would be one in ha - tred of all wrong,
3 O clothe us with your heaven - ly ar - mor, Lord,
of cir - cling plan - ets sing - ing on their way;
one in our love of all things true and fair,
your trust - y shield and sword of love be ours;
guide of the na - tions from the night pro - found
one with the joy that finds a voice in song,
for in - spi - ra - tion clothe us in your word;
in - to the glo - ry of the per - fect day;
one with the grief that trem - bles in - to prayer,
we ask no vic - to - ries that are not yours:
rule in our hearts, that we may live a - new,
one in the power which sets your chil - dren free
give or with - hold, let pain or plea - sure fall;

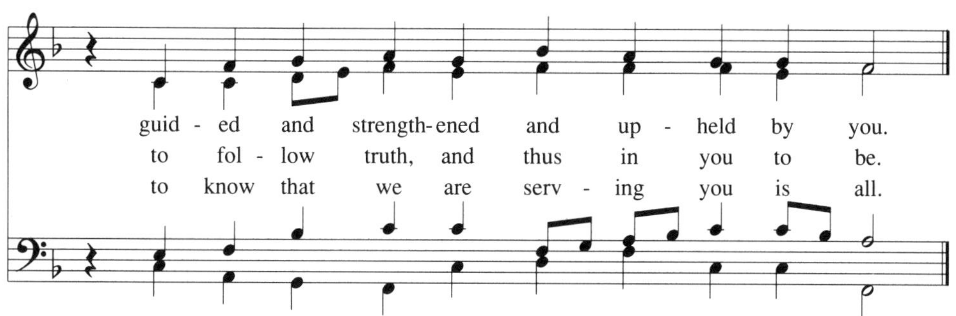
guid - ed and strength-ened and up - held by you.
to fol - low truth, and thus in you to be.
to know that we are serv - ing you is all.

499 Lord of our growing years

David Mowbray, 1982

Music: *Little Cornard*, 666688; Martin Shaw, 1915

1 Lord of our grow - ing years, with us from in - fan - cy,
2 Lord of our strong - est years, stretch - ing our youth - ful powers,
3 Lord of our mid - dle years, giv - er of stead - fast - ness,
4 Lord of our old - er years, steep though the road may be,

laugh - ter and quick - dried tears, fresh - ness and en - er - gy:
lov - ers and pi - o - neers when all the world seems ours:
cour - age that per - se - veres when there is small suc - cess:
rid us of fool - ish fears, bring us se - ren - i - ty:

Refrain

your grace sur-rounds us all our days—for all your gifts we bring our praise.

5 Lord of our closing years,
always your promise stands;
hold us, when death appears,
safely within your hands:

Refrain

500 Here, O Lord, your servants gather

Sekai no tomo to

Tokuo Yamaguchi, 1958; translated by Everett M. Stowe, 1958

Music: *Tokyo*, 7575D; Isao Koizumi, 1958

1 *Se - ka - i no to - mo to te o tsu - na - gi,*
1 Here, O Lord, your ser - vants gath - er, hand we link with hand;
2 Man - y are the tongues we speak, scat - tered are the lands,
3 Na - ture's se - crets o - pen wide, chang - es nev - er cease.
Jyu - ji - ka no mo - to ni ta - tsu wa - re - ra,
look - ing toward our Sa - vior's cross, joined in love we stand.
yet our hearts are one in God, one in love's de - mands.
Where, O where, can wea - ry souls find the source of peace?
Ka - mi no mi - ku - ni o me a te to shi,
As we seek the realm of God, we u - nite to pray:
In the dark - ness hope ap - pears, call - ing age and youth;
Un - to all those sore dis - tressed, torn by end - less strife,

Shu Ye - su no mi - chi o su - su - mi yu - kan.
Je - sus, Sa - vior, guide our steps, for you are the Way.
Je - sus, Teach - er, dwell with us, for you are the Truth.
Je - sus, Heal - er, bring your balm, for you are the Life.

4 Grant, O God, an age renewed,
filled with deathless love;
help us as we work and pray,
send us from above

truth and courage, faith and power,
needed in our strife;
Jesus, Master, be our Way,
be our Truth, our Life.

501 Teach me, my God and King

"The Elixir," George Herbert, 1633 (posth.)

Music: *Carlisle*, 6686; melody and most of the harmony by Charles Lockhart, 1769

1 Teach me, my God and King, in all things thee to see,
2 Per - chance I look on glass, and on it stay my eye,
3 All may of thee par - take; no - thing can be so mean
4 A ser - vant with this clause makes drudg - er - y di - vine:
and what I do in an - y - thing, to do it as for thee.
or, if it please me, through it pass, and then the heaven es - py.
which with this tinc - ture, "For thy sake," will not grow bright and clean.
who sweeps a room as for thy laws, makes that and the ac - tion fine.

5 This is the famous stone
that turneth all to gold;
for that which God doth touch and own
cannot for less be told.

502 Living Word of God eternal

Jeffery Rowthorn, 1983

Music: *Julion*, 878787; David Hurd, 1974

These words can also be sung to *Regent Square*, no. 246.

1 Liv-ing Word of God e-ter-nal, lay-ing claim to ev-ery age,
Je-sus, speak through all our speak-ing, bring to life the Bi-ble's page;
2 Lov-ing Sa-vior, whose em-brac-es our true selves a-lone un-mask,
in this fel-low-ship's small com-pass train us for our com-mon task:
3 Liv-ing Bread come down from heav-en, brok-en, shared, dis-tri-but-ed,
feed us, gath-ered at this ta-ble, with your grace un-lim-it-ed,
4 Lov-ing Spir-it, pray-ing in us, giv-ing voice to all our sighs,
show the wide-ness of your mer-cy to deaf ears and blind-ed eyes;

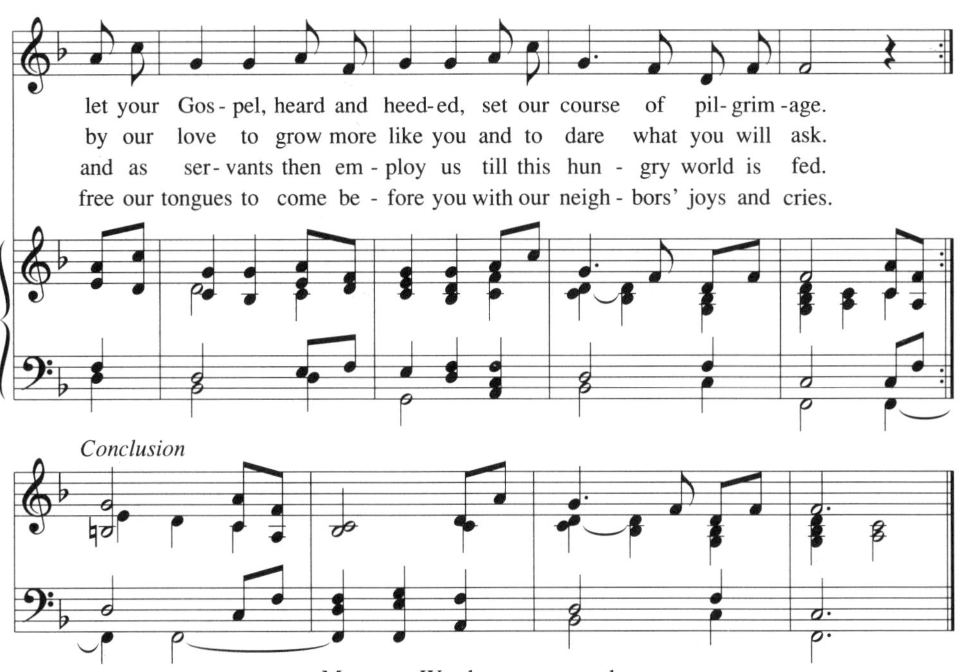
let your Gos - pel, heard and heed-ed, set our course of pil- grim -age.
by our love to grow more like you and to dare what you will ask.
and as ser- vants then em - ploy us till this hun - gry world is fed.
free our tongues to come be - fore you with our neigh - bors' joys and cries.

Conclusion

5 May your Word among us spoken,
may the loving which we dare,
may your Bread among us broken,
may the prayers in which we share
daily make us faithful people,
living signs, Lord, of your care.

503 Help us, O Lord, to learn

William Watkins Reid, Jr., 1959

Music: *St. Ethelwald*, 6686; William H. Monk, 1861

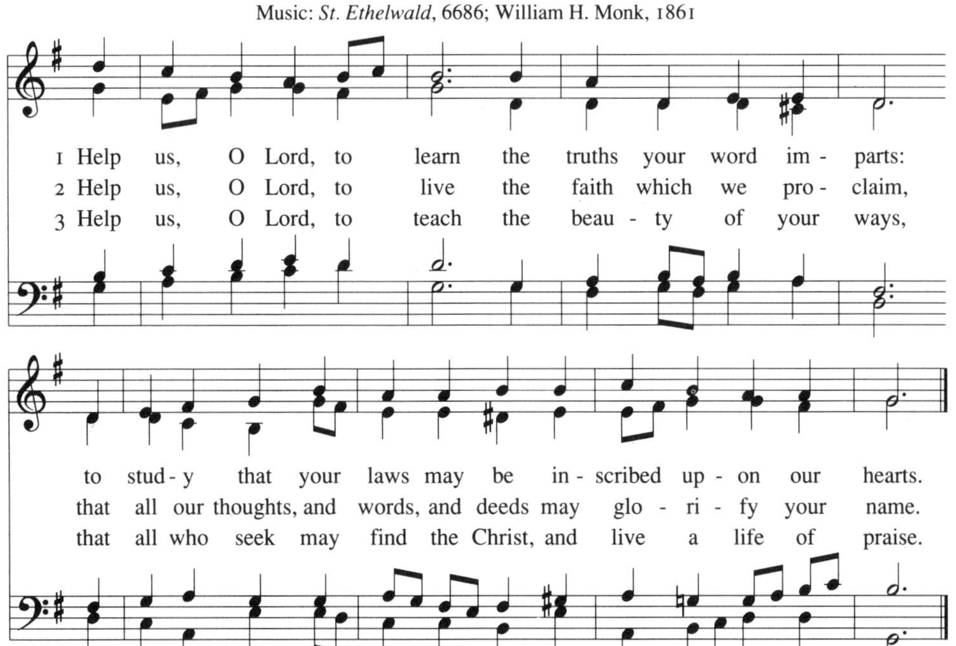
1 Help us, O Lord, to learn the truths your word im - parts:
2 Help us, O Lord, to live the faith which we pro - claim,
3 Help us, O Lord, to teach the beau - ty of your ways,
to stud - y that your laws may be in - scribed up - on our hearts.
that all our thoughts, and words, and deeds may glo - ri - fy your name.
that all who seek may find the Christ, and live a life of praise.

504 Lord, whose love through humble service

Albert F. Bayly, 1961

Music: *Beach Spring*, 8787D; melody in *The Sacred Harp*, Philadelphia, 1844; attributed to Benjamin F. White; harmony by Ronald A. Nelson, 1978

1 Lord, whose love through hum - ble ser - vice bore the weight of hu - man need, who up - on the cross, for - sak - en, of - fered mer - cy's per - fect deed, we, your ser - vants, bring the wor - ship not of voice a - lone, but heart, con - se - crat - ing
2 Still your chil - dren wan - der home - less; still the hun - gry cry for bread; still the cap - tives long for free - dom; still in grief we mourn our dead. As, O Lord, your deep com - pas - sion healed the sick and freed the soul, use the love your
3 As we wor - ship, grant us vi - sion, till your love's re - veal - ing light, in its height and depth and great - ness, dawns up - on our quick-ened sight, mak - ing known the needs and bur - dens your com - pas - sion bids us bear, stir - ring us to
4 Called by wor - ship to your ser - vice, forth in your dear name we go, to the child, the youth, the a - ged, love in liv - ing deeds to show; hope and health, good will and com - fort, coun - sel, aid, and peace we give, that your ser - vants,

to your pur - pose ev - ery gift that you im - part.
Spir - it kin - dles still to save and make us whole.
tire - less striv - ing, your a - bun - dant life to share.
Lord, in free - dom may your mer - cy know and live.

505 Awake, my soul, stretch every nerve

Philip Doddridge, 1775 (posth.)

Music: *Siroe*, 86866; melody in James Hewitt's *Harmonia Sacra*, 1812; adapted from an aria in G. F. Handel's *Siroe*, 1728

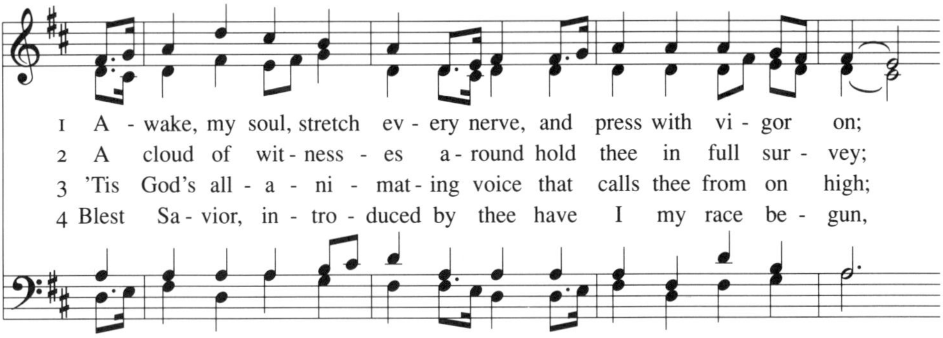

1 A - wake, my soul, stretch ev - ery nerve, and press with vi - gor on;
2 A cloud of wit - ness - es a - round hold thee in full sur - vey;
3 'Tis God's all - a - ni - mat - ing voice that calls thee from on high;
4 Blest Sa - vior, in - tro - duced by thee have I my race be - gun,

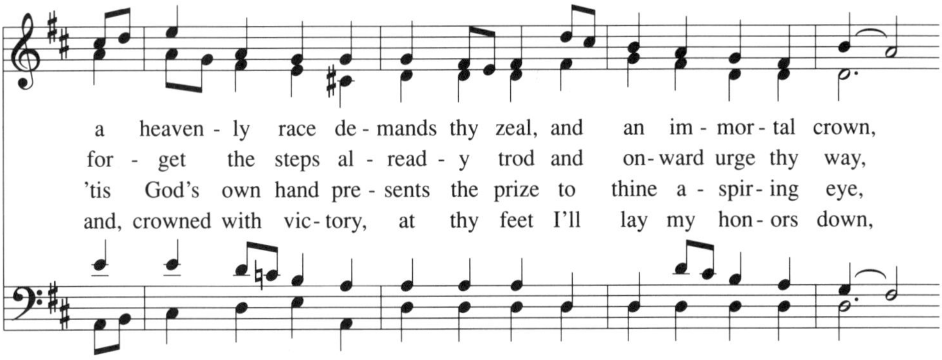

a heaven - ly race de - mands thy zeal, and an im - mor - tal crown,
for - get the steps al - read - y trod and on - ward urge thy way,
'tis God's own hand pre - sents the prize to thine a - spir - ing eye,
and, crowned with vic - tory, at thy feet I'll lay my hon - ors down,

and an im - mor - tal crown.
and on - ward urge thy way.
to thine a - spir - ing eye.
I'll lay my hon - ors down.

506 How clear is our vocation, Lord

"Our Christian Vocation," Fred Pratt Green, 1981

Music: *Repton*, 868866; arranged in George Gilbert's *Repton School: Hymns for Use in Chapel*, 1924, from a song in C. Hubert H. Parry's *Judith*, 1888

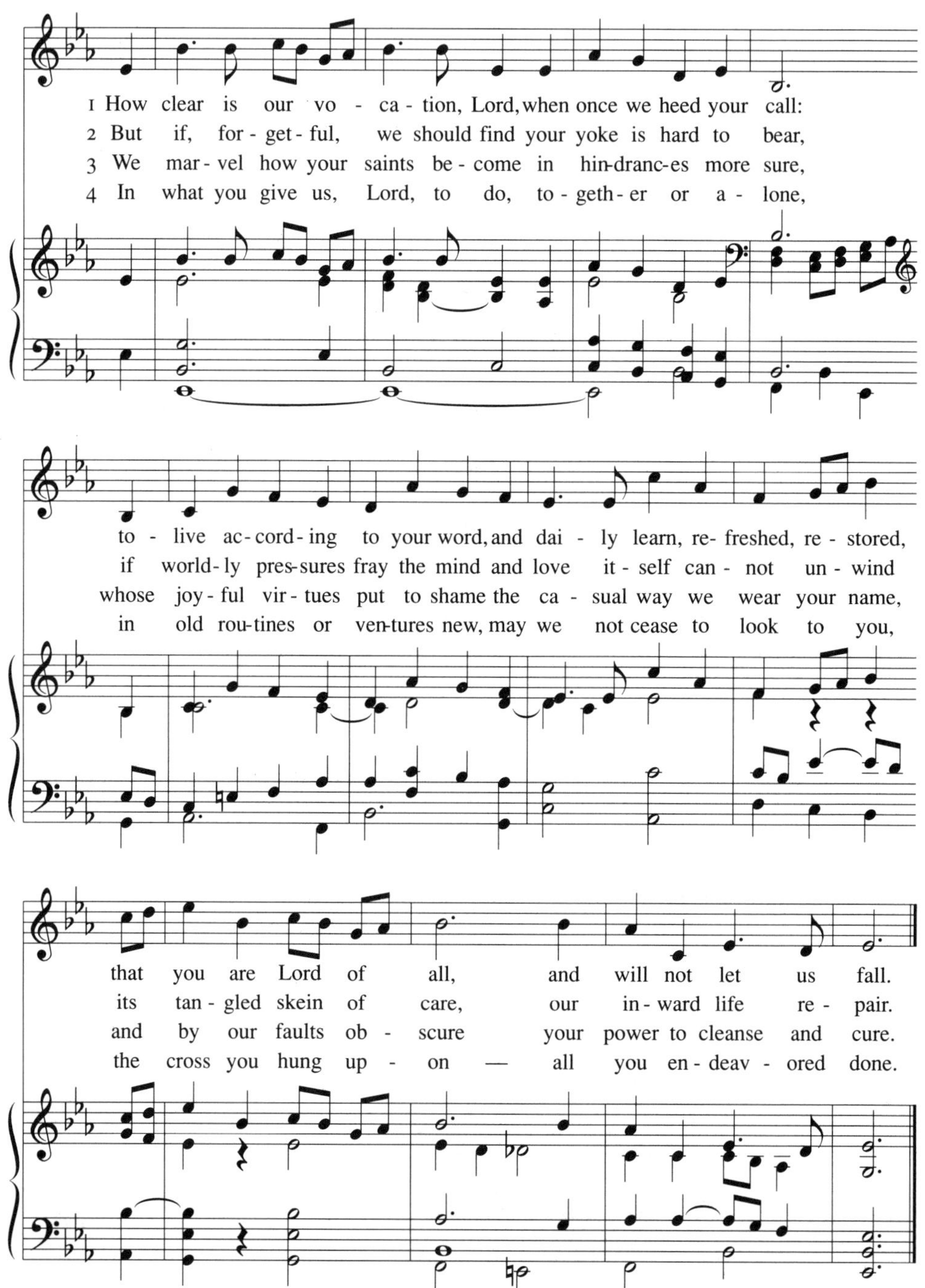
1 How clear is our vo - ca - tion, Lord, when once we heed your call:
2 But if, for - get - ful, we should find your yoke is hard to bear,
3 We mar - vel how your saints be - come in hin-dranc-es more sure,
4 In what you give us, Lord, to do, to - geth - er or a - lone,
to - live ac - cord - ing to your word, and dai - ly learn, re - freshed, re - stored,
if world - ly pres-sures fray the mind and love it - self can - not un - wind
whose joy - ful vir - tues put to shame the ca - sual way we wear your name,
in old rou-tines or ven-tures new, may we not cease to look to you,
that you are Lord of all, and will not let us fall.
its tan - gled skein of care, our in - ward life re - pair.
and by our faults ob - scure your power to cleanse and cure.
the cross you hung up - on — all you en - deav - ored done.

507 Shepherd of all who inhabit the earth

Jeffery Rowthorn, 1980

Music: *O quanta qualia*, 10.10.10.10; melody in *Paris Antiphoner*, 1681

1 Shep - herd of all who in - hab - it the earth,
2 Lov - er of souls, un - der - min - ing our pride,
3 Con - queror of death, o - ver - com - ing de - spair,
4 Her - ald of God and the king - dom to be,
dy - ing you showed us hu - man - i - ty's worth;
heal and for - give each of - fense we would hide.
strength - en us, lest, by our ceas - ing to care,
grant us the vi - sion to see as you see;
call - ing all home in their own mo - ther tongue,
Par - don and grace are the fruits of your tree;
truth yield to false - hood and jus - tice to wrong;
risk - ing the new to give life to the old,
Lord, by your life - giv - ing word, make us one.
Lord, by your self - giv - ing love, make us free.
Lord, by your ris - ing to life, make us strong.
Lord, by your gos - pel of hope, make us bold.

5 Host at the feast and our Guide on the way,
yours is the glory redeeming earth's day;
teach us to serve and with joy to depend,
Lord, on your Spirit-filled life without end.

508 Eternal Father, strong to save

"For Those at Sea," William Whiting, 1860, 1869

Music: *Melita*, 888888; John B. Dykes, 1861

1 E - ter - nal Fa - ther, strong to save, whose arm doth bind the rest - less wave,
2 O Sa - vior, whose al - might - y word the winds and waves sub - mis - sive heard,
3 O Ho - ly Spir - it, who didst brood up - on the cha - os dark and rude,
4 O Tri - ni - ty of love and power, our kin - dred shield in dan - ger's hour;

who bidd'st the might - y o - cean deep its own ap - point - ed lim - its keep:
who walked up - on the foam - ing deep, and calm a - mid its rage could sleep:
who bade its an - gry tu - mult cease, and called forth light, and life, and peace:
from rock and tem - pest, fire and foe, pro - tect them where - so - e'er they go;

O hear us when we cry to thee for those in per - il on the sea.
O hear us when we cry to thee for those in per - il on the sea.
O hear us when we cry to thee for those in per - il on the sea.
and ev - er let there rise to thee glad hymns of praise from land and sea.

509 Lord of all nations

Olive Wise Spannaus, 1960

Music: *Breslau*, 8888; German traditional melody; arranged and harmonized by Felix Mendelssohn in his *St. Paul*, 1836

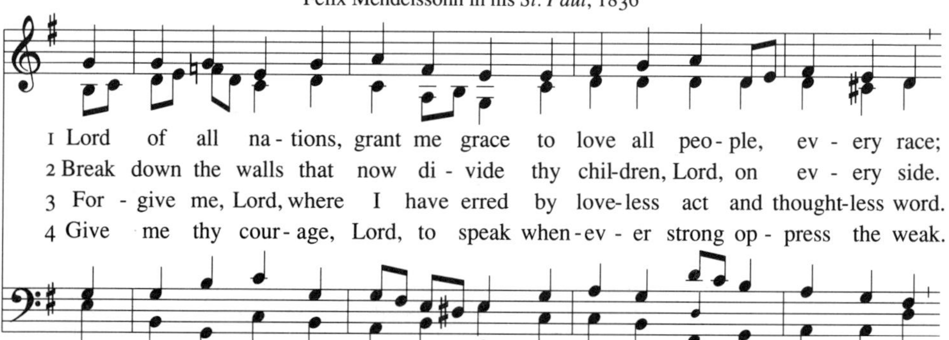
1 Lord of all na - tions, grant me grace to love all peo - ple, ev - ery race;
2 Break down the walls that now di - vide thy chil - dren, Lord, on ev - ery side.
3 For - give me, Lord, where I have erred by love - less act and thought - less word.
4 Give me thy cour - age, Lord, to speak when - ev - er strong op - press the weak.

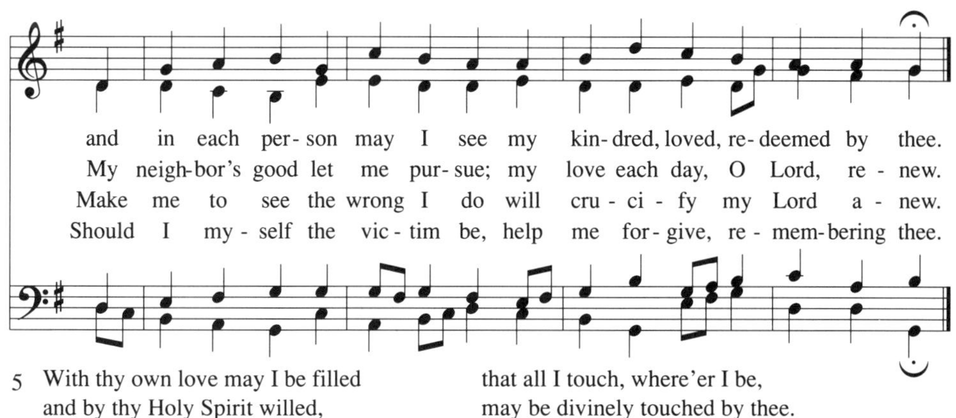
and in each per- son may I see my kin- dred, loved, re- deemed by thee.
My neigh-bor's good let me pur- sue; my love each day, O Lord, re - new.
Make me to see the wrong I do will cru - ci - fy my Lord a - new.
Should I my - self the vic - tim be, help me for- give, re - mem- bering thee.

5 With thy own love may I be filled
and by thy Holy Spirit willed,
that all I touch, where'er I be,
may be divinely touched by thee.

510 Be thou my vision

Rob tu mo bhoile, a Comdi cride

Irish, c. 8th century; translated by Maire ni Bhroin (Mary Byrne), 1905, and versified by Eleanor Hull, 1912

Music: *Slane*, 10.10.9.10; Irish traditional melody; harmonized by Martin Shaw, 1925

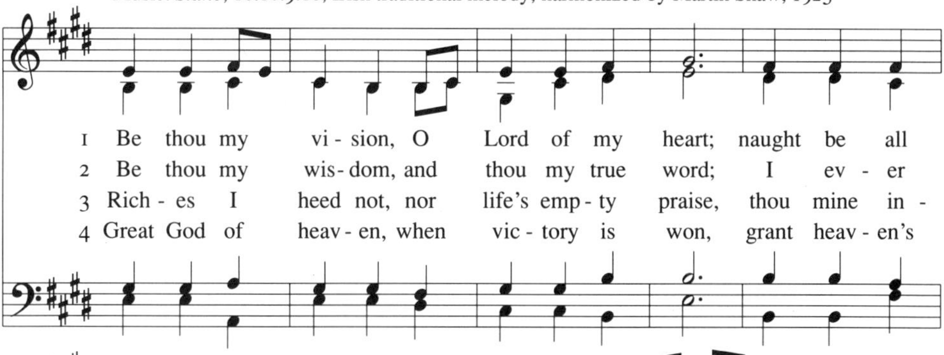

1 Be thou my vi - sion, O Lord of my heart; naught be all
2 Be thou my wis- dom, and thou my true word; I ev - er
3 Rich - es I heed not, nor life's emp - ty praise, thou mine in -
4 Great God of heav - en, when vic - tory is won, grant heav - en's

else to me save that thou art — thou my best thought, by
with thee, and thou with me, Lord. Thou, and thou on - ly,
her - i - tance, now and al - ways; thou my soul's shel - ter,
joys to me, O bright heaven's Sun! Heart of my heart, what -

day or by night, wak - ing or sleep - ing, thy pres- ence my light.
first in my heart; great God of heav - en, my trea- sure thou art.
thou my high tower, raise thou me heaven- ward, O Power of my power.
ev - er be - fall, still be my vi - sion, O Ru - ler of all.

511 Lord, as you have lived for others

Somerset Lowry, 1893, and others

Music: *In Babilone*, 8787D; Dutch traditional melody; harmony by Julius Roentgen, 1906

These words can also be sung to *Blaenwern*, no. 522.

1 Lord, as you have lived for oth - ers, so may we for oth - ers live.
2 Come, O Christ, and reign a - mong us, King of love and Prince of Peace;
3 Son of God, e - ter - nal Sa - vior, source of life and truth and grace,
Free - ly have your gifts been grant - ed; free - ly may your ser - vants give.
hush the storm of strife and pas - sion, bid its cru - el dis - cords cease.
Word made flesh, whose birth a - mong us hal - lows all our hu - man race:
Yours the gold and yours the sil - ver, yours the wealth of land and sea;
By your pa - tient years of toil - ing, by your si - lent hours of pain,
by your pray - ing, by your will - ing that your peo - ple should be one,
as the stew - ards of your boun - ty may we act re - spon - si - bly.
quench our fe - vered thirst of plea - sure, stem our sel - fish greed of gain.
grant, O grant our hope's fru - i - tion: here on earth your will be done.

512 Our Parent, by whose name

F. Bland Tucker, 1939, and others

Music: *Rhosymedre*, 6666888; melody by John David Edwards, c. 1840

1 Our Par - ent, by whose name all par - ent - hood is known,
2 O Je - sus, who, a child with - in an earth - ly home,
3 Blest Spir - it, who can bind our hearts in u - ni - ty,
you in your love pro - claim each fam - i - ly your own:
with heart still un - de - filed did to a - dult - hood come:
and teach us so to find the love from self set free:
di - rect all par - ents, guard - ing well, with con - stant love as
all chil - dren bless in ev - ery place, that they may each be -
in all our hearts such love in - crease that ev - ery home, by
sen - ti - nel, the homes in which your peo - ple dwell.
hold your face, and know - ing you may grow in grace.
this re - lease, may be the dwell - ing place of peace.

513 Lord, you give the great commission

Jeffery Rowthorn, 1978

Music: *Abbot's Leigh*, 8787D; Cyril V. Taylor, 1941

These words can also be sung to *Hyfrydol*, no. 560.

1 Lord, you give the great com - mis - sion: "Heal the sick and
2 Lord, you call us to your ser - vice: "In my name bap -
3 Lord, you make the com - mon ho - ly: "This my bod - y,
4 Lord, you show us love's true mea - sure: "Fa - ther, what they
preach the word." Lest the Church ne - glect its mis - sion
tize and teach." That the world may trust your prom - ise,
this my blood." Let us all, for earth's true glo - ry,
do, for - give." Yet we hoard as pri - vate trea - sure
and the Gos - pel go un - heard, help us wit - ness
life a - bun - dant meant for each, give us all new
dai - ly lift life heav - en - ward, ask - ing that the
all that you so free - ly give. May your care and
to your pur - pose with re - newed in - teg - ri - ty;
fer - vor, draw us clos - er in com - mun - i - ty;
world a - round us share your chil - dren's lib - er - ty:
mer - cy lead us to a just so - ci - e - ty;

Refrain

with the Spir-it's gifts em-power us for the work of min - is - try.

5 Lord, you bless with words assuring:
"I am with you to the end."
Faith and hope and love restoring,
may we serve as you intend,
and, amid the cares that claim us,
hold in mind eternity;

Refrain

514 O thou who camest from above

Charles Wesley, 1762

Music: *Hereford*, 8888; Samuel Sebastian Wesley, 1872

1 O thou who cam-est from a-bove, the fire ce-les-tial to im-part, kin-dle a flame of sa-cred love on the mean al-tar of my heart.

2 There let it for thy glo-ry burn with in-ex-tin-guish-a-ble blaze, and trem-bling to its source re-turn in hum-ble prayer and fer-vent praise.

3 Je-sus, con-firm my heart's de-sire to work, and speak, and think for thee; still let me guard the ho-ly fire, and still stir up thy gift in me.

4 Read-y for all thy per-fect will, my acts of faith and love re-peat, till death thy end-less mer-cies seal, and make the sac-ri-fice com-plete.

515 Jesu, Jesu

Tom Colvin, 1969

Music: *Chereponi*, 779 with refrain; Ghanaian folksong, adapted by Tom Colvin, 1969

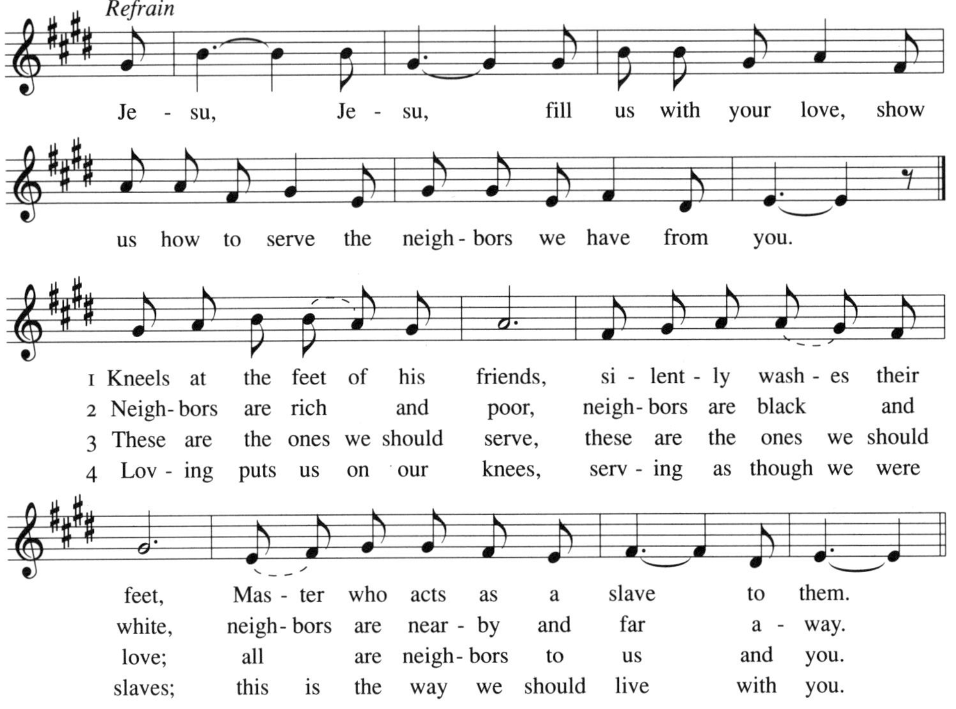
Refrain
Je - su, Je - su, fill us with your love, show
us how to serve the neigh-bors we have from you.
1 Kneels at the feet of his friends, si - lent - ly wash - es their
2 Neigh-bors are rich and poor, neigh-bors are black and
3 These are the ones we should serve, these are the ones we should
4 Lov - ing puts us on our knees, serv - ing as though we were
feet, Mas - ter who acts as a slave to them.
white, neigh-bors are near - by and far a - way.
love; all are neigh-bors to us and you.
slaves; this is the way we should live with you.

516 It is God who holds the nations

"A Hymn for the Nation," Fred Pratt Green, 1976

Music: *Vision*, 15.15.15.7; H. Walford Davies, 1915; arranged by John Wilson, 1977

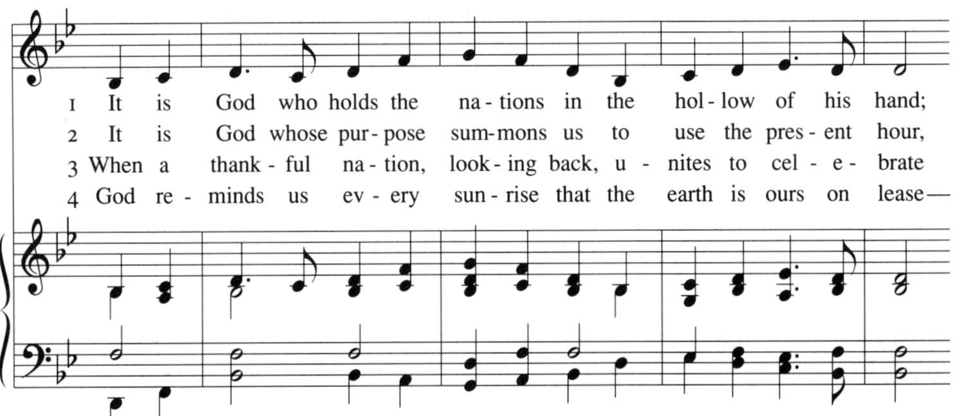
1 It is God who holds the na - tions in the hol - low of his hand;
2 It is God whose pur - pose sum-mons us to use the pres - ent hour,
3 When a thank - ful na - tion, look - ing back, u - nites to cel - e - brate
4 God re - minds us ev - ery sun - rise that the earth is ours on lease—

it is God whose light is shin-ing in the dark-ness of the land;
who re-calls us to our sens-es when a na-tion's life turns sour;
those who win our ad-mir-a-tion by their ser-vice to the state,
for the sake of life to-mor-row may our love for it in-crease;
it is God who builds his Cit-y on the rock and not on sand:
in the dis-ci-pline of free-dom we shall know God's sav-ing power:
when self-giv-ing is a mea-sure of the great-ness of the great,
may all rac-es live to-geth-er, share its rich-es, be at peace:
Congregation
(God be praised!....)
may the liv-ing God be praised!
may the liv-ing God be praised!
may the liv-ing God be praised!
may the liv-ing God be praised!
Choir ad lib
may the liv-ing God be praised! God be praised!
may the liv-ing God be praised! God be praised!
may the liv-ing God be praised! God be praised!
may the liv-ing God be praised! God be praised!

517 To those who knotted nets of twine

Thomas H. Troeger, 1983

Music: *Storm-swept Way*, 8686; Carol Doran, 1983

1 To those who knot-ted nets of twine to comb a fish-filled sea, Christ called a-loud: "Put down that line and come and fol-low me!"
2 Ac-cus-tomed to the tug of rope en-snared in rocks and weeds, they felt from Christ a pull of hope a-midst their tan-gled needs.
3 They left their boats, their sails and oars, but e-ven more than these, they left the lake's en-cir-cling shores and its fa-mil-iar breeze.
4 They braved the ty-rant's bru-tal blast and hate's un-bound-ed rage, while res-cue lines of faith they cast to save their sink-ing age.
1–4

5
your storm-swept way.

5 O Christ, who called beside the sea,
still call to us today.
Like those who fished in Galilee,
we'll risk your storm-swept way.

518 God, you have given us power

"The New Peril," George W. Briggs, 1954

Music: *Culross*, 8686; melody in *Scottish Psalter*, 1634

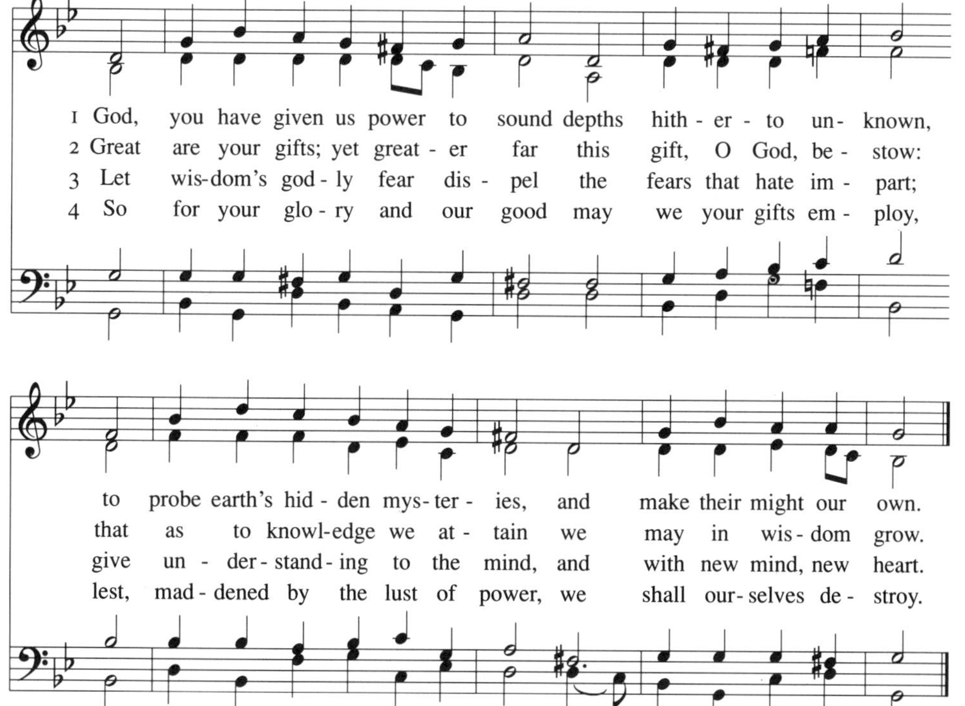
1 God, you have given us power to sound depths hith - er - to un- known,
2 Great are your gifts; yet great - er far this gift, O God, be - stow:
3 Let wis-dom's god - ly fear dis - pel the fears that hate im - part;
4 So for your glo - ry and our good may we your gifts em - ploy,
to probe earth's hid - den mys- ter - ies, and make their might our own.
that as to knowl-edge we at - tain we may in wis - dom grow.
give un - der - stand - ing to the mind, and with new mind, new heart.
lest, mad - dened by the lust of power, we shall our- selves de - stroy.

519 Where science serves and art inspires

Jane Manton Marshall, 1976

Music: *Venerable*, 14.14; Vincent Persichetti, 1956

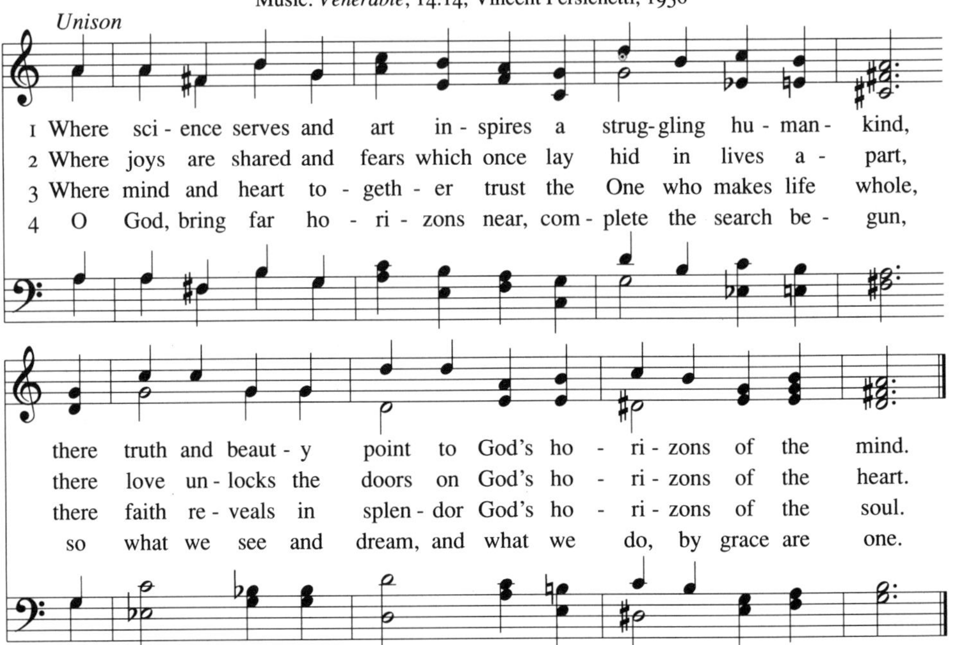
Unison
1 Where sci - ence serves and art in - spires a strug - gling hu - man - kind,
2 Where joys are shared and fears which once lay hid in lives a - part,
3 Where mind and heart to - geth - er trust the One who makes life whole,
4 O God, bring far ho - ri - zons near, com - plete the search be - gun,
there truth and beaut - y point to God's ho - ri - zons of the mind.
there love un - locks the doors on God's ho - ri - zons of the heart.
there faith re - veals in splen - dor God's ho - ri - zons of the soul.
so what we see and dream, and what we do, by grace are one.

520 Tú has venido a la orilla

Lord, you have come to the lakeshore

Cesareo Gabaraín; translated by Gertrude C. Suppe, George Lockwood, and Raquel Gutiérrez-Achon, 1987

Music: *Pescador de hombres*, 8.10.9 with refrain; Cesareo Gabaraín; harmony by Skinner Chavez-Melo, 1987

Unison
1 *Tú has ve - ni - do a la o - ri - lla, no has bus -*
2 *Tú sa - bes bien lo que ten - go; en mi*
1 Lord, you have come to the lake - shore, look - ing
2 You know so well my pos - ses - sions; my boat
ca - do ni a sa - bios ni a ri - cos, tan só - lo
bar - ca no hay o - ro ni es - pa - das, tan só - lo
nei - ther for wealth - y nor wise ones; you on - ly
car - ries no gold and no weap - ons; you will

quie - res que yo te si - ga.
re - des y mi tra - ba - jo.
asked me to fol - low hum - bly.
find there my nets and la - bor.
Refrain
Se - ñor, me has mi - ra - do a los o - jos
O Lord, with your eyes you have searched me,
y son - rien - do has di - cho mi nom - bre;
and while smil - ing have spok-en my name;
en la a - re - na he de - ja - do mi bar - ca;
now my boat's left on the shore-line be - hind me;
jun - to a ti bus - ca - ré o - tro mar.
by your side I will seek oth - er seas.

3 *Tú necesitas mis manos,*
mi cansancio que a otros descanse,
amor que quiera seguir amando.

Refrain

3 You need my hands, full of caring,
through my labors to give others rest,
and constant love that keeps on loving.

Refrain

521 Christ is the Way

W. H. Auden, 1945, and others

Music: *New Dance*, irregular meter; Richard Wetzel, 1972

1 Christ is the Way. Fol - low him through the
2 Christ is the Truth. Seek him in the
3 Christ is the Life. Love him in the
Land of Un - like - ness; you will see
King - dom of An - xi - e - ty: you will come to a great
World of the Flesh: and at your
rare beasts and have u - nique ad - ven - tures.
ci - ty that has ex - pec - ted your re - turn for years.
mar - riage all its oc - ca - sions shall dance for joy.

522 Lord of light

Howell Elvet Lewis, 1916

Music: *Blaenwern*, 8787D; William P. Rowlands, c. 1904–1905

These words can also be sung to *In Babilone*, no. 511.

1 Lord of light, your name out-shin-ing all the stars and suns of space,
use our tal-ents in your king-dom, make us ser-vants of your grace;
use us to ful-fill your pur-pose in the gift of Christ your Son:
2 Grant that knowl-edge, still in-creas-ing, at your feet may low-ly kneel;
with your grace our tri-umphs hal-low, with your char-i-ty our zeal;
lift the na-tions from the shad-ows to the glad-ness of the sun:
3 By the prayers of faith-ful watch-ers, nev-er si-lent day or night;
by the cross of Je-sus, bring-ing peace to all and heal-ing light;
by the love that pass-es knowl-edge, mak-ing all your chil-dren one:
Refrain
Fa-ther, as in high-est heav-en, so on earth your will be done.

523 Holy Spirit, truth divine

Samuel Longfellow, 1864

Music: *Song 13*, 7777; adapted from by Orlando Gibbons, 1623

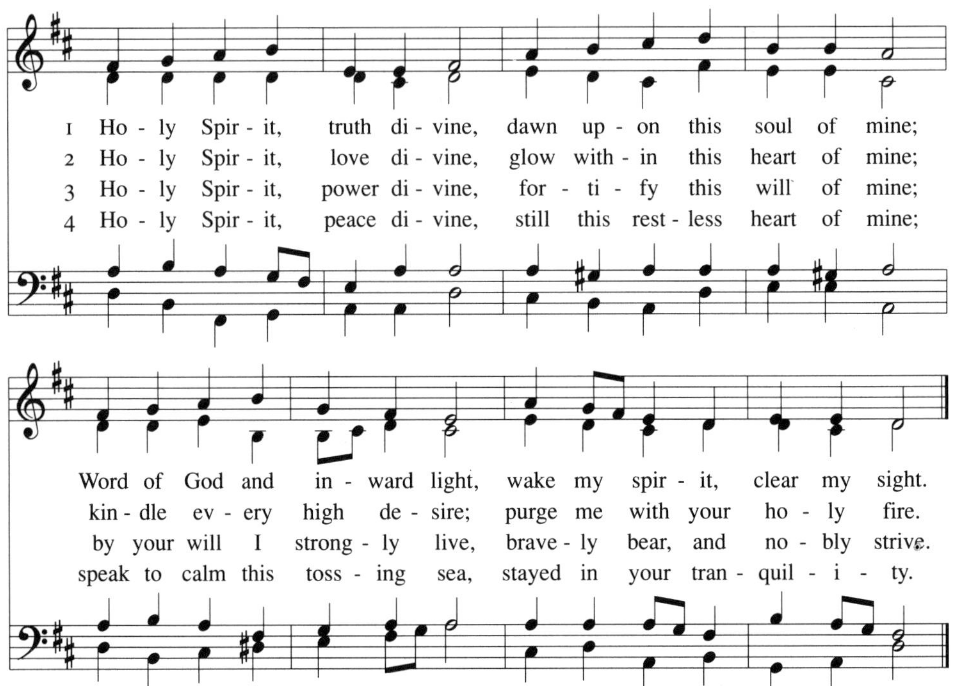
1 Ho - ly Spir - it, truth di - vine, dawn up - on this soul of mine;
2 Ho - ly Spir - it, love di - vine, glow with - in this heart of mine;
3 Ho - ly Spir - it, power di - vine, for - ti - fy this will of mine;
4 Ho - ly Spir - it, peace di - vine, still this rest - less heart of mine;
Word of God and in - ward light, wake my spir - it, clear my sight.
kin - dle ev - ery high de - sire; purge me with your ho - ly fire.
by your will I strong - ly live, brave - ly bear, and no - bly strive.
speak to calm this toss - ing sea, stayed in your tran - quil - i - ty.

5 Holy Spirit, right divine,
sovereign in my conscience reign;
be my Lord, and I shall be
firmly bound, forever free.

524 Christ the worker

Tom Colvin, 1969

Music: *Christ the Worker*, 4449; traditional work song from Southern Africa, adapted by Tom Colvin, 1969

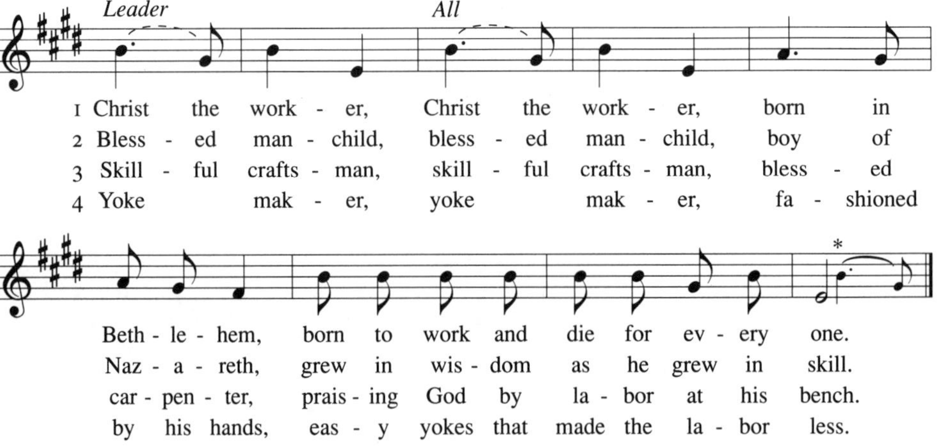
Leader
All
1 Christ the work - er, Christ the work - er, born in
2 Bless - ed man - child, bless - ed man - child, boy of
3 Skill - ful crafts - man, skill - ful crafts - man, bless - ed
4 Yoke mak - er, yoke mak - er, fa - shioned
*
Beth - le - hem, born to work and die for ev - ery one.
Naz - a - reth, grew in wis - dom as he grew in skill.
car - pen - ter, prais - ing God by la - bor at his bench.
by his hands, eas - y yokes that made the la - bor less.

**The leader begins successive stanzas here.*

5 *All who labor,*
all who labor,
listen to his call,
he will make that heavy burden light.

6 *Heavy laden,*
heavy laden,
gladly come to him,
he will ease your load and give you rest.

7 *Christ the worker,*
Christ the worker,
Love alive for us,
teach us how to do all work for God.

525 We pattern our Heaven

John Updike, b. 1932

Music: *Little Venice*, 5555D; Gerald H. Knight (1908–1979)

1 We pat-tern our Heaven on bright but-ter-flies, but it must be that even in
2 God bless-es him; he gives praise with his toil, lends com-fort to me, and
earth Heav-en lies. The worm we up-root in turn-ing a spade re-
aër-ates the soil. Im-mersed in the facts, one must wor-ship there; claus-tro-
turns, care-ful brute, to the peace he has made.
pho-bia at-tacks us e-ven in air.

526 Weary of all trumpeting

Martin H. Franzmann, 1971; written for this melody

Music: *Distler*, 7676D; melody by Hugo Distler, 1938, celebrating the Anschluss of Austria with Germany; harmony by Richard Proulx, 1975

1 Wea - ry of all trum - pet - ing, wea - ry of all kill - ing,
2 Cap - tain Christ, O low - ly Lord, Ser - vant King, your dy - ing
3 To the tri - umph of your cross sum - mon all the liv - ing;
wea - ry of all songs that sing prom - ise, non - ful - fil - ling,
bade us sheathe the fool - ish sword, bade us cease de - ny - ing.
sum - mon us to live by loss, gain - ing all by giv - ing,
we would raise, O Christ, one song; we would join in sing - ing
Trum - pet with your spir - it's breath through each height and hol - low;
suf - fering all, that we may see tri - umph in sur - ren - der;
that great mu - sic pure and strong, where - with heaven is ring - ing.
in - to your self - giv - ing death, call us all to fol - low.
leav - ing all, that we may be part - ners in your splen - dor.

527 God the Omnipotent

Stanzas 1 and 2: Henry Fothergill Chorley, 1842; stanzas 3 and 4: John Ellerton, 1870

Music: *Russian Anthem*, 11.10.11.9; Alexis Lvov, 1833, for the national hymn of Russia

1 God the Om - ni - po - tent! Thou who or - dain - est
2 God the All - mer - ci - ful! earth has for - sak - en
3 God the All - righ - teous One! earth has de - fied thee,
4 God the All - prov - i - dent! earth by thy chas - tening
thun - der thy clar - ion and light - ning thy sword,
thy ways all ho - ly, and slight - ed thy word;
yet to e - ter - ni - ty stand - eth thy word;
yet shall to free - dom and truth be re - stored;
show forth thy pi - ty on high where thou reign - est:
bid not thy wrath in its ter - rors a - wak - en:
false - hood and wrong shall not tar - ry be - side thee:
through the thick dark - ness thy king - dom is hasten - ing:
give to us peace in our time, O Lord.
give to us peace in our time, O Lord.
give to us peace in our time, O Lord.
thou wilt give peace in thy time, O Lord.

528 In Bethlehem a new-born boy

Rosamond E. Herklots, c. 1980

Music: *In Bethlehem*, 8888; Wilbur Held, 1984

1 In Beth-le-hem a new-born boy was hailed with songs of praise and joy. Then warn-ing came of dan-ger near: King Her-od's troops would soon ap-pear.
2 The sol-diers sought the child in vain: not yet was he to share our pain. But down the a-ges rings the cry of those who saw their chil-dren die.
3 Still rage the fires of hate to-day, and in-no-cents the price must pay, while ach-ing hearts in ev-ery land cry out, "We can-not un-der-stand!"
4 Lord Je-sus, through our night of loss shines out the won-der of your cross, the love that can-not cease to bear our hu-man an-guish ev-ery-where.
5 (May)
1–4
5

5 May that great love our lives control
and conquer hate in every soul,
till, pledged to build and not destroy,
we share your pain and find your joy.

529 To us all, to every nation

Adapted from "The Present Crisis," James Russell Lowell, 1844

Music: *Ebenezer*, 8787D; Thomas J. Williams, 1890

1 To us all, to ev - ery na - tion comes the mo - ment to de - cide,
2 Then to side with truth is no - ble, when we share its wretch - ed crust,
3 By the light of burn - ing mar - tyrs Je - sus' bleed - ing feet we track,
4 Though the cause of e - vil pros - per, yet 'tis truth a - lone is strong;
in the strife of truth with false - hood, for the good or ev - il side;
ere the cause bring fame and pro - fit and 'tis pros-perous to be just;
toil - ing up new Cal - varies ev - er with the cross that turns not back;
though its por - tion be the scaf - fold, and up - on the throne be wrong,
some great cause, some mod - ern pro - phet, offer - ing each the bloom or blight,
then it is the brave who choos-es, while the cow - ard stands a - side
new oc - ca - sions teach new du - ties, time makes an - cient good un - couth;
yet that scaf - fold sways the fu - ture, and, be - hind the dim un - known,
and the choice goes by for ev - er 'twixt that dark - ness and that light.
till the mul - ti - tude make vir - tue of the faith they had de - nied.
they must up - ward still, and on - ward, who would keep a - breast of truth.
stand - eth God with - in the shad - ow, keep - ing watch a - bove God's own.

530 Judge eternal, throned in splendor

Henry Scott Holland, 1902

Music: *Rhuddlan*, 878787; Welsh traditional melody in Edward Jones's *Musical Relicks of the Welsh Bards*, 1800; harmony from *The English Hymnal*, 1906

1 Judge e - ter - nal, throned in splen- dor, Lord of lords and King of kings,
2 Still the wea - ry folk are pin - ing for the hour that brings re - lease,
3 Crown, O God, your own en- deav - or; cleave our dark- ness with your sword;

with your liv - ing fire of judg- ment purge this land of bit - ter things:
and the ci - ty's crowd - ed clam - or cries a - loud for sin to cease,
feed the faint and hun - gry peo - ple with the rich- ness of your word;

so - lace all its wide do - min - ion with the heal- ing of your wings.
and the home- steads and the wood- lands plead in si- lence for your peace.
cleanse the bo - dy of this na - tion through the glo - ry of the Lord.

531 Father eternal, Ruler of creation

Laurence Housman, 1919

Music: *Langham*, 11.10.11.10 with refrain; Geoffrey Shaw, 1921

1 Fa - ther e - ter - nal, Rul - er of cre - a - tion,
2 Rac - es and peo - ples, lo, we stand di - vid - ed,
3 En - vious of heart, blind - eyed, with tongues con- found - ed,
4 Lust of pos - ses - sion ends in des - o - la - tions;

Spir - it of life, which moved ere form was made,
and, shar - ing not our griefs, no joy can share;
na - tion by na - tion still goes un - for - given,
there is no meek - ness in the powers of earth;
through the thick dark - ness cover - ing ev - ery na - tion,
by wars and tu - mults love is mocked, de - rid - ed;
in wrath and fear, by jeal - ous - ies sur - round - ed,
led by no star, the rul - ers of the na - tions
light for our blind - ness, O be now our aid:
Love's con - quering cross no na - tion wills to bear:
build - ing proud towers which shall not reach to heaven:
still fail to bring us to the bliss - ful birth:
Refrain
your king - dom come, O Lord, your will be done.

5 How shall we love you, holy hidden Being,
if we love not the world which you have made?
O give us deeper love for better seeing
your Word made flesh, and in a manger laid. *Refrain*

532 Where cross the crowded ways of life

Frank Mason North, 1903

Music: *Gardiner*, 8888; melody "from Beethoven" in William Gardiner's *Sacred Melodies*, 1815

1 Where cross the crowd - ed ways of life, where sound the
2 In haunts of wretch - ed - ness and need, on shad - owed
3 From ten - der child - hood's help - less - ness, from hu - man
4 The cup of wa - ter given for you still holds the
cries of race and clan, a - bove the noise of
thresh - olds dark with fears, from paths where hide the
grief and bur - dened toil, from fam - ished souls, from
fresh - ness of your grace; yet long these mul - ti -
self - ish strife, we hear your voice, O Son of Man.
lures of greed, we catch the vi - sion of your tears.
sor - row's stress, your heart has nev - er known re - coil.
tudes to view the sweet com - pas - sion of your face.

5 O Savior, from the mountainside
make haste to heal these hearts of pain;
among these restless throngs abide,
O tread the city's streets again;

6 till all the world shall learn your love,
and follow where your feet have trod;
till glorious from your heaven above
shall come the city of our God.

533 O God of every nation

William Watkins Reid, Jr., 1958

Music: *Llangloffan*, 7676D; melody in Daniel Evans's *Hymnau a Thonau*, 1865; harmony by David Evans, 1927

1 O God of ev - ery na - tion, of ev - ery race and land,
2 From search for wealth and pow - er, from scorn of truth and right,
3 Keep bright in us the vi - sion of days when war shall cease,
re - deem the whole cre - a - tion with your al - might - y hand;
from trust in bombs that show - er de - struc - tion through the night,
when hat - red and di - vi - sion give way to love and peace,
where hate and fear di - vide us and bit - ter threats are hurled,
from pride of race and na - tion and blind - ness to your way,
till dawns the morn - ing glo - rious when truth and jus - tice reign
in love and mer - cy guide us and heal our strife - torn world.
de - liv - er ev - ery na - tion, e - ter - nal God, we pray!
and Christ shall rule vic - to - rious o'er all the world's do - main.

534 What does the Lord require

Albert F. Bayly, 1950

Music: *Sharpthorne*, 6666336; Erik Routley, 1968

1 What does the Lord re - quire for praise and of - fer - ing?
2 Rul - ers of earth, give ear! Should you not jus - tice show?
3 All who gain wealth by trade, for whom the work - er toils,
4 Still down the a - ges ring the pro - phet's stern com - mands.
What sac - ri - fice, de - sire, or tri - bute bid you
Will God your plead - ing hear, while crime and cruel - ty
think not to win God's aid, if greed your com - merce
Of mer - chant, work - er, king God makes these high de -
bring? Do just - ly; love mer - cy; walk
grow? Do just - ly; love mer - cy; walk
soils. Do just - ly; love mer - cy; walk
mands. Do just - ly; love mer - cy; walk

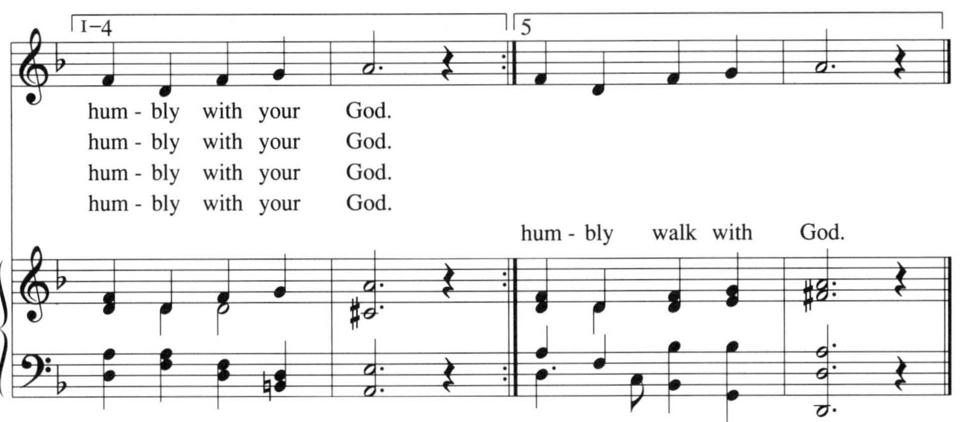
1–4
5
hum - bly with your God.
hum - bly with your God.
hum - bly with your God.
hum - bly with your God.
hum - bly walk with God.

535 For the healing of the nations

"A hymn of human rights," Fred Kaan, 1965

Music: *Fortunatus New*, 878787; Carl Schalk, 1966

Unison

1 For the healing of the nations,
Lord, we pray with one accord;
for a just and equal sharing
of the gifts which you afford.
To a life of love in action
help us rise and pledge our word.

2 Lead us forward into freedom,
from despair your world release;
that, redeemed from war and hatred,
all may come and go in peace.
Show us how through care and goodness
fear will die and hope increase.

3 All that kills abundant living,
let it from the earth be banned;
pride of status, race or schooling,
dogmas that obscure your plan.
In our common quest for justice
may we hallow life's brief span.

4 You, Creator-God, have written
your great name on humankind;
for our growing in your likeness
bring the life of Christ to mind;
that by our response and service
earth its destiny may find.

536

O God of earth and altar

G. K. Chesterton, c. 1905

Music: *King's Lynn*, 7676D; English traditional melody, arranged and harmonized by Ralph Vaughan Williams, 1906

Unison
1 O God of earth and al - tar, bow down and hear our cry,
2 From all that ter - ror teach - es, from lies of tongue and pen,
3 Tie in a liv - ing teth - er the prince and priest and thrall,
our earth - ly rul - ers fal - ter, our peo - ple drift and die;
from all the eas - y speech - es that com - fort cru - el men,
bind all our lives to - geth - er, smite us and save us all;
the walls of gold en - tomb us, the swords of scorn di - vide,
from sale and pro - fan - a - tion of hon - or, and the sword,
in ire and ex - ul - ta - tion a - flame with faith, and free,
take not thy thun - der from us, but take a - way our pride.
from sleep and from dam - na - tion, de - liv - er us, good Lord!
lift up a liv - ing na - tion, a sin - gle sword to thee.

537 O beautiful for spacious skies

Katherine Lee Bates, 1893, 1904

Music: *Materna*, 8686D; Samuel A. Ward, 1882 or 1885

1 O beau - ti - ful for spa - cious skies, for am - ber waves of grain;
2 O beau - ti - ful for he - roes proved in lib - er - at - ing strife,
3 O beau - ti - ful for pa - triot dream that sees be - yond the years
for pur - ple moun - tain ma - jes - ties a - bove the fruit - ed plain!
who more than self their coun - try loved, and mer - cy more than life!
thine al - a - bast - er ci - ties gleam, un - dimmed by hu - man tears!
A - mer - i - ca! A - mer - i - ca! God shed his grace on thee,
A - mer - i - ca! A - mer - i - ca! may God thy gold re - fine,
A - mer - i - ca! A - mer - i - ca! God mend thine ev - ery flaw,
and crown thy good with bro - ther - hood from sea to shin - ing sea.
till all suc - cess be no - ble - ness, and ev - ery gain di - vine.
con - firm thy soul in self - con - trol, thy lib - er - ty in law.

538 They cast their nets in Galilee

William Alexander Percy, 1924

Music: *Georgetown*, 8686; David McK. Williams, 1941

1 They cast their nets in Gal - i - lee just off the hills of brown; such hap - py, sim - ple fish - er - folk, be - fore the Lord came down.
2 Con - tent - ed, peace - ful fish - er - men, be - fore they ev - er knew the peace of God that filled their hearts brim - ful, and broke them too.
3 Young John, who trimmed the flap - ping sail, home - less, in Pat - mos died. Pe - ter, who hauled the teem - ing net, head - down was cru - ci - fied.
4 The peace of God, it is no peace, but strife closed in the sod. Yet let us pray for but one thing — the mar - velous peace of God.

539 Lord, save your world

Albert F. Bayly, 1947

Music: *Kedron*, 8888; melody in Amos Pilsbury's *United States Sacred Harmony*, 1799

1 Lord, save your world; in bit - ter need to
2 Lord, save your world; our souls are bound in
3 Lord, save your world; we strive in vain to
4 Lord, save your world; yet you have sent the
you your chil - dren raise their plea; we wait your lib - er -
i - ron chains of fear and pride; high walls of ig - nor -
save our - selves with - out your aid; what skill and sci - ence
Sa - vior whom we sore - ly need; for us his tears and
at - ing deed to sig - nal hope and set us free.
ance a - bound, and fac - es from each oth - er hide.
slow - ly gain is soon to e - vil ends be - trayed.
blood were spent that from our bonds we might be freed.

5 Then save us now by Jesus' power,
and use the lives your love sets free
to bring at last the glorious hour
when all shall find your liberty.

540 All who love and serve your city

Erik Routley, 1966, reflecting upon the riots in the Watts district of Los Angeles

Music: *Charlestown*, 8787; melody in Stephen Jenks's *American Compiler of Sacred Harmony, No. 1*, 1803; harmony by Carlton R. Young, 1964

Unison

1 All who love and serve your ci - ty, all who
2 in your day of loss and sor - row, in your
3 In your day of wealth and plen - ty, wast - ed
4 For all days are days of judg-ment, and the

bear its dai - ly stress, all who cry for peace and
day of help - less strife, hon - or, peace, and love re -
work and wast - ed play, call to mind the word of
Lord is wait - ing still, draw - ing near to all who

jus - tice, all who curse and all who bless,
treat - ing, seek the Lord, who is your life.
Je - sus, "I must work while it is day."
spurn him, offer - ing peace from Cal - vary's hill.

5 Risen Lord! shall yet the city
be the city of despair?
Come today, our Judge, our Glory;
be its name, "The Lord is there!"

541 Dona nobis pacem

Traditional canon

1
Do - na no - bis pa - cem, pa-cem. Do - na no - bis

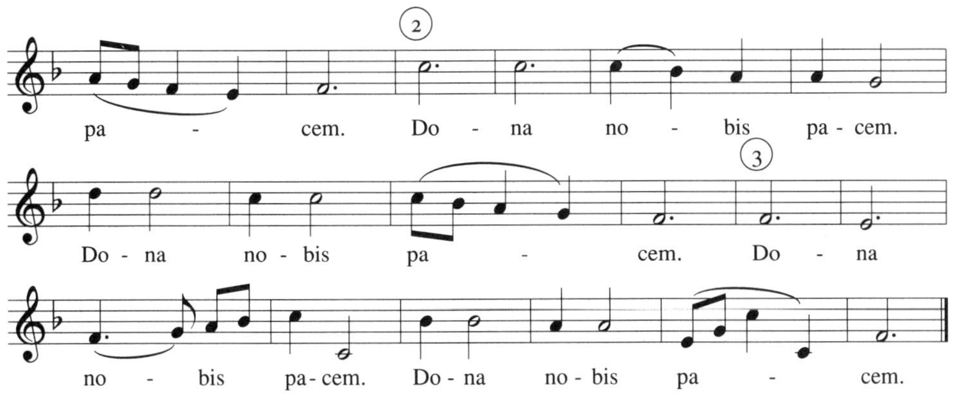
2
pa - cem. Do - na no - bis pa - cem.
3
Do - na no - bis pa - cem. Do - na
no - bis pa - cem. Do - na no - bis pa - cem.

542 Christ is alive

Brian Wren, 1968, reflecting upon the assassination of Martin Luther King, Jr.; revised in 1988

Music: *Truro*, 8888; melody in Thomas Williams's *Psalmodia Evangelica*, vol. 2, 1789

1 Christ is a - live! Let Chris - tians sing. The cross stands
2 Christ is a - live! No long - er bound to dis - tant
3 Not throned a - far, re - mote - ly high, un - touched, un -
4 In ev - ery in - sult, rift, and war where col - or,

emp - ty to the sky. Let streets and homes with
years in Pal - es - tine, but sav - ing, heal - ing,
moved by hu - man pains, but dai - ly, in the
scorn or wealth di - vide, Christ suf - fers still, yet

prais - es ring. Love, drowned in death, shall nev - er die!
here and now and touch - ing ev - ery place and time.
midst of life, our Sa - vior in the God - head reigns.
loves the more, and lives where e - ven hope has died.

5 Christ is alive, and comes to bring
good news to this and every age,
till earth and sky and ocean ring
with joy, with justice, love and praise.

543 This is my song

Lloyd Stone, 1934

Music: *Finlandia*, 11.10.11.10.11.10; arranged from Jean Sibelius's symphonic poem *Finlandia*, 1899, for *The Hymnal*, 1933

1 This is my song, O God of all the na-tions, a song of peace for
2 My coun-try's skies are blu-er than the o-cean, and sun-light beams on
lands a-far and mine. This is my home, the coun-try where my heart is;
clo-ver-leaf and pine; but oth-er lands have sun-light too, and clo-ver,
here are my hopes, my dreams, my ho-ly shrine; but oth-er hearts in
and skies are ev-ery-where as blue as mine. O hear my song, O
oth-er lands are beat-ing with hopes and dreams as true and high as mine.
God of all the na-tions, a song of peace for their land and for mine.

544 God of grace and God of glory

Harry Emerson Fosdick, 1930, for the opening of Riverside Church in New York City

Music: *Cwm Rhondda*, 8787877; melody by John Hughes, 1905

1 God of grace and God of glo - ry, on your peo - ple pour your power;
2 Lo! the hosts of e - vil round us scorn your Christ, as - sail his ways!
3 Cure your chil - dren's war - ring mad- ness, bend our pride to your con - trol;
4 Set our feet on loft - y plac - es; gird our lives that we may be
crown your an - cient church - 's sto - ry; bring its bud to glo- rious flower.
From the fears that long have bound us free our hearts to faith and praise.
shame our wan - ton, self - ish glad- ness, rich in things and poor in soul.
strength-ened with all Christ - like grac - es in the quest for lib - er - ty.
Grant us wis - dom, grant us cour - age, for the fac - ing of this
Grant us wis - dom, grant us cour - age, for the liv - ing of these
Grant us wis - dom, grant us cour - age, lest we miss your king-dom's
Grant us wis - dom, grant us cour - age, as we seek to set all
hour, for the fac - ing of this hour.
days, for the liv - ing of these days.
goal, lest we miss your king - dom's goal.
free, as we seek to set all free.

5 Save us from weak resignation
to the evils we deplore;
let the search for your salvation
be our glory evermore.
Grant us wisdom, grant us courage,
serving you whom we adore,
serving you whom we adore.

545 When Jesus came preaching the Kingdom of God

Fred Pratt Green, 1969

Music: *Samanthra*, 11.8.11.8.D; melody in *Southern Harmony*, 1835; harmony by Austin C. Lovelace, 1986

Unison
1 When Je - sus came preach - ing the King - dom of God, with the
2 Since Je - sus came preach - ing the King - dom of God, what a
3 Still Je - sus comes preach - ing the King - dom of God in a
love that has power to per- suade, the sick were made whole, both in
change in our lives he has made! How ma - ny have shared in the
world that is sick and a - fraid; his gos - pel has spread like the
bod - y and soul, and e - ven the de - mons o - beyed.
joy of their Lord, in self - giv - ing have loved and o - beyed!
leav - en in bread by the love that has power to per- suade.
But he need - ed a few he could trust to be true, to
But let none of us doubt what re - li - gion's a - bout, or by
So let none of us swerve from our mis - sion to serve that has
share in his work from the start: when Je - sus came preach - ing the
what it is shamed and be- trayed: do just - ly, love mer - cy, walk
made us his Church from the start; may Je - sus, the light of the

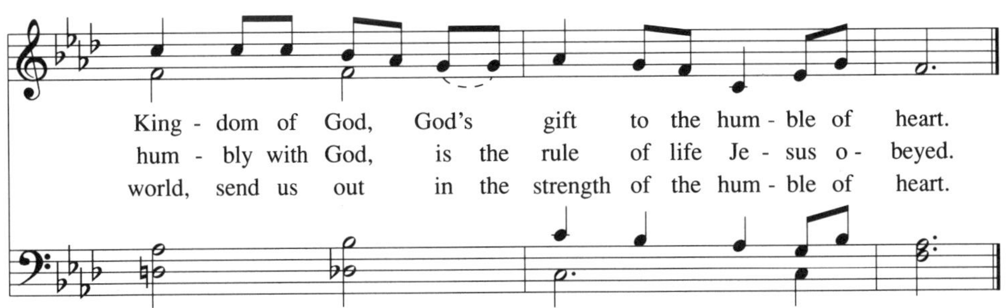
King - dom of God, God's gift to the hum - ble of heart.
hum - bly with God, is the rule of life Je - sus o - beyed.
world, send us out in the strength of the hum - ble of heart.

546 Lift every voice and sing

James Weldon Johnson, 1921; this is the official song of the NAACP

Music: *Lift Every Voice*, irregular meter; J. Rosamond Johnson, 1921

1 Lift ev - ery voice and sing till earth and hea - ven ring,
2 Ston - y the road we trod, bit - ter the chasten - ing rod,
3 God of our wea - ry years, God of our sil - ent tears,

ring with the har - mon - ies of lib - er - ty.
felt in the days when hope un - born had died;
thou who hast brought us thus far on the way;

Let our re - joic - ing rise high as the listen - ing skies;
yet, with a stead - y beat, have not our wear - y feet
thou who hast by thy might led us in - to the light;
let it re - sound loud as the roll - ing sea.
come to the place for which our par - ents sighed?
keep us for ev - er in the path, we pray.
Sing a song full of the faith that the dark past has taught us;
We have come o - ver a way that with tears has been wa - tered;
Lest our feet stray from the pla - ces, our God, where we met thee;
(♭)
3

sing a song full of the hope that the pres-ent has brought us;
we have come, tread-ing our path through the blood of the slaugh - tered,
lest, our hearts drunk with the wine of the world, we for-get thee;
fac-ing the ris - ing sun of our new day be - gun,
out from the gloom - y past, till now we stand at last
sha-dowed be-neath thy hand may we for ev - er stand,
let us march on, till vic - to - ry is won.
where the white gleam of our bright star is cast.
true to our God, true to our na - tive land.

547 Hope of the world

Georgia Harkness, 1952, for the Second Assembly of the World Council of Churches, Evanston, Illinois

Music: *Donne secours, Seigneur*, 11.10.11.10; melody in *Genevan Psalter*, 1551; harmony adapted from Claude Goudimel, 1565

1 Hope of the world, O Christ of great com - pas - sion,
2 Hope of the world, God's gift from high - est heav - en,
3 Hope of the world, a - foot on dust - y high - ways,
4 Hope of the world, who by your cross has saved us
speak to our fear - ful hearts by con - flict rent;
bring - ing to hun - gry souls the bread of life,
show - ing to wan - dering souls the path of light;
from death and dark de - spair, from sin and guilt;
save us, your peo - ple, from con - sum - ing pas - sion,
still let your Spir - it un - to us be giv - en
walk now be - side us lest the tempt - ing by - ways
we ren - der back the love your mer - cy gave us;
who by our own false hopes and aims are spent.
to heal earth's wounds and end its bit - ter strife.
lure us a - way from you to end - less night.
take now our lives, with them your king - dom build.

5 Hope of the world, O Christ, o'er death victorious,
who by this sign has conquered grief and pain,
we would be faithful to your gospel glorious.
You are our Lord! You shall forever reign!

548 Filled with the Spirit's power

John R. Peacey, 1969

Music: *Sheldonian*, 10.10.10.10; Cyril V. Taylor, 1943

1 Filled with the Spir - it's power, with one ac - cord
2 Now with the mind of Christ set us on fire,
3 Wid - en our love, good Spir - it, to em - brace
the in - fant church con - fessed its ris - en Lord.
that u - ni - ty may be our great de - sire.
in your strong care all those of ev - ery race.
O Ho - ly Spir - it, in the Church to - day
Give joy and peace; give faith to hear your call,
Like wind and fire with life a - mong us move,
no less your power of fel - low - ship dis - play.
and read - i - ness in each to work for all.
till we are known as Christ's, and Chris - tians prove.

549 "Let my people seek their freedom"

Herbert O'Driscoll, 1971

Music: *Shir Hamaalot*, 8787D; Jewish folksong; harmony by Samuel Adler, 1974

These words can also be sung to *Ebenezer*, no. 9.

1 "Let my peo - ple seek their free - dom in the wil - der -
2 When we mur - mur on the moun - tains for the old E -
3 In the mael - strom of the na - tions, in the jour - ney
ness a - while, from the slave pens of the Del - ta,
gyp - tian plains, when we miss our an - cient bond - age,
in - to space, in the clash of gen - er - a - tions,
from the ghet - tos on the Nile": so God spoke from
and the hope, the prom - ise, wanes, then the rock shall
in the hun - ger - ing for grace, in our a - go -
out of Si - nai, so God spoke and it was done,
yield its wa - ter and the man - na fall by night,
ny and glo - ry, we are called to new - er ways
l.h.

and a peo - ple crossed the wa - ters toward the ris - ing of the sun.
and with vi - sions of a fu - ture we shall march to - ward the light.
by the Lord of our to - mor - rows and the God of earth's to - days.

550 Ye servants of God

Charles Wesley, 1744

Music: *Paderborn*, 10.10.11.11; melody in *Catolisch-Paderbornisches Gesangbuch*, 1765, based on a folk melody; harmony by Sydney H. Nicholson, 1916

These words can also be sung to *Hanover*, no. 6.

1 Ye ser - vants of God, your Mas - ter pro - claim, and pub - lish a -
2 God rul - eth on high, al - might - y to save; and still he is
3 "Sal - va - tion to God who sits on the throne!" Let all cry a -
4 Then let us a - dore, and give him his right, all glo - ry and

broad his won - der - ful name; the name, all vic - to - rious, of
nigh, his pres - ence we have: the great con - gre - ga - tion his
loud and hon - or the Son: the prais - es of Je - sus the
power, and wis - dom and might, all hon - or and bless - ing, with

Je - sus ex - tol; his king - dom is glo - rious and rules o - ver all.
tri - umph shall sing, a - scrib - ing sal - va - tion to Je - sus, our King.
an - gels pro - claim, fall down on their fac - es and wor - ship the Lamb.
an - gels a - bove, and thanks nev - er ceas - ing and in - fin - ite love.

551 Your hand, O God, has guided

Edward H. Plumptre, 1889

Music: *Thornbury*, 7676D; Basil Harwood, 1898

1 Your hand, O God, has guid - ed your flock from age to age;
2 Your her-alds brought glad tid - ings to great - est as to least;
3 Through many a day of dark - ness, through many a scene of strife,
4 And we, shall we be faith - less? Shall hearts fail, hands hang down?
the won-drous tale is writ - ten, full clear, on ev - ery page.
they bade them rise, and has - ten to share the heaven-ly feast.
the faith - ful few fought brave - ly to guard your peo-ple's life.
Shall we e - vade the con - flict and cast a - way our crown?
Our fore-bears owned your good - ness, and we their deeds re - cord;
And this was all their teach - ing, in ev - ery deed and word,
Their gos - pel of re - demp - tion, sin par-doned, earth re - stored,
Not so: in God's deep coun - sels some bet - ter thing is stored;

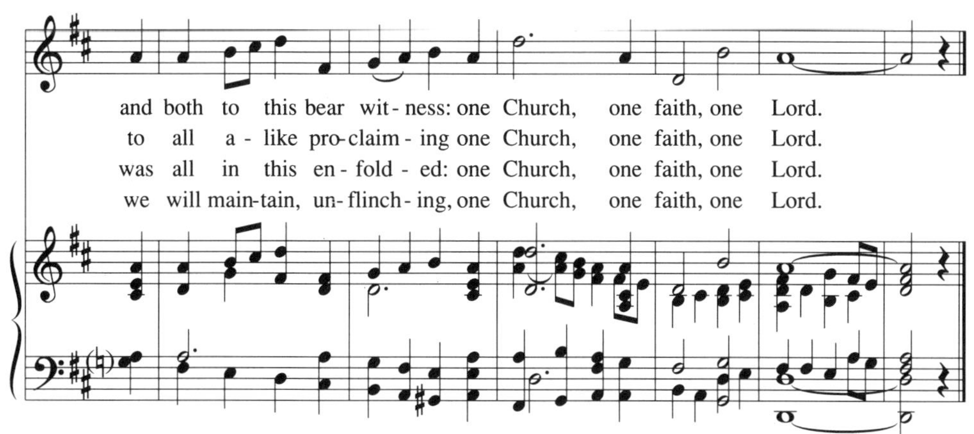
and both to this bear wit - ness: one Church, one faith, one Lord.
to all a - like pro-claim - ing one Church, one faith, one Lord.
was all in this en - fold - ed: one Church, one faith, one Lord.
we will main-tain, un- flinch - ing, one Church, one faith, one Lord.

5 Your mercy will not fail us,
nor leave your work undone;
with your right hand to help us,
the victory shall be won;

and then, by earth and heaven,
your name shall be adored,
and this shall be our anthem:
one Church, one faith, one Lord.

552 Where charity and love prevail

Ubi caritas et amor

Ninth century; paraphrased by Omer Westendorf, 1960

Music: *St. Fulbert*, 8686; Henry J. Gauntlett, 1852

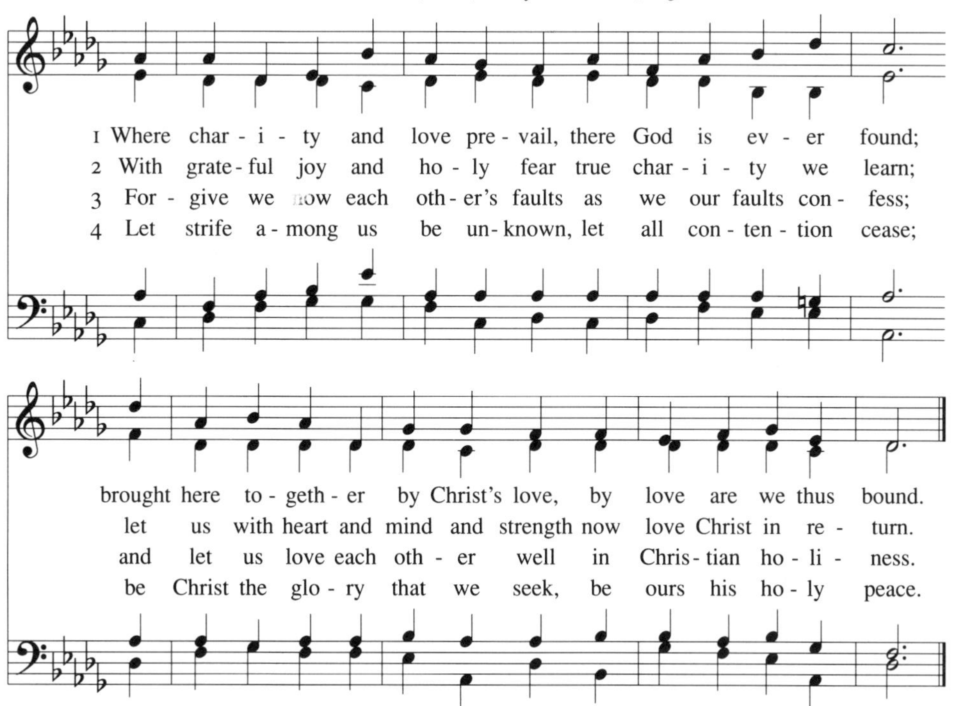
1 Where char - i - ty and love pre - vail, there God is ev - er found;
2 With grate - ful joy and ho - ly fear true char - i - ty we learn;
3 For - give we now each oth - er's faults as we our faults con - fess;
4 Let strife a - mong us be un - known, let all con - ten - tion cease;
brought here to - geth - er by Christ's love, by love are we thus bound.
let us with heart and mind and strength now love Christ in re - turn.
and let us love each oth - er well in Chris - tian ho - li - ness.
be Christ the glo - ry that we seek, be ours his ho - ly peace.

5 Let us recall that in our midst
dwells God's begotten Son;
as members of his Body joined,
we are in him made one.

6 Love can exclude no race or creed
if honored be God's name;
our common life embraces all
whose Maker is the same.

553 Where charity and love prevail

Ubi caritas et amor

Ninth century; paraphrased by Omer Westendorf, 1960

Music: *Cheshire*, 8686; melody and bass from *Est(e)'s Psalmes*, 1592

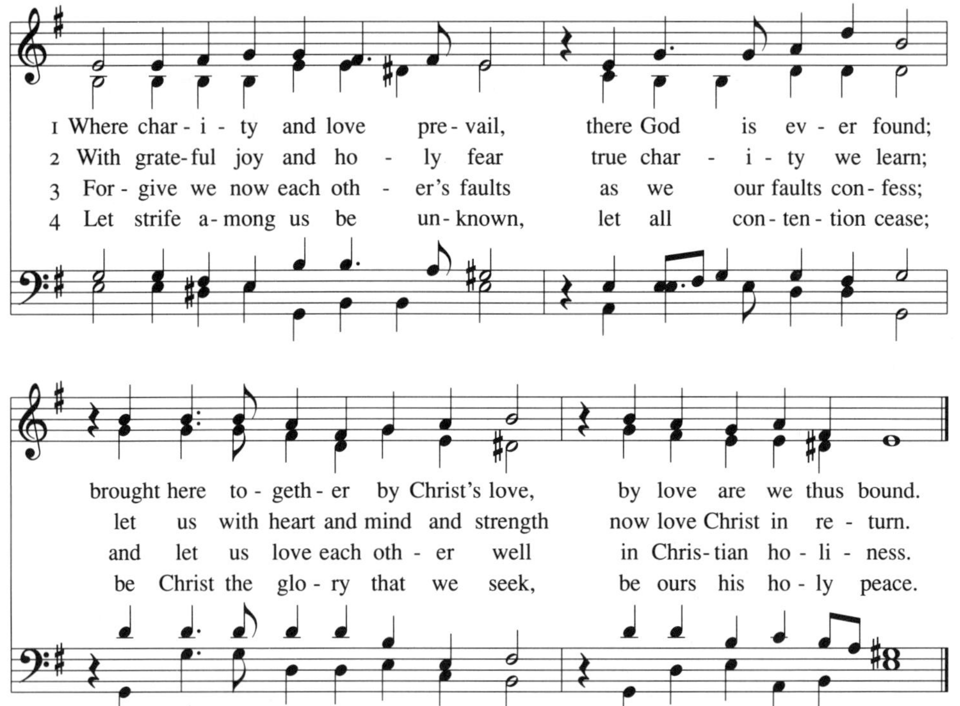
1 Where char - i - ty and love pre - vail, there God is ev - er found;
2 With grate-ful joy and ho - ly fear true char - i - ty we learn;
3 For - give we now each oth - er's faults as we our faults con - fess;
4 Let strife a - mong us be un - known, let all con - ten - tion cease;
brought here to - geth - er by Christ's love, by love are we thus bound.
let us with heart and mind and strength now love Christ in re - turn.
and let us love each oth - er well in Chris - tian ho - li - ness.
be Christ the glo - ry that we seek, be ours his ho - ly peace.

5 Let us recall that in our midst
dwells God's begotten Son;
as members of his Body joined,
we are in him made one.

6 Love can exclude no race or creed
if honored be God's name;
our common life embraces all
whose Maker is the same.

554 In Christ there is no East or West

Stanzas 1, 2, and 4: John Oxenham, 1913; stanza 3: Laurence Hall Stookey, 1987

Music: *McKee*, 8686; African American melody, adapted by Harry T. Burleigh, 1939

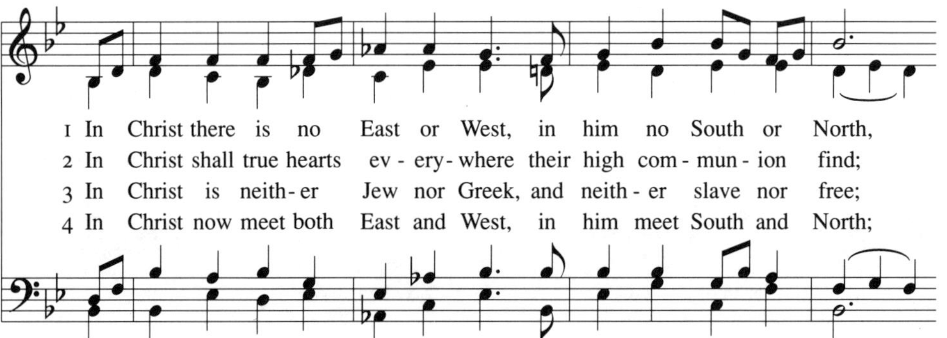
1 In Christ there is no East or West, in him no South or North,
2 In Christ shall true hearts ev - ery - where their high com - mun - ion find;
3 In Christ is neith - er Jew nor Greek, and neith - er slave nor free;
4 In Christ now meet both East and West, in him meet South and North;

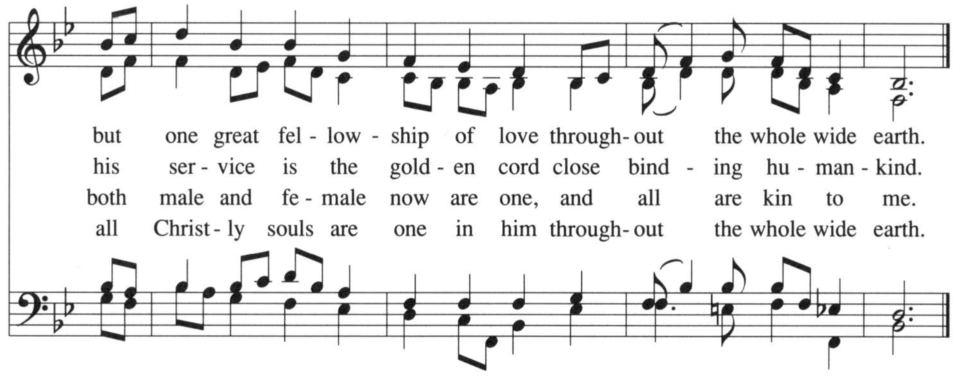
but one great fel - low - ship of love through- out the whole wide earth.
his ser - vice is the gold - en cord close bind - ing hu - man - kind.
both male and fe - male now are one, and all are kin to me.
all Christ - ly souls are one in him through- out the whole wide earth.

555 The Church of Christ, in every age

"The Caring Church," Fred Pratt Green, 1969

Music: *Babylon's Streams*, 8888; melody by Thomas Campion, 1613; adapted and arranged by E. H. Fellowes (1870–1951)

These words can also be sung to *Wareham*, no. 422.

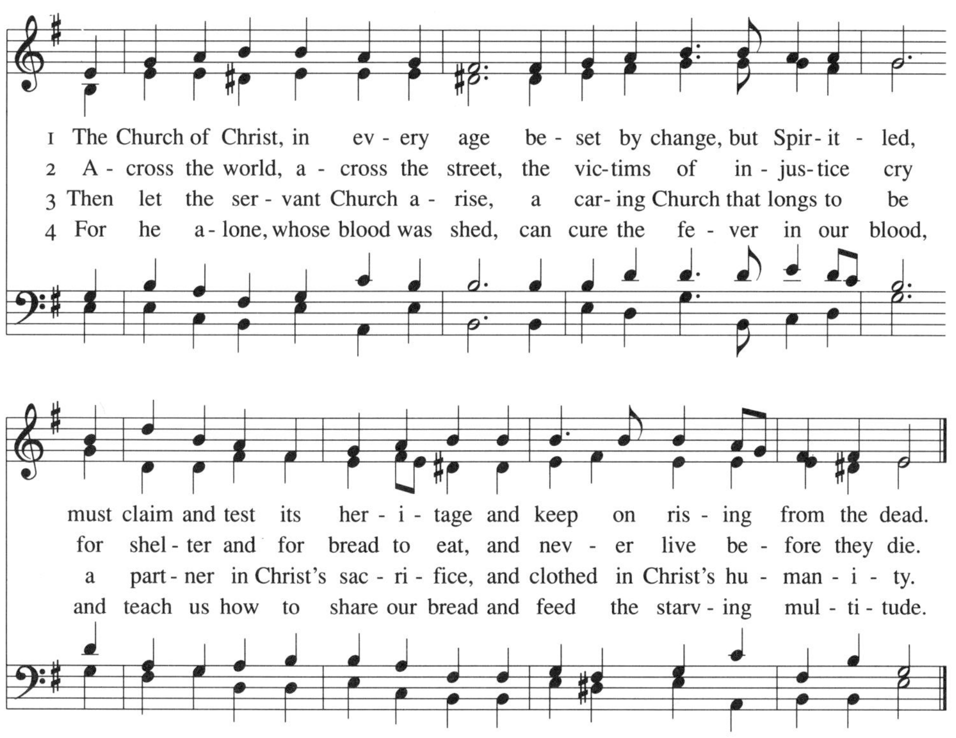
1 The Church of Christ, in ev - ery age be - set by change, but Spir - it - led,
2 A - cross the world, a - cross the street, the vic- tims of in - jus- tice cry
3 Then let the ser - vant Church a - rise, a car- ing Church that longs to be
4 For he a - lone, whose blood was shed, can cure the fe - ver in our blood,
must claim and test its her - i - tage and keep on ris - ing from the dead.
for shel - ter and for bread to eat, and nev - er live be - fore they die.
a part - ner in Christ's sac - ri - fice, and clothed in Christ's hu - man - i - ty.
and teach us how to share our bread and feed the starv - ing mul - ti - tude.

5 We have no mission but to serve
in full obedience to our Lord;
to care for all, without reserve,
and spread his liberating word.

556 Lift high the cross

George W. Kitchen, 1887, and Michael R. Newbolt, 1916

Music: *Crucifer*, 10.10 with refrain; Sydney H. Nicholson, 1916

Refrain
Lift high the cross, the love of Christ pro - claim
till all the world a - dore his sa - cred name.
Fine
1 Led on their way by this tri - um - phant sign,
2 Each new - born ser - vant of the Cru - ci - fied
3 O Lord, once lift - ed on the glo - rious tree,
4 Set up thy throne, that earth's de - spair may cease
the hosts of God in one great hymn com- bine:
bears on the brow the seal of him who died.
as thou hast prom - ised, draw the world to thee.
be - neath the shad - ow of its heal - ing peace.
D.C.

5 So shall our song of triumph ever be:
praise to the Crucified for victory.

Refrain

557 The Lord will come and not be slow

John Milton, 1648; selected lines from psalm paraphrases

Music: *Donnez au Seigneur gloire*, 8686D; melody in *Genevan Psalter*, 1547; harmony adapted from Claude Goudimel, 1565

1 The Lord will come and not be slow; his foot-steps can - not err;
2 Truth from the earth, like to a flower, shall bud and blos - som fresh,
3 The na- tions, all whom thou hast made, shall come and all shall frame
be - fore him righ-teous- ness shall go, his roy - al har - bing - er.
and jus - tice from her heaven- ly bower look down on mor - tal flesh.
to bow them low be - fore thee, Lord, and glor - i - fy thy name.
Mer - cy and truth that long were missed, now joy - ful - ly are met;
Rise, God, judge thou the earth in might; this wick - ed earth re - dress,
For great thou art, and won - ders great by thy strong hand are done;
sweet peace and righ-teous-ness have kissed, and hand in hand are set.
for thou art God and shalt by right the na- tions all pos - sess.
thou in thy ev - er - last - ing seat re - main-est God a - lone.

558 Lo, he comes with clouds descending

"Thy Kingdom come," Charles Wesley, 1758

Music: *Helmsley*, 878747 extended; melody in John Wesley's *Select Hymns with Tunes Annext*, 1765

1 Lo, he comes with clouds de-scend-ing, once for fa-vored sin-ners slain; thou-sand, thou-sand saints at-tend-ing swell the tri-umph of his train. Al-le-lu-ia! Al-le-lu-ia! Al-le-lu-ia! God ap-pears on earth to reign.
2 Ev-ery eye shall now be-hold him, robed in dread-ful ma-jes-ty; those who set at naught and sold him, pierced and nailed him to the tree, deep-ly wail-ing, deep-ly wail-ing, deep-ly wail-ing, shall the true Mes-si-ah see.
3 Those dear to-kens of his pas-sion still his daz-zling bo-dy bears; cause of end-less ex-ul-ta-tion to his ran-somed wor-ship-ers; with what rap-ture, with what rap-ture, with what rap-ture, gaze we on those glo-rious scars!
4 Yea, a-men, let all a-dore thee, high on thy e-ter-nal throne; Sa-vior, take the power and glo-ry, claim the king-dom for thine own. Come, Lord Je-sus! Come, Lord Je-sus! Come, Lord Je-sus! Ev-er-last-ing God, come down!

559 O holy city, seen of John

Walter Russell Bowie, 1909

Music: *Sancta Civitas*, 868686; Herbert Howells, 1936

These words can also be sung to *Morning Song*, no. 349.

1 O ho - ly ci - ty, seen of John, where Christ, the Lamb, doth reign,
2 O shame to us who rest con- tent while lust and greed for gain
3 Give us, O God, the strength to build the ci - ty that hath stood
4 Al - read - y in the mind of God that ci - ty ris - eth fair:
with - in whose four-square walls shall come no night, nor need, nor pain,
in street and shop and ten - e - ment wring gold from hu - man pain,
too long a dream, whose laws are love, whose crown is ser - vant - hood,
lo, how its splen - dor chal - leng - es the souls that great - ly dare —
and where the tears are wiped from eyes that shall not weep a - gain!
and bit - ter lips in blind de - spair cry, "Christ hath died in vain!"
and where the sun that shin - eth is God's grace for hu - man good.
yea, bids us seize the whole of life and build its glo - ry there.

560 Love divine, all loves excelling

Charles Wesley, 1747

Music: *Hyfrydol*, 8787D; melody by Rowland Hugh Prichard, 1844

1 Love di - vine, all loves ex - cell - ing, joy of heaven, to
2 Breathe, O breathe thy lov - ing Spir - it in - to ev - ery
3 Come, Al - might - y to de - liv - er, let us all thy
4 Fin - ish, then, thy new cre - a - tion; pure and spot - less
earth come down; fix in us thy hum - ble dwell - ing;
trou - bled breast! Let us all in thee in - her - it;
life re - ceive; sud - den - ly re - turn and nev - er,
let us be. Let us see thy great sal - va - tion
all thy faith - ful mer - cies crown! Je - sus, thou art
let us find our pro - mised rest. Take a - way our
nev - er - more thy tem - ples leave. Thee we would be
pre - fect - ly re - stored in thee; changed from glo - ry
all com - pas - sion, pure, un - bound - ed love thou art; vis - it
bent to sin - ning; Al - pha and O - me - ga be; end of
al - ways bless - ing, serve thee as thy hosts a - bove, pray and
in - to glo - ry, till in heaven we take our place, till we

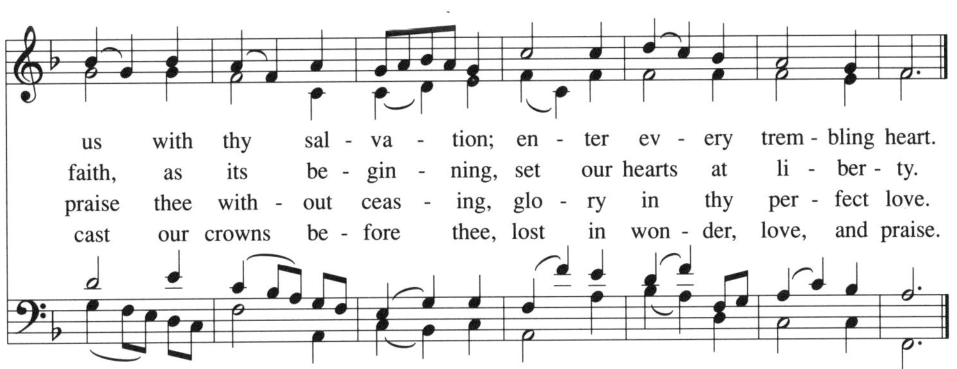
us with thy sal - va - tion; en - ter ev - ery trem - bling heart.
faith, as its be - gin - ning, set our hearts at li - ber - ty.
praise thee with - out ceas - ing, glo - ry in thy per - fect love.
cast our crowns be - fore thee, lost in won - der, love, and praise.

561 Jesus lives

Jesus lebt

Christian Gellert, 1757; translated by Frances Cox, 1841

Music: *St. Albinus*, 78784; Henry J. Gauntlett, 1852

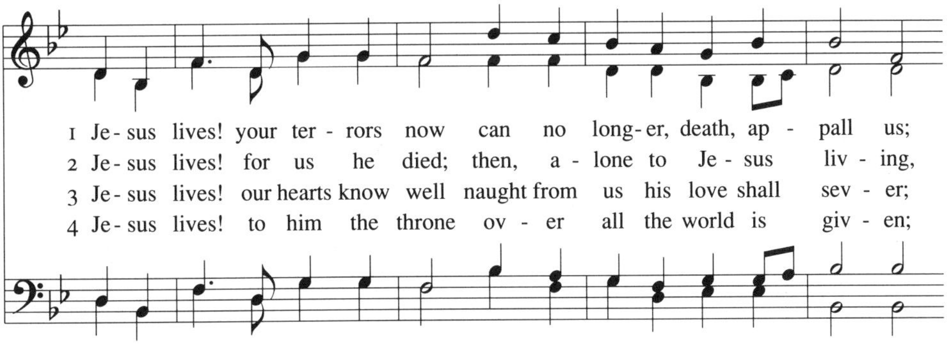

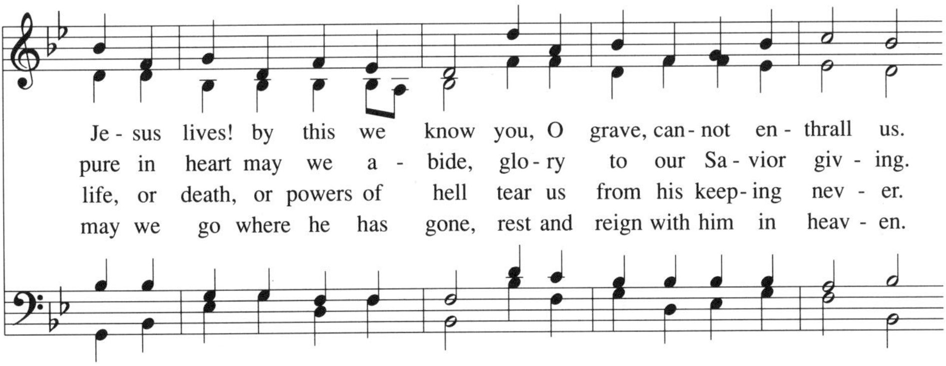

1 Je - sus lives! your ter - rors now can no long - er, death, ap - pall us;
Je - sus lives! by this we know you, O grave, can - not en - thrall us.
Al - le - lu - ia!

2 Je - sus lives! for us he died; then, a - lone to Je - sus liv - ing,
pure in heart may we a - bide, glo - ry to our Sa - vior giv - ing.
Al - le - lu - ia!

3 Je - sus lives! our hearts know well naught from us his love shall sev - er;
life, or death, or powers of hell tear us from his keep - ing nev - er.
Al - le - lu - ia!

4 Je - sus lives! to him the throne ov - er all the world is giv - en;
may we go where he has gone, rest and reign with him in heav - en.
Al - le - lu - ia!

562 Faith looking forward

"A living hope," Brian Wren, 1982

Music: *Martyrs' Memorial*, 57855; Peter Cutts, 1983

1 Faith looking forward from the cross and empty tomb knows that whatever may happen, Jesus is risen, hope of the kingdom.
2 Experts or tyrants plan a future cut and dried. Faith looking forward surmises hopeful surprises, signs of the kingdom.
3 Though terror rages and oppression blocks their way, hope knows the poor will awaken and thrones be shaken, building the kingdom.
4 And if our action, running risks or taking sides, burns all our bridges behind us, Christ longs to find us free for the kingdom.

5 Hope keeps in vision,
though the dust and ashes fall,
love's final transfiguration
of all creation,
new in the kingdom.

563 Hail to the Lord's Anointed

James Montgomery, 1821, based on Psalm 72

Music: *Wolvercote*, 7676D; William H. Ferguson, c. 1910

These words can also be sung to *Ave Maria, klarer*, no. 278.

1 Hail to the Lord's A - noint - ed, great Da-vid's great-er Son!
2 Christ comes with suc - cor speed - y to those who suf - fer wrong,
3 Christ shall come down like show - ers up - on the fruit-ful earth,
4 Kings shall bow down be - fore him, and gold and in-cense bring;
Hail, in the time ap - point - ed, his reign on earth be - gun!
to help the poor and need - y, and bid the weak be strong;
and love, joy, hope, like flow - ers, spring in his path to birth;
all na-tions shall a - dore him, his praise all peo - ple sing;
Christ comes to break op - pres - sion, to set the cap-tive free;
to give them songs for sigh - ing, their dark-ness turn to light,
be - fore him on the moun - tains shall peace, the her-ald, go;
to him shall prayer un - ceas - ing and dai - ly vows as-cend;
to take a - way trans - gres - sion, and rule in e - qui - ty.
whose souls, con-demned and dy - ing, are pre-cious in his sight.
and righ-teous-ness in foun - tains from hill to val - ley flow.
his king-dom still in - creas - ing, a king-dom with-out end.

5 O'er every foe victorious,
Christ on his throne shall rest;
from age to age more glorious,
all-blessing and all-blest;
the tide of time shall never
his covenant remove;
his name shall stand for ever,
the changeless name of Love.

564 Camina, pueblo de Dios

Walk on, O people of God

Cesareo Gabaraín; translated by George Lockwood, 1987

Music: *Nueva Creación*, 7878D with refrain; Cesareo Gabaraín; harmony by Juan Luis García, 1987

Refrain
Unison
Ca - mi - na, pue- blo de Dios, ca - mi - na, pue- blo de Dios.
Walk on, O peo- ple of God; walk on, O peo- ple of God!
Nue-va ley, nue - va a - lian- za, en la nue- va cre- a - ción.
A new law, God's new al - li- ance, all cre - a- tion is re- born.
Fine
Ca - mi - na, pue- blo de Dios, ca - mi - na, pue- blo de Dios.
Walk on, O peo- ple of God; walk on, O peo- ple of God!
1 Mi - ra a- llá en el Cal - va - rio en la ro - ca hay u - na cruz;
2 Cris - to to- ma en su cuer- po el pe - ca - do, la es - cla - vi - tud.
1 Look on Cal - va - ry's sum-mit; on the rock there tow - ers a cross;
2 Christ takes in - to his bod - y all our sin, en- slave- ment, and pain;

© 1979, Ediciones Paulinas. Sole U.S. Agent: OCP Publications, 5536 N.E. Hassalo, Portland, Oreg. 97213. All rights reserved. Used with permission. English translation © 1989 by The United Methodist Publishing House. From *The United Methodist Hymnal*. Used by permission.

muer- te que en- gen - dra la vi - da, nue- vos hom- bres, nue- va luz.
Al des- tru - ir - los, nos tra - e u - na nue - va ple- ni - tud.
death that gives birth to new liv - ing, a new peo - ple, a new light.
as he des-troys them, he brings us life's a - bun-dance, life's new joy.
Cris - to nos ha sal - va - do con su muer- te y re - su- rrec- ción.
Po - ne en paz a los hom-bres, a las co - sas y al Cre - a - dor.
Christ has brought us sal - va - tion with his death and ris- ing a - gain.
Christ brings rec - on- cil - ia - tion to all things and peo- ple with God.
D.C.
To- das las co - sas re - na - cen en la nue- va cre- a - ción.
To- do re - na- ce a la vi - da en la nue- va cre- a - ción.
Ev - ery- thing comes to new birth - ing, all cre - a- tion is re- born.
Na- ture bursts in - to new flow-ering, all cre - a- tion is re- born.

3 *Cielo y tierra se abrazan,*
nuestra alma halla el perdón.
Vuelven a abrirse los cielos
para el hombre pecador.
Israel peregrino,
vive y canta tu redención.
Hay nuevos mundos abiertos
en la nueva creación.

Refrain

3 Heaven and earth are embracing,
and our souls find pardon at last.
Now heaven's gates are reopened
to the sinner, to us all.
Israel walks a journey;
now we live, salvation's our song;
Christ's resurrection has freed us.
There are new worlds to explore.

Refrain

565 Shall we gather at the river

Robert Lowry, 1864

Music: *Hanson Place*, 8787 with refrain; melody by Robert Lowry, 1864; arranged by Aaron Copland, 1954

1 Shall we ga-ther at the riv - er,
2 Ere we reach the shin-ing riv - er,
3 Soon we'll reach the shin-ing riv - er,
where bright an - gel feet have trod;
lay we ev - ery bur - den down;
soon our pil - grim - age will cease,
with its crys - tal tide for
grace our spir - its will de -
soon our hap - py hearts will
ev - er flow-ing by the throne of God?
liv - er, and pro - vide a robe and crown.
quiv - er with the mel - od - y of peace.
Refrain
Yes, we'll ga-ther at the riv - er, the beau-ti-ful, the beau-ti-ful riv - er;

566 Shall we gather at the river

Robert Lowry, 1864

Music: *Hanson Place*, 8787 with refrain; Robert Lowry, 1864

gath-er with the saints at the riv - er that flows by the throne of God.
1 Shall we ga-ther at the riv - er, where bright an-gel feet have trod;
2 Ere we reach the shin-ing riv - er, lay we ev-ery bur-den down;
3 Soon we'll reach the shin-ing riv - er, soon our pil-grim-age will cease,
with its crys-tal tide for ev - er flow-ing by the throne of God?
grace our spir-its will de - liv - er, and pro - vide a robe and crown.
soon our hap-py hearts will quiv - er with the mel-od - y of peace.
Refrain
Yes, we'll ga-ther at the riv - er, the beau-ti-ful, the beau-ti-ful riv - er;
gath-er with the saints at the riv - er that flows by the throne of God.

567 O day of peace

Carl P. Daw, Jr., 1982

Music: *Jerusalem*, 8888D; C. Hubert H. Parry, 1916; harmony by Richard Proulx, 1983

1 O day of peace that dim-ly shines through all our hopes and prayers and dreams, guide us to jus - tice, truth, and love, de-liv-ered from our self - ish schemes. May swords of hate fall from our hands, our hearts from
2 Then shall the wolf dwell with the lamb, nor shall the fierce de - vour the small; as beasts and cat - tle calm-ly graze, a lit-tle child shall lead them all. Then en - e - mies shall learn to love, all crea-tures

en - vy find re - lease, till by God's grace our war - ring world
find their true ac - cord; the hope of peace shall be ful - filled,
shall see Christ's prom - ised reign of peace.
for all the earth shall know the
1
2
Lord.

568 Lord Christ, when first you came to earth

Walter Russell Bowie, 1928, and others

Music: *Mit Freuden zart*, 8787887; melody in *Kirchengesang*, Berlin, 1566; harmony by Heinrich Reimann, 1895

1 Lord Christ, when first you came to earth, up - on a cross they bound you, and mocked your sav - ing king-ship's worth by thorns with which they crowned you: and still our wrongs may fash-ion now new thorns to pierce that
2 O awe-some love, which found no room in life where sin de - nied you, and, doomed to death, must bring to doom the powers which cru - ci - fied you, till not a stone was left on stone, and all an em - pire's
3 New ad - vent of the love of Christ, shall we a - gain re - fuse you, till in the night of hate and war we per - ish as we lose you? From old un - faith our souls re-lease to seek the king - dom
4 O wound-ed hands of Je - sus, build in us your new cre - a - tion; our pride is dust, our vaunt is stilled, we wait your re - ve - la - tion: O Love that tri - umphs o - ver loss, we bring our hearts be -

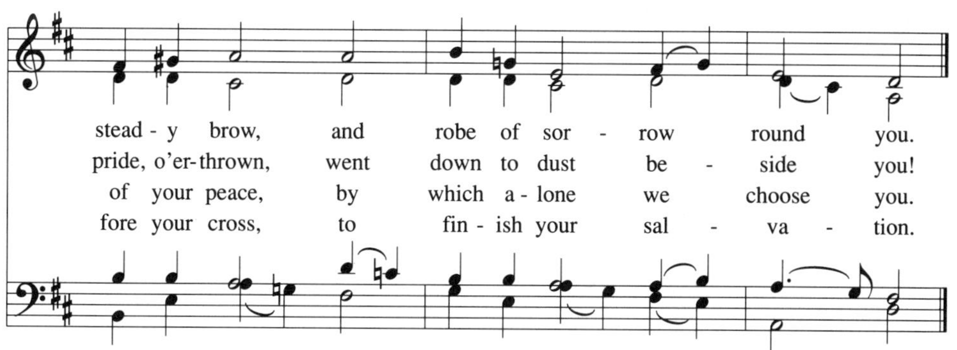
stead - y brow, and robe of sor - row round you.
pride, o'er-thrown, went down to dust be - side you!
of your peace, by which a - lone we choose you.
fore your cross, to fin - ish your sal - va - tion.

569 The head that once was crowned with thorns

Thomas Kelly, 1820

Music: *St. Magnus*, 8686; melody in Henry Playford's *The Divine Companion*, 1709; probably by Jeremiah Clark(e) (c. 1673–1707)

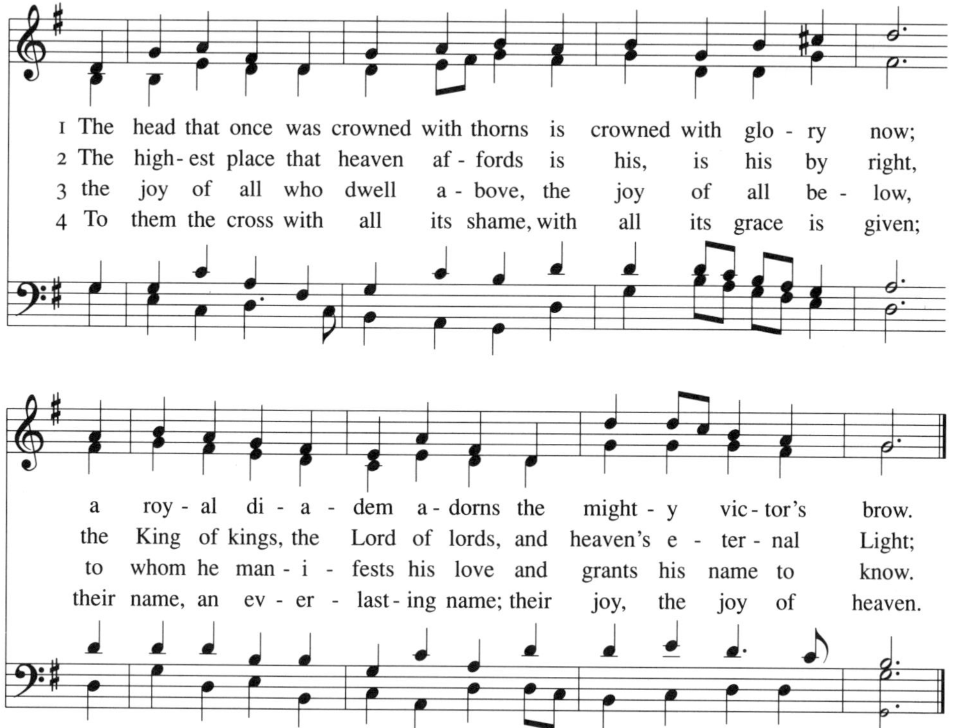
1 The head that once was crowned with thorns is crowned with glo - ry now;
2 The high-est place that heaven af - fords is his, is his by right,
3 the joy of all who dwell a - bove, the joy of all be - low,
4 To them the cross with all its shame, with all its grace is given;
a roy - al di - a - dem a - dorns the might - y vic - tor's brow.
the King of kings, the Lord of lords, and heaven's e - ter - nal Light;
to whom he man - i - fests his love and grants his name to know.
their name, an ev - er - last - ing name; their joy, the joy of heaven.

5 They suffer with their Lord below,
they reign with him above,
their profit and their joy to know
the mystery of his love.

6 The cross he bore is life and health,
though shame and death to him:
his people's hope, his people's wealth,
their everlasting theme.

570 Glorious the day

"The Glorious Work of Christ," Fred Pratt Green, 1967

Music: *Diemer*, 8888 with refrains; Emma Lou Diemer, 1989

1 Glo-rious the day when Christ was born
2 Glo-rious the day when Christ a-rose,
3 Glo-rious the days of gos-pel grace
4 Glo-rious the day when Christ ful-fills
Al-le-lu-ia!
to wear the crown that Cae-sars scorn,
the sur-est friend of all his foes;
when Christ re-stores the fal-len race,
what self re-jects yet feeb-ly wills;
Al-le-lu-ia!
whose life and death that love re-veal
who for the sake of those he grieves
when doubt-ers kneel and waver-ers stand,
when that strong Light puts out the sun
Al-le-lu-ia!
which mor-tals need and need to feel.
tran-scends the world he nev-er leaves.
and faith a-chieves what rea-son planned.
and all is end-ed, all be-gun.
Al-le-lu-ia!

Al - le - lu - ia! Al - le - lu - ia! Al - le - lu - ia!

571 I Glorious the day

"The Glorious Work of Christ," Fred Pratt Green, 1967

Music: *Frohlockt mit Freud*, 8888 with refrain; adapted slightly from Heinrich Schütz, *Der Beckersche Psalter*, 1628

1 Glorious the day when Christ was born
to wear the crown that Caesars scorn,
whose life and death that love reveal
which mortals need and need to feel.

2 Glorious the day when Christ arose,
the surest friend of all his foes;
who for the sake of those he grieves
transcends the world he never leaves.

3 Glorious the days of gospel grace
when Christ restores the fallen race,
when doubters kneel and waverers stand,
and faith achieves what reason planned.

4 Glorious the day when Christ fulfills
what self rejects yet feebly wills;
when that strong Light puts out the sun
and all is ended, all begun.

Refrain
Alleluia! Alleluia! Alleluia!

572 Songs of praise the angels sang

James Montgomery, 1819

Music: *Northampton*, 7777; Charles J. King, c. 1904

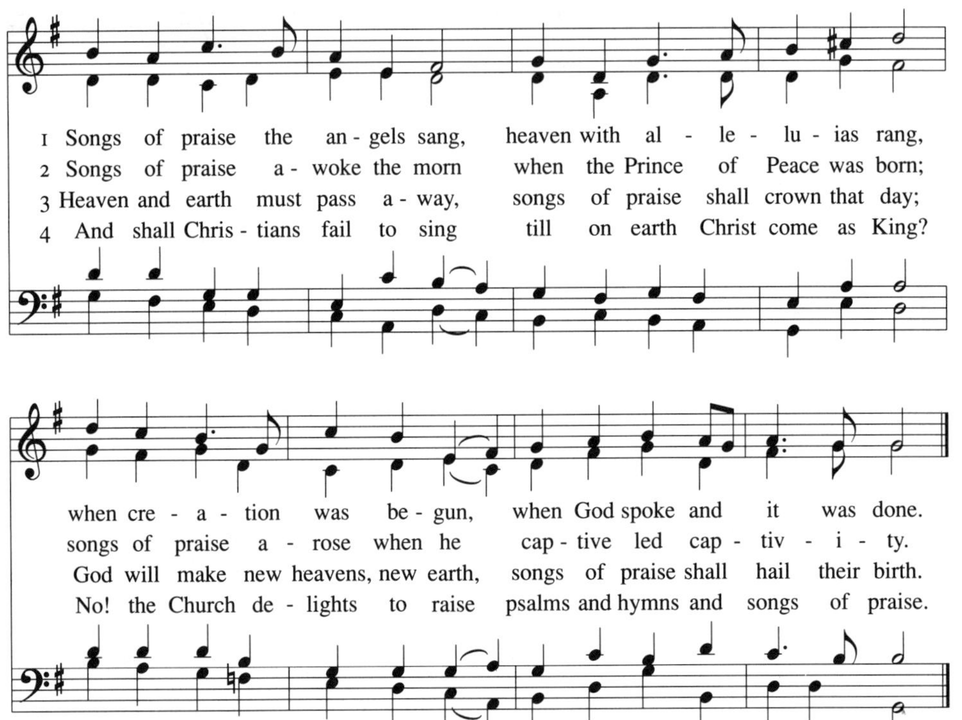
1 Songs of praise the an - gels sang, heaven with al - le - lu - ias rang,
2 Songs of praise a - woke the morn when the Prince of Peace was born;
3 Heaven and earth must pass a - way, songs of praise shall crown that day;
4 And shall Chris - tians fail to sing till on earth Christ come as King?
when cre - a - tion was be - gun, when God spoke and it was done.
songs of praise a - rose when he cap - tive led cap - tiv - i - ty.
God will make new heavens, new earth, songs of praise shall hail their birth.
No! the Church de - lights to raise psalms and hymns and songs of praise.

5 Saints below, with heart and voice,
still in songs of praise rejoice,
learning here, by faith and love,
songs of praise to sing above.

6 Borne upon their final breath,
songs of praise shall conquer death;
then, amidst eternal joy,
songs of praise their powers employ.

573 Mine eyes have seen the glory

Julia Ward Howe, 1861

Music: *Battle Hymn*, 15.15.15.6 with refrain; American traditional melody

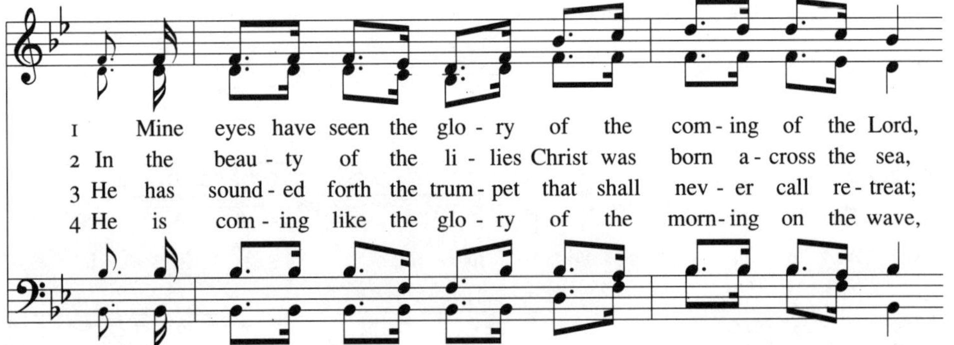
1 Mine eyes have seen the glo - ry of the com - ing of the Lord,
2 In the beau - ty of the li - lies Christ was born a - cross the sea,
3 He has sound - ed forth the trum - pet that shall nev - er call re - treat;
4 He is com - ing like the glo - ry of the morn - ing on the wave,

who is tram-pling out the vin-tage where the grapes of wrath are stored,
with a glo-ry in his bos-om that trans-fig-ures you and me;
he is sift-ing out each hu-man heart be-fore his judg-ment seat;
he is wis-dom to the might-y, he is hon-or to the brave;
who has loosed the fate-ful light-ning of his ter-ri-ble swift sword;
as he died to make all ho-ly, let us live to make all free:
O be swift, my soul, to an-swer him, be ju-bi-lant, my feet:
so the world shall be his foot-stool, ev-ery e-vil power his slave:
his truth is march-ing on.
our God is march-ing on.
our God is march-ing on.
our God is march-ing on.
Refrain
Glo-ry, glo-ry, hal-le-lu-jah!
Glo-ry, glo-ry, hal-le-lu-jah!
Glo-ry, glo-ry, hal-le-lu-jah! His truth is march-ing on.

574 The King of glory comes to earth

Timothy Dudley-Smith, 1987

Music: *Jordan*, 8686D; melody by William Billings, 1786

These words can also be sung to *Kingsfold*, no. 379.

1 The King of glo-ry comes to earth from God the Fa-ther given,
2 The King of glo-ry comes un-known, the in-fant Lord of all;
3 The King of glo-ry comes to die in pov-er-ty and scorn,
4 The King of glo-ry comes in peace, and hope is ours a-gain,
the her-alds of his roy-al birth the an-gel host of heaven;
a mo-ther's lap his on-ly throne, his state a cat-tle stall.
up-on a don-key rid-ing by to claim a crown of thorn.
as life and love and joy in-crease and faith and free-dom reign.
his king-ly robe the swath-ing bands, his hom-age Ma-ry's gaze,
Be-fore their nak-ed new-born King the ox and ass are dumb,
Cre-a-tion's Lord of time and space is come to meet his hour,
The Child of all our Christ-mas songs, his cross and pas-sion past,
be-yond the stars his king-dom stands to ev-er-last-ing days.
while count-less choirs of an-gels sing to see his king-dom come.
his tri-umph-song the word of grace, and love his on-ly power.
will right the sum of hu-man wrongs, and bring us home at last.

575 Turn back, turn back, forswear thy foolish ways

Clifford Bax, 1916, and others

Music: *Old 124th*, 10.10.10.10.10; melody in *Genevan Psalter*, 1551; harmony adapted from Claude Goudimel, 1565

1 Turn back, turn back, for - swear thy fool - ish ways. Old now is
2 Earth might be fair, and all be glad and wise. Age af - ter
3 Earth shall be fair, and all her peo - ple one: nor till that
earth, and none may count her days, yet thou, her child, whose
age their trag - ic em - pires rise, built while they dream, and
hour shall God's whole will be done. Now, e - ven now, once
head is crowned with flame, still wilt not hear thine in - ner God pro -
in that dream - ing weep: would we but wake from out our haunt - ed
more from earth to sky peals forth in joy the old, un - daunt - ed
claim, "Turn back, turn back, for - swear thy fool - ish ways."
sleep, earth might be fair, and all be glad and wise.
cry: "Earth shall be fair, and all her folk be one."

INDEX OF NAMES OF TUNES

INDEX OF COMPOSERS, SOURCES, AND ARRANGERS

INDEX OF AUTHORS, SOURCES, AND TRANSLATORS

METRICAL INDEX

COPYRIGHT ACKNOWLEDGMENTS

The following twenty-two psalms (in whole or in part) are from *An Inclusive Language Lectionary* (*Readings for Year A, B, C*), copyright 1983, 1984, 1985 by the Division of Education and Ministry, National Council of Churches of Christ in the USA, and are used by permission:
Psalms 20, 21, 22, 23, 26, 35, 44, 53, 57, 69, 70, 71, 72, 82, 94, 101, 111, 125, 127, 128, 145, and 149.

Two psalms are from the Revised Standard Version of the Bible, copyright 1946, 1952, 1971 by the Division of Christian Education, National Council of Churches of Christ in the USA, and are used by permission:
Psalms 74 and 86.

The remaining ninety psalms (in whole or in part) are from *The United Methodist Liturgical Psalter*, edited by Harrell Beck, John Holbert, S. T. Kimbrough, Jr., and Alan Luff, © 1989 The United Methodist Publishing House, based on the New Revised Standard Version of the Bible, 1989, and adapted by permission of the Division of Christian Education, National Council of Churches of Christ in the USA, all rights reserved:
Psalms, 1, 2, 3, 4, 5, 8, 9, 10, 13, 14, 15, 16, 17, 19, 24, 25, 27, 28, 29, 30, 31, 32, 33, 34, 36, 37, 39, 40, 41, 42, 43, 46, 47, 48, 50, 51, 62, 63, 65, 66, 67, 68, 76, 77, 78, 80, 81, 84, 85, 89, 90, 91, 92, 93, 95, 96, 97, 98, 99, 100, 102, 103, 104, 105, 106, 107, 112, 113, 114, 115, 116, 118, 119, 121, 122, 124, 126, 130, 132, 133, 134, 135, 137, 138, 139, 143, 146, 147, 148, and 150.

Psalm tones A and B (Mark Bangert) are reprinted from *Lutheran Book of Worship,* copyright © 1978, by permission of Augsburg Fortress.

Psalm tones C, D, and E (Paul G. Bunjes) are from *Lutheran Worship,* copyright © 1982 Concordia Publishing House. Reprinted by permission.

The eight psalm antiphons (composed for this collection by Richard Proulx) are copyright © 1992 by Yale University Press.

Individual acknowledgments are as follows:

1 Words: French translation copyright Roger Chapal. From "Cantate Domino," World Council of Churches Publications, Geneva, Switzerland.

3 Music: Harmonization copyright © 1964 Abingdon Press. From *The Book of Hymns.* Used by permission.

4 Music: Setting copyright 1969 Concordia Publishing House. Reprinted by permission.

5 Music: Copyright © 1960 by Central Conference of American Rabbis.

7 Words: Copyright © 1992 Gracia Grindal. Music: Copyright © 1980 by GIA Publications, Inc., Chicago, Ill. All rights reserved.

8 Music: From "A Song to David" (Edition Peters 67020), © 1985 by Henmar Press, Inc. Used by permission of C. F. Peters Corporation, New York.

9 Words: Copyright © 1969 Concordia Publishing House. Reprinted by permission.

12 Music: Harmonization copyright © 1991 by Hope Publishing Company, 380 S. Main Pl., Carol Stream, Ill. 60188. All rights reserved. Used by permission.

13 Words: Translation copyright Boris and Clare Anderson. Music: Harmonization © 1983 assigned to The United Methodist Publishing House. From *The United Methodist Hymnal.* Used by permission.

15 Words: Copyright © 1986 by Hope Publishing Company, 380 S. Main Pl., Carol Stream, Ill. 60188. All rights reserved. Used by permission. Music: Copyright © Jane M. Marshall. Used by permission.

18 Words: Copyright 1973 The Word of God. All rights reserved. Music: Melody copyright 1973 The Word of God, P.O. Box 8617, Ann Arbor, Mich. 48107. All rights reserved.

19 Music: From *Enlarged Songs of Praise 1931,* by permission of Oxford University Press.

23 Music: Copyright © 1985 by Hope Publishing Company, 380 S. Main Pl., Carol Stream, Ill. 60188. All rights reserved. Used by permission.

27 Music: From *The Hymnal 1982,* © The Church Pension Fund, 800 Second Avenue, New York, N.Y. 10017. Used by permission.

28 Music: Copyright © 1976 by Hinshaw Music, Inc. Used by permission.

29 Words: Copyright J. W. Shore. Music: Copyright Dorothy Sheets. All rights reserved. Used by permission.

30 Music: By permission of Dieter Kugler.

31 Music: Copyright © 1924 John Ireland. Used by permission of the Executors of N. Kirby, deceased.

33 Words: Copyright © 1982 by Hope Publishing Company, 380 S. Main Pl., Carol Stream, Ill. 60188. All rights reserved. Used by permission.

40 Words: Copyright © 1962. Renewal 1990 by Hope Publishing Company, 380 S. Main Pl., Carol Stream, Ill. 60188. All rights reserved. Used by permission.

43 Music: Harmonization copyright © 1991 by Hope Publishing Company, 380 S. Main Pl., Carol Stream, Ill. 60188. All rights reserved. Used by permission.

44 Music: Copyright © 1983 by Hope Publishing Company, 380 S. Main Pl., Carol Stream, Ill. 60188. All rights reserved. Used by permission.

48 Music: Accompaniment copyright by Bruce Neswick. Used by permission.

49 Music: Harmonization copyright © 1991 by Hope Publishing Company, 380 S. Main Pl., Carol Stream, Ill. 60188. All rights reserved. Used by permission.

50 Words: Copyright © 1984 by Hope Publishing Company, 380 S. Main Pl., Carol Stream, Ill. 60188. All rights reserved. Used by permission. Music: Copyright © 1992 by GIA Publications, Inc., Chicago, Ill. All rights reserved.

51 Words: Copyright © 1979 by The Hymn Society, Texas Christian University, Fort Worth, Tex. 76129. All rights reserved. Used by permission.

52 Music: Harmonization from *The English Hymnal,* by permission o Oxford University Press.

53 Words and music: Copyright © 1979 by Hope Publishing Compan 380 S. Main Pl., Carol Stream, Ill. 60188. All rights reserved. Us by permission.

54 Words and music: Copyright © 1987 The Shadyside Presbyterian Church, Pittsburgh, Pa. Used by permission.

56 Words: Copyright 1967 assigned to The United Methodist Publishi House. From *The United Methodist Hymnal.* Used by permission. Music: Harmonization copyright 1989 The United Methodist Publishing House. From *The United Methodist Hymnal.* Used by permission.

57 Words: Copyright © 1983 Jaroslav J. Vajda. Used by permission. Music: Copyright © 1983 by GIA Publications, Inc., Chicago, Ill. All rights reserved.

58 Music: From *The English Hymnal,* by permission of Oxford University Press.

59 Music: Harmonization copyright © 1991 by Hope Publishing Company, 380 S. Main Pl., Carol Stream, Ill. 60188. All rights reserved. Used by permission.

61 Words: Copyright © 1973 by The Hymn Society, Texas Christian University, Fort Worth, Tex. 76129. All rights reserved. Used by permission. Music: Copyright © 1974 Augsburg Publishing House Reprinted by permission of Augsburg Fortress.

62 Music: From *The English Hymnal,* by permission of Oxford University Press.

64 Words: Copyright © 1981 by Hope Publishing Company, 380 S. Main Pl., Carol Stream, Ill. 60188. All rights reserved. Used by permission. Music: Copyright © 1985 by GIA Publications, Inc., Chicago, Ill. All rights reserved.

65 Words: Copyright © 1992 by Hope Publishing Company, 380 S. Main Pl., Carol Stream, Ill. 60188. All rights reserved. Used by permission. Music: Harmonization copyright © 1990 Praise Publications.

66 Words: Copyright © 1967 by Hope Publishing Company, 380 S. Main Pl., Carol Stream, Ill. 60188. All rights reserved. Used by permission.

68 Music: From *The Oxford Book of Carols,* © 1964 Oxford Universit Press. Used by permission.

71 Music: Copyright © 1970 by Hope Publishing Company, 380 S. M Pl., Carol Stream, Ill. 60188. All rights reserved. Used by permission. Music: Copyright © 1978 *Lutheran Book of Worship.* Reprinted by permission of Augsburg Fortress.

73 Words: Copyright © 1961. Renewal 1989 by The Hymn Society, Texas Christian University, Fort Worth, Tex. 76129. All rights reserved. Used by permission. Music: From *The English Hymnal,* b permission of Oxford University Press.

74–196 (Copyright information regarding the psalms, psalm tones, and psal antiphons can be found at the beginning of this index.)

198 Music: Copyright © 1949 by H. W. Gray, a division of Belwin-Mil Pub. Corp. All rights reserved. Used with permission.

199 Words: Copyright 1988 Keith Landis. Music: Copyright © 1971 Faber Music Limited. Reprinted from *The New Catholic Hymnal* b permission.

201 Words: By permission of Juan Luis Garcia. English translation copyright © 1989 The United Methodist Publishing House. From *T United Methodist Hymnal.* Used by permission. Music: By permission of Juan Luis Garcia.

202 Words and music: Copyright 1973 Editorial Apostolado de la Prensa Sole U.S. agent: OCP Publications, 5536 N.E. Hassalo, Portland, Oreg. 97213. All rights reserved. Used with permission.

204 Words: Verses 3 and 4 copyright © 1982 by Hope Publishing Company, 380 S. Main Pl., Carol Stream, Ill. 60188. All rights reserved. Used by permission. Music: From *The Oxford Book of Carols,* © 1964 Oxford University Press. Used by permission.

206 Words: Copyright © 1974 by Hope Publishing Company. All rights reserved. Used by permission. Music: Harmonization copyright © 1977 by Hope Publishing Company, 380 S. Main Pl., Carol Stream, Ill. 60188. All rights reserved. Used by permission.

209 Words and music: English translation and harmonization copyright 1960 Transcontinental Music Publications, 838 Fifth Avenue, New York, N.Y. 10021. Used by permission from the Central Conference of American Rabbis.

210 Words: Copyright © 1974 by Hope Publishing Company, 380 S. Main Pl., Carol Stream, Ill. 60188. All rights reserved. Used by permission.

214 Words: Copyright © 1982 Charles P. Price.

215 Music: Copyright © 1938 H. Hugh Bancroft.

216 Music: Accompaniment copyright Bruce Neswick. Used by permission.

218 Music: Harmonization copyright © 1975 by GIA Publications, Inc., Chicago, Ill. All rights reserved.

221 Words: Stanzas 3b–5 copyright Concordia Publishing House. Reprinted by permission.

222 Words: By permission of Hingham Associates Limited, London, England. Music: Arrangement copyright © Barry Rose.

223 Music: Harmonization used by permission as published in *The Pilgrim Hymnal,* copyright 1958 The Pilgrim Press, New York, N.Y.

224 Words: "A Christmas Hymn" from *Advice to a Prophet and Other Poems,* copyright 1961 and renewed 1989 by Richard Wilbur, reprinted by permission of Harcourt Brace Jovanovich, Inc. Music: Copyright © 1984 by GIA Publications, Inc., Chicago, Ill. All rights reserved.

226 Words: Copyright © 1978 *Lutheran Book of Worship.* Reprinted by permission of Augsburg Fortress.

233 Words: English version copyright © 1978 *Lutheran Book of Worship.* Reprinted by permission of Augsburg Fortress. Spanish translation © 1987 Skinner Chavez-Melo. Music: Harmonization © 1987 Skinner Chavez-Melo.

234 Words: Copyright © 1989 by Hope Publishing Company, 380 S. Main Pl., Carol Stream, Ill. 60188. All rights reserved. Used by permission.

236 Music: From *The English Hymnal,* by permission of Oxford University Press.

238 Music: Copyright P. A. Howgil, International Music Publications, Woodford Trading Estate, Southend Road, Woodford Green, Essex IG8 8HN, England.

239 Words: English text of the "Huron Carol" by J. E. Middleton. Used by permission of The Frederick Harris Music Co., Limited, Oakville, Ontario, Canada. All rights reserved. Music: Setting copyright © 1978 *Lutheran Book of Worship.* Reprinted by permission of Augsburg Fortress.

249 Words: Copyright © The Church Pension Fund, 800 Second Avenue, New York, N.Y. 10017. Used by permission.

251 Words and music: Copyright © 1977 by Hope Publishing Company, 380 S. Main Pl., Carol Stream, Ill. 60188. All rights reserved. Used by permission.

252 Words: Copyright © 1978 *Lutheran Book of Worship.* Reprinted by permission of Augsburg Fortress.

253 Words: Text revised for *Hymns for Today's Church.* Copyright © 1982 by Hope Publishing Company, 380 S. Main Pl., Carol Stream, Ill. 60188. All rights reserved. Used by permission.

254 Words: From *The English Hymnal,* by permission of Oxford University Press.

257 Words: Text paraphrase copyright © 1976 by Hinshaw Music, Inc. Reprinted by permission.

261 Music: Arrangement copyright Ivan Florjanc. Used by permission.

262 Words: Copyright 1971 John Webster Grant. Music: Harmonization copyright © 1991 by Hope Publishing Company, 380 S. Main Pl., Carol Stream, Ill. 60188. All rights reserved. Used by permission.

263 Words: Copyright © 1973 by Hope Publishing Company, 380 S. Main Pl., Carol Stream, Ill. 60188. All rights reserved. Used by permission.

264 Words: Copyright Herbert O'Driscoll. Used by permission. Music: Copyright 1989 Selah Publishing Co., Accord, N.Y. 12404. All rights reserved. Used by permission.

265 Music: Harmonization from *The Hymnal 1982,* © The Church Pension Fund, 800 Second Avenue, New York, N.Y. 10017. Used by permission.

270 Music: Harmonization from *The Oxford Book of Carols,* © 1964 Oxford University Press. Used by permission.

273 Words: Copyright © 1980 by John Bennett. Music: Copyright © 1983 by Henmar Press, Inc. Used by permission of C. F. Peters Corporation from *Six New Hymns* (Edition Peters 66968).

277 Words: Reprinted by permission of Mowbray, a division of Cassell PLC, Artillery House, Artillery Row, London SW1P 1RT, England.

279 Words: Copyright World Student Christian Federation. Used by permission. Music: Copyright © 1983 by Hope Publishing Company, 380 S. Main Pl., Carol Stream, Ill. 60188. All rights reserved. Used by permission.

281 Music: Reprinted from *The Cambridge Hymnal,* with the permission of Cambridge University Press.

282 Words: Copyright Society of the Sacred Mission. Music: Arrangement copyright © 1992 Margaret Irwin-Brandon. Used by permission.

283 Words and music: Methodist Press Ltd., c/o Ediciones La Aurora; Dean Funes 1823, 1244 Buenos Aires, Argentina. English translation copyright © 1974 by Hope Publishing Company, 380 S. Main Pl., Carol Stream, Ill. 60188. All rights reserved. Used by permission.

287 Words: Copyright © 1971 John Webster Grant.

288 Words: Copyright © 1982 by Hope Publishing Company. All rights reserved. Used by permission. Music: Copyright © 1969 by Hope Publishing Company, 380 S. Main Pl., Carol Stream, Ill. 60188. All rights reserved. Used by permission.

290 Words: Adaptation copyright 1983 assigned to The United Methodist Publishing House. From *The United Methodist Hymnal.* Used by permission.

292 Words and music: Copyright © 1969 by Hope Publishing Company, 380 S. Main Pl., Carol Stream, Ill. 60188. All rights reserved. Used by permission.

293 Words: Copyright Community of the Resurrection, Mirfield, West Yorkshire WF14 0BN, England. Music: Reproduced by permission of Novello and Company Limited.

295 Words: Copyright 1963 Galliard Ltd. Used by permission of Galaxy Music, Boston. Music: Harmonization copyright Margaret W. Mealy. Used by permission.

296 Music: From *The English Hymnal,* by permission of Oxford University Press.

297 Words and music: Copyright © 1980, 1983 Linda Wilberger Egan, 302 Woodward Road, Moyland, Pa. 19065.

298 Music: Copyright © 1968 Derek Williams.

299 Words and music: Copyright by GIA Publications, Inc., Chicago, Ill. All rights reserved.

301 Music: From *The English Hymnal,* by permission of Oxford University Press.

303 Words: Copyright © 1983 by Hope Publishing Company, 380 S. Main Pl., Carol Stream, Ill. 60188. All rights reserved. Used by permission. Music: Copyright 1989, Selah Publishing Co., Accord, N.Y. 12404. All rights reserved. Used by permission.

304 Words: Copyright © 1973, 1980 by Hope Publishing Company, 380 S. Main Pl., Carol Stream, Ill. 60188. All rights reserved. Used by permission.

305 Words: From *English Praise 1975,* by permission of Oxford University Press.

306 Music: Copyright © 1985 Skinner Chavez-Melo.

307 Music: Copyright © 1971 by GIA Publications, Inc., Chicago, Ill. All rights reserved.

308 Music: Copyright Royal School of Church Music as publisher to Church Music Society.

312 Words: Copyright © The Church Pension Fund, 800 Second Avenue, New York, N.Y. 10017. Used by permission.

313 Music: From *Communion Service* (S598), © 1972 Oxford University Press. Reprinted with permission.

314 Music: Harmonization copyright © 1991 by Hope Publishing Company, 380 S. Main Pl., Carol Stream, Ill. 60188. All rights reserved. Used by permission.

315 Music: Copyright © 1971 by GIA Publications, Inc., Chicago, Ill. All rights reserved.

316 Music: Copyright © 1971 by GIA Publications, Inc., Chicago, Ill. All rights reserved.

318 Music: Adaptation copyright © 1985 by GIA Publications, Inc., Chicago, Ill. All rights reserved.

320 Music: Copyright © 1976 E. C. Schirmer, Boston. Used by permission.

326 Words: Copyright © 1990 by Hope Publishing Company, 380 S. Main Pl., Carol Stream, Ill. 60188. All rights reserved. Used by permission.

328 Words: Copyright 1969 Concordia Publishing House. Reprinted by permission.

330 Words: Copyright © 1989 by Hope Publishing Company, 380 S. Main Pl., Carol Stream, Ill. 60188. All rights reserved. Used by permission.

333 Words: Copyright © 1979 by Hope Publishing Company. All rights reserved. Used by permission. Music: Copyright © 1942. Renewal 1970 by Hope Publishing Company, 380 S. Main Pl., Carol Stream, Ill. 60188. All rights reserved. Used by permission.

335 Music: Arrangement by Margaret W. Mealy. Used by permission.

336 Words: Copyright © 1977 by Hope Publishing Company, 380 S. Main Pl., Carol Stream, Ill. 60188. All rights reserved. Used by permission. Music: Harmonization copyright © 1965 Abingdon Press. From *The Book of Hymns.* Used by permission.

337 Words: Copyright © 1972 by Hope Publishing Company, 380 S. Main Pl., Carol Stream, Ill. 60188. All rights reserved. Used by permission.

338 Words: Copyright John E. Bowers. Used by permission. Music: Copyright © 1984 Richard W. Dirksen.

340 Words: Copyright © 1984, TEAM Publications. Published by OCP Publications, 5536 N.E. Hassalo, Portland, Oreg. 97211. All rights reserved. Used with permission.

342 Words: Copyright 1964 World Library Publications, Inc. All rights reserved. Used with permission. Music: Setting copyright © 1972 *Contemporary Worship 4: Hymns for Baptism and Holy Communion.* Reprinted by permission of Augsburg Fortress.

344 Words: Copyright Methodist Publishing House. Music: From *The English Hymnal,* by permission of Oxford University Press.

347 Music: From *The Hymnal 1982,* © The Church Pension Fund, 800 Second Avenue, New York, N.Y. 10017. Used by permission.

348 Words: By permission of Hingham Associates Limited, London, England. Music: From *The Hymnal 1982,* © The Church Pension Fund, 800 Second Avenue, New York, N.Y. 10017. Used by permission.

349 Music: From *The Hymnal 1982,* © The Church Pension Fund, 800 Second Avenue, New York, N.Y. 10017. Used by permission.

352 Words: Copyright © 1965 Bliss Wiant.

353 Words: Copyright © 1971 Faber Music Limited. Reprinted from *The New Catholic Hymnal* by permission.

355 Music: Arrangement copyright © 1983 by Hope Publishing Company, 380 S. Main Pl., Carol Stream, Ill. 60188. All rights reserved. Used by permission.

357 Words: Revised translation Anne LeCroy (1982). Music: Copyright © 1985 by GIA Publications, Inc., Chicago, Ill. All rights reserved.

361 Words: Copyright © The Church Pension Fund, 800 Second Avenue, New York, N.Y. 10017. Used by permission.

362 Words: Stanza 3 copyright James Waring McCracy. Used by permission.

363 Music: Setting copyright © 1958 *Service Book and Hymnal.* Reprinted by permission of Augsburg Fortress.

365 Music: Copyright Paraclete Press, Orleans, Mass. Used by permission.

370 Words: Copyright © 1989 by Hope Publishing Company, 380 S. Main Pl., Carol Stream, Ill. 60188. All rights reserved. Used by permission. Music: Copyright Jane M. Marshall. Used by permission.

372 Words: Copyright Methodist Publishing House.

375 Music: Harmonization from *Enlarged Songs of Praise 1931,* by permission of Oxford University Press.

377 Music: Copyright © The Church Pension Fund, 800 Second Avenue, New York, N.Y. 10017. Used by permission.

378 Words: By permission of Oxford University Press. Music: Arrangement by Margaret W. Mealy. Used by permission.

379 Words: Copyright © 1975 by Hope Publishing Company, 380 S. Main Pl., Carol Stream, Ill. 60188. All rights reserved. Used by permission.

381 Words: Copyright © 1954. Renewal 1982 by Hope Publishing Company. All rights reserved. Used by permission. Music: Copyright © 1966 by Hope Publishing Company, 380 S. Main Pl., Carol Stream, Ill. 60188. All rights reserved. Used by permission.

382 Music: Arrangement copyright © by GIA Publications, Inc., Chicago, Ill. All rights reserved.

383 Words: Copyright © 1966, 1985 by Willard F. Jabusch. Music: Copyright © 1985 by GIA Publications, Inc., Chicago, Ill. All rights reserved.
384 Words: Copyright © 1976 Norman P. Olsen. Used by permission. Music: Tune and setting copyright © 1978 *Lutheran Book of Worship.* Reprinted by permission of Augsburg Fortress.
385 Words: Copyright John B. Geyer. Used by permission of the author.
388 Words: Copyright Thomas E. Herbranson. Used by permission. Music: Copyright 1964 Abingdon Press. From *The Book of Hymns.* Used by permission.
389 Words: Copyright © 1979 by Hope Publishing Company, 380 S. Main Pl., Carol Stream, Ill. 60188. All rights reserved. Used by permission.
391 Music: Copyright 1970 Warren Swenson.
392 Words: By permission of Oxford University Press.
393 Music: Harmonization copyright © 1986 by GIA Publications, Inc., Chicago, Ill. All rights reserved.
394 Words and music: Copyright © 1974 by Hope Publishing Company, 380 S. Main Pl., Carol Stream, Ill. 60188. All rights reserved. Used by permission.
396 Words: From *Enlarged Songs of Praise 1931,* by permission of Oxford University Press. Music: The H. W. Gray Co., a division of CCP/Belwin, Inc., P.O. Box 4340, Miami, Fla. 33014. All rights reserved. Used by permission.
397 Words: Copyright © The Church Pension Fund, 800 Second Avenue, New York, N.Y. 10017. Used by permission.
398 Words: Copyright © The Church Pension Fund, 800 Second Avenue, New York, N.Y. 10017. Used by permission. Music: Copyright 1973 Elkan-Vogel, Inc. Reprinted by permission of the publisher and sole representative, Theodore Presser Company.
401 Words and music: Copyright permission obtained, Archdiocese of Philadelphia, 1977. All rights reserved.
403 Words: Copyright © 1971 by Hope Publishing Company, 380 S. Main Pl., Carol Stream, Ill. 60188. All rights reserved. Used by permission.
404 Music: Harmonization copyright Ivan Florjanc. Used by permission.
405 Music: Harmonization from *Songs of Praise 1925,* by permission of Oxford University Press.
406 Words: English translation copyright © 1989 The United Methodist Publishing House. From *The United Methodist Hymnal.* Used by permission. Music: Copyright 1973 Ediciones Musical PAX. Sole U.S. agent: OCP Publications, 5536 N.E. Hassalo, Portland, Oreg. 97213. All rights reserved. Used by permission. Harmonization copyright 1973 Skinner Chavez-Melo.
407 Words and music: Copyright © 1969 by Hope Publishing Company, 380 S. Main Pl., Carol Stream, Ill. 60188. All rights reserved. Used by permission.
409 Music: Harmonization copyright 1978 *Lutheran Book of Worship.* Reprinted by permission of Augsburg Fortress.
411 Words: Copyright © 1983 Augsburg Publishing House. Reprinted by permission of Augsburg Fortress. Music: Tune and setting copyright © 1983 Augsburg Publishing House. Reprinted by permission of Augsburg Fortress.
412 Words: Phonetic transcription copyright 1989 The United Methodist Publishing House. From *The United Methodist Hymnal.* Used by permission. Music: Copyright I-to-Loh, P.O. Box 3167, Manila 1099, Philippines. Harmonization copyright 1989 The United Methodist Publishing House. Used by permission.
413 Words: Copyright © 1969 by Hope Publishing Company. All rights reserved. Used by permission. Music: Harmonization copyright © 1991 by Hope Publishing Company, 380 S. Main Pl., Carol Stream, Ill. 60188. All rights reserved. Used by permission.
414 Words and music: Copyright © 1984 Oxford University Press. Used by permission.
417 Words: Copyright © 1985 by Hope Publishing Company, 380 S. Main Pl., Carol Stream, Ill. 60188. All rights reserved. Used by permission.
418 Words: Copyright © 1983 by Hope Publishing Company. All rights reserved. Used by permission. Music: Arrangement copyright 1983 by Hope Publishing Company, 380 S. Main Pl., Carol Stream, Ill. 60188. All rights reserved. Used by permission.
420 Words: Copyright 1969 Galliard Ltd. Used by permission of Galaxy Music, Boston.
423 Words: Copyright © 1989, Oxford University Press, Inc. Used by permission. Music: From *The Hymnal 1982,* © The Church Pension Fund, 800 Second Avenue, New York, N.Y. 10017. Used by permission.
424 Music: Copyright © 1985 by Hope Publishing Company, 380 S. Main Pl., Carol Stream, Ill. 60188. All rights reserved. Used by permission.
425 Words: Copyright © 1990 by Hope Publishing Company, 380 S. Main Pl., Carol Stream, Ill. 60188. All rights reserved. Used by permission.
426 Music: Copyright © 1990 by Hope Publishing Company, 380 S. Main Pl., Carol Stream, Ill. 60188. All rights reserved. Used by permission.
428 Music: From *The English Hymnal,* by permission of Oxford University Press.
430 Words: Reprinted by permission of Mowbray, a division of Cassell PLC, Artillery House, Artillery Row, London SW1P 1RT, England. Music: Copyright © 1942. Renewal 1970 by Hope Publishing Company, 380 S. Main Pl., Carol Stream, Ill. 60188. All rights reserved. Used by permission.
431 Words: Copyright © 1989 by Hope Publishing Company, 380 S. Main Pl., Carol Stream, Ill. 60188. All rights reserved. Used by permission.
432 Words: Copyright © 1982 by Hope Publishing Company, 380 S. Main Pl., Carol Stream, Ill. 60188. All rights reserved. Used by permission. Music: Copyright © 1988 by GIA Publications, Inc., Chicago, Ill. All rights reserved.
433 Words: Copyright © 1982 by Hope Publishing Company, 380 S. Main Pl., Carol Stream, Ill. 60188. All rights reserved. Used by permission.
434 Music: Copyright © 1976 David Charles Walker. Used by permission.
435 Music: From *The English Hymnal,* by permission of Oxford University Press.
437 Music: Walton Music Corporation. Used by permission.
438 Music: Arrangement copyright Transcontinental Music Publications 838 Fifth Avenue, New York, N.Y. 10021.
439 Words: From *Enlarged Songs of Praise 1931,* by permission of Oxford University Press.
440 Music: Copyright © by Hope Publishing Company, 380 S. Main Pl., Carol Stream, Ill. 60188. All rights reserved. Used by permission.
441 Music: Harmonization copyright © 1991 by Hope Publishing Company, 380 S. Main Pl., Carol Stream, Ill. 60188. All rights reserved. Used by permission.
442 Words: Copyright © 1974 by The Hymn Society, Texas Christian University, Fort Worth, Tex. 76129. All rights reserved. Used by permission.
444 Words and music: Copyright Walton Music Corporation.
445 Words: Copyright Herbert O'Driscoll. Used by permission. Music: Copyright © 1990 Alice Parker.
449 Music: Setting copyright © 1983 Augsburg Publishing House. Reprinted by permission of Augsburg Fortress.
451 Music: Harmonization copyright © 1991 by Hope Publishing Company, 380 S. Main Pl., Carol Stream, Ill. 60188. All rights reserved. Used by permission.
453 Words: Copyright © 1978 *Lutheran Book of Worship.* Reprinted by permission of Augsburg Fortress. Music: Setting copyright © 1978 *Lutheran Book of Worship.* Reprinted by permission of Augsburg Fortress.
459 Words: Copyright © 1984 by Hope Publishing Company, 380 S. Main Pl., Carol Stream, Ill. 60188. All rights reserved. Used by permission.
461 Words: Copyright © 1987 Morning Star Publishers. Used by permission. Music: Reprinted from *The Cambridge Hymnal,* with th permission of Cambridge University Press.
462 Words: Copyright © 1987 Morning Star Publishers. Used by permission. Music: Copyright © 1990 Ione Press, Inc., Boston. Us with permission.
463 Words: Copyright © 1976 by Hinshaw Music, Inc. Text paraphrase reprinted by permission.
464 Music: Copyright © 1971 Faber Music Limited. Reprinted from *The New Catholic Hymnal* by permission.
465 Music: Reproduced by permission of Novello and Company Limited
467 Words: Copyright © 1974 by Hope Publishing Company, 380 S. Main Pl., Carol Stream, Ill. 60188. All rights reserved. Used by permission.
469 Words and music: Copyright © 1986 by GIA Publications, Inc., Chicago, Ill. All rights reserved.
470 Music: From "Eternal Light" by Erik Routley. Copyright © 1971 by Carl Fischer, Inc., New York. Used by permission.
472 Music: Copyright © 1983 assigned to The United Methodist Publishing House. From *The United Methodist Hymnal.* Used by permission.
473 Music: Copyright © 1977 by GIA Publications, Inc., Chicago, Ill. All rights reserved.
474 Words and music: Copyright © 1975 by Hope Publishing Company, 380 S. Main Pl., Carol Stream, Ill. 60188. All rights reserved. Used by permission.
475 Words: Copyright © 1978 *Lutheran Book of Worship.* Reprinted by permission of Augsburg Fortress.
476 Words: Copyright © 1977 by Hinshaw Music, Inc. Text paraphrase reprinted by permission. Music: Copyright © 1977 by Hinshaw Music, Inc. Reprinted by permission.
478 Music: Harmonization copyright Calvin Hampton. Used by permission of Marcella Pambrun.
479 Words: Copyright © 1964 by Hope Publishing Company, 380 S. Main Pl., Carol Stream, Ill. 60188. All rights reserved. Used by permission. Music: Harmonization from *Enlarged Songs of Praise 1931,* by permission of Oxford University Press.
480 Words and music: Copyright © 1975 by Hope Publishing Company, 380 S. Main Pl., Carol Stream, Ill. 60188. All rights reserved. Used by permission.
482 Words: From *The Poetry of Robert Frost,* edited by Edward Connery Lathem. Copyright 1916, 1969 by Holt, Rinehart and Winston. Copyright 1944 by Robert Frost. Reprinted by permission of Henry Holt and Company, Inc. Music: Copyright 1960, renewed 1988, E. C. Schirmer, Boston. Used by permission.
485 Words: From *Enlarged Songs of Praise 1931,* by permission of Oxford University Press. Music: From *The Hymnal 1982,* © The Church Pension Fund, 800 Second Avenue, New York, N.Y. 10017. Used by permission.
486 Words: Copyright 1979 Concordia Publishing House. Reprinted by permission.
487 Words and music: Copyright © 1984 Oxford University Press, Inc. Used by permission.
488 Words: Copyright © 1971 Faber Music Limited. Reprinted from *The New Catholic Hymnal* by permission. Music: By permission of Oxford University Press.
489 Words: Copyright © 1984 by Hope Publishing Company, 380 S. Main Pl., Carol Stream, Ill. 60188. All rights reserved. Used by permission. Music: By permission of the APCK, Dublin.
490 Music: Copyright Mrs. V. M. Caird. Used by permission.
491 Music: Arrangement copyright © 1985 by GIA Publications, Inc., Chicago, Ill. All rights reserved.
496 Words: Copyright © 1989 Oxford University Press, Inc. Used by permission.

499 Words: Copyright David Mowbray.
500 Words: Phonetic transcription © 1989 The United Methodist Publishing House. From *The United Methodist Hymnal.* Used by permission. Music: Used by permission of JASRAC, License no. 9071755.
502 Words: Copyright © 1983 by Hope Publishing Company, 380 S. Main Pl., Carol Stream, Ill. 60188. All rights reserved. Used by permission. Music: Copyright © 1983 by GIA Publications, Inc., Chicago, Ill. All rights reserved.
503 Words: Copyright © 1959. Renewal 1987 by The Hymn Society, Texas Christian University, Fort Worth, Tex. 76129. All rights reserved. Used by permission.
504 Words: By permission of Oxford University Press. Music: Setting copyright © 1978 *Lutheran Book of Worship.* Reprinted by permission of Augsburg Fortress.
506 Words: Copyright © 1982 by Hope Publishing Company, 380 S. Main Pl., Carol Stream, Ill. 60188. All rights reserved. Used by permission.
507 Words: Copyright © 1992 by Hope Publishing Company, 380 S. Main Pl., Carol Stream, Ill. 60188. All rights reserved. Used by permission.
509 Words: Copyright 1969 Concordia Publishing House. Reprinted by permission.
510 Music: Harmonization from *Enlarged Songs of Praise 1931,* by permission of Oxford University Press.
512 Words: Copyright © The Church Pension Fund, 800 Second Avenue, New York, N.Y. 10017. Used by permission.
513 Words: Copyright © 1978 by Hope Publishing Company. All rights reserved. Used by permission. Music: Copyright © 1942. Renewal 1970 by Hope Publishing Company, 380 S. Main Pl., Carol Stream, Ill. 60188. All rights reserved. Used by permission.
515 Words and music: Copyright © 1969 by Hope Publishing Company, 380 S. Main Pl., Carol Stream, Ill. 60188. All rights reserved. Used by permission.
516 Words: Copyright © 1976 by Hope Publishing Company, 380 S. Main Pl., Carol Stream, Ill. 60188. All rights reserved. Used by permission. Music: By permission of Oxford University Press.
517 Words: Copyright 1983 Thomas H. Troeger. Used by permission of Oxford University Press, Inc. Music: Copyright 1985 Carol Doran. Used by permission of Oxford University Press, Inc.
518 Words: By permission of Oxford University Press.
519 Words: Copyright Highland Park United Methodist Church, Dallas, Tex. Music: From *Hymns and Responses for the Church Year,* © 1956 Elkan-Vogel, Inc. Reprinted by permission of the publisher.
520 Words and music: Copyright 1979 Ediciones Paulinas, Sole U.S. agent: OCP Publications, 5536 N.E. Hassalo, Portland, Oreg. 97213. All rights reserved. Used by permission. Translation © 1989 The United Methodist Publishing House. From *The United Methodist Hymnal.* Used by permission. Harmonization © 1987 Skinner Chavez-Melo.
521 Words: From W. H. Auden, *Collected Poems,* edited by Edward Mendelson. Copyright © 1976 by Edward Mendelson, William Meredith, and Monroe K. Spears, Executors of the Estate of W. H. Auden. Reprinted by permission of Random House, Inc. Music: Copyright 1972 by The Westminster Press. From *The Worshipbook: Services and Hymns.* Used by permission of Westminster/John Knox Press.
524 Words and music: Copyright © 1969 by Hope Publishing Company, 380 S. Main Pl., Carol Stream, Ill. 60188. All rights reserved. Used by permission.
525 Words: Copyright © 1960 by John Updike. Reprinted from *Telephone Polls and Other Poems* by John Updike, by permission of Alfred A. Knopf, Inc. Music: Reprinted by permission of the Executors of G. H. Knight.
526 Words: Used by permission of the Inter-Lutheran Commission on Worship. Music: Melody copyright © 1972 by Chantry Music Press, Inc. Used by permission.
528 Words: By permission of Oxford University Press.
531 Words: From *The English Hymnal,* by permission of Oxford University Press. Music: United Nations Association, 3 Whitehall Court, London SW1A 2EL, England.
533 Words: Copyright © 1958. Renewal 1986 by The Hymn Society, Texas Christian University, Fort Worth, Tex. 76129. All rights reserved. Used by permission. Music: From the *Revised Church Hymnary 1927,* by permission of Oxford University Press.
534 Words: By permission of Oxford University Press. Music: Copyright © 1969 by Hope Publishing Company, 380 S. Main Pl., Carol Stream, Ill. 60188. All rights reserved. Used by permission.
535 Words: Copyright © 1968 by Hope Publishing Company, 380 S. Main Pl., Carol Stream, Ill. 60188. All rights reserved. Used by permission. Music: Tune and setting copyright 1967 Concordia Publishing House. Reprinted by permission.
536 Music: From *The English Hymnal,* by permission of Oxford University Press.
538 Words: Copyright © 1964 Regent Music Corporation. Reprinted by permission. All rights reserved. Music: From *The Hymnal 1982,* © The Church Pension Fund, 800 Second Avenue, New York, N.Y. 10017. Used by permission.
539 Words: By permission of Oxford University Press.
540 Words: Copyright 1969 Galliard Ltd. Used by permission of Galaxy Music, Boston. Music: Harmonization © 1965 Abingdon Press. From *The Book of Hymns.* Used by permission.
542 Words: Copyright © 1975 by Hope Publishing Company, 380 S. Main Pl., Carol Stream, Ill. 60188. All rights reserved. Used by permission.
543 Words: Copyright The Lorenz Corporation. Reproduced by permission.
544 Words: Used by permission of Elinor Fosdick Downs.
545 Words: Copyright © 1974 by Hope Publishing Company, 380 S. Main Pl., Carol Stream, Ill. 60188. All rights reserved. Used by permission. Music: Copyright © 1986 by GIA Publications, Inc., Chicago, Ill. All rights reserved.
546 Words and music: Copyright © 1921 by Edward B. Marks Music Company. Copyright renewed. International copyright secured. Made in USA. All rights reserved. Used by permission.
547 Words: Copyright © 1954. Renewal by The Hymn Society, Texas Christian University, Fort Worth, Tex. 76129. All rights reserved. Used by permission.
548 Words: Mrs. M. E. Peacey (M. J. Hancock). Music: Copyright © 1985 by Hope Publishing Company, 380 S. Main Pl., Carol Stream, Ill. 60188. All rights reserved. Used by permission.
549 Words: Copyright © 1971 assigned to The United Methodist Publishing House. From *The United Methodist Hymnal.* Used by permission. Music: Arrangement copyright © 1974 by Hope Publishing Company, 380 S. Main Pl., Carol Stream, Ill. 60188. All rights reserved. Used by permission.
552 Words: Copyright 1961, 1962 World Library Publications, Inc. All rights reserved.
553 Words: Copyright 1961, 1962 World Library Publications, Inc. All rights reserved.
554 Words: Verse 3 copyright © 1989 The United Methodist Publishing House. From *The United Methodist Hymnal.* Used by permission.
555 Words: Copyright © 1971 by Hope Publishing Company, 380 S. Main Pl., Carol Stream, Ill. 60188. All rights reserved. Used by permission.
556 Words and music: Copyright © 1974 by Hope Publishing Company, 380 S. Main Pl., Carol Stream, Ill. 60188. All rights reserved. Used by permission.
559 Music: Reproduced by permission of Novello and Company, Limited.
562 Words and music: Copyright © 1983 by Hope Publishing Company, 380 S. Main Pl., Carol Stream, Ill. 60188. All rights reserved. Used by permission.
564 Words and music: Ediciones Paulinas. Sole U.S. agent: OCP Publications, 5536 N.E. Hassalo, Portland, Oreg. 97213. All rights reserved. Used by permission. English translation: Copyright © 1989 The United Methodist Publishing House. From *The United Methodist Hymnal.* Used by permission. Harmonization by Juan Luis Garcia. Used by permission.
565 Music: Arrangement copyrighted 1954 by Aaron Copland. Sole publishers: Boosey and Hawkes, Inc.
567 Words: Copyright © 1982 by Hope Publishing Company, 380 S. Main Pl., Carol Stream, Ill. 60188. All rights reserved. Used by permission.
568 Music: Harmonization copyright © 1991 by Hope Publishing Company, 380 S. Main Pl., Carol Stream, Ill. 60188. All rights reserved. Used by permission.
570 Words: Copyright © 1969 by Hope Publishing Company, 380 S. Main Pl., Carol Stream, Ill. 60188. All rights reserved. Used by permission. Music: Copyright Emma Lou Diemer.
571 Words: Copyright © 1969 by Hope Publishing Company, 380 S. Main Pl., Carol Stream, Ill. 60188. All rights reserved. Used by permission.
574 Words: Copyright © 1988 by Hope Publishing Company, 380 S. Main Pl., Carol Stream, Ill. 60188. All rights reserved. Used by permission.
575 Words: Reprinted by permission of the Peters Fraser and Dunlop Group Ltd.

INDEX OF FIRST LINES

HIEBERT LIBRARY
3 6877 00127 4645